INTERDISCIPLINARITY

INTERDISCIPLINARITY

History, Theory, and Practice

Julie Thompson Klein

 Wayne State University Press   Detroit   1990

Library of Congress Cataloging-in-Publication Data

Klein, Julie Thompson
    Interdisciplinarity : history, theory, and practice / Julie
Thompson Klein.
      p.   cm.
    Bibliography: p.
    Includes index.
    ISBN 0-8143-2087-2
    1. Interdisciplinary approach to knowledge. I. Title.
BD255.K54 1990
  001 – dc20   89-35166
                                                                    CIP

Grateful acknowledgment is made for permission to use the items listed below. The elephant fable from Lawrence Wheeler's "Multidisciplinary Approach to Planning," Paper presented at Council of Educational Facilities Planners Forty-seventh Conference, in Oklahoma City, Oklahoma, October, 1970, ERIC ED 044814. Reprinted by permission of the author.
The graphic material on page 68 and Figures 2, 3, and 4, from R. Wasniowski, "Futures Research as a Framework for Transdisciplinary Research," in *Managing Interdisciplinary Research,* S. R. Epton, R.L. Payne, and A.W. Pearson, eds., copyright © 1983 by John Wiley and Sons Limited. Reproduced by permission of John Wiley and Sons Limited.
Figure 8, Joseph A. Steger's "Conceptualization of the IDR Manager's Role" is reproduced from *Interdisciplinary Research Groups,* copyright © 1979 (Vancouver: IRGIP). By permission of Joseph A. Steger and IRGIP.
Figures 5 and 6, from Donald T. Campbell's "Ethnocentrism of Disciplines and the Fish-scale Model of Omniscience," in *Interdisciplinary Relationships in the Social Sciences,* copyright © 1969 (Chicago: Aldine). By permission of the author.
Figure 1, from *Interdisciplinarity: Problems of Teaching and Research in Universities* (Paris: OECD, 1972). By permission of the publishers.
Figure 10, from Barbara Hursh, Paul Haas, and Michael Moore, "An Interdisciplinary Model to Implement General Education," originally in the *Journal of Higher Education.*
Figure 7, from F. Rossini, A. Porter, P. Kelley, and D. Chubin, "Interdisciplinary Integration within Technology Assessments" originally in *Knowledge: Creation, Diffusion, Utilization.*
Figures 11 and 12, by Maurice deWachter, "Interdisciplinarity Bioethics: But Where Do We Start? A Reflection on Epochè as Method," *Journal of Medicine and Philosophy.* Copyright © 1982 by Reidel Publishing Company. Reprinted by permission of Kluwer Academic Publishers.
Figure 9, from Stephen Kendall and E. E. Mackintosh, *Management Problems of Poly-disciplinary Environmental Research Projects in the University Setting,* (Canada MAB Report 13). By permission of E. E. Mackintosh.
Portions of chapters 4, 6, and 7 originally appeared in somewhat altered form in Julie Thompson Klein, "The Dialectic and Rhetoric of Disciplinarity and Interdisciplinarity," in *Issues in Integrative Studies.*
Portions of chapter 8 originally appeared in somewhat altered form in Julie Thompson Klein, "The Evolution of a Body of Knowledge: Interdisciplinary Problem-focused Research," in *Knowledge: Creation, Diffusion, Utilization.*
Portions of chapter 1 originally appeared in somewhat altered form in Julie Thompson Klein, "The Broad Scope of Interdisciplinarity" in *Interdisciplinary Research and Analysis: A Book of Readings,* D. Chubin, A. Porter, F. Rossini, and T. Connolly, eds. Copyright © 1986 by Lomond Publications, Inc. Reprinted by permission of the publisher.

To my daughter,
  Sarah Thomasen Klein

Contents

Acknowledgments   9

Introduction: The Problem of Interdisciplinary Discourse   11

Part I   Definitions of Interdisciplinarity   17

    1   The Evolution of Interdisciplinarity   19

    2   The Interdisciplinary Archipelago   40

    3   An Interdisciplinary Lexicon   55

Part II   Disciplinarity/Interdisciplinarity   75

    4   The Rhetoric of Interdisciplinarity   77

    5   Borrowing   85

    6   The Critique of Limitation   95

    7   The Disciplinary Paradox   104

Part III   The State of the Art   119

    8   IDR: Problem-focused Research   121

    9   Interdisciplinary Care   140

    10   IDS: Interdisciplinary Education   156

Conclusion: The Integrative Core   182

Notes   197

Selected Bibliography   229

            Introduction   231

            Essential References   232

Problem-focused Research	243
Interdisciplinary Care and Services	255
Education	271
The Humanities	286
The Social Sciences	298
The Sciences	315
Index	326

Acknowledgments

THROUGHOUT this book I cite the many people who have provided information on individual programs and activities. Here, however, I want to acknowledge my greatest debts.

From the start I have benefited from the generous support of three remarkable friends: Joseph Kockelmans (The Pennsylvania State University), William Newell (Miami University), and Raymond Miller (San Francisco State University). Their unflagging belief in the value of my work has meant a great deal to me.

I am also grateful to those who read drafts of individual chapters. C. Jan Swearingen (University of Texas, Arlington), Thomas Benson (St. Andrews College), Guy Beckwith (Auburn University), Mark Blum (University of Louisville), and Ronald Aronson (Wayne State University) advised me on drafts of the Introduction and the first part of Chapter one, which defines "the problem of knowledge." Joseph Kockelmans and Ray Miller reviewed parts of Chapters one and two as well as preliminary material for Chapters four through seven. Later, Stanley Bailis (San Francisco State University) read a revised version of Chapters four through seven. In addition, a number of people read parts of "The State of the Art" section. Philip Birnbaum (University of Southern California) and Daryl Chubin (Office of Technology Assessment, United States Congress) reviewed an early draft of the chapter on problem-focused research. A number of individuals checked pertinent sections of the chapter on interdisciplinary education: Tony Becher (University of Sussex), Keith Clayton (University of East Anglia), David Jowett and Richard Logan (University of Wisconsin, Green Bay), Soren Kjørup (University Center of Roskilde and University of Trondheim), Sato Tadashi (University of Tsukuba), Anthony Mountain (Sonoma State University), Bill Newell, George Helling (St. Olaf College), Arnold Binder (University of California, Irvine), Nelson Bingham (Earlham College), Ivan Kovacs (California State University, Hayward), Joseph Kockelmans, and Ingemar Lind (University of Linköping). My greatest debt, however, is to Bill Newell, who read almost the entirety of the manuscript.

In addition, I want to acknowledge several institutional debts. Wayne State University provided generous support in the form of a sabbatical leave, a research grant, travel grants to attend the OECD conference on interdisciplinarity in Sweden and the fourth INTERSTUDY conference on interdisciplinary research, plus several opportunities to rearrange my teaching schedule to accommodate my research. Along with the Association for Integrative Studies, the Office of the Dean of the College of Lifelong Learning as well as the Office of the Dean and Vice President for Research and Graduate Studies at Wayne State also provided financial assistance for the actual publication of the book. The National Science Foundation provided a travel stipend to attend the third INTERSTUDY conference on interdisciplinary research, and the OECD and Swedish National Board of Universities and Colleges provided support in Sweden. I also want to acknowledge the University of Michigan Libraries for granting me full access to their research libraries as a visiting scholar.

Several individuals deserve mention as well. For bringing my work to wider attention, I thank John Nichols (St. Joseph's College), Ray Ortali (State University of New York, Albany, and the Institute for Renaissance Interdisciplinary Studies), Donald Baldwin (of the University of Washington and INTERSTUDY), Alan Porter and Frederick Rossini (both of Georgia Institute of Technology and INTERSTUDY), Lennart Levin (Swedish National Board of Universities and Colleges) and Pierre Duguet and Hans Schütze (OECD). I also want to acknowledge the good counsel that has grown out of several friendships: with Fred Wacker (Wayne State University), Thomas Murray (Case Western Reserve University), Beth Casey (Bowling Green State University), György Darvas (Hungarian Academy of Sciences), Ernest Lynton (University of Massachusetts-Boston, Harbor campus), Wilhelm Vosskamp (Center for Interdisciplinary Research at the University of Bielefeld and University of Cologne, West Germany), and Bazel Allen (University of Michigan).

Finally, I thank George and Sarah for understanding how important this project has been to me and my editors, Laurel Brandt and Anne Adamus, for guiding the book through production.

Introduction: The Problem of Interdisciplinary Discourse

THERE is a subtle restructuring of knowledge in the late twentieth century. New divisions of intellectual labor, collaborative research, team teaching, hybrid fields, comparative studies, increased borrowing across disciplines, and a variety of "unified," "holistic" perspectives have created pressures upon traditional divisions of knowledge. There is talk of a growing "permeability of boundaries,"[1] a blurring and mixing of genres,[2] a postmodern return to grand theory[3] and cosmology,[4] even a "profound epistemological crisis."[5] To echo Clifford Geertz, there is indeed something happening "to the way we think about the way we think." These pressures have many origins and serve many purposes. However, they share one important commonality. At one time or another, they have all been labeled "interdisciplinary."

This label appears across a remarkably broad plane, giving the underlying concept of interdisciplinarity a universality and complexity that seem to defy definition. Still, all interdisciplinary activities are rooted in the ideas of unity and synthesis, evoking a common epistemology of convergence.[6] Educators, researchers, and practitioners have all turned to interdisciplinary work in order to accomplish a range of objectives:

- to answer complex questions;
- to address broad issues;
- to explore disciplinary and professional relations;
- to solve problems that are beyond the scope of any one discipline;
- to achieve unity of knowledge, whether on a limited or grand scale.

Given this range of activities it is hardly surprising that interdisciplinarity is a concept of wide appeal. However, it is also one of wide confusion.

11

There are several reasons for the confusion.

First, there is general uncertainty about the meaning of the term. Many fields were pronounced "interdisciplinary" with no clear definition of what that meant. As interdisciplinary curricula emerged in the United States during the World War I and II eras, there was no consensus on theory, methodology, or pedagogy. Social psychology and biochemistry, the most frequently cited examples of "interdisciplines," were touted as interdisciplinary fields well before recognized definitions emerged in the 1970s. Even today the interdisciplinary approach is often praised with no clear indication of what it is.

The confusion is only heightened by a pervasive tendency to associate interdisciplinarity with particular ranges of experience. A physicist may use the term *interdisciplinary* to describe converging theory levels among parts of modern physics, biology, and chemistry, yet be unaware of its rather substantial role in the social sciences. An economist may condemn all interdisciplinarians as dilettantes because of suspicions about a particular curriculum, yet overlook interdisciplinary investigations of development in the Third World. An engineer may extol the virtues of collaborative research on environmental problems, yet fail to see parallels in the professional practice of medicine, law, business, and social work. A geneticist may dismiss interdisciplinarity because of problems encountered on a public health project, but neglect to consider the interdisciplinary nature of biochemistry. Not surprisingly then, generalizations about *the* nature of interdisciplinarity emerged prematurely.

Interdisciplinarity has been described as both nostalgia for lost wholeness and a new stage in the evolution of science. Some people associate interdisciplinarity with the historical quest for unified knowledge, others with developments at the "frontiers" of knowledge. Technologists, engineers, and scientists are especially inclined to associate the concept with innovation, change, and the unexpected, though educators are split on whether interdisciplinarity is an old concept or a new one. Some consider interdisciplinarity primarily an educational concept; others contend the best interdisciplinary work lies outside the university — in government, industry, and the professions. There are also national differences in definition. In the United States, there is a tendency to associate interdisciplinarity primarily with undergraduate general education, but that is not the case in Europe. Certain disciplines are also thought to have a more "interdisciplinary" character in some countries, a more "disciplinary" character in others. Geoffrey Squires even suggested there is something "vaguely continental" about interdisciplinarity, that certain concepts such as unity and totality are more deeply embedded in continental than in Anglo-Saxon traditions.[7] Many U.S. scholars concur, noting a greater tendency towards theory than discipline in their European counterparts.

The *second* major reason for confusion stems from widespread un-familiarity with interdisciplinary scholarship. Given all the talk about interdisciplinarity, published work on the subject is used by a relatively small group of people. The reasons are understandable. Reliable bibliographies have only emerged within the last decade, and interdisciplinary professional groups are still quite young. Moreover, some of the most visible proponents of the concept are doubtful about whether or not there should be professional interdisciplinary movements, fearing the insularity that has accompanied the professionalization of other areas. Most of all, there is a general disinclination to place individual activities within a larger conceptual framework or wider body of knowledge.

The *third* and related reason for confusion is the lack of a unified body of discourse. Discussion of interdisciplinarity literally sprawls across general, professional, academic, governmental, and industrial literatures. All three reasons for the confusion—general uncertainty over definition, lack of professional identity, and dispersion of discourse—are the realities that prefigure any attempt to define the concept of interdisciplinarity. It is, however, the dispersion of discourse that is most fundamental.

"The interdisciplinary issue," Joseph Kockelmans explains, "is not made by the interdisciplinarians who write about it."[8] The need for meaningful interaction is everywhere. As a result the discourse on interdisciplinarity is widely diffused. The basic signals of discourse are texts, texts that are spoken, listened to, written, or read.[9] These written and spoken forms of communication embody a further property of discourse, that of commonality: common values, beliefs, perceptions, concepts, ideas, and questions.[10] There are interdisciplinary "texts," in fact a massive body of speeches, conference papers, institutional reports and working papers, reviews, notes, articles, and even a number of books on the subject. However, they are not read in common, even though they address common issues that cut across classrooms, laboratories, offices, archives, and field sites. Some degree of text-sharing is occurring in the subdomains that have developed: in interdisciplinary education, problem-focused research, health care, the social sciences, and a variety of problem communities and subject areas. However, there is a recognized bibliography in only one of those subdomains, that of problem-focused research. The majority of people engaged in interdisciplinary work lack a common identity. As a result, they often find themselves homeless, in a state of social and intellectual marginality.[11]

That marginality has led to a lot of unnecessary wheel-spinning and a generally diminished capacity for reflection on the nature of interdisciplinarity. Asian scholars using a regional research center generally do not explore parallels between their work and the work of biochemists, gerontologists, or environmentalists. Yet, in each area there are common methodological and epistemological problems created by borrowing from other disciplines. An engineer on a large-scale urban transportation project does not discuss interdisciplinary theory with a speech therapist on an interdisciplinary health-care team, an African historian on a large-scale archaeological project, or a social psychologist on a child development team. Yet all four experience the social and intellectual dynamics of interdisciplinary teamwork. Members of a large-scale social history project and members of a consortium for off-shore drilling projects in the Gulf of Mexico have not compared their use of computerized data bases. Yet each has struggled with the problems and reaped the benefits of machine-readable data accessible to specialists from different disciplines. A humanist trying to design an interdisciplinary curriculum at a small college, a pharmacist working at an interdisciplinary health clinic, and a bioethicist teaching courses that bridge the humanities and sciences ordinarily do not draw from the published literature on the management of problem-focused research or the educational "fugitive" literature comprised of conference papers, institutional working papers, committee reports, and project summaries. Yet those literatures contain a wealth of information about designing projects and managing teamwork. Obviously these people encounter organizational and intellectual phenomena unique to their own fields, but they also share common problems and ideas born of their involvement in interdisciplinary work.

The costs of ignoring these commonalities are enormous. Instead of sharpened methodologies, broadened theories, and improved communication, there are disputed borrowings, aborted projects, frayed nerves, and continued skepticism about the whole interdisciplinary enterprise. This need not continue. Since the 1970s there has been an exponential growth of publications on interdisciplinarity, a variety of interdisciplinary networks have formed, and discussion of the concept has widened considerably. Good scholarship on the subject does exist, but it is underused and much in need of synthesis. The purpose of this book is to provide that synthesis. Inevitably there will be debate over principles of selection. Every single interdisciplinary project, conference, symposium, course, program, and idea cannot be included in a single volume. It is possible, however, to provide a sound framework for future discussion and research by analyzing the internal and external forces that have shaped the concept of interdisciplinarity in the twentieth century. In conducting this analysis, I have drawn upon a variety of historical, sociological, economic, political, and philosophical insights, though my primary focus is on the interplay of arguments that constitute the modern discourse on interdisciplinarity. To understand the unity and diversity of the discourse is to understand the concept of interdisciplinarity.

The analysis itself is structured around a fundamental set of questions:

How is interdisciplinarity defined? How did the concept evolve in the twentieth century? What kinds of activities are associated with it, and why did they emerge? What are the different types and levels of integrative activity? (Part 1)

What is the relationship between disciplinarity and interdisciplinarity? What are the problems and implications of borrowing from other disciplines? How has interdisciplinarity functioned as a critique of disciplinarity? What happens when interdisciplinary fields begin to assume disciplinary characteristics? (Part II)

What is the state-of-the-art in such major areas as problem-focused research, health care, and education? (Part III)

What qualities characterize an "interdisciplinary person"? What is the nature of the interdisciplinary process? (Conclusion)

What constitutes a basic English-language literature on interdisciplinarity? (Bibliography)

A word about terminology: lack of agreement on terminology has been a recurring issue in the discourse. I take up the issue of descriptive labels in Chapter 1 and Chapter 3, though in general practice I use the terms *interdisciplinary* and *integrative* interchangeably, as adjectives signifying an attempt or desire to integrate different perspectives. Whenever it is necessary to distinguish the two terms, or to distinguish "interdisciplinary" from "multidisciplinary" or other levels of integrative work, I place the terms in quotation marks.

PART I

Definitions of Interdisciplinarity

1   The Evolution of Interdisciplinarity

> The need for interdisciplinarity has been reflected in epistemological writings ever since the origins of Western science.
>
> — Georges Gusdorf

The Problem of Knowledge

ANY attempt to understand the concept of interdisciplinarity is complicated by a considerable difference of opinion about its origin. For some it is quite old, rooted in the ideas of Plato, Aristotle, Rabelais, Kant, Hegel, and other historical figures who have been described as "interdisciplinary thinkers." For others it is entirely a phenomenon of the twentieth century, rooted in modern educational reforms, applied research, and movement across disciplinary boundaries. The actual term did not emerge until the twentieth century, and that is the history being traced here. However, the basic ideas are in fact quite old, and, for that reason, it is important to take a moment to clarify the underlying problem of knowledge that informs the modern concept of interdisciplinarity.

The roots of the concept lie in a number of ideas that resonate throughout the modern discourse—the ideas of a unified science, general knowledge, synthesis, and the integration of knowledge. Plato was the first to advocate philosophy as a unified science and, correspondingly, named the philosopher as the one who is capable of synthesizing knowledge. Plato also noted the prominence of certain subjects, namely mathematics and dialectic, and argued that a general idea or concept is timeless and immutable because it exists independently. His pupil Aristotle moved more in the direction of specificity by delineating clearer divisions of inquiry, such as "Politics," "Poetics," and "Metaphysics." Yet, Aristotle also believed it is the philosopher who has the ability to collect all forms of knowledge,

Portions of this chapter originally appeared in somewhat altered form in *Interdisciplinary Research and Analysis: A Book of Readings*, D. Chubin, A. Porter, F. Rossini, and T. Connolly, eds. Copyright © 1986 by Lomond Publications, Inc. Reprinted by permission of the Publisher.

to organize them and to know "all" in a general, encyclopedic sense. Though Aristotle denied the possibility of a universal science in the Platonic sense, there was for him a form of thinking logically prior to all others—the "first philosophy." Even as they were revised and challenged in later periods, these ideas were to remain part of the cultural heritage of the West.

The concept of interdisciplinarity has been shaped not only by ideas but also the way ideas were structured in the curriculum. Concern about the dangers of overspecialization arose quite early. Although rhetoric prevailed at the core of Roman higher education, some doubted whether one discipline was in and of itself a satisfactory form of advanced education, and Quintilian openly advocated more advanced studies over the whole range of the traditional curriculum.[1] As the modern university evolved from the medieval cathedral schools, a unified whole had come to include both letters and sciences in the customary divisions of the *trivium* (grammar, logic, and rhetoric) and the *quadrivium* (music, geometry, arithmetic, and astronomy). The idea was not that a student should study everything and forgo specialization but that specialization would occur in a community of general studies, " a little city."[2] The integration of knowledge was to be the occasion for the union of men, an ideal embodied in the twin notions of a community of disciplines of knowledge (*universitas scientiarum*) and a community of teachers and students (*universitas magistrorum et scholarium*).[3]

Unfortunately, there was a gap between the real and the ideal. Education remained for the most part a purely literary experience. Formal treatises on the liberal arts continued to pay homage to the encyclopedic ideal, but they did not reflect the actual shape of medieval education. There was a mass of general knowledge that did not fall within the range of any particular specialty, and many subjects still remained part of a much wider field.[4] However, by the late Middle Ages, the term *discipline* was being applied preeminently in three areas: at Paris, to theology and the arts; at Bologna, to the law; and at Salerno, to medicine.[5] Both the legal and medical faculties were responding to pressures to harness education to professional, ecclesiastical, and governmental needs.[6] These demands for specialization were *external* to educational institutions, in contrast to later divisions promoted by the *internal* growth of knowledge in the nineteenth century.[7]

The idea of unity persisted in a variety of ways, including preservation of the classical heritage and the work of the Renaissance Humanists, who demonstrated how unity can be defined not in terms of the divine but of human talent and consciousness. Still, the growth of specialization drew increasing attention to the problem of the parts. Though not yet phrased in terms of interdisciplinarity per se, the problem was apparent in the work of a number of writers from the sixteenth through nineteenth centuries, including Francis Bacon, Descartes, the French Encyclopedists,

Kant, Hegel, and Comte. Each of them expressed concern about the fragmentation of knowledge, and each, in his own way, articulated a vision of the unity of knowledge. However, Wilhelm Vosskamp notes, by the mid-eighteenth century universalistic ways of thinking no longer prevailed. Individuals continued to offer integrative systems though, over time, spiritually and philosophically based systems were gradually replaced by more materialistic, empirical systems based on a hierarchy or delineation of particular principles. Exhortations to achieve scientific and value-neutral theories in the nineteenth century only accelerated the movement away from grand philosophical systems. There was, in the nineteenth century, a strong synthetic thrust to several movements, including the theory of internal relations, vitalism, creative evolution, and organicism.[8] However, the cumulative effect of the growing particularization of knowledge was to accelerate the forces of differentiation, slowing down conceptual assimilation. More and more the problem of *Wissenschaft* — the totality of institutionalized scholarly and scientific pursuits — was perceived as no longer readily solvable in either theoretical or practical terms.[9]

The growing particularization of knowledge was also to have a profound impact on the structure of higher education. The reconstitution of the universities — during the eighteenth and nineteenth centuries in Germany, with the Napoleonic reforms in France, in the middle of the nineteenth century in Britain, and at the end of the nineteenth century in the United States[10] — altered the bifurcation of traditional knowledge, transmitted in universities, and new research, conducted in scientific societies. The University of Göttingen was an excellent example of the trend. Göttingen, founded in 1737, boasted a broad curriculum, an anatomical institute, a physical-mathematic institute, a botanical garden, a pharmacy, and, most indicative of the new trend, a scientific society.[11]

The modern connotation of *disciplinarity* is a product of the nineteenth century and is linked with several forces: the evolution of the modern natural sciences, the general "scientification" of knowledge, the industrial revolution, technological advancements, and agrarian agitation.[12] As the modern university took shape, disciplinarity was reinforced in two major ways: industries demanded and received specialists, and disciplines recruited students to their ranks. The trend toward specialization was further propelled by increasingly more expensive and sophisticated instrumentation within individual fields. Some subspecialties were also becoming distinct branches of knowledge, though certain fields remained connected with other fields. The parts of psychology now known as personality theory and social psychology, for example, remained linked with philosophy well into the second decade of the twentieth century, a trend evident in the work of Dewey, James, and others.[13]

Although the "Renaissance Man" may have remained an ideal for the well-educated baccalaureate, it was not the model for the new professional, specialized research scholar. Formalization of the pursuit of knowledge in various fields — history in 1884, economics in 1885, political science in 1903, and sociology in 1905 — paved the way for the "professionalization" of knowledge in the twentieth century.[14] A rare combination of a combined philosophical and institutional attempt to deal with the problem of fragmented knowledge did occur when the University of Berlin was founded at the beginning of the nineteenth century, in Wilhelm von Humboldt's concept of "universal education" (*allgemeine Menschenbildung*). There were enormous problems, however, in applying the concept, the very same problems that confront interdisciplinary programs today: the structural organization of universities, the politics of individual disciplines, the question of whether connections can be made between individual disciplines, and the question of whether any one concept could be so general as to include all the disciplines.[15]

The beginning of the modern period, Vosskamp suggests, is marked by three important points:

1. institutional (and therefore political) establishment of the disciplines as a "system of *Wissenschaft*";
2. differentiation in scholarly and scientific institutions for the sake of progress in individual disciplines; and
3. cooperation between individual disciplines, especially of the sort that intends to solve the problem of applying *Wissenschaft* and technology and to attain thereby at least a partial unity of *Wissenschaft*.[16]

These changes have raised the question of whether unity of knowledge is still possible. It is, Nicholas Rescher suggests, not the *unity* of science that has been lost but the *simplicity*.[17] In the shift towards "atomistic multiplicity," the tree of knowledge has become magnificently brachiated. But has the tree become dismembered in the process,[18] or, even as its branches grow outward in different directions, is the tree itself growing upward in one direction?[19] The modern concept of interdisciplinarity is centered on this problem of knowledge.

The Evolution of Interdisciplinarity

In what is a decidedly rich and crowded history, the modern concept of interdisciplinarity has been shaped in four major ways:

1. by attempts to retain and, in many cases, reinstill historical ideas of unity and synthesis;

2. by the emergence of organized programs in research and education;
3. by the broadening of traditional disciplines;
4. by the emergence of identifiable interdisciplinary movements.

It was no accident that the most visible momentum for interdisciplinarity in the first part of the twentieth century was in general education and the social sciences. Disciplinary cooperation was not unknown in the natural sciences, but a "fissiparous tendency" dominated the infrastructure of science until approximately mid-century. It was characterized by the splitting of some disciplines into new subspecialties.[20]

As liberal arts colleges were becoming dominated by disciplinary structure and the proliferation of specialties continued, it was becoming increasingly more difficult to educate the "whole person." In response many proponents of "liberal" and "general" culture promoted "general" education as an antidote to specialization. One of their goals was to offer students broad, nonspecialized education in a set of common courses seated in the unspecialized part of the curriculum and focused on a common viewpoint or common set of values.[21] There were several precedents for their curricular objectives, including the Greek program of *enkuklios paedeia* and the Roman *orbis doctrinae* (programs reflecting the belief that an educated person is one who has surveyed the disciplines), Cicero's concept of the *doctus orator* (the man who combines extensive knowledge of all sciences with wide experience of the problems of everyday life), and the ideas of a "Renaissance man" and, its modern counterpart, the "generalist." The "general" education reform also incorporated such forthrightly interdisciplinary objectives as addressing the difficulties created by specialization and devising a curriculum to help solve modern problems by marshalling disciplinary resources.

William Mayville associates many of the reforms of this era with Bouwsma's *civic model* of the educated person. The basis for many interdisciplinary programs today, the civic model is associated with general culture rather than a particular group. It assumes, in part, that the collective ideals of a culture are manifested in a literary culture that includes both literary and nonliterary "classics." This assumption was evident in Meiklejohn's belief that books form the basis of "intelligence," Eliot's "five-foot shelf" of classics, and Erskine and Hutchins's "Great Books" curricula at the University of Chicago and Columbia University.[22] The concept of interdisciplinarity was also linked with several additional programs: a survey course on "Social and Economic Institutions" (introduced in 1914 at Amherst by Alexander Meiklejohn), a program for freshmen and sophomores based on comparing and contrasting an ancient and a modern civilization (introduced after the war at the University of Wisconsin, by Meiklejohn), and the "war-aims" and "peace-aims" courses at Columbia (the model for many general-education programs around the country). In addition, the concept was linked with adaptations of the Progressive views of Alfred North Whitehead and John Dewey. Dewey himself was educated in the Hegelian tradition of internal, organic relations and, in his collaboration with Arthur Bentley, discussed the same problem of relations that lies at the heart of systems theory.[23]

Ernest Boyer considers the educational reforms of this era a response to several historical problems, including misplaced vocational emphasis in the 1920s, overemphasis on individual interests, disillusionment among youth, and the need for a national sense of unity.[24] Although the new programs clearly had an impact on the educational system, the general momentum for interdisciplinarity was undermined in the postwar era both externally, by a depression, and internally, by ever-increasing specialization.

Interdisciplinarity in the social sciences was propelled by parallel concerns. In the 1920s the Social Science Research Council (SSRC) was established to promote integration across disciplines that were being increasingly isolated by specialization. Though jurisdictional disputes continued to inhibit interdisciplinary contact, scholars who objected to the "craft exclusiveness" of specialization followed their problems across disciplinary lines. They included Dewey, Mead, Veblen, Angell, Boas, and Merriam—all at the University of Chicago. The "interactionist" framework at Chicago encouraged cross-fertilization, and later, in the 1930s and 1940s, the culture-personality movement proved a vital unifying force.[25] It was also becoming increasingly apparent that many problems in the postwar period were larger than the scope of any one discipline, among them war, labor, propaganda, population shifts, housing, social welfare, and crime. A spirit of reform encouraged integrative thinking in both governmental and private agencies, and, though the concept of an applied social science initially emerged from outside the university, academic social scientists began to see its importance and inherently interdisciplinary nature.[26]

Landau, Proshanky, and Ittelson speak of two interdisciplinary movements in the social sciences. The first movement, which extended from the close of World War I to the 1930s, was characterized by the borrowing of techniques and instruments for primarily instrumental purposes. There was a particular attraction to the quantitative methods of the natural sciences, evident in the movement of politics and sociology toward psychology, a field that appeared to have developed its own research instruments. Occasionally, disciplinary "spillage" did lead to the evolution of hybrid disciplines to fill gaps, in the case of social psychology, political sociology, physiological psychology, and social anthropology. However, the relationship between fields remained essentially empirical. There was "no direct challenge to the status quo of social science" and existing categories remained intact.

The 1930s and 1940s were also marked by an effort to integrate scientific inquiry. This effort had been preceded by the founding of the Vienna Circle in 1924, part of a broad unity of science movement aimed at achieving common terminology and laws.[27] In the 1930s members of the Chicago school of social sciences tried to unify the rational and empirical domains through logical positivism, emphasizing a logical analysis of language anticipated by Decartes's earlier *mathesis universalis.* Encyclopedism and physicalism were the pillars of the new movement.[28] The *International Encyclopedia of Unified Science* was a project marked by Otto Neurath, Rudolf Carnap, and Charles Morris's vision of a foundation for the philosophy of the natural and social sciences. They attempted to integrate scientific statements with all their discrepancies and difficulties, rather than using a system based on a priori principles. Scientific statements might be axiomatized, but that would not necessarily yield a model of the scientific knowledge of a given age. It was, Neurath reported, "the maximum of integration which we can achieve."[29] Although the movement eventually dwindled, it gained widespread attention in the 1930s.

There was, in addition, a much-heralded synthetic movement known as the "area" approach. Area studies began appearing in American universities in the late 1930s as efforts to provide comprehensive, integrated knowledge about other geographical areas. The area approach is an example of the second interdisciplinary movement in the social sciences, which dates from the close of World War II. The second movement was also apparent in the form of integrated social science courses, integrated departments, and, its most significant outcome, the concept of behavioral science. The movement was based not on the instrumental integration of knowledge but on a more ambitious conceptual premise. By bridging gaps between disciplines, teams of scholars hoped to work towards unity of knowledge. Yet, despite its promise, the area approach led to disappointment. Many disciplinarians were inclined to "default,"[30] to fall back on their disciplinary perspectives instead of creating new synthetic perspectives. As a result, a demand for new "integrative" categories arose in the social sciences.

The older "interdisciplinary" approach has been likened to "the old Baconian belief that broader basic generalizations will almost automatically drop out of the vast accumulation of discrete fact." Given past experience, it was a naïve conviction. In the absence of an automatic breakthrough, there must be a deliberate search for new "integrative" concepts that allow for treating problems in the most effective manner. Landau and colleagues explain: "'Area,' when not reified, may be such a concept. And by its proper use it replaces the categories of the older traditions. It is a new category deemed to have greater analytic power and if it promises to eliminate the older disciplines because of this power, this—in the logic of scientific inquiry—is as it should be."[31]

The same may be said of other concepts, such as "role," "reference group," "mobility," "status," and "self," as well as game theory, "decision-making," "action," "information," and "communication." As they cross the "vertical pillars" of the disciplines, they promote theoretical convergence. Although clearly more difficult than the more instrumental form of inter-disciplinarity, this task derives from the first stage of interdisciplinary contact. Logically, it may lead to several consequences: restructuring fields in theoretic terms, transcending institutionalism by providing a theoretical coherence, producing a new system for the division of labor, or distributing resources based on a set of explicit ordering principles. In this context both the area approach and the behavioral-science movement were considered more than just an extension of "interdisciplinary" work. They were alternative methods of organizing social inquiry, anticipating, but never effecting, a cumulative science.[32] Clearly, "integrative" was a higher and more powerful category than "interdisciplinary," which signified in this case the combining of established categories, methods, and perspectives.

A similar distinction also evolved in educational circles, where the correlation theories of the Herbartians provided the germ of the modern integration movement in education.[33] "Correlation" was associated primarily with Herbartism, a set of philosophical and psychological ideas applied to instructional method. The "doctrine of concentration" held that a mind advances when wholly immersed in one interest, but it was supplemented by the "doctrine of correlation," which held that connections should be made with related subjects.[34] Although some theorists tried to distinguish "integration" and "correlation," most of them used the terms synonymously. By the 1930s "integration" had acquired a number of meanings, though it was used specifically as a slogan for an educational movement associated with changing social conditions. In 1935, at a meeting on the concept of integration, members of the National Education Association concluded that complete unity was impossible. They proposed, instead, to think in terms of "unifying" rather than "unified" experiences. The meeting also produced a book that was to become a watershed in development of the concept of "integrative" education: *Integration: Its Meaning and Application.*[35]

The more pertinent distinction arose from the Foundation (later Center) for Integrative Education. Through conferences, a book (*Integrative Principles of Modern Thought*), and a journal (*Main Currents in Modern Thought*), its members worked to overcome divisiveness in modern education. They included a remarkable group of philosophers and scientists — among them Northrup, Margenau, Sinnot, Mather, Maslow, Laszlo, Sorokin, and Kluckhorn. In 1948, when the year-old foundation convened a workshop on integrated education, participants formally recognized a belief that had appeared recurrently in the 1930s: they distinguished *con-*

tent integration, the integration of physical sciences with arts and letters, from *process integration,* the "interplay of individual and environment." They also noted a difference between *integration,* defined as synthesizing presently accepted postulates, and an *integrative* building of new conceptual modes capable of producing a holistic educational philosophy.[36] Clearly, "integration" had taken on a much wider meaning than "correlation." It had come to mean a broad concept in education, not a specific structure or teaching method. Moreover, the focus had shifted from transmitting traditional fields of knowledge and linking existing disciplinary categories — akin to the "interdisciplinary" distinction in the social sciences — to an integrative transmutation that emphasized the individual's learning process and the development of new conceptual approaches, new pedagogy, and even a new corpus of universal principles — akin to the "integrative" distinction in the social sciences.

Despite these technical distinctions, "interdisciplinary" remained an ambiguous term. It was applied to both the idea of grand unity and a more limited integration of existing disciplinary concepts and theories. It was used for both instrumental borrowing across disciplines and the development of new conceptual categories. By the 1940s and 1950s, and even into the 1960s, the only formal distinctions were in the education and social science literatures, and even those distinctions were not observed consistently. Still, as late as 1971, Richard Pring argued that "integrated" and "interdisciplinary" descriptions of the curriculum are on different logical levels. "Integration" raises certain epistemological questions to which "interdisciplinary" remains indifferent. "Integration" incorporates the idea of unity between forms of knowledge and their respective disciplines, whereas "interdisciplinary" simply refers to the use of more than one discipline in pursuing a particular inquiry. Hence, in Pring's view, "interdisciplinary" does not raise questions about the unity of knowledge, though further thinking might show such questions are unavoidable.[37]

Even in the absence of widespread consensus on terminology, though, a fundamental distinction had emerged in the dispersed discourse. It was reflected, technically, in the "interdisciplinary"/"integrative" distinction and, more generally, in two basic metaphors noted in the 1970s by the British Group for Research and Innovation in Higher Education. They are "bridge building" and "restructuring." The first, "bridge building," takes place between complete and firm disciplines. The second, "restructuring," involves changing parts of several disciplines. Bridge-building seems more common and is less difficult, since it preserves disciplinary identities. Restructuring is more radical and often embodies a criticism of not only the state of the disciplines being restructured but, either implicitly or explicitly, the prevailing structure of knowledge. Bridge-building usually assumes a grounding in the constituent disciplines and often has an applied orientation. Restructuring usually assumes the need for new organizing concepts and the methodologies or skills common to more than one discipline. Clearly, there is a difference between an external, applied focus and an internal, methodological or conceptual basis for interdisciplinarity, though they are not necessarily found in pure form. The British Group also noted a third possibility for integration, one that comes from a new overarching concept or theory. This overarching integration subsumes the theories and concepts of several existing disciplines[38] and corresponds to what was to be labeled "transdisciplinarity" in a widely used typology of definitions that emerged in the early 1970s from the work of the Organization of Economic Cooperation and Development (OECD). At least in intention, this third level of integration has functioned as a modern equivalent of the older, comprehensive unity of knowledge.

Interdisciplinarity at Mid-Century

By mid-century interdisciplinarity was being promoted in several ways. There was, to begin with, a second major reform, symbolized by the 1945 Harvard "redbook," *General Education in a Free Society*. It called for core curricula covering Western civilization, literary texts, scientific principles, and English composition, with an additional course in each of the humanities, social sciences, and natural sciences. Designed in part to nullify the problems of excessive concentration, this innovation had already been attempted in a series of introductory courses at Columbia University.[39] In 1944 Columbia historian Frank Tannenbaum was using the term *holistic* to indicate the need for studying whole systems. Tannenbaum sought a force capable of unifying fragmented expertise in order to deal with the challenges of the time. Just after World War II, Columbia launched a seminar program that has continued, to this day, providing a forum for the discussion of common problems and issues.[40] Until the late 1960s, most American colleges and universities developing programs of general and interdisciplinary education tended to emulate the Harvard, Columbia, and Chicago models.[41]

The second general education reform, like the earlier one, moved in the direction of community: towards shared values, shared responsibilities, shared governance, shared heritage, and a shared world vision.[42] "General" education continued to be interdisciplinary in several respects: when it functioned as a revolt against fragmentation, when it attempted to reorganize and integrate knowledge along other than disciplinary lines, when it tried to deal with contemporary issues and problems by drawing on more than one discipline, and when it continued to address the human problems created by specialization. Once again, however, the momentum was checked.

Though the movement had a strong impact on a gifted generation of students, the Hutchins reforms of Chicago were challenged by accelerating specialization, and the experiments at Columbia and Harvard were confined, at the time, to the undergraduate level.[43]

A number of synthetic theories were also having an impact on the structure of inquiry at mid-century. Synthetic theories such as Marxism, structuralism, and general systems theory operate on several levels. They have been used to strengthen theory in one discipline, to unify a single discipline, to provide an integrative methodology or theory for a cluster of disciplines, and even to function as a unified science by integrating all disciplines around a single transcendent paradigm. Marxism has raised a broad range of questions about economic, social, and political forces in a wide variety of fields, ranging from biology to art history. General systems theory, which emerged at mid-century, is concerned with patterns and interrelations in wholes. Structuralism is concerned with the deep structures underlying human thought, formal structures believed to reflect a basic cognitive, biologically derived structure of the thought process. Structuralism shares some assumptions with general systems theory, including the relatedness of all things, their organization into levels of isomorphic structure with laws of transformation, structures (or systems) manifesting homeostatic self-regulation, and holism.[44] In the early 1970s, Piaget was to make the idea of common structures the starting point for a theory of interdisciplinarity,[45] though systems theory has tended to be the most widely influential of modern synthetic theories. General systems theory revived "organismic thinking" as a complement to analytical thinking. With its attendant concepts of symmetry, feedback, steady state, entropy, and negentropy (a numerical measure of information content), and their correlates of information gain and loss,[46] general systems theory promoted a holistic approach to both a conception of reality and a theory of cognition.[47] Since the 1950s, it has also been associated with several forms of holistic thinking in the social sciences.[48]

The power of synthetic theories increased significantly with their dispersion. Shannon's information theory is a good example. Seven years after its initial appearance in the field of communications engineering, references had appeared in the publications of nine different disciplines: psychology, physiology, optics, physics, linguistics, biology, sociology, statistics, and journalism. Both academic and nonacademic centers played an important role in disseminating the theory and bringing together people from different disciplines. The idea spread rapidly because of its relevance. The problem of measuring information transmission was widespread, and Shannon's explanation had great appeal, though Shannon's eminence and the prestige of the *Bell System Technical Journal,* in which his work appeared, certainly contributed to the speed of adoption.[49]

Interdisciplinarity was also being promoted by a rich variety of cross-fertilizations still visible today. Theology was moving in the direction of sociology, analytic psychology, and philosophic positivism.[50] In geography the man-land thesis was creating a wider perspective at a time when economic history was finding its way into economics and history departments. History itself was the clear beneficiary of progress in the "imperialistic human sciences,"[51] though only after 1945 and then quite slowly did the new approaches gain prominence. In the 1920s "New History" had emerged as part of a movement towards the social sciences. Led by Marc Bloch, Lucien Febvre, and later Fernand Braudel, the *synthèse historique* of the *Annales* school of history built the foundation for a "global" history that they hoped would promote a synthesis of social history. Drawing on demographic data, the *annales* historians based many of their studies on a region rather than a political or national unit. In many cases they wound up producing what has been termed a "retrospective anthropology."[52] The new interdisciplinary history found its firmest institutional base in France. In 1946 the sixth section of the Ecole Pratique des Hautes Etudes (since 1975 the Ecole des Hautes Etudes en Sciences Sociales) was established as a research and teaching center for the integration of history and the social sciences. It also assumed publication of *Annales: Economies, Sociétés, Civilisations*. In 1952, in England, the journal *Past and Present* began appearing; and in the United States, a number of other new interdisciplinary journals emerged, including *Comparative Studies in Society and History* (1958) and, later, the *Journal of Social History* (1967) and the *Journal of Interdisciplinary History* (1970). In socialist countries Marxist ideology and the coordinating role of the academies of science played an important role in promoting the integration of historical research and social history.

During this period the SSRC remained a significant integrative force. An SSRC committee on research in economic history was instrumental in creating the Center for Entrepreneurial Studies at Harvard and, in 1954, its Committee on Historiography published a study entitled *The Social Sciences in Historical Study*.[53] At first historians associated with the SSRC continued their prewar commitment to building social science research skills, supported by SSRC Bulletin 64, a 1954 work validating social science theory and methods of proof. A different view, however, was to emerge from a separate conference of leading historians that the council sponsored in 1953. Its participants focused on what historians were, not on what they should become, and they cautioned historians not to become social scientists. In 1956 a third SSRC committee on historiography moved on from the work of the first two, influenced by rising respect for the humanistic complexity of historical thought.[54]

This was not the only turn towards the humanities,[55] where a concern for values has long promoted relationships with the social and natural sciences. The discourse on interdisciplinarity grew wider as social scientists debated whether their proper model ought to be the natural sciences or the humanities. The argument for "interpretation" has been prominent in this debate, and, as Clifford Geertz has shown, analogies from the humanities—game, drama, text, speech-act analysis, discourse models, and representationalist approaches related to cognitive aesthetics—have been playing an increasingly visible role in sociological and anthropological explanation.[56] These and other trends are evident in the work of individual scholars.

Richard Harvey Brown has returned to the humanities—to point of view, metaphor, and irony—to discover how an understanding of language and history can structure explanation in the discipline of sociology, creating *A Poetic for Sociology*. In conceiving of *Society as Text,* Brown has found in critical rhetoric a method for not only showing how experience and knowledge are produced through the persuasive use of language but also providing canons of judgment in science as well as political and moral discourse.[57] Hayden White has utilized rhetorical categories to examine the deep structure of historical imagination, creating a poetic for history,[58] and James Boyd White has demonstrated the relationship between humanities and law through a study of the language, rhetoric, and explanation of the law.[59]

Though not always highly visible, the impact of these changes has been widespread. Within the past few decades there has been a transformation that constitutes, Beth Casey suggests, a "quiet revolution" within the humanities and social sciences. Centered on a view of the humanities as language-oriented connective disciplines, this transformation is rooted in the gradual absorption of Saussurean linguistics and is evident in demonstrations of how the social world is discursively constructed and rooted in specifically historical situations. As linguistic models have replaced models borrowed from the natural sciences, there has been a movement toward reintegration of the humanistic disciplines of linguistics, literature, rhetoric, philosophy, aesthetics, history, and art history with each other and with the social sciences. The evidence is widespread, though it has been particularly apparent in the critical movements known as structuralism and deconstruction, especially in the work of Claude Lévi-Strauss, Roland Barthes, Jacques Derrida, and Michel Foucault.[60]

The changes in literary studies demonstrate how such pluralistic movement can alter the shape of a discipline, a discipline that was grounded traditionally in philology and biography. The most visible interdisciplinary effort at mid-century was the American Studies movement, a combined field that arose out of English and history departments. Taken as a whole, the new movements in literary study were characterized by social explanation and attention to psychology, anthropology, political history, linguistics, and the general history of ideas. In the years after 1945, the voices of methodological reintegration were still rather isolated, but they were to grow. In Europe interdisciplinary research was promoted as the model for a regenerated study of literature and, by the mid-1950s, similar voices were being heard in the United States. There was talk of "multiple interpretation," "multiple parallelism," and "multiple causation."[61] One of the leading critics in the United States, Kenneth Burke, sought a gradual integration of sociological, psychoanalytical, and purely linguistic factors. A man of truly "catholic scope,"[62] Burke drew on Marxism, psychoanalysis, and Gestalt theory. Burke's concept of symbolic action appeared subsequently in a number of different fields, including poetry, theology, metaphysics, diplomacy, and historiography.

There has been no single interdisciplinary approach in any of these fields. Literature, history, and anthropology, especially, fit LeRoy Ladurie's description of history as a "crowded multiple crossing." In literature some of the forces advocating pluralism have wanted to counteract the narrow interpretation of works with an eclectic combination of two or three methods. Others argue for historical awareness, with increasing emphasis on social or literary history over phenomenological, existential, formal, and structural approaches. Still others endorse current attempts to reintegrate the humanities through linguistic, rhetorical, semiotic, and hermeneutic theories. Currently the study of literature is being energized by a wide spectrum of interests, ranging across psychoanalysis, Marxism, history, sociology, and a complex set of interpretive stances that have evolved from structuralism, post-structuralism, and expanding interest in "textualism."[63]

In the realm of applied research, World War II proved an even greater catalyst for interdisciplinarity than World War I, on technological, political, and intellectual grounds. During World War II, the military's need for a new turbo-engine led to cooperative work among physicists and chemists, an effort now regarded as part of the early history of the field of solid-state physics.[64] Operations research evolved as operating problems were experienced with a new system of radar. They were not simple, technical problems. Any scientist who might be useful was pressed into service by the Royal Air Force, whether biologist, physicist, or engineer.[65] Spurred by an interest in the politics and economics of science that stemmed from heavy governmental involvement in science during World War II, science policy studies also began finding a place in the subfields of history, philosophy, and sociology of science.[66] By the 1950s, the growth of interdisciplinary "hyphenated sciences" was creating a palpable tension within universities. Straining to serve multiple communities, librarians faced new pressures from area studies as well as partial and extensive consolidations in biophysics, biochemistry, and biomedical engineering.[67]

New developments in the natural sciences were also promoting cross-fertilization. Since the 1940s analogies between the machine and the organism[68] had been functioning as root metaphors promoting interdisciplinary thought. There were also a variety of cross-fertilizations among the different subbranches of physics,[69] and scientific subgroups were seeking fusion through grand simplifying concepts such as the second law, the mass-energy equivalence, and quantum mechanics.[70] They constituted, Rustum Roy explains, "an intellectual pediment strangely at variance with the increasing administrative and pedagogic specialization."[71] They reflected a view of science recently reaffirmed by Gerald Holton, who noted, "The underlying epistemological thrust of science is towards a program of omniscience, the development of a scientific world picture that is so powerful and so simple in its fundamental assumptions that, from it, you can deduce all the phenomena of nature."[72] This search for unity continues at the same time a new field, loosely termed "chaos theory," is gaining wider recognition. Reflecting a concern for not only pattern but also randomness and complexity in systems, chaos theory is evident in mathematics, biology, and physics, as well as astronomy, business, political theory, and other disciplines.

There were also new fields. The new science of radioastronomy and dendrochronology (tree-ring dating) were integrative in nature,[73] and there was a heightened interdisciplinarity to the post-World War II earth sciences. The shift from the classical theory of continental drift to modern plate tectonics involved paleontology, geochemistry, marine geology and geophysics, seismology, volcanology, and paleomagnetism.[74] Moreover, as interest in existentialism, phenomenology, and post-structuralism spread, the sharp distinction between science and humanism was questioned. With the publication of Thomas Kuhn's *The Structure of Scientific Revolutions* in 1962, inquiry into the social, cultural, and political dimensions of science expanded,[75] accelerating skepticism about received notions of scientific rationality and truth criteria. Kuhn's book has been called a "major text for interdisciplinary discourse."[76] The description is appropriate, for the book stimulated an ever-widening inquiry into the nature of knowledge in both disciplinary and interdisciplinary communities.

The role of mission-oriented projects cannot be overstated, for it has had, in a very real sense, the greatest impact on current definitions of interdisciplinarity. Mission-oriented projects are not unique to the twentieth century. In 1803 the Congress of the United States appropriated $2,500 to support a multidisciplinary investigation of the upper Missouri River led by Meriwether Lewis, who broadened his expertise by studying celestial navigation, zoology, botany, and ethnography with members of the American Philosophical Society in Philadelphia.[77] The first research grant from the federal government, in support of the Franklin Institute's 1930 effort to explain the causes of steam boiler explosions, went to a research group that included representatives from chemistry, engineering, physics, meteorology, and other fields.[78] In addition, the mission orientation of the U.S. Department of Agriculture has long promoted collaboration across disciplines.[79] In the early part of the century, interdisciplinary research was not formally organized. The small size of agricultural research staffs encouraged interactions, but formal interdisciplinary research in agriculture did not begin until the 1940s. The earliest work is dated at 1942, on studies of input-output relationships in milk. By the 1950s and 1960s, there was a great deal of interest in this type of research going on among agricultural economists and biological scientists, especially at Iowa State University and Michigan State University. Inevitably, though, the degree of collaboration varied from project to project.[80]

The significant factor at mid-century was the size and scope of problem-focused research. The most famous mission was the Manhattan Project to build an atomic bomb, a cooperative effort among science, industry, and the United States Army. It was the beginning of a mission focus that would, by the 1960s and 1970s, create a visible interdisciplinary presence on campuses in the form of organized research teams, institutes, and centers. They focused, most often, on problems of defense, aerospace, and industry. After the 1957 launching of Sputnik by the U.S.S.R., as federal funding of mission-oriented projects expanded in the United States, organizations such as the National Science Foundation (NSF) and the National Institutes of Health (NIH) were established to support both basic and applied research in universities.[81] Governmental and industrial laboratories as well as non-profit research groups such as the Rand Corporation and the Princeton Institute for Advanced Study also engaged in interdisciplinary research. During the Sputnik era, mission-oriented research was dominated by interdisciplinary engineering centers, though by the 1970s the "driving force" had shifted to nonmarket goods and social concerns, such as product safety, environmental quality, mobility, and technology assessment. As a result, interdisciplinary engineering centers became "sociotechnical think tanks."[82] Correspondingly, the mission-based information systems that emerged during World War II — focused on engineering, science, and technology — were joined by problem-based information systems in the 1960s and 1970s — focused on sociotechnical problems.[83] Now, in the 1980s, the NSF is once again focusing on engineering in a new series of multidisciplinary engineering centers, and interdisciplinary research is also envisioned in another series of U.S. science and technology centers. It is also promoted in a variety of NATO-sponsored cooperative programs in science and technology.

Mark Kann contends that "there was no effective demand for general explanations prior to World War II." There has been a demand for general explanation since the beginnings of Western philosophy. However, as Kann points out, the postwar status of the United States heightened the demand for interdisciplinary discourse across state political lines, corporate decision-making and planning, and a variety of social and political movements. By the 1970s "an odd combination of liberal intellectuals, conservative elites, and radicals expressed an interest in breaking down disciplinary boundaries and in pursuing more fully and consciously the interdisciplinary idea." The university responded in two ways: by sponsoring joint programs and by legitimizing joint subfields.[84] There are two major reasons why mission-oriented projects became so prominent. There was, first of all, considerable financial incentive for universities, in the form of government and foundation grants. There was also the *"inexorable logic that the real problems of society do not come in discipline-shaped blocks."* In Rustum Roy's view, the major force in changing university structures toward interdisciplinarity was not intellectual but political and financial.[85]

In the postwar decades, the NSF was to play a particularly significant role. It began, in 1969, when the foundation organized a program called Interdisciplinary Research Relevant to Problems of Our Society (IRROPS). Later, in 1971, IRROPS evolved into the Research Application Directorate and the Research Applied to National Needs Program (RANN), an effort that placed more emphasis on problem-solving research.[86] Despite the considerable amount of funding that went into interdisciplinary problem-focused research (IDR), however, funding agencies were often disappointed in the results. Like area studies, mission-oriented projects often fell short of genuine integration. Born of pressure to solve problems outside the narrow scope of individual specialties, IDR itself was plagued by disciplinary chauvinism and the psychological, social, and epistemological problems of working across disciplines. In the early 1970s, the NSF resolved to do something about the problem by establishing the Research Management Improvement Program (RMI), a unit charged with the task of improving the ability of nonprofit research organizations to manage federally funded research projects. By the time its funding was terminated by the U.S. Congress, RMI had distributed $3,880,000 across thirty-five projects, almost half of them interdisciplinary.[87] In creating the RMI unit, the NSF also became a major catalyst in the creation of a new phenomenon, the organized investigation of interdisciplinary research. Along with Stifting Volkswagenwerk (Federal Republic of Germany), the NSF would sponsor the first international conference on interdisciplinary problem-focused research in 1979.

The Watershed Era

The 1960s and 1970s constituted a remarkable era, "a slot in history when innovations could get support."[88] Identification of interdisciplinarity with reforms of the sixties and seventies is so strong that many people are inclined to associate the very concept of interdisciplinarity with that remarkable era. Ingemar Lind, for one, declared "Interdisciplinarity was born of a sudden demand for the universities to renew themselves,"[89] and the OECD, in calling an international conference on interdisciplinarity in 1984, spoke of interdisciplinarity as a concept that developed in the late 1960s.[90] Many of the current educational programs were founded in that era, as "experimental," "cluster," and "satellite" programs attached to existing colleges and universities. The majority were alternatives to the traditional curriculum. They were "telic" institutions in the sense that Grant and Riesman used the term to describe purposive reforms charged with a sense of mission and distinctiveness. Telic reforms approached the status of social movements or generic protests against contemporary life. They pointed towards a different conception of the ends of undergraduate education, ends that could not be met by simply reforming existing curricula or inventing new instructional technology. New programs and, in some cases, entirely new institutions were required.[91]

During this period general awareness of interdisciplinarity was heightened by major funding. In the United States, a variety of agencies supported interdisciplinary activities, including the NSF, the Carnegie Foundation, the National Endowment for the Humanities (NEH),[92] and the Fund for the Improvement of Post-Secondary Education (FIPSE). In Europe the OECD, the London-based Society for Research into Higher Education, and the United Nations Educational, Social, and Cultural Organization (UNESCO) played major roles. It was, however, the OECD that was to have the greatest influence on how the concept is currently defined. In the late 1960s, the OECD's Centre for Educational Research and Innovation organized the first international investigation of the concept of interdisciplinarity, an effort that culminated in a 1970 seminar on the problems of interdisciplinary teaching and research in universities. The seminar capped an investigation provoked by worldwide reform in education, renewed protests against the fragmentation of knowledge, and heightened demands for the university to fulfill its social mission.

Marked as it was by the appearance of the OECD seminar results in book form, the year 1972 was to become a major date in the history of interdisciplinarity. Entitled *Interdisciplinarity: Problems of Teaching and Research in Universities,* the book is dominated by the general systems and structuralist thinking of the seminar's major theorists, among them Erich Jantsch, Guy Berger, Jean Piaget, and Leo Apostel. Their work was truly seminal. It was a "preliminary balance sheet," a "working tool" that did indeed become "the starting point for new thought and action."[93] Even now this book remains the most widely cited reference on the subject of interdisciplinarity because it "channeled"[94] hitherto sporadic, dispersed discussions of interdisciplinarity. Across the disciplines teachers and scholars began reflecting on their own interdisciplinary activities aided by a new theoretical framework and typology of definitions for "multidisciplinary," "pluridisciplinary," "interdisciplinary" and "transdisciplinary" work.

The period of 1979–80 was also to prove significant, with the appearance of a second major book, the evolution of two professional associations, and a new OECD definition of interdisciplinarity. The book is *Interdisciplinarity and Higher Education,* a full-length collection of essays by participants in a postdoctoral seminar on interdisciplinarity held in 1975–76 under the auspices of the Interdisciplinary Graduate Program in the Humanities at Pennsylvania State University. Its authors concentrated on definitions of interdisciplinarity, interdisciplinary methodology, problems of designing and sustaining interdisciplinary research projects, historical perspectives on interdisciplinary education, and critiques of structuralism, general systems, and the unity of science movement as foundations for an adequate theory of interdisciplinarity. By an intriguing coincidence, two professional organizations also emerged in 1979, the Association for Integrative Studies (AIS) and the International Association for the Study of Interdisciplinary Research (INTERSTUDY). The AIS is a U.S.-based organization that promotes the study of interdisciplinary theory, methodology, curricula, and administration. Most of its members are teachers and scholars engaged in interdisciplinary education. It is the most broadly based of current organizations devoted to interdisciplinary issues and has published a directory of undergraduate interdisciplinary programs in the United States. INTERSTUDY is an international organization that formed after the first NSF-sponsored international conference on interdisciplinary problem-focused research. It has continued to sponsor periodic international conferences and has produced books from each of those conferences, focused primarily on the management of research. Most of its members come from government, industry, and primarily business and social science departments in universities.

All five episodes in the contemporary history of interdisciplinarity — the publication of two major books on interdisciplinarity, the emergence of the AIS and INTERSTUDY, as well as the new OECD formulation — occurred in isolation, though by 1984 all affiliated organizations were at least in some fashion aware of the existence of the others. Even so, there has been no real consolidation of efforts.

The new OECD definition emerged after a 1976–78 survey of relationships between the university and the community in their member countries, followed by a 1980 international conference on that subject. The OECD concluded there is increased demand for interdisciplinarity outside the university. As a result, they surmised, *interdisciplinarity exogenous to the university* must now be given more weight. Exogenous interdisciplinarity originates in the continuous momentum provided by "real" problems of the community, enriching and interrogating *endogenous university interdisciplinarity,* which is based on the production of new knowledge with the aim, more or less explicit, of realizing unity of science.[95] Their conclusion parallels a growing "primacy of the practical."[96] A complex technological society, in the logic of the exogenous argument, has problems that require interdisciplinary solution. It is an argument that has been heard since the start of the century, but it has assumed an increased sense of urgency as the magnitude of the problems mounts and calls for praxis increase.

The events that have occurred since the late 1960s raise an important question about interdisciplinarity in the late twentieth century—that of the balance between specialization and integration. At a 1975 conference on interdisciplinarity in London, Hans Klette spoke of a constant swing between unity and diversity in Western civilization.[97] On other occasions, Stephen Toulmin has invoked the images of a folkdance and a pendulum, signifying movement between cooperation and isolation, between practical and abstract research.[98] Gerald Holton has also suggested that the human mind proceeds by two steps: first, analysis, which produces highly specialized work, and then, synthesis.[99] The swings, the marching, and the shifts are by no means uniformly spaced, and they do not account for the growing complexity and diffusion of the concept of interdisciplinarity.

Both complexity and diffusion are readily apparent in the exponential growth of published scholarship on interdisciplinarity since 1970. Chubin, Rossini, and Porter found the literature on interdisciplinary problem-focused research is just over thirty years old, dating from a 1951 paper on problems of collaboration between an anthropologist and a psychiatrist. After 1969, however, the literature grew significantly: doubling from 1969 to 1972, then growing 120 percent from 1973 to 1977, and an additional 95 percent from 1978 to 1982.[100] There has also been a corresponding increase in the discussion of interdisciplinarity across disciplinary, professional, and general literatures. The changing nature of that literature is quite striking. Whereas earlier work tended to focus primarily on educational programs, the social sciences, and traditional ideas about unity, the focus has now widened. Since 1970 scholars have been paying closer attention to the problems of designing and managing interdisciplinary curricula and research projects, the practical and philosophical consequences of relations between particular disciplines, the dynamics of interdisciplinary problem-solving, and the nature of interdisciplinary theory and method.

The momentum is undeniable. The discussion of interdisciplinarity is becoming both broader and deeper. However, the institutional obstacles to interdisciplinary programs remain formidable. Reflecting on the concept of interdisciplinarity since the 1970s, Georges Papadopoulos concluded there has been a clear shift from the optimism of the seventies to an "empirical realism" in the eighties, from developing concepts to experimenting with practical applications and dealing with the reality of disciplinary restraints. The "quest for academic responsibility," he concluded, "leads inevitably to a regression back to individual disciplines," leaving interdisciplinarity "a hostage to the disciplines."[101] Paradoxically, then, the discourse is widening and there is a heightened sense of urgency about the need for interdisciplinarity at the same time interdisciplinary programs are struggling for legitimacy in the academy. Moreover, the "reformists" who support interdisciplinary movements are far outnumbered by "traditionalists," who support interdisciplinary work but have doubts about interdisciplinary programs. Even the reformists do not agree. "Progressive reformists," Harry Hermanns points out, want control over the direction of change in society, whereas "conservative reformists" want better adaptations.[102] These and other differences of opinion only complicate the attempt to define interdisciplinarity. In order to arrive at a fuller understanding of the concept, it is necessary to look more closely at how interdisciplinarity has been defined in the discourse and to consider what role visibility and formality have played in the assessment of its worth.

2　The Interdisciplinary Archipelago

> . . . das ist ein *zu* weites Feld.
>
> —Theodor Fontane, *Effi Briest*

GUY BERGER once envisioned interdisciplinarity as an archipelago, a number of scattered or regrouped islands broken away from a system that both provokes and rejects them.[1] The archipelago metaphor makes a rather useful model, for it invites us to map the intelligible surface structure of interdisciplinarity. Mapping the archipelago is not an easy task, for interdisciplinarity has appeared so widely that definitions vary from country to country, institution to institution, from one part of a campus to another, and even among members of the same team. Furthermore, the relative size and visibility of interdisciplinary activities vary greatly, ranging from formal, "overt" structures to a "concealed" presence that may flourish where it is not even labeled an interdisciplinary activity.[2]

Prior to its 1970 seminar on interdisciplinarity, the OECD conducted a survey to determine whether interdisciplinary activities in particular countries tended to be primarily in general education, professional education, the training of researchers, basic research, or applied research. General education was the most frequent answer, though there were national differences. Canadian answers favored the sciences and applied research, with biology as the most frequently cited area. The answers that came from Japan also tended to be in the sciences. In France the social sciences appeared most often and professional training hardly at all, though the French answers tended to come from such experimental centers as the University of Paris IX (Centre Paris-Dauphine) and VIII (Paris-Vincennes), institutions created in October 1968 for the expressed purpose of setting up "pluridisciplinary" activities. In West Germany general education was not represented, suggesting that interdisciplinarity was seldom part of education and training. In contrast, professional training was the leading area in the United Kingdom and science the most frequently cited example. In the United States, where the greatest diversity of disciplines was cited, general education was the leading activity.[3] Clearly, interdisciplinarity has a varied geography.

Most attempts to define the concept are partial at best, though two of them offer a fairly comprehensive account of why interdisciplinary activities appear where they do. Corinna Delkeskamp defined the concept as a set of four arguments: common interest in an object of study, social concerns, the existential belief that society must be restored to wholeness, and an ethical concern for the contrast between ideal and actual academic humanism in university structures.[4] The most comprehensive account, to date, is the one that emerged from the pioneer work of the OECD, which found interdisciplinarity arises from five demands:[5]

1. *The development of science* as the result of two movements:
   first, increasing specialization leading to the intersection of two disciplines, splitting up of an over-rigid discipline, or setting off into new fields of knowledge;
   second, the result of attempts to define elements common to disciplines.
2. *Student demand:*
   The result of direct student pressure or faculty anticipation, most of the time as a protest against parcelization and artificial subdivisions of "reality."
3. *Problems of university operation or even administration:*
   The result of increasingly elaborate equipment in research centers and the need for budget management in universities, especially in regard to contracts with government or the advent of a major technology such as a computer.
4. *Vocational and professional training requirements:*
   Educational needs based on student demand and, in some cases, the result of a contract extending outside the university, thereby linked with the fifth demand.
5. *The original social demand:*
   Particular needs and new subjects which cannot, by definition, be contained within a single disciplinary frame, such as environmental research.

These demands reflect not only external and internal reasons for interdisciplinarity—the endogenous versus exogenous distinction made by the OECD—but also a related distinction apparent in the history of the concept—the distinction between a conceptually based, "synoptic" justification and a pragmatically based "instrumental" justification.[6]

The synoptic claim is evident in several forms: historically informed arguments for unity and synthesis, modern synthetic theories and integrative concepts, and the work of individual synthesizers. The instrumental claim arises from the need to solve problems that may be either social or intellectual in origin, though instrumental interdisciplinarity is associated most often with the need to solve "practical" problems. The instrumental claim also incorporates the borrowing of tools, methods, concepts, and theories. In mathematics, to illustrate, this instrumentality has included not only traditional tools[7] but also new tools such as "fuzzy sets," for dealing with the ambiguity and vagueness of complex decision-making.[8] Statistics and computer modeling have also spanned the disciplines,[9] and, elsewhere, a variety of methodologies have promoted movement across disciplinary borders—including surveys, interviews,[10] questionnaires, direct observation techniques, and the tools of demography on which the "social mathematics" of history are based.[11] There is also a considerable amount of tool-borrowing going on in the natural sciences, ranging from the use of cyclotrons to positron annihilation, X-rays, polymer tools, lasers,[12] statistical mechanics,[13] and mathematical methods for understanding shock waves.[14]

The escalation of instrumental interdisciplinarity since mid-century has created an inevitable tension in the discourse between those who define interdisciplinarity as a philosophically conceived synopsis and those who believe interdisciplinarity is not a theoretical concept but a practical one, one that arises from the unsolved problems of society rather than from science itself.[15] Instrumental work has a tendency to accentuate external interactions and is often finite in nature. Synoptic work, on the other hand, has a tendency to be more introspective, with an emphasis on internal coherence, methodological unification, and long-term exploration.[16] Yet these are not absolute states. Although there is a general disinclination towards epistemology among instrumentalists—even an antiphilosophical operationalism among some of them—the "practical" argument has been cast in philosophical terms, linking the instrumental claim with the idea of unity. Discussing interdisciplinarity as an innovation in school curricula, Giovanni Gozzer cited a 1979 Italian Ministry of Education formulation entitled "Unity of Knowledge: Interdisciplinarity." The ministry called for a more "relevant and down-to-earth cultural approach to reality, directed at acquiring knowledge that has unity in its interconnected diversity."[17] That call has been echoed in a number of areas, including fields with a planning and policy dimension as well as problem-focused research within both industrialized and developing countries.[18] The act of tool borrowing has also led in some cases to an appreciation of conceptual ties, promoting a fuller, more synoptic view of relationships among participating disciplines.

Ultimately both forms of instrumentality and many synoptic attempts to achieve unity in the twentieth century are part of a far more comprehensive reason for interdisciplinarity—the evolution of knowledge. Many modern developments, such as holography and chemotherapy, fit poorly within existing disciplines;[19] and, as investigators interested in such areas as cellular biology, tumor virology, political behavior, and environmental physics have applied their methods and skills to problems that interest them, they have moved beyond their traditional domains.[20] The interdisciplinary thrust of the neurosciences[21] has had a strong influence on the current field of anatomy,[22] and molecular biology was born of movements within physics and chemistry into areas previously labeled "biology."[23] The net result, in many cases, has been a lag between conventional definitions of a given discipline and what is really happening, especially in new research areas. The definition of boundaries among anthropology, history, and ethnohistory, for example, depends very much on the context. Anthropology and history are sharply distinct as fields of training and in the social and political organization of their practitioners. Yet distinctions of subject matter are not made so easily. On occasion specialists in either field define their boundaries in a way that includes the other as a subdivision or, in rarer cases, have even characterized one field as the other.[24]

Changes in disciplines occur as a result of both differentiation and integration. Through fission existing disciplines split into subdivisions that may become disciplines in their own right. Fusion is an overtly integrative process. Although specialization is often vilified in the discourse, as a negative force promoting fragmentation, specialization has in fact fostered a number of interactions as disciplinarians approach each other's borders. The depth of disciplinary study may open up relationships at the intersection or parts of two disciplines,[25] especially when contiguous problems are involved.[26] This has been readily apparent in the forensic disciplines, especially forensic anthropology. It is also apparent in biochemistry, which has interacted from its very origin with such fields as immunology, endocrinology, bacteriology, pharmacology, and physiology.[27] Observing modern changes in biology, Paul-Emile Pilet concluded the *emergence of complexity* "leads to the gradual erosion of boundaries of the special branch."[28]

The most prominent examples of fusion are the "interdisciplines," a term that covers a variety of interactions ranging from informal groups of scholars to well-established research and teaching communities. Social psychology and biochemistry are the most frequently cited examples, though the list also includes biophysics, physical chemistry, materials science, environmental engineering, geochemistry, psycholinguistics, sociolinguistics, psychohistory, psychoanthropology, psychological economics, political economy, political sociology, geopolitics, psychiatric sociology, sociobiology, ethnomusicology, economic anthropology, cultural anthropology, systems engineering, and American Studies. Some theorists maintain an interdiscipline is the highest form of interdisciplinary inquiry. However, there is growing skepticism about predicating the success of interdisciplinary inquiry upon the achievement of disciplinary status. In 1970, at the OECD seminar on interdisciplinarity in Nice, France, the rallying cry was "The 'inter-discipline' of today is the 'discipline' of tomorrow."[29] By 1984, at an international reassessment of the interdisciplinary concept, the rallying cry of the early 1970s was regarded in some quarters as the "Nice nonsense."[30]

There is no single pattern of disciplinary interactions. Because disciplines are responsive to so many spatial, temporal, demographic, and epistemological variables, it is difficult to predict how disciplines will interact. Sometimes it is on the basis of their proximity or complementarity. At other times mutual differences may assist the combining of disciplines. Guy Berger found eight regrouping patterns based on homogeneity and heterogeneity,[31] and Neale Mucklow identified no less than nineteen areas that may be grounds for grouping disciplines. They range from concepts, methods, skills, processes, criteria, and theoretical frameworks to kinds of arguments, discipline-conditioning attitudes, and expressions used to formulate, express, or embody thought.[32] In general, though, the OECD found that regrouping tends to take place around a field of study and particular clusters, rather than the grand structure of knowledge or learning of algorithms.

The degree of formality varies greatly in new areas. If there are enough practitioners, eventually they may constitute a recognized research community. This has happened in areas as diverse as immunopharmacology, demography, oral history, linguistics, military history, operations research, gerontology, and various ethnic, minority, regional, and national studies. In subdisciplines such as economic history and physical chemistry, there is sufficient control of subject that the fields function sociologically as disciplines, even though they not be classed taxonomically as separate disciplines. Some areas, including psychohistory and sociobiology, may be the objects of considerable dispute, and others are so new they are not widely recognized as fields. That is true of psychogeography, political gerontology, thanatology (the study of death and dying), human population biology, pastoralism (efforts to combat desertification), and behavioral teratology (the integration of elements of obstetric and pediatric medicine, development, physiology, and psychology). Many areas, by their very existence, question the prevailing structure of knowledge. The emergence of the field of public health, for example, challenged traditional subject divisions in medicine, as teachers and researchers developed interests in behavioral, social, ecological, economic and communication sciences.

Whether interactions occur for synoptic or instrumental purposes, there is a common pattern of justification—that of "necessity" or "complexity." These justifications are so strong, in fact, that there is a tendency to speak of inquiries and problems anthropomorphically "demanding" interdisciplinary perspective. In the area of materials science, researchers have necessarily drawn upon chemistry and physics in order to understand the property of materials.[33] Behavioral medicine, to cite another example, gained momentum because of an increased need for theory, research, and applications of behavioral factors in the etiology, treatment, and prevention of disease.[34] The most compelling example, though, is physics. The level of boundary-crossing in physics alone underscores the truth of Wolf Lepenies's contention that the exchange of subdisciplines back and forth between established fields is often more important than the emergence of new disciplines in appraising current interdisciplinary trends.[35]

In the early part of the century, physics was based on a foundation of quantum and atomic theory. By the 1960s, however, physics had become a federation of disciplines, incorporating such areas as nuclear physics and solid-state physics, areas that had more in common with chemistry and engineering than with traditional physics.[36] By 1972 the Physics Survey Committee of the National Research Council concluded there is "no definable boundary" between physics and other disciplines. Biophysics is recognized as a formal "interface" based on new combinations of skills from both of its parent disciplines. Experimental chemistry is influenced by physical methods, and, the committee found, there is even a "characteristic pattern associated with the assimilation of any physical method into chemistry." Both physicists and chemists have contributed to a variety of studies, ranging from biomolecules and photosynthesis to new methods of materials preparation, geographics, and work on the upper atmosphere and astrophysics, including the entire complex set of problems associated with the earth's atmosphere and the problem of the formation of molecules in interstellar space.[37] The committee also reported that there were roughly 5,000 U.S. research scientists in the early 1970s who "would not be out of place in either a physics or a chemistry department." Some called themselves physicists and designated their specialties as chemical physics or just physics. Others called themselves physical chemists. These labels usually reflected their original graduate training and correlated with differences of interest and style.[38] (J.T. Lemon made a similar observation about urban history, where he found that identifying themselves by department affiliations is, for some people in the field, "pretty much reduced to administrative inertia.")[39]

With "necessity" and "complexity" cited so frequently as justifications, there is a frequent sense of "inevitability" in the discourse. Ronald Grele found the practice of collecting and using oral data produces "its own impetus toward interdisciplinarity," leading inevitably to synthetic levels of analysis and discussion.[40] Jeroom Vercruysee noted a similar inevitability in studies of the Enlightenment,[41] and many environmental psychologists consider their field interdisciplinary almost "by definition" because it is conceived as a problem-centered discipline that deals with personal and environmental issues in the urban setting.[42] Necessity and complexity have also been cited as reasons for interdisciplinary research in and about developing countries. Shinichi Ichimura cautioned that the conceptual frameworks of traditional disciplines are often too narrow and too compartmentalized for the study of problems in other areas.[43] Norman Dinges made a similar observation about cross-cultural research, suggesting interdisciplinary perspective grows as the "indigenization" of research sensitive to local norms takes place;[44] and Lawrence Murphy, using the example of the Social Research Center of the American University of Cairo (Egypt), has traced the movement from narrow, academically oriented research projects to more appropriate long-term interdisciplinary, multifaceted studies that analyzed problems of immediate concern to the host nation.[45] Others have also found interdisciplinarity warranted in research involving developing countries because of the multiplicity of interrelated variables.[46]

When interdisciplinarity is justified on the basis of "complexity," it is not uncommon to find several reasons for crossing disciplines. Robert Chen found research on increasing carbon dioxide levels in the atmosphere to be interdisciplinary because the problem is not only *unique* in scale and complexity but also inescapably *normative* and *unprecedented.*[47] Complexity of the problem domain has also been linked with interdisciplinarity in a number of applied areas, in arid land studies, ecotoxicology, aerobiology, mycorrhizal fungi research; in agricultural history, where there are no less than seven interacting systems;[48] and in material history, which incorporates a broad range of ecological, economic, and sociocultural factors involved in the production, diffusion, acceptance, longevity, and use of the artifact.[49]

Interdisciplinarity is further linked with scarcity of resources in both academic and nonacademic settings. Arnold de Mayer suggested that people who work in a small company often become interdisciplinary by default, for lack of sufficient resources.[50] John Reid reported the very scarcity of documentation on Maritime regional history forced a radically new approach to sources and a willingness to accept whatever insights could be offered by different disciplines.[51] A comparable sense of necessity and inevitability has also been noted in areas as diverse as rural Indian economics, genetic epistemology, sociolinguistics, discovery of the point-contact transistor, criminology, social history and material history, organizational productivity, the socioeconomic dimensions of reindeer herding, and the impact of increasing levels of carbon dioxide in the atmosphere.[52]

In short, interdisciplinarity has resulted from several kinds of change, from the development of practical, applied dimensions to a more synoptic, conceptually based exploration of commonalities. This is particularly true at what Talcott Parsons called the "zone of interpenetration," where more than one theoretical scheme may apply to the same concrete set of phenomena.[53] Very often disciplinary interactions are also the inevitable result of the broadening of disciplines, in, for example, movement past exhausted modes of analysis and narrow definitions, as well as the shift from an empirical to a theoretical orientation or from a monistic to a pluralistic perspective.

A Matter of Visibility

Awareness of interdisciplinarity—its presence and its importance—has a lot to do with its relative visibility. In the past most discussion has focused on the more "overt" forms, obscuring the less visible forms.

Interdisciplinary Institutions

The most visible form of interdisciplinarity is the "overt" interdisciplinary institution, not only educational institutions but also a variety of research centers. Some of them are autonomous, but the majority are smaller units within larger, more traditional institutions. Interdisciplinary study tracks and graduate/professional programs also have a certain institutional visibility, and there are literally thousands of interdisciplinary courses offered in the context of general, disciplinary, and professional education. In some institutions a single "umbrella" organization bestows increased visibility and legitimacy on interdisciplinary activities. In its history Stanford University's Center for Interdisciplinary Studies has incorporated a variety of areas, including transportation, information transmission, telecommunication and television, in addition to centers for the study of women, drugs, and crime and the community. In other institutions there may be a variety of opportunities but no central office. The University of Southern California maintains interdisciplinary programs in nine areas, and San Francisco State University offers over fifty undergraduate and graduate interdisciplinary programs. At Pennsylvania State University, interdisciplinary research has been conducted in centers and institutes focused on a variety of areas, including transportation, public policy analysis and evaluation, and information systems. Interdisciplinarity is also formally recognized in the form of joint appointments and joint departments, arrangements made for both economic and intellectual reasons. Recently, the University of Chicago Medical Center merged a number of its departments, while eliminating others. John E. Ultmann, the dean of research and development within the division of biological sciences, commented that science itself has been moving more quickly than the organizational structure of the medical school. As a result, "There was too much overlap in the knowledge being taught in different departments."[54]

Certain institutions have cultivated an "interdisciplinary milieu" that lends a distinctive hue to both teaching and scholarship.[55] At Hobart and William Smith Colleges, interdisciplinarity is considered "a fundamental daily way of doing business."[56] At the University of Chicago, it is difficult to find many areas of intellectual activity that are *not* interdisciplinary in some fashion, from general education courses to dissertation committees and faculty seminars.[57] Certain departments and "schools" have also been conducive environments for interaction, including the Department of Social Relations at Harvard and the University of Chicago's Committee on Social Thought as well as the Chicago school of social science. In addition a number of collections and museums have been natural centers for inter-disciplinary work, attracting scholars with a common interest in their resources. Because it is not "locked in" to structures that inhibit cross-fertilization, the Smithsonian Institution has been a catalyst for exploring relationships between disciplines and acting on those relationships with an appropriate curriculum.[58]

Some research centers and institutes have also tended to function as interdisciplinary "think tanks." The premier example is the Center for In-terdisciplinary Research, a central research institute at the University of Bielefeld (West Germany). The Bielefeld center initiates and supports in-terdisciplinary work on problems that lie beyond the scope of a single discipline or traditional set of methods. Though the Bielefeld center is an exception in its devotion to interdisciplinary research, any list of inter-disciplinary centers would necessarily include the Institute for Advanced Study in Princeton and the Stanford Research Institutes. The more typical example, though, is a facility that sponsors integrative work in a particular area, such as the Center for Genetic Epistemology, the Tavistock Clinic and Cavendish Laboratories, the U.S. agricultural field stations, the School of Pacific Studies and the East/West Center, centers for urban studies, and such technical and scientific centers as the Institute of Fundamental Technical Research of the Polish Academy of Sciences,[59] the International Center of Insect Physiology and Ecology,[60] and the International Rice Research Institute.[61] In recent years, centers for humanistic studies have also served as "homes" for interdisciplinary research. They include the University of California Humanities Research Institute at Irvine, the In-stitute for the Humanities at the University of Illinois at Chicago, the Na-tional Humanities Center in North Carolina, and other centers and insti-tutes located at the Universities of New Hampshire, Wisconsin, and Oregon, as well as Stanford, Harvard, Dartmouth, Vanderbilt, Brandeis, Wesleyan, and the State University of New York at Stony Brook.

Forums for Interdisciplinary Dialogue

Organizations devoted exclusively to interdisciplinary approaches are rare. Beyond the most "overt" examples, there is great deal of dialogue taking place in forums that serve particular communities on either an occasional or a steady basis. The term *hidden university* has been used to describe a variety of study groups, symposia, conferences, and institutes.[62] It would not be inappropriate to consider some of them "invisible colleges," a term Diana Crane used to define a subgroup or communication network of scientists who define important problems, interpret seminal work, and link collaborators in a given research area.[63] Stephen Toulmin also used the term to describe a community of researchers who are in close personal contact. They study one another's work and engage in a "respectful but competitive rivalry." Lacking such visible social and cognitive structures as departments and recognized professional associations, they are defined by "invisible" patterns of communication: relationships among key productive scholars, conferences, core activities, and vehicles for the diffusion of information.[64]

The term can also apply to funded projects and subgroups within organizations that have had an interest in issues with an interdisciplinary component, such as the Comparative Interdisciplinary Studies Section of the International Sociological Association (CISS/ISA), the Society for Cross Cultural Research (SCCR), the Social Science History Association, (SSHA), the Society for Social Studies of Science, and the Society for Literature and Science. In addition, there are many networks within larger organizations focused on subjects of interest to scholars in more than one discipline, including diplomatic history, health and science policy, and psychohistory. On an occasional basis, a number of organizations, including the Modern Language Association and the American Association for the Advancement of Science, also sponsor special panels and sessions about interdisciplinary topics and issues.

Interdisciplinary publications constitute another important forum, although their scope and visibility vary greatly. Beyond the more overt examples — the publications of AIS, INTERSTUDY, and the Bielefeld center — there are many area-specific publications, such as *Cell Calcium,* the *Journal of Immunopharmacology, Interdisciplinary Science Reviews, Systems Research,* the *Journal of Interdisciplinary History,* the *Journal of the History of Ideas, Signs: Journal of Women in Culture and Society,* and, in American Studies, *American Quarterly* and *Prospects.* Some journals also publish interdisciplinary pieces within a selected range of disciplines, including the *International Social Science Journal, Representations, Humanities and Society,* and *Critical Inquiry.* In addition a number of mainstream publications have devoted special issues on interdisciplinary topics and perspectives.

Many of these publications provide an important bibliographical service. *American Quarterly,* for example, codes its annual bibliography to highlight articles of interest to individuals in several areas, and it periodically features bibliographical essays. *Signs* provides bibliographical essays and lists to acquaint readers interested in women's studies with current work in different fields, and the *American Journal of Physics* has sponsored resource letters covering particular fields. From time to time, the *Journal of Popular Culture* has published special in-depth issues on the relevance of such fields as history and sociology, and one particular issue of *Soundings,* devoted to the impact of women's studies and the feminist perspective in scholarship on the humanities and social sciences, ultimately appeared as a book, *A Feminist Perspective in the Academy: The Difference It Makes.* The more frequent case, however, is the individual review essay. *Signs, American Quarterly,* and the *Journal of Interdisciplinary History* have been particularly reliable in providing this kind of service. John Lankford's article "The Writing of American History in the 1960s" is an excellent example of the value such essays have. Subtitled "A Critical Bibliography of Material of Interest to Sociologists," it appeared in the *Sociological Quarterly*[65] as a sample of recent scholarship in American history that may be of interest to sociologists. Lankford indicated the types of problems that concern historians, the variety of materials they use, and new departures in method and technique, while offering suggestions on how sociologists can keep track of developments in history.

Peter Mullen considers the emergence of interdisciplinary journals part of the revival of interest in interdisciplinary publications that stems from recognition of important interfaces and growing appreciation of work in other fields. Occupying a middle position between the all-inclusive general publication and the specialty journal, an interdisciplinary journal can play a vital role in determining the future direction of a new field, serving as a platform for new ideas and providing an epistemic ground for testing theory and methodology. It may also be one of the few avenues for advancing aspects of research that do not find favor in mainstream journals.[66] One intriguing example involved the separation of polymer synthesis (organic chemistry), polymer characterization (physical chemistry and physics), and polymer processing (mechanical and chemical engineering) into independent parts of several key journals: the *Journal of Macromolecular Science, Part A — Chemistry, Part B — Physics,* and *Part D — Reviews in Polymer Technology.* In 1973, the name of *Part D* was changed to *Polymer Plastics Technology and Engineering;* and a number of areas of polymer application have also developed independent literatures and technologies, including the plastics, coatings, rubber, adhesive, electronics, surfactants, and additive industries. Several of these industries deal with a fertile area for interdisciplinary approaches, that of thermosetting materials.[67] Bioelectrochemistry and bioenergetics is another case in point.[68]

Interdisciplinary publications also play a vital role in consolidating discourse that is scattered across several journals. In 1980 *Cell Calcium* started providing a steady forum for work previously dispersed across publications in biochemistry, chemistry, endocrinology, medicine, pharmacology, physiology, zoology, and a number of other fields.[69] The lack of such an interdisciplinary journal has been identified as a major impediment in the development of behavioral medicine, where interdisciplinary communication is hampered by the spread of research over diverse behavioral and biomedical publications, even though parts of specialized journals do represent parts of the field of behavioral medicine.[70]

The American College of Chest Physicians (ACCP) provides an excellent example of both organizational and journal support in a particular area. Described as a *"university without walls,"* the ACCP incorporates pulmonologists, cardiologists, thoracic and cardiac surgeons, immunologists, allergists, anesthesiologists, radiologists, and pathologists. By 1979 the organization had reached a membership exceeding 10,000 and a journal circulation of 20,000. The journal *Chest* functions as a "balance wheel" for a variety of member interests. Yet the lack of an adequate faculty and curriculum continue to inhibit the evolution of a successful interdisciplinary approach to diagnosis and therapy. The pathological isolation that plagues the field was demonstrated when two pioneer cardiac surgeons operated at the same hospital in adjacent rooms, without having seen the other work.[71]

Interdisciplinary dialogue also achieves a partial consolidation within the numerous interdisciplinary conferences and symposia that dot the academic calendar. The more "overt" examples are far outnumbered by one-time meetings that have spanned such topics as internal medicine, cellular automata, dairy housing, volcanology, Victorian studies, pluralism in literary criticism, the psychoanalytical theory of aggression, and the rhetoric of inquiry. Expeditions and major projects also have been focal points, occurring as part of an ongoing large-scale program — such as the Man and the Biosphere program conducted under the auspices of UNESCO — or within local regions — such as the Lake Mungo expedition in Australia, the joint Indian-American Satellite Instructional Television Experiment, estuarine studies of the Severn and Thames, and the International Polar Year expeditions. The relative visibility of these conferences, symposia, and expeditions varies greatly. Sometimes a collection of papers will emerge, but it is usually a "multidisciplinary" collection rather than an "interdisciplinary" synthesis. Synthesis is often limited to the editor's remarks and the opening and closing remarks of individual participants. Very often the greatest value is not what is said or printed but the new attitudes that participants gain as a result of these opportunities — a "concealed" benefit that can be very difficult to measure.

A variety of informal faculty forums must also be counted, many of them launched as private study groups among teachers and scholars who feel the need to expand beyond their disciplinary confines. In 1984, to illustrate, a group of professors at Bryn Mawr College formed a private study group known as the Committee on Interpretation. They wanted to address questions larger than the scope of their individual specialties. They wanted to know how other disciplines interpret the human world of language, knowledge, and culture, while acquainting themselves with European theorists whose writings have influenced several fields in the United States. Similar voluntary associations have formed at the Universities of California and Virginia, Stanford, Wesleyan, and many smaller institutions. Some of these gatherings have even generated new courses, new journals, and new interdisciplinary programs.[72] A good many of them have been organized to deal with the multitudinous borrowings of tools, methods, concepts, theories, and paradigms that are being used across disciplines. This form of interdisciplinarity tends to have what Raymond Miller calls a "much longer and quieter history."[73]

There is an additional "concealed" presence in the thousands of individual articles and notes that appear in a wide variety of disciplinary, professional, and general publications. The majority are isolated pieces, and most have remained relatively invisible because there has never been a systematic attempt to identify them. They vary considerably, ranging from descriptions of the interdisciplinary nature of a particular field, curriculum, or project to attempts to define common nomenclature, proposals for integrative concepts and methods, and theoretical essays. Beyond these publications there is an even more deeply concealed reality in the vast and unrecorded "oral history" of interdisciplinarity. Its most visible form is the conference presentation, but there is a substantial amount of knowledge being transmitted in the day-to-day working relationships of interdisciplinary research teams and in the conversations of teachers and scholars, including those who do not label their work "interdisciplinary." Unfortunately not enough of this wisdom makes its way into published form.

There is a wide range of opinion on the relative importance of interdisciplinarity in the twentieth century. Some place interdisciplinarity at the periphery of modern knowledge, a series of catalysts, second-order effects, jerry-built structures, and ad hoc enterprises. For them interdisciplinarity will continue to linger at the fringes of disciplinary hegemony, a "tolerated margin" that is "too productive to be dismissed and too deviant to be incorporated into the mainstream."[74] "Isolated pockets of borrowing" may even be considered dangerous because they create a further fragmentation of knowledge.[75] Others see a more significant phenomenon, "not an exotic fungus" but a "natural healthy growth." "Any living community of scholars," Bryce Crawford contended, "will turn up and pursue transdisciplinary questions out of the very nature of scholarship," creating changing patterns, new alignments, shared problems, and merging interests.[76] Still others see a more profound consequence—if not a retrieval of the seamless web of knowledge, at least the gradual integration of particular concepts and theories. György Darvas sees interdisciplinarity as a characteristic phenomenon of modern science, caught in an apparent paradox of self-contradiction as interdisciplines become disciplines. Every differentiation postulates the existence of integrated elements.[77] Others believe interdisciplinarity is the next phase in the development of the social sciences,[78] that increasing acceptance of interdisciplinary study marks a "paradigm shift" under way in academe.[79]

Clearly, the level at which interdisciplinarity is conceived to take place influences one's judgment about its value; however, current history does suggest two conclusions. The first is related to the synoptic quest for unity of knowledge. Stanley Bailis cautions that progressive emphasis on the instrumental aspects of education and research, divorced from philosophical contemplation, constitutes a threat to a broader conceptual concern for identifying relationships that might direct inquiry in a general fashion. Undeniably, the shift towards an instrumental perspective has yielded a "rich mix of what is known to bear upon crucial problems." However, he cautions, the modification and in some cases outright demise of the experiments of the 1960s and 1970s, the pull of disciplinary loyalties, the progressive buildup of disciplinary training in interdisciplinary universities, and the shift to more "instrumental," thematic and problem-based units have all created a problem of "limited futures" for interdisciplinarians in universities. The instrumental shift has produced units that look as if they have only limited scope and duration, while muting the question of how people who have different ways of regarding the world can learn to learn from each other more effectively.[80] Thus, the synoptic challenge remains unfulfilled.

The second conclusion moves in an opposite direction, towards the reality of pervasive cross-fertilization. Although he eschewed "interdisciplinary brotherhood" as the answer, Clifford Geertz put his finger on an important phenomenon when he observed a refiguration of social thought that goes beyond "the moving of a few disputed borders, the marking of some more picturesque mountain lakes." Conventions of interpretation persist, but there is an increasing need to accommodate "a situation at once, fluid, plural, uncentered, and ineradicably untidy." With philosophical inquiries that look like literary criticism, scientific discussions that look like belles lettres *morceaux,* histories consisting of equations and tables or law court testimony, parables posing as ethnographies, theoretical treatises set out as travelogues, ideological arguments cast as historiographical inquiries, and epistemological studies constructed like political tracts, there is clearly a widespread "jumbling of the varieties of discourse" that defies classification.[81] Some of these movements, Geertz argues, are taking place at highly eccentric angles. However, many of them are not. A significant percentage of interactions today are based on the perception of "natural" connections, kindred alliances, and family clusters. Some of them are overt, highly visible, "institutionalized" examples of interdisciplinarity, but many more of them are "quiet revolutions," shifts in perspective and new ways of seeing that often take place without fanfare or upheaval.[82] Until there is a fuller analysis of these shifts within their respective problem communities and disciplines, we cannot hope to have a full understanding of either interdisciplinarity or disciplinarity itself. There is often a distinctly "local" nature to interdisciplinary activity, and the analysis must also come from the practitioners rather than interdisciplinary theorists alone.

3 An Interdisciplinary Lexicon

"That's a great deal to make one word mean,"
Alice said in a thoughtful tone. "When I make a
word do a lot of work like that," said
Humpty Dumpty, "I always pay it extra."
— Lewis Carroll, *Alice in Wonderland*

INTERDISCIPLINARITY is usually defined in one of four ways:

1. *by example,* to designate what form it assumes;
2. *by motivation,* to explain why it takes place;
3. *by principles of interaction,* to demonstrate the process of how disciplines interact; and
4. *by terminological hierarchy,* to distinguish levels of integration by using specific labels.

Each is a legitimate strategy. The first and second ones, by example and by motivation, tend to cut across the entire published literature on interdisciplinarity, though the third, that of process, has been a more specialized topic. It is the fourth, however, that has been the most popular approach in recent decades, despite Guy Berger's warning that hierarchies are ill-advised in the absence of well-developed theory.[1]

Berger was right. The literature on interdisciplinarity is littered with labels and disputes about their appropriateness. The popular term *cross-disciplinary* provides a good example of the problem. It has been used for several different purposes: to view one discipline from the perspective of another, rigid axiomatic control by one discipline, the solution of a problem with no intention of generating a new science or paradigm, new fields that develop between two or more disciplines, a generic adjective for six different categories of discipline-crossing activities, and a generic adjective for all activities involving interaction across disciplines. These differences occur because labels are not neutral. Any nomenclature, Kenneth Burke once pointed out, acts as a "terministic screen" that filters, directs, and redirects attention in certain directions rather than others. Thus, terminology is not only a *reflection* of reality but, by its very nature, also a *selection* and a *deflection* of reality. Much of what we take to be observations about reality may well be the "spinning out of possibilities implicit in our particular choice of terms."[2]

For some, terminology has become a stale issue. They have tired of debates over labels. Nevertheless, terminological hierarchy has played a major role in shaping the way people think about interdisciplinarity; and there is a general agreement on two core distinctions: between "multidisciplinarity" and "interdisciplinarity" and, in turn, between "interdisciplinarity" and "transdisciplinarity."

The Multidisciplinary/Interdisciplinary Distinction

Most purportedly "interdisciplinary" activities are not "interdisciplinary" but "multidisciplinary" or "pluridisciplinary." "Multidisciplinarity" signifies the juxtaposition of disciplines. It is essentially *additive,* not *integrative.* Even in a common environment, educators, researchers, and practitioners still behave as disciplinarians with different perspectives. Their relationship may be mutual and cumulative but not interactive, for there is "no apparent connection,"[3] no real cooperation or "explicit" relationships,[4] and even, perhaps, a "questionable eclecticism."[5] The participating disciplines are neither changed nor enriched,[6] and the lack of "a well-defined matrix" of interactions[7] means disciplinary relationships are likely to be limited and "transitory."[8]

These characteristics are frequently associated with undergraduate courses that present different specialists either in serial fashion or on different days. Heinz Heckhausen labeled this encyclopedic approach *"indiscriminate interdisciplinarity,"*[9] though it has also been dubbed a "hodgepodge" or "cafeteria-style" education. Whatever synthesis may occur, if it occurs at all, is usually in the student's own mind. Encyclopedic curricula are usually associated with the lower-division and nonspecialist parts of undergraduate study, but the term also applies to a number of programs at the master's level. In the field of public health, for example, students are prepared for a variety of situations because public health teams encompass a range of specialties.[10] Likewise, schools of public administration call for at least some training in economics, sociology, psychology, political science, and other disciplines implied by the very name "public administration." So do graduate programs in family studies, museum management, and hotel and restaurant management. Usually the overall format is "multidisciplinary," though there may be an overtly "interdisciplinary" component in the form of an integrative thesis or capstone seminar on a particular problem, topic, theory, or methodology.

Forrest Armstrong distinguishes four different levels of integration and synthesis in education. At the *first level,* students take a selection of courses from different departments, counting them toward a particular disciplinary major. Though this may be the cheapest, least demanding, and probably the most easily achieved interdisciplinary variant, it may also be the least effective. At the *second level,* there is an institutionally provided opportunity for students to meet and share insights from various disciplinary courses, often in a capstone seminar. However, the responsibility for achieving integration may be left largely to the students. At the *third level,* a significant change occurs as faculty join students in the process of synthesizing knowledge. This implies the creation of courses focused on interdisciplinary topics and, in Armstrong's view, requires the participation of more than one faculty member. However, the degree of interaction varies, and these courses are often characterized by serial rather than integrated team teaching, since individual faculty simply "bring their disciplinary wares to be displayed in a different context." At the *fourth and highest level* there is a conscious attempt to integrate material from various fields of knowledge into "a new, single, intellectually coherent entity." This demands an understanding of the epistemologies and methodologies of other disciplines and, in a team effort, requires building a common vocabulary.[11]

A number of disciplines are also thought to be in "multidisciplinary" relation to each other. Archaeologists and historians, for example, share an interest in diachronic, historical explanations.[12] Archaeologists have also made several important contributions by filling in lacunae from incomplete records, corroborating or disputing what is known from those records, and, at times, even providing entirely new ways of viewing historical questions. In the case of the eighteenth-century Fort Michilimackinac (Michigan), archaeologists were able to demonstrate that when the British took the fort over from the French in 1761, at the end of the French and Indian War, French trade goods were not immediately replaced by British goods. Instead, goods continued to come into the outpost through English Canada. Even though complex British navigation laws now extended to Canada, basic trade lines were not altered. In this instance archaeologists raised questions about not only relations between these two countries after their struggle for the North American continent but also the rigidity and inertia of long-standing patterns, regardless of significant changes in overall political and military control.[13] In this and other cases, archaeology has facilitated a picture that may exist only in broad outlines and may even be controversial, but, M. I. Finley points out, hardly any of it could be derived from the ancient traditions alone or from archaeology alone.[14]

Joseph Kockelmans contends that in the West, at least, "all education is inherently multidisciplinary," and the term has no genuine meaning in a research context.[15] Still, it is used to describe a certain type of research setting. Daniel Alpert cites two representative examples: *a materials research lab,* where metallurgists, solid-state physicists, and solid-state chemists share facilities; and *an Asian Studies center,* where specialists from Oriental history, economics, and sociology use the same Asian library.[16] Even in these common environments, however, scholars still work on problems posed by their original disciplines. Individuals using the same materials research lab or the same Asian library are in "multidisciplinary" relation by virtue of mere logistics. If they begin interacting on the basis of each other's data, information, concepts, methods, or theories, then they are in what OECD theorists called a "pluridisciplinary" relation because the juxtaposition of disciplines is assumed to be more or less related. Should one or more of them achieve a synthesis greater than any single disciplinary approach — say, a geographer incorporating economic concepts of development into regional analysis or a chemist becoming dependent upon explanations or instruments borrowed from physics — then "interdisciplinarity" is taking place. In problem-focused research, it is the difference between a "contractual" mode — carrying out tasks within separate units — and a "consulting" mode — carrying out tasks within a single unit and producing a common product. The former leads to a series of separate reports joined only by external, editorial linkages; the latter, joint reports that reflect an internal, substantive linkage.[17]

"Multidisciplinary" research is often a "spontaneous answer" in carrying out problem-focused projects. Their "multidisciplinary" character is guaranteed by the "sheer variety" of contributing disciplines.[18] Joint facilities and favorable environments for the exchange of information across disciplines are also key factors. In the early 1960s, an open spirit of dialogue and inquiry proved a major catalyst for interdisciplinary research on a disease that appeared in corn plantings in the north central and southern parts of the United States. Regional research projects and federal funding further enhanced the prospects for collaboration and ultimately led to new knowledge about the complex problem of corn viruses.[19] Similarly, during the 1940s, reorganization of the Bell Telephone Laboratories around "multidisciplinary" team research resulted in a hospitable environment for collaboration, followed thirty months later by the discovery of the point contact transistor.[20] Even in favorable environments, however, the excitement generated by parallel investigations and borrowed information is no guarantee of ultimate convergence. Neither is the mere perception of relationships, nor the most promising intimation of cohesion and synergy.

These problems were quite evident to the pioneers of African history, who believed in the "interdisciplinary" approach. Some scholars, in most cases expatriates, extracted data from joint projects and published independently. As a result of this "safari-type of research," Bernard Wilpert's term for jet-set data collectors who sweep in and out of a country in pursuit of "multi-national research,"[21] none of the projects in Benin achieved "interdisciplinarity," despite occasional exchanges between anthropologists, archaeologists, art historians, and historians. In contrast an archaeological survey planned under the general Rivers Research Scheme was designed as a more consciously "interdisciplinary" effort. Planned by a historian to cover places indicated by the collection and analysis of oral traditions, the Rivers scheme involved a palynologist and a historian who took part in excavations with the archaeologist. They studied together and attempted to interpret events on a joint basis. Moreover preliminary accounts of test excavations were published in the same journal.[22]

The Philadelphia Social History Project (PSHP) is perhaps the most instructive example of the core distinction between "multidisciplinarity" and "interdisciplinarity." Organized along "collaborative," "multidisciplinary," and "interdisciplinary" lines, the PSHP was a collaborative investigation of how urbanization and industrialization shaped the development of the nineteenth-century metropolis and the experience of its diverse population. Research began in April 1968, with funds earmarked for a comparative study of black, Irish, and German immigrants. Eventually the project grew so large that one commentator dubbed it "a beacon for multi- and interdisciplinary urban history."[23]

The first phase, from 1969 to roughly 1973, was clearly a *disciplinary phase,* characterized by the development of a data base with the necessary software, methodology, and conceptual categories. Researchers wanted to know whether the burdens and disabilities of black Americans were peculiar to their historical experience or typical of immigrant experience. Like other "new urban" historians at the time, PSHP researchers found that initial data from manuscript schedules of the federal census described only the personal attributes of the people being studied. In order to learn how micro-level behavior and the urban-industrial environment interacted systematically, in addition to how group experiences were differentially affected, researchers expanded the data base. Eventually the data base came to include a great deal of information on Philadelphia's industrial base, spatial arrangements, facilities, institutions, and vital statistics.

The second phase of the project, from 1973 to about 1978, was a *"multidisciplinary" phase,* characterized by the voluntary addition of social scientists who possessed the skills necessary for a systematic analysis of the city's basic demographic processes, spatial arrangements, and economic activities. They were drawn by the project's "machine readable" data base, a resource that constitutes a new kind of "research laboratory" supportive of both "multidisciplinary" and "interdisciplinary" research.[24] It is, in project director Theodore Hershberg's words, "an instrument with the potential to serve scholars in the humanities and the social sciences as the microscope served researchers in the biological sciences."[25] (Elsewhere, James Sharp has described the use of large-scale computerized data banks in multi-university ecosystem management, paying special attention to peer group appraisal in evaluating and synthesizing data.)[26]

At first, only social historians were involved with the PSHP, but the gradual addition of new data attracted pre- and post-doctoral scholars from a variety of social science backgrounds. By 1981 there were more than thirty people affiliated with the project, representing economics, sociology, demography, geography, city planning, and history. In its "multidisciplinary" phase, the PSHP shifted from a methodological orientation as researchers undertook a series of studies in four substantive areas: the nature of work, uses of urban space, the family, and the experience of subgroups within the larger population. Still, characteristic of "multidisciplinary" work, researchers preserved the paradigmatic concerns of their own disciplines:

> An economist might look at location in terms of cost minimization and use equilibrium theory to balance the competing tugs of transportation costs among raw materials, production, and market sites; a sociologist might consider location in terms of social distance, of social control, and of symbolic land use; a geographer might deal with location in terms of central place theory and use diffusion or space-time convergence models, or might stress environmental over economic factors; a historian might focus on antecedent and adjacent land-use patterns.[27]

Phase three began in 1978 with the intention of moving into an "interdisciplinary" phase based not on the *group* work of phase two but genuine *team* work. *"Interdisciplinary"* work was set in motion by the establishment of new analytic goals emphasizing integrative over discrete studies. Attention shifted from the four substantive areas of the "multidisciplinary phase" to interrelationships within and among the formation of the urban environment, a wide range of behaviors, and the experience of diverse population groups. Unfortunately, "interdisciplinarity" was to remain an "unrealized potential" in the PSHP, due in part to the juggling of professional loyalties and the sheer difficulty of maintaining a large-scale project that crossed several disciplines. Key researchers were confronted with the demand for disciplinary credentials. Hence, a 1981 book of essays from the project represents the "fruits" of "multidisciplinary" rather than "interdisciplinary" labor. As a result, the PSHP was criticized for failing to achieve synthesis, for opting to treat the city as a "process" rather than establishing a fully developed, holistic framework that would facilitate the interaction of quantitative and qualitative empirical efforts.[28] Yet, Hershberg had anticipated that objection when he considered why a theoretical model had not developed. In 1981 the research was too diverse. Moreover, the working of the city as a whole was too complex to be forced into a single theoretical model. Researchers agreed on the desirablity of such a framework, but a "middle ground" seemed more realistic than grand theory.

There is an important lesson here about the danger of trying to predetermine interdisciplinary outcomes, a lesson often overlooked by critics of interdisciplinary projects. Premature imposition of a particular model has hindered the development of a viable synthesis in a number of projects. Based on their experience with environmental impacts on estuaries, Bella and Williamson concluded that imposing a particular conceptual framework at the beginning of a project may mean basing the entire project on something inappropriate for the problem at hand.[29] A large ecosystem project in Sweden provides a much fuller example of this rather fundamental problem.[30]

Initiated in 1970, the project sought a scientific basis for understanding the structure, function, and management of the most important coniferous forest ecosystem in Sweden. It took two years to launch the actual project. In the initial working phase, from July 1972 to December 1973, biologists, meteorologists, and data specialists concentrated on formulating operative goals and research problems. They spent a great deal of time at this point working on their conflicting interests, but, as they discovered the extent to which they shared the same world-picture assumptions about the territory under study, initial terminological differences were overcome. Still, conflicts persisted. The empirical scientists were a heterogeneous group. Some were used to thinking in mathematical terms and focusing on processes and flows, but others came from disciplines where mathematics and statistics were regarded with suspicion.

Although this particular project might seem analogous to the Apollo project, where goals were formulated in operational terms, it was actually more analogous to cancer research projects, which have the goal of discovering new knowledge. Consequently the project had the character of a research program in pure science, where it is not possible to formulate results beforehand. The goal of teaching systems theory to all participating scientists was a dramatic case in point. Participating scientists were supposed to learn systems theory from engineers skilled in mathematical modeling, in order to provide a global model of the pine forest ecosystem. However, that did not happen. Some of the disciplines were not mature enough for mathematical work, and some of the scientists were not motivated to learn systems models, finding them too complicated, too difficult, or of no heuristic value. As a result there were two views on the systems paradigm, and there was, correspondingly, a division of labor between theoreticians and empiricists. Research leaders had failed to consider that learning systems theory is more complicated than just learning a new method or technique, since it implies the adoption of a new paradigm with its respective methodology and epistemology. As empirically inclined researchers continued to work as they were accustomed to working, they began to feel cast in the role of mere data deliverers. Even some of the scientists with prior interdisciplinary experience and a degree of familiarity with systems theory preferred to work without the models.

The next phase of the project, from January 1974 to December 1975, was marked by empirical dominance. In 1973 the difficulties of doing cooperative work and failure to adhere to the modeling process had led to reorganization of the project around problem areas such as gas exchanges, litter fall, and consumption. This shift from cooperation between disciplines to problem groups turned out to be successful for both planning purposes and empirical work. Comparing the Swedish forest project to other interdisciplinary projects, Barmark and Wallen found that groups which did not change to a problem-oriented structure failed to achieve an integrated output. Yet, even with this change, there were still problems. By this time the sheer size of the project was making it impossible to steer subgroups. In addition, the field work was not very integrated, though in problem-oriented groups there was theoretical integration taking place at the planning level and empirical integration at an intermediate level. The problem with systems theory also continued. Only project managers and theoretical biologists remained committed to steering the project by its original goals and systems theory. Modeling had proved more difficult than expected, and empiricists were encountering difficulties in delivering data adapted to modeling, due largely to their lack of theoretical biological knowledge. Empirical scientists and modelers had rather different views on delivering data. Modelers needed data quickly and sometimes wound up using them in a manner unrecognizable to the empirical scientists, who wanted to obtain longer series of measurements in order to have data that would fulfill their criteria of knowledge, brought from their own disciplines.

In the next phase of the project, from 1976 to 1978, most of the empirical work continued as before, though modeling began to prove more successful. By the beginning of 1976, the idea of *one* global model was abandoned. It was replaced by a family of partial, more detailed models closer to fieldwork and traditional knowledge of growth in plants. The initial models, which did not fit project data, were based on empirical data from the literature. The new models were built to answer specific questions and suggest certain applications. It turned out that a plant stand model of 150 years can function as an adequate global model. Work on the effects of acid rain from burning oil in forest ecosystems also suggested that successful solutions to practical problems can, in some cases, be found by using problem-oriented models, without a complete pure-science background.

The final phase, from 1979 to 1980, was dominated by synthesizing reports and integrating knowledge. Although the overly ambitious scope of the project had caused problems, the project nevertheless suggested the possible beginning of a new discipline, *theoretical ecosystem-ecology*. The main theme of ecosystem was even beginning to "institutionalize" in the permanent appointment of some project personnel and preservation of main parts of the equipment. Veterans of the project drew several conclusions. Hakan Törnebohm and colleagues concluded that organizational changes in a project have to be made in step with cognitive development.[31] Barmark and Wallen concurred, warning that the organization of a project must be adjusted to its own scientific development.[32] Administrative problems cannot be separated from scientific ones. Although steering and coordination are necessary, especially in large-scale projects, the more project leaders steer, the less opportunity there is for innovation by participants.

There was also another important realization. Although the attempt to steer the project by systems theory and global models did not succeed at the field level, other kinds of interdisciplinary cooperation grew spontaneously among empirical scientists, who made unexpected discoveries regarding root production while working in an environment of relative freedom. Cooperative research tended to occur most often among those with prior interdisciplinary experience and those with the initiative to engage in such work. Veterans of previous interdisciplinary projects who went into the project intending to work in teams exchanged methods and results on a mutual basis and were able to help in conducting experiments. The experiment station at Jadraas also proved an ideal creative atmosphere conducive to informal discussions. Scientists were motivated to adopt new kinds of competence, widen their perspectives, and even establish networks for future interdisciplinary exchange. Although informal cooperation between scientists seldom led to full integration of knowledge in group work, in most cases it did lead to a widening of individual competence, one of the secondary aims of the project.

The Interdisciplinary/Transdisciplinary Distinction

The original OECD definition of "interdisciplinarity" was rather broad, ranging from "simple communication of ideas to the mutual integration of organising *concepts, methodology, procedures, epistemology, terminology, data,* and organisation of research and education in a fairly large field."[33] However, the "simple communication of ideas" can hardly be said to constitute a truly integrative act; and there are, of course, different opinions about what constitutes "genuine" interdisciplinarity. Piaget believed it meant reciprocal assimilation among the participating disciplines.[34] Alpert considered a *problem* the fundamental ground for interaction,[35] and Gusdorf believed teamwork is essential.[36]

Signifying a particular activity by attaching a label to it has an obvious danger. Many activities and theories have been labeled "interdisciplinary." The most commonly cited examples include general systems theory, structuralism, Marxism, and American studies. Yet, American studies programs, to take one example, vary across institutions and the work of individual scholars: from "multidisciplinary" conglomerations, to well-defined integrative paradigms for the study of American culture, to "transdisciplinary" visions of culture and history. The same is true of eighteenth-century studies, which may center on disciplinary texts — what Richard Schwartz considers a "contextual" approach — or approaches that lie beyond those texts — an "interdisciplinary" approach.[37] They range from a "soft approach" — David Sheehan's term for turning to another discipline to illustrate something already clear in the disciplinary text — to a "hard approach" — turning out of necessity to the materials and methods of another discipline.[38]

Rather than listing examples, it is more fruitful to note the kinds of interaction that have constituted "interdisciplinary" interaction in actual practice. The four most basic ones are (1) borrowing, (2) solving problems, (3) increased consistency of subjects or methods, and (4) the emergence of an interdiscipline.

Borrowing has been given several technical labels. Heinz Heckhausen used *pseudo interdisciplinarity* to describe the borrowing of analytical tools, such as mathematical models and computer simulation. He also used *auxiliary interdisciplinarity* for borrowing disciplinary methods, whether for an occasional transitional purpose or a more mature and enduring relationship between participating disciplines.[39] Marcel Boisot used *linear interdisciplinarity* to describe one discipline becoming "legalised" by a law belonging to another discipline,[40] and in their work at the Center for Interdisciplinary Research at Bielefeld, Huerkamp and colleagues used *method interdisciplinarity* to denote methods that can be used in other disciplines. As examples, they cited the use of psychology in behavioral zoology and the use of game theory in evolutionary biology. They also used *concept interdisciplinarity* for cases in which a model or concept either supplements or supplants the models or concepts of another discipline. The theory of evolution, for instance, has had obvious appeal to psychologists, since biological and historical perspectives greatly enhance psychological research. Psychological concepts, in turn, have added some useful aspects to evolution theory, particularly regarding the individuality of behavior.[41]

There are also special terms for the solution of problems with no intention of achieving a conceptual unification of knowledge. Heckhausen used *composite interdisciplinarity* for the instrumental solution of a problem, such as the Apollo space project or a city-planning project. Similarly, Boisot used *restrictive interdisciplinarity* to describe restricted interactions between disciplines focused on a concrete object, such as a city planning project. Heurkamp and her colleagues used *problem interdisciplinarity* for research centered on a complex, problematic question that cannot be assigned to a given discipline or find its solution in a border area between two fields. Each of these theorists believes, however, that it is not out of the question for one kind of interdisciplinarity to lead to another.

There are, in addition, special terms for the increased consistency of subject matters and methods. Heckhausen used *supplementary interdisciplinarity* to describe the partial overlapping of disciplines in the same material field, usually in the borderline areas of a discipline. He cited psycholinguistics as an example. Heckhausen also used *unifying interdisciplinarity* to describe an increased consistency in subject matter paralleled by "an approximation of the respective theoretical integration levels and method." This happened when biology reached the subject-matter level of physics, creating biophysics. *Interdisciplinary* has also been used to signify knowledge that exists within groups of closely related disciplines.[42] For Heurkamp and her colleagues *border interdisciplinarity,* or *interdisciplinarity of neighboring disciplines,* signifies two disciplines that have approached each other to the extent that an overlapping area is created. Both disciplines can make a contribution because each has worked in the area, yet neither one can supply sufficient concepts, methods, and tools by itself.

A Bielefeld research project on comparative behavioral ontogenesis in humans and animals illustrates what is meant by "border interdisciplinarity." The project involved an area that concerns both psychologists and biologists, behavioral ontogenesis. Its growing visibility was evident in the creation of a division for developmental psychobiology at the Max Planck Institute for Psychiatry in Munich and the publication of a new American journal, *Developmental Psychobiology.* Increased consistency is often signaled by a significant number of major publications dealing with a particular problem, appearing in this case in journals of biology and psychology. "Border interdisciplinarity" originates in the disciplines and may even lead to the next kind of interdisciplinarity, a new branch of knowledge. A new formal discipline or speciality is usually called a hybrid "interdiscipline," though Heckhausen used *unifying interdisciplinarity* and Boisot used *structural interdisciplinarity* to describe interactions leading to the creation of a new body of laws forming the basic structure of an original discipline.

"Transdisciplinary" approaches are far more comprehensive in scope and vision. Raymond Miller cites general systems, structuralism, Marxism, phenomenology, policy sciences, and sociobiology as leading examples. Many proponents of Marxism, neo-evolutionary theory, cybernetic and systems theory, behaviorism and exchange theory, structuralism, and social phenomenology hold out the promise of the kind of "overarching synthesis"[43] implied by the term "transdisciplinarity." "Transdisciplinary" approaches, Miller explains, are conceptual frameworks that transcend the narrow scope of disciplinary world views, metaphorically encompassing the several parts of material handled separately by specialized disciplines.[44] A "transdisciplinary" approach literally transcends a particular range,[45] "breaking through disciplinary barriers, and disobeying the rules of disciplinary etiquette."[46] Disciplines become "irrelevant," "subordinate," or "instrumental" to the larger framework. Others have used the terms "non-disciplinary," "adisciplinary," "metadisciplinary," "supra-disciplinary," "omnidisciplinary" and "trans-specialization"[47] to describe a variety of activities and paradigms that subordinate disciplines to a particular issue, problem, or holistic scheme. Some have also used the term "transdisciplinary" to signify the breadth of certain fields. Richard Coe used the term in discussing the broad applications of rhetoric,[48] and it has also been used for cultural futuristics,[49] human population biology,[50] and peace research.[51] In a similar vein, anthropology has been called a "supra-discipline" spanning virtually all established fields of knowledge.[52]

It is with "transdisciplinarity" that gaps between the real and the ideal are most apparent, whether the context is a unified society or a comprehensive system of medical care. Of all the definitions that have appeared, Erich Jantsch's vision of "interdisciplinary" and "transdisciplinary" coordination[53] has been the most influential. It has appeared in a wide variety of contexts, ranging from organizational models for managing research[54] to an interdisciplinary approach to environmental resources.[55] In Jantsch's multi-level, multi-goal system, "interdisciplinary" links cause scientific disciplines to change their concepts and structures as they move towards a higher level of coordination based on the axiomatics of a common viewpoint or purpose focused on human action.[56] (See Figure 1.)

The ultimate degree of coordination, for Jantsch, is a "transdisciplinary" system that facilitates the mutual enhancement of epistemologies, what Ozbekhan called "synepistemic cooperation." In Jantsch's view the whole education/innovation system embraces a multitude of interdisciplinary two-level systems that move in the direction of overall coordination. Whereas "interdisciplinarity" signifies the synthesis of two or more disciplines, establishing a new metalevel of discourse, "transdisciplinarity" signifies the interconnectedness of all aspects of reality, transcending the dynamics of a dialectical synthesis to grasp the total dynamics of reality as a whole. It is a vision of interdisciplinarity penetrating the entire system of science. Jantsch himself conceded the idea will always be beyond the complete reach of science, though he believed, nevertheless, that it could guide science in its evolution.[57]

The full spectrum of definitions may now be pictured, using the examples of child development, education of the handicapped, and futures research.

In the area of child development,[58] members of a "multidisciplinary

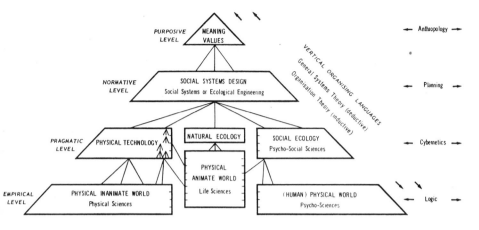

Figure 1. The Education/Innovation System,
Viewed as a Multi-level Multi-goal
Hierarchical System
Branding lines between levels and sub-levels
indicate possible forms of interdisciplinary
coordination

team" work side by side. The social worker takes a social history, the nutritionist evaluates nutrition, the occupational therapist evaluates feeding skills, the psychologist provides IQ information, and the pediatrician offers a medical explanation. Likewise, in education of the severely and profoundly handicapped, there is a separation of professional roles.[59] The child is seen by different professionals at different times, usually away from the classroom, and the professionals issue separate reports that may be left for the teacher to interpret and implement. In contrast, members of an "interdisciplinary" team may substitute for each other, building on, and complementing, each other's skills while becoming aware of their own limitations. On an "interdisciplinary" child development team, the nurse may take a social history alone on one occasion or, on another occasion, in conjunction with the social worker. The physician may suggest that the social worker explore specific issues, or the entire team may ask the nurse, the occupational therapist, or the nutritionist to explore a feeding problem. If the problem is complicated, they may even do it together. In contrast, a "transdisciplinary" team engages in a more thorough assimilation of knowledge. In the area of child development, a teacher is placed in a central role, using the technique of "role release" to communicate with the client. Role release authorizes one person to act as primary therapist in order to deliver services in a clear and trustful manner. Members of the team still offer consultative backup, but the systematic teaching and learning experiences built into teamwork enable one person to represent adequately the different disciplines. "Transdisciplinarity," therefore, implies a true totality, and, for that reason, "transdisciplinary" approaches are quite rare.

Ryszard Wasniowski pictured the entire spectrum in describing the metamorphosis of work at the Futures Research Centre (FRC) of the Technical University of Wroclaw (Poland).[60] Established in 1971, the FRC was a scientific center for systematic, complex studies on the development of science and technology in their social and economic environments. Initally researchers were involved in three types of interaction. Those who worked in *multidisciplinary* fashion did not interact cooperatively and tended to write papers from their own individual perspectives (pictured after Jantsch):

Others interacted in a *pluridisciplinary* manner, without coordination. They wrote forecasts on problems, such as constructional materials.

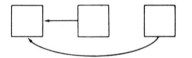

Still others worked in a polarized, unidirectional cooperation that corresponds to Jantsch's own definition of *crossdisciplinarity*. Researchers using this approach developed forecasts for subjects such as biochemistry.

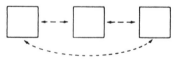

Graphic material reproduced from R. Wasniowski, "Futures Research as a Framework for Transdisciplinary Research," in *Managing Interdisciplinary Research*, S. R. Epton, R. L. Payne, and A. W. Pearson, eds., copyright © 1983 by John Wiley and Sons, Inc.

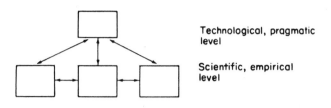

Technological, pragmatic
level

Scientific, empirical
level

Figure 2

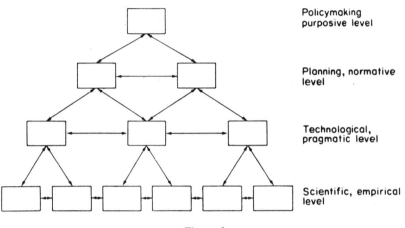

Policymaking
purposive level

Planning, normative
level

Technological,
pragmatic level

Scientific, empirical
level

Figure 3

Eventually, some staff members were compelled to work towards more intense cooperation in the form of *interdisciplinary teams* centered on a common problem-solving purpose, as illustrated in Figure 2.

In subsequent years research developed further along multilevel interactions. There was a horizontal and vertical coordination of disciplines that led to the kind of encompassing common purpose that characterizes *"transdisciplinarity."* Feedback mechanisms facilitated communication among basic sciences, applied sciences, and decision-making. The system was pictured as a Jantschian pyramid built on a scientific, empirical base, moving to a pragmatic level (technology), to a normative level (planning), to a purposive level at the apex (policy-making). (See Figure 3.) Specialists from both Poland and abroad worked on projects such as the role of technology in the advancement of social progress. (See Figure 4.) Manag-

Figure 2 and Figure 3 reproduced from R. Wasniowski, "Futures Research as a Framework for Transdisciplinary Research," in *Managing Interdisciplinary Research,* S. R. Epton, R. L. Payne, and A. W. Pearson, eds., copyright © 1983 by John Wiley and Sons, Inc.

ing this complex system involved very intense cooperation among teams
and the implementation of tasks in a hierarchical system.

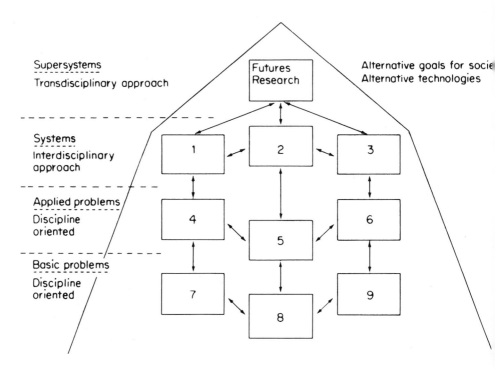

Figure 4. Scheme of the Place of Futures Research
as Transdisciplinary Research

The particular fields and research trends numbered in Figure 4 are as
follows:

1. Technological systems
   food production
   waste disposal
2. Sociotechnological systems
   controlling the environment development
3. Social system: developing countries
   factory

Figure 4 reproduced from R. Wasniowski, "Futures Research as a Framework for
Transdisciplinary Research," in *Managing Interdisciplinary Research,* S. R. Epton, R. L.
Payne, and A. W. Pearson, eds., copyright © 1983 by John Wiley and Sons, Inc.

4. Engineering
5. Assistance in decision-making
   analysis of decision
   methods of forecasting
6. Sciences on behavior
   law
7. Physics
   structure of life
   geology
8. Mathematics
   logics
   theory of sets
9. Social science
   sociology
   history

There is no inevitable progression from "multidisciplinarity" through "interdisciplinarity" to "transdisciplinarity." Even so, it is useful to keep in mind Sverre Sjölander's account of the ten stages in the development of an "interdisciplinary" project. Although Sjölander's remarks apply directly to groups, they have obvious implications for individuals as well, demonstrating as they do the importance of communicating with other specialists and checking the validity of one's conclusions.[61]

At Stage 1 participants often spend their time *"singing the old songs,"* presenting themselves, their work, and their answers to any conceivable criticism. Short-term meetings and workshops attended by large groups may never get past this stage. At Stage 2 as individuals begin detecting deficiencies in each other's positions, *"Everyone on the other side is an idiot."* Many people quit at this point, regarding the whole effort as a waste of time. At Stage 3, participants begin *"retreating into abstractions"* in order to find a common ground. The more abstract things are, the easier it is to agree. However, the general feeling of progress may crumble as soon as questions are asked about the concrete results of discussions. If participants are unable to account for the content and results of discussions, a project may remain indefinitely at this stage. At Stage 4, *"the definition sickness"* sets in as colleagues ask each other to define technical terms, only to discover that use of more general, philosophical terms varies. Developing a group-specific jargon is a common solution, though jargon can be an obstacle to new members of a group. At Stage 5, participants can begin to concentrate on fruitful discussion areas, if the earlier stages have been passed successfully. The areas are usually quite disparate, however: with perhaps one in methods, another in the use of statistics, a third in a general attitude towards experimental work, or in a holistic framework. As a result, discussion will tend to jump from one area to another, like *"jumping the tussocks"* in a quagmire.

At Stage 6 participants may be playing *"the glass bead game."* This is an undeniably positive step, since they are building on common jargon and common ground. It may well be the starting point for something really new and fruitful. Yet, this is a time-consuming process, and may prove no more successful than earlier methods of proceeding. By Stage 7 *"the great failure"* often surfaces. After wallowing in abstractions and playing glass bead games, participants may despair of their time and effort. Yet when asked to produce some kind of report of their activity and results, they often find their interest rekindled. Projects that stop at this stage are usually considered to have stopped just when they could have really turned fruitful. Those who make it to Stage 8 may find themselves wondering *"What's happening to me?"* They have changed more than they may be aware of consciously, a realization that often comes when they return to their original place of work or when they describe the results of a project to colleagues in their own disciplines. In many cases they have become better advocates or at least reluctant defenders of the disciplines with which they have interacted, strengthening and rekindling their interest in further interdisciplinary work. Those who left a project in a pessimistic mood may deplore their failure to spend more time on the project or to have a follow up activity, a beneficial event months or even years after a project. Evaluations made immediately upon termination of a project may be far more negative than evaluations measuring long-term growth, a tactical measure to consider when seeking funds for projects. Stage 9 is *"getting to know the enemy,"* moving towards more in-depth knowledge of other disciplines not only for the sake of the immediate project but also getting to know the general structures, principles, and ways of thinking in other disciplines. Stage 10 is *"the real beginning,"* reached after long-term work or repeated meetings and often quite productive of results at an astounding rate.

Making it to Stage 10 is neither easy nor inevitable. Moreover, in many cases the ultimate benefit, as the Swedish forest project demonstrated, may not be measured in terms of the immediate "success" or "failure" of a project but less tangible and more "concealed" benefits, especially changes in the way individuals work and think. Making it to Stage 10 also has a lot to do with realizing that criteria differ from project to project. In the absence of widely accepted criteria, there are several lessons that can be drawn from criteria Ernest Lynton has proposed.[62] It is important to remember that all projects must try to strike a balance between interdisciplinary breadth and the capabilities of the participants, ensuring both comprehensiveness and coherence. The chosen methodologies and variables must also be appropriate to the task. Within organizations cooperation and interaction must be balanced with state-of-the-art knowledge in the component disciplines, ensuring flexibility, adequate rewards, and opportunities for wider collaboration. Within degree programs depth in at least one area must be balanced with an adequate synthesis, and, in technology transfer, there must be bridging mechanisms between interdisciplinary efforts and the pertinent constituencies, both inside and outside the university. There is no formula for interdisciplinary work at any stage, but greater awareness of what the different levels of integration entail will help participants conceptualize both their objectives and the possibility of achieving them.

PART II

Disciplinarity /Interdisciplinarity

4 The Rhetoric of
Interdisciplinarity

The attempt to rescue Clio from pitiable
maidenhood by artificial insemination [historians]
know is nothing new. The exhortations to become
a science are an old nineteenth-century habit.
These precedents suggest that perhaps the time has
come for a noble abdication.
— Jacques Barzun, *Clio and the Doctors*

THERE is an inevitable paradox when talking about interdisciplinarity.
Our vocabulary — indeed, our entire logic of classification — predisposes us
to think in terms of disciplinarity. This predisposition has created a set of
metaphoric structures in the discourse. The dominant image — the surface
structure — is that of geopolitics. The major activity is dispute over territory, not only in education and research but also on health-care teams,
where a patient becomes the "turf" of specialists. In the logic of the geopolitical metaphor, a discipline is "private property," an "island fortress"[1]
staked off by its own "patrolled boundaries," and "no trespassing notices."[2]
A discipline is the "mother lode."[3] A field is an "empire" and "oligarchy,"
a graduate division a "territory," and each separate scientific domain a "man-
darin culture,"[4] a "balkanized region of research principalities."[5] These "domains" are "feudalized" into separate "fiefdoms"[6] occupied by "great hives
of capricious faculty specialists."[7] Locked in their "bastions of medieval
autonomy," these specialists nurture "academic nationalism,"[8] keeping
departmental turf "jealously protected"[9] and "domain assumptions" intact.[10] The dominant policy is that of "protectionism," the governing
philosophy a "tariff mentality,"[11] and the local mission a "territorial im-
perative."[12] Disciplinary jargon is "the shibboleth of adequate professional
training by the ingroup."[13]

However, there is unrest: the mounting of a "third-party challenge,"[14]
the "breaching" of boundaries,[15] "cross-cultural exploration[s],"[16] "flounder-
ing expeditions" into other disciplinary territories, and excursions to the
"frontiers" of knowledge. Where once "no interdisciplinary interlopers in-

vaded,"[17] no "intellectual scavengers" pilfered,[18] there is "alien intrusion."[19] Where once no one "looked over the hedge,"[20] there is "border traffic," "intellectual migration," and "transient authorship." It is rather like "fishing in a posted pond."[21] Asking "cutting-edge questions," researchers, teachers, and practitioners cross the "no man's land" between the disciplines,[22] making their way across the "academic Demilitarized Zone."[23] Like ancient mariners, educators embark on the "poorly charted waters of non-disciplinary or interdisciplinary study," lured by the beguiling "siren songs" of values, problem-solving, simplicity, usefulness, modernism, skills, and subject coverage.[24]

Some will come to rest in the "bureaucratic foothills of interdepartmental cooperation"[25] or in designated interdisciplinary programs, the "Switzerland of academia."[26] Others form "enclaves" of interdisciplinarity, "little islands"[27] where there is open talk of "transdisciplinary cosmopolitanism," new structures, "global strategy," and the "common-law marriage" of allied disciplines. The expeditions and "annexing" of "sattelite disciplines"[28] do not go unnoticed, for no discipline willingly abdicates its "mandated sovereignty."[29] Disciplinarians are warned to "stay out . . . or pay the price."[30] Inevitably, interdisciplinary ventures lead to problems of "foreign policy"[31] and "complex boundary readjustments." In some cases "bilateral treaties" may even be in order,[32] and the beginnings of a "common market" will be sketched out.[33]

Geopolitics are central to the conception of interdisciplinarity because, as Robert L. Scott put it, there is a "distinctly political face to the circumstances in which interdisciplinary efforts must thrive or not."[34] Disciplinary structure is so deeply embedded in academic institutions that it is unusual to find an argument for interdisciplinarity that does not acknowledge that sociopolitical reality. The concept, the activity — indeed, the very language of argument — are partially structured by the metaphor of war: claims are "indefensible," criticisms land "right on target," positions are wiped out by "strategy," arguments are "attacked," "demolished," "won," or "shot down."[35] This tendency is only heightened in the case of interdisciplinarity. If the disciplines have become "warring fortresses between which envoys are sent and occasional temporary alliances formed," then calls for "truce and synthesis" are inevitably charged with political overtones.[36]

Given this surface structure, it should not be surprising to find the rhetoric of belief affixed to the rhetoric of suzerainty and war. The "sheer force of orthodoxy" has driven disciplinarity into a fixed hole,"[37] leading disciplinarians to "sing out of the same prayerbook"[38] and seek "right doctrine" in their journals.[39] To experiment with disciplinary knowledge is to tamper, to "meddle with" the "preordained," to disturb the "intellectual idols," to tear off the "labels which still decorate the pediments of the university temples"[40] — even to challenge the "awe-inspiring pontiffs."[41] Disciplinarians are exhorted to "stop whoring after strange gods,"[42] and interdisciplinarity itself is regarded as a "hedonic calculus,"[43] a "black art kept in check by disciplinary Luddites"[44] who are members of a lost tribe cast adrift.[45] Disciplinarians may talk about the value of interdisciplinary perspectives, yet their words are only "pious but ritualized obeisances."[46]

And yet, the interdisciplinary impulse is to do the same, to "convert" the specialists into generalists just as they themselves were once "baptize[d]" into specialization. Specialists are not the only ones to have "worked their alchemy."[47] The generalists also have certain powers and even had a "Bible" in the Harvard "redbook" on general education. Interdisciplinarians have staged their own "revivals" and dispatched their own share of "missionaries." They even have their own "frequent strain" of "millenial interdisciplinarity," advanced by a "scornful prophetic minority" with its own corner on "some special Truth."[48]

The belief turns ideological for those who see interdisciplinarity as ontological polemic. Interdisciplinarity has been "the implement for a blithe liberation"[49] and a banner for "vehement protest" against fragmentation. Universities are described as "prisons with hermetically sealed cells for inmates with the same record."[50] Disciplinary jargon becomes the "suitable discourse" for translating new "arsenal concepts,"[51] and laboratory research in psychology is not just a prominent paradigm but "the most efficient and powerful weapon" in the "social psychological research armamentarium."[52] Little wonder, once the dust has settled, that some will have "moved their careers to safety within traditional departmental boundaries."[53]

The results are both negative and positive. While resisting attempts to usurp their data and theory in the name of interdisciplinarity, disciplinarians may well assert their own imperialistic claims. Semiotics, for example, has been touted as "'the only game in town,'" an "inherently" unified doctrine of signs that reconceptualizes and transforms the traditional disciplines.[54] Imperialistic claims like these have a certain value. They force matters into "the courts of communal discourse,"[55] into an arena where separate rationalizations can be "transmuted." Just as cross-pressures in voting can free individuals from traditional views, the "intellectual cross-pressures" of interdisciplinarity may yield new outlooks.[56] Disciplinary imperialism is not altogether unhealthy, for it obliges other disciplines to assess their own points of view, to use concepts, methods, and techniques that come from elsewhere. The danger of "ethnocentrism" is thereby lessened, the "master words" and "master concepts" of one discipline less likely to turn into "intellectual idols."[57]

The Machine and the Organism

Beneath the combative surface structure, there is another conceptual structure that has epistemological implications. There is, at first glance, what we might expect. The physicist describes knowledge in terms of elements and particles, the mathematician in terms of subsets and vectors, the biologist of symbiotic ideals and fecundity, the economist of market strategies, the anthropologist of disciplinary ethnocentrism and tribal rivalries, the systems theorist of feedback and cybernetic relations, the sociologist of sibling rivalries — and predictably so on. Still, there is common terminology. The language of mathematics, physics, biology, and general systems have found a popular fusion in the discourse, as knowledge is described in terms of "clusters" and "sets." "Material fields" are described at their "overlapping patterns" and "nexus" points. Converging forces approach a "center of gravity," a "critical mass." These are not static sets, for knowledge is pictured as a dynamic system moving vigorously at the "frontiers of convexity," propelled by "fission" and "fusion."

The most prominent images are the machine and the organism. There is a lot of talk about "interfacing," the most popular term borrowed from computer language. When questions and problems arise, they require "interfacing" of concepts and methods. Stored programs must be adapted to new information, the "through flow" of people used productively, and the "operators" and "entrepreneurs" marshalled. To do that, however, generalists must synthesize and address the "dynamics of specialized knowledge, whose sudden thrusts within a limited sector of a social system create imbalances in the whole."[58] Leo Apostel, one of the original OECD theorists, has in fact developed an elaborate market productivity metaphor to illustrate the best possible "operations" for interdisciplinarity within society as a whole.

Still, the dominant metaphor of a system is an organism. The organic metaphor enjoys great favor in the discourse because it establishes interdisciplinarity as a natural, generative process. It stresses evolution and fluctuation of knowledge rather than rigid architectural taxonomies and states of equilibrium. The image of an organism puts knowledge into "live relationships," emphasizing a fecundity that spawns new disciplines.[59] The "hybrid vigor" of interdisciplines, the "symbiotic ideal" of the Meikeljohn curriculum, the "symbiosis" of an interdisciplinary curriculum: all demonstrate the synergistic worth of interdisciplinarity. Synthesis has "taken root," and interdisciplinary education is "in the wind," a "growing swell." It becomes easy — in fact, organically proper — for biologist Lewis Thomas to see a poem as a healthy organism.[60] The model of the bodily paradigm as a system of knowledge regains its appeal.

And yet, the organic metaphor has a dark side, inviting the rhetoric of pathology. On the one hand, the generalist is viewed as a "broken-down specialist."[61] On the other, the wrong kind of knowledge is "dead" knowledge. Professors are pictured "authoritatively performing their appropriate mortuary rites," cast as undertakers threatened by changes that are perceived as "destructive disasters to be resisted," not "natural" or "benign" processes.[62] In the logic of the metaphor, the "dreaded poison" of specialization can only be expunged with the "antidote" of interdisciplinarity. The university is beset by "hardening of the arteries," and the patient needs "surgery." However, there is a risk. "How can new organs capable of changing the whole organism be transplanted without killing him?"[63] If specialization is a disease, then interdisciplinarity is not progress but a "symptom of the pathological situation in which man's theoretical knowledge finds itself today."[64]

The tendency to describe knowledge in the language of natural, organic properties is pervasive in the discourse because it directs attention to "links," "symmetry," "convergence," "conjuncture," "interactions," "interfaces," and "integration" itself. Interdisciplinary work is described as a natural mediation along "intercultural," "interdependent," "interstitial," "intersectional," and "interdepartmental" lines. Problems anthropomorphically elude the "grasp" of a single discipline and "refuse" to stay within boundries. Ultimately the cumulative effect of the organic metaphor is to assert interdisciplinarity's "natural" place and "inherent" need in a predominantly geopolitical environment.

Diffusion and Nonlinearity

Interdisciplinarity is further signified by a set of images reflecting how knowledge and information move across disciplines. The underlying problem of knowledge is reflected in the tendency to liken research in one specialty to "the deeper and deeper drilling of a mine shaft." Correspondingly the transfer of information across disciplines is likened to "interconnecting tunnels" drilled between vertical shafts."[65] There is a horizontal diffusion between the vertical pillars of knowledge,[66] a certain heterozygosity of knowledge and crossbreeding that lies below the surface of all sciences, with the possible exception of mathematics. Vertically structured disciplines may be "loosened" enough to allow horizontal diffusion and "spill over." Few know this better, Aronoff suggested, than the biologist, "who has seen his area grown . . . from an almost completely descriptive one, where only human physiology had the beginnings of qualitative levels, to today's arena involving, at the populational levels, the most sophisticated aspects of applied mathematics and, at the subcellular levels, combinations of physics, chemistry, and mathematics which, not too long ago, were considered the sacred domains of those disciplines alone."[67] This development resulted from the "spill-over" of physics and chemistry into biology.

*Figure 5. Present Situation: Disciplines as
clusters of specialties, leaving
interdisciplinary gaps*

There are other comparable images that reinforce a certain picture of
knowledge: overlapping neighborhoods, chain links, overlapping fish scales,
honeycombs, a spiral structure, conical shapes, fluctuating systems, a telephone network, a journey, concentric circles, and poly-ocularity. Many of
these images are associated with new ecological, cosmological, and network
models that emphasize interdependence and a non-dualistic synthesis. Perhaps the best-known visual image is Donald Campbell's fish-scale model of
omniscience. Campbell pictured the current structure of knowledge as clusters of specialties, with each narrow specialty represented by a fish-scale. The
redundant piling up of specialties leaves interdisciplinary gaps (Figure 5).
The ideal model would discourage disciplinary ethnocentrism in favor of
novel specialties, novel ranges of competence, and new administrative structures that facilitate communication across disciplines (Figure 6).[68]

Nonlinear images also characterize the view of interdisciplinary process. Lucien Pye likened the growth of knowledge in interdisciplinary area
studies to a pattern of zigzags,[69] and in describing the interdisciplinary
study of American culture, Gene Wise used the images of a journey and
concentric circles. Wise argued that experience "takes place within a range
of particular environments, or surrounds"[70] that radiate outward from a
center in widening circles of influence. The scholar must locate connecting links while journeying through those fields of experience. The process
is neither singular nor closed but multiple and open, a point John Adams
made in explaining the importance of interdisciplinary communication for

Figure 6. Ideal Situation: Fish-scale model of omniscience

understanding the circular, cumulative nature of causation in rural India.[71] Likewise, Emile Hadač, speaking for the collective of the Czechoslovakian Institute of Landscape Ecology, called the emerging integrative paradigm of the anthropoecological system a "model of an open, circular process of acquiring knowledge."[72] Scholarship, Wise added, is not a series of discrete *contributions*—"like building blocks in a pyramid"—but a series of *dialogues*—"transactions with an unfinished, an inherently unfinishable world of cultural experience."[73] In all of these models of interdisciplinary knowledge, circularity has replaced linearity.

Two final metaphors illustrate the two major perspectives on how interdisciplinary knowledge is achieved. Julian Huxley used a popular image when he advocated reforming science along a "centripetal, convergent pattern" in order to alleviate the damage caused by centrifugal, divergent trends. Huxley believed changing to a centripetal pattern required a problem focus, "a concentrated attack on specified problems."[74] Similarly, Les Humphreys and many others have argued that interdisciplinary thought has "centripetal power."[75] Huxley himself was uncomfortable with interdisciplinary terminology. To avoid using what he considered the "fashionable" term "multidisciplinary," he preferred to use just "plain *cooperative*." Terminological quibbles aside, Huxley arrived at the centripetal position for a commonly cited reason. Intercommunication and cross-fertilization constitute "a kind of reproductive union, producing new generations of scientific offspring, like biophysics or cytogenetics." They stand in contrast to the separate sciences, pictured as galaxies in an expanding universe: "diverging at increasing rates from some central position towards some limiting frontier."[76]

B. M. Kedrov, who spoke at the same UNESCO colloquium on science and synthesis as Huxley did, posited a different metaphoric image of the advancement of science, a symmetrically truncated cylinder: "According to the angle it makes with the plane, its projection on the plane may be a circle, a triangle, a square, or all three at once—like shadows projected upon the ceiling and two different walls." Thus, "from the point of view of simple analysis, the aspect of the object-model changes according to the standpoint from which it is viewed. But from the synthetic point of view, the different aspects of the model can be seen to belong to the same object by relationships which can be determined." Integration depends upon synthesis, yet synthesis takes account of analytic data. By first studying the projections individually, then breaking down the geometrical image of the body into its "constituent elements," and finally reconstructing them on a theoretical level, science can move "from the one to the many, and from the simple to the compound."[77]

Huxley's view is more organic in that he sees interdependency and intercommunication as centripetal *forces,* as natural processes of reproduction. Kedrov achieves integration by manipulating the cylinder and by moving from part to whole. The organic image assumes there are linkages which have been obscured and even damaged by *arbitrary* divisions. The belief that natural connecting forces will reestablish existing relationships is the dominant ideal of interdisciplinary discourse. Yet, it is for the most part just that, an ideal. The day-to-day reality of interdisciplinary work is that centripetal power does not function of its own accord. The interdisciplinarian must construct and project a synthesis.

Thus, whereas the organic metaphor asserts the natural place and inherent need for interdisciplinarity, the geopolitical structure of the discourse makes it clear that interdisciplinarity is an architechtonic, productive process, something constructed rather than given. This is particularly apparent in the next three chapters, which explore the relationship between disciplinarity and interdisciplinarity in greater depth. They deal with the problems and consequences of borrowing across disciplines, some of the ways interdisciplinarity has functioned as a critique of disciplinary limitations, and the "disciplinary" nature of interdisciplinary inquiry.

5 Borrowing

There are better ruts and cart-tracks to follow than
are at present being used.

—P. J. Perry

BORROWING is not a new phenomenon. Recent econometric history, for
instance, is only the most recent wave in a recurrent cycle of borrowing[1]
that includes the introduction of mechanical models into economics, the
use of economic models in electoral anaylsis, and the application of
cybernetic models in decision-making.[2] Any history of borrowing would
also note the role of geography and geology in the development of geomor-
phology, Harvey's use of the principles of volume and force in explaining
the circulation of blood, Darwin's use of geological evidence in the theory
of biological evolution, the use of thermodynamics in the theory of chemical
reactions, the use of knowledge about line spectra from radiant energy in
the discovery of helium on the sun, and the role of quantum mechanics
and crystallography in the discovery of DNA.[3] It would also recognize the
magnitude of borrowing from physics, including medical applications of
techniques developed in the area of elementary particles, the use of pattern-
recognition devices and image intensifiers in biological research,[4] and applications of radioactive dating methods in archaeology, the fine arts, and
criminology.[5]

Borrowing takes place for a number of reasons, though, as James Kinneavy pointed out, the great value in importing a model lies in the fact that
a borrowed system represents an area that has already been analyzed. Thus,
it is more familiar, more secure, and more complete than the system under
investigation. The transfer of knowledge may occur for several reasons:

1. to help structure a relatively unstructured domain;
2. to simplify a domain;
3. to complete a domain;
4. to explain a domain;
5. to enable a domain to get a complete picture of its own framework;
6. to allow for experimentation where the domain does not permit it.[6]

Though it is dangerous to generalize about a phenomenon that appears so widely, there is some agreement on the role of status and prestige

in borrowing. Muzafer and Carolyn Sherif observed a pattern of *upward modeling:* "an uncritical selectivity that is overawed in favor of models from disciplines more prestigeful than one's own."[7] Likewise, in the context of modernization, Samuel Huntington found that a discipline will usually tend to copy the more structured and "scientific" of its neighboring disciplines.[8] The more successful a theory is in its ability to describe, explain, predict, and systematize, the more tempting it is to extend its validity outside its original boundaries. As a result, the most successful theories tend to become "obsessive paradigms" for other fields of knowledge.[9]

There is no single pattern of borrowing. Some borrow for instrumental purposes, others in search of a new conceptual unity. In some cases borrowing is a temporary phenomenon; in others, it leads to a more permanent assimilation or general pattern of interactions, or even, in a few cases, a formal alliance. Borrowing may stem from a serendipitous alliance[10] or be part of the wide "conceptual spillage" from fashionable or powerful theories.[11] The degree of participation also varies, ranging from the work of a lone researcher to the kind of large-scale cross-fertilization implied in Michael Schiffer's characterization of archaeologists as "chronic" borrowers.[12] In addition, the direction varies. In geography and in urban affairs, there tends to be more importing than exporting. History and sociology, in contrast, are characterized by a more mutual and general borrowing of categories and methods, to such an extent, in fact, that Philip Abrams feels "even the unconvinced have had to familiarize themselves with the other side in order to withstand its advances."[13] Some borrowing is quite arbitrary and even illogical, but much of it is not. It is, for example, considered quite "natural" for political scientists to borrow concepts from sociologists and to imitate economic concepts in trying to understand political development, or for the sociological concept of modernization to be extended and applied to political analysis.[14]

Given the recognition of "natural" alliances, it is not unusual for patterns of borrowing to develop along some lines rather than others. In the late 1970s, for example, Marvin Mikesell found it reasonably safe to assume that a geographer who specializes in urban analysis will be fairly well informed on the postulates of "classical human ecology." However, the same geographer would not necessarily be able to differentiate between what is "classical" or "neoorthodox," nor understand the rationale for the placement of geographic studies in anthologies edited by sociologists. Moreover, with a few notable exceptions, it would have been hard to prove "human ecologists" were knowledgeable about the evolution of geographic thought in recent years or well versed in geographic research conducted outside the subfield of urban geography. Conversely, references to the work of rural sociologists seldom appeared in the writings of American geographers, though a comprehensive view of the interaction of human geography and sociology was evident in the writings of European geographers. The narrow bridge between the two disciplines in the past could be explained, in large part, by the failure of American geographers to develop a field of social geography and the preoccupation of American sociologists with the urban environment of modern America.[15]

Folklore provides another, more extended example.[16] David Hufford has shown how folklorists came to identify psychology with Freud's psychoanalytic theory and its offspring. Not only are the temptations of symbolic interpretation obvious, but clinical theorists have also tended to use interview materials as the basis for speculation, making psychoanalytic subjects and methods accessible to both anthropologists and folklorists. Furthermore, whereas academic psychologists tended to have a more molecular concern for limited aspects of behavior, particularly those observed in the laboratory, clinical depth psychologists and personality theorists tended to have more molar concerns. Thus, an overarching concept such as "personality" proved of greater interest to scholars in a field traditionally concerned with grand problems, such as the origins of culture. As a result, the primary area of psychological concern in anthropology, that of personality and culture, came to be linked with psychoanalysis. It is the psychoanalytic approach that has received attention in surveys of the field and the work of personality and culture theorists that has had an impact on folklore scholarship. There have been exceptions, of course, but no other theory has attracted the same degree of attention.

Even with a "natural" alliance, however, there may be problems, including, in this particular case, imprecise definitions and a lack of appreciation for both historical and contemporary connotations within psychology, in particular, and the behavioral sciences, in general. Exclusive use of depth psychologies can also lead to overreliance on the interpretation of symbols as a primary method. Moreover, terms carrying a specific meaning in psychoanalytic theory have been used without operational definitions in folklore and anthropology, implying in some cases a commitment to specific portions of psychoanalytic theory. "Repression," for example, might be used to indicate the forcing of material out of conscious awareness for a number of reasons, though in psychoanalytic theory "repression" is regarded as an act powered by specifically libidinal and aggressive energies. Similar difficulties arise from using "anxiety" to denote "nervousness" or feelings of "tension," and from applying "psychotherapy" to descriptions of folk religion and healing, an application increasingly more common as psychiatric anthropology (or transcultural psychiatry) gains momentum. The borrowing goes beyond simple description and empirical matters, since these terms carry with them a "heavy load of theory."

Clearly, there are several difficulties associated with borrowing. Hasty and indiscriminate borrowing have been especially troublesome, for many borrowed concepts have proved less empirically sound than they appeared at first glance.[17] Resorting to "an alien expertise" to solve an immediate problem[18] is often evidence of a "quick-fix mentality" rather than a long-term, integrated solution. Though different contexts create different problems, there are six common problems:[19]

1. distortion and misunderstanding of borrowed material;
2. use of data, methods, concepts, and theories out of context;
3. use of borrowings out of favor in their original context (including an overreliance on "old chestnuts");
4. "illusions of certainty" about phenomena treated with caution or skepticism in their original disciplines;
5. overreliance on one particular theory or perspective; and
6. a tendency to dismiss contradictory tests, evidence, and explanations.

In order to deal with these problems, borrowers must assume the core responsibility of borrowing. The "burden of comprehension"[20] requires that borrowers acquire at least a basic understanding of how something is used in its original context. Failure to assume this "burden" can lead to considerable problems of confidence. Mikesell found the personality of the statistically sophisticated and theoretically minded economic geographer to be "frankly schizoid." Confident in his discourse with fellow geographers, he tended to be "diffident in the company of economists." Yet the opposite problem, false confidence, also creates problems. Andrew Appleby cited the example of a book on insects and history. The author knew his biological subject well enough but displayed insufficient knowledge of history, leading him to assert inappropriately the historical importance of insects and insect-borne diseases.[21]

Problems with borrowing led Leon Pomerance to recommend that guidelines and general rules for interdisciplinary conferences be established. The catalyst was an International Scientific Congress on Thera. Prior to the conference, interdisciplinary exchanges between geologists and archaeologists were envisioned as a way of answering questions about the chronology of the volcanic climax of Thera. After observing confusion and even outright errors, Pomerance urged nonscientists to conduct more intensive consultations on scientific facts *before* they publish material involving such highly complex fields as seismology and volcanology.[22] Marilyn Robinson Waldman observed similar problems in Islamic Studies, where data and insights have been borrowed sometimes with the same reductivist "nuggeting" and "mining" of sources that plague other fields. Like Pomerance, Waldman considers it essential to check references with specialists in other fields. Interplay with more problem-oriented disciplines would encourage more careful construction of categories of analysis, forestalling conceptual isolation and impoverishment. Even the passing remarks of nonphilological, nonhistorical, and even non-Islamic scholars would cut away many of the myths that have encrusted the field. Islamic scholars, she suggests, would surely mistrust the work of historians who relied on translations rather than their own reading of original languages. They would also be likely to question incorporating results of archaeological, linguistic, numismatic, and statistical techniques without an understanding of their languages, their uses, and their limitations.[23]

A Case Study in Borrowing

Though the dynamics of borrowing are apparent in many fields, archaeology provides a particularly instructive example. Like anthropologists, archaeologists have borrowed instruments and concepts for some time. The nature of that borrowing is indicated, in part, by the Fryxell Award for interdisciplinary research in archaeology. Past awards have gone to Peter J. Mehringer, for his work in environmental archaeology;[24] John Guilday, for work on a wide range of problems shared by archaeology and paleontology;[25] and James Bennett Griffin, for applying postwar scientific techniques to archaeology. Griffin, in particular, was cited for his ability to convince physicists, chemists, biologists, and geologists of the value of archaeological work. He also brought technical devices such as computers, statistical procedures, earth-moving equipment, X-rays, and metallurgical analyses to the attention of archaeologists.[26] Gumerman and Phillips found that archaeologists have used interdisciplinary approaches in two quite different ways. The first and more successful involves the *results* of other disciplines; for example, using botany and zoology to help answer questions about the origin of maize agriculture or the changing degree of dependence on certain animals for food. The second involves borrowing concepts and models of causation from other academic disciplines. In the first instance, archaeologists are hiring the services of specialists in other disciplines. In the second instance, they are more like "do-it-yourself handymen."[27]

Borrowing has been propelled by changes in the nature of the field itself. In the late 1960s, as "New Archaeology" was reorienting the field, a number of archaeologists became concerned about methodology and epistemology.[28] Their concerns, which appeared entirely in the archaeological literature, were characterized by prescriptive statements supported by appeals to authority, especially G. G. Hempel, a philosopher of science. There was no consensus, however, and other archaeologists appealed to other authority figures with different methodological and epistemological positions. As philosophers themselves reacted, chiding archaeologists for flawed analyses and misused concepts, they assumed what Michael Schiffer calls the role of an "indulgent parent, reluctantly applying corrective measures to an errant offsping." At the same time, they did not acquaint themselves thoroughly with the unique problems or the literature of archaeology, reducing their own credibility and effectively thwarting an opportunity to develop an explicit philosophy of modern archaeology.

Since the initial debates, new issues have arisen, including heightened interest in archaeological inference, adequacy criteria for theory-building, possible uses of general systems theory, analogy in archaeological reasoning, and laws of cultural evolution. However, the relationship between archaeology and philosophy of science has tended to remain one-sided. There is also a further problem. Many archaeologists are charged with a feeling of progress. Their interest in sampling, behavioral chains, microwear analysis, and other improvements in technique is fed by the prospect of upgrading the quality of archaeological information and bridging the gap between data and models. Yet, in a number of cases, computer packages and philosophy of science have been used mechanically, and systems theory, ecology, and other disciplines have been raided for concepts. The quality and precision of the models and methods being borrowed are not so much at fault as the abuse of models, a problem that has led to "elegant but faulty conclusions."[29]

Borrowing from ecology provides an excellent example of both the benefits and problems of borrowing. Modern cultural ecology emerged in both archaeology and cultural anthropology during the early 1960s.[30] They have shared concepts to such an extent that cultural ecologists were said to "readily pass" through the disciplinary boundary between archaeology and sociocultural anthropology. Cultural ecologists view culture as a behavioral system through which a human population adapts to its environment. When principles of biological ecology have been applied to cultural systems in archaeological studies, there have been several results. They have implied laws common to all ecological systems and have also been seen as part of a commitment to general systems theory. Cultural ecologists, in fact, are largely responsible for introducing general systems theory into archaeology. There is also a more far-reaching claim that principles of biological ecology are indispensable, perhaps even self-sufficient, means of explaining important aspects of cultural behavior.

There is, then, great promise. Several factors, however, have impeded the development of a unified perspective. One is the reluctance of ecologically oriented collaborators to leave the "comfortable realm of empirical data." In some cases ecological problems have also been given only token acknowledgement or been used in ignorance. In addition, Karl Butzer has observed a tendency to stress broad organizational models in theoretical writings explicitly devoted to ecology, even though the complex relationships between culture and environment have not been explicitly formulated and fully explored. He also found that the ecological models implicit in archaeological writings in the mid 1970s were being drawn from increasingly defunct notions of synchronic cultural ecology.[31] These general issues are apparent in the borrowing of two specific concepts, "ecotone" and "edge."

The "ecotone" concept generated considerable excitement in the 1930s and 1940s. Developed originally by wildlife management specialists as a limited explanatory tool, the ecotone concept relates transition zones between larger biological regions to increases in the population density of certain species and increases in the number of species. Many archaeologists using the terms "ecotone" and "edge effect" have relied upon a basic definition from Eugene Odum's introductory textbook *Fundamentals of Ecology* (1959), which indicates "ecotone" is a transition between two or more diverse communities, such as a forest and grassland or a soft-bottom marine community. It is a junction zone or tension belt that may have considerable linear extent but is narrower than the adjoining community areas themselves. Usually an ecotonal community contains many organisms from each of the overlapping communities, in addition to organisms characteristic of, and often restricted to, the ecotone. Both the number of species and population density of some of the species are often greater in the ecotone than in adjacent communities.

"Edge effect" refers to a tendency for increased variety and density at community junctions, and "edge species" refers to organisms occurring primarily or most abundantly in junctional communities.[32] The edge philosophy was derived primarily from research observations on farm and preserve game, where the creation of human-made "edge" by conservationists and farmers significantly altered animal behavior. From there it was carried over into general ecology, where it seemed to lose some of its original precision. Subsequently it was borrowed for archaeological use, where it helped explain the character of cultural boundaries. In the process of borrowing, though, biological systems and cultural variability were uncritically equated. Relationships between two archaeological "cultures" were treated as relationships between life zones, with "ecotone" being used to cover almost any kind of biological transition zone, even broad classificatory categories of life zones rather than actual communities.[33]

A significant part of the problem encountered in borrowing "ecotone" and "edge" has been failure to appreciate its original context. Although the ecological perspective has opened up new avenues for research, the alignment of ecology and animal studies has been slowed by inadequate communication between anthropology and those natural sciences, making it difficult to judge the validity of numerous specialized terms now populating anthropological writings. Moreover, there is debate on the current status of the concepts not only within archaeology[34] but within ecology as well. Their phenomenal status has been questioned by ecology's "continuum school," which denies that ecosystems must have distinct boundaries, as living cells do. There is also considerable ambiguity about how the terms are to be defined. They have been applied to rather diverse boundaries, ranging from a shore or small pond to a vast transition area extending from the African tropical rain forest to the Sahara. Archaeologists should not avoid the terms because of these differences, but they must be careful how they use them.

The development of cultural and ecological principles may one day lead to a truly general ecological theory, different from current formulations in both biological and cultural ecology. At present, however, none has been systematized or put into axiomatic form. The example of borrowing from ecology only underscores the necessity of communication not only across disciplines but also within disciplines, where individuals may place rather different values on what is being borrowed. Adopting models just because they are useful is not sufficient. There must be more adequate justification and thorough understanding of both the logic and validity of the model in its original context. Archaeologists can learn from the example of historians and sociologists, who have inappropriately applied ill-digested anthropological concepts such as "tribe," "band," "culture," and "race."[35]

To promote less asymmetrical, more symbiotic relationships, Schiffer advocates a change in discourse strategy, concentrating on shared concerns rather than disputes. Butzer echoes the need for more carefully focused dialogue, lamenting that basic patterns of interaction between excavators and collaborating scientists in the 1970s were pretty much the same as they were in the 1950s. Site reports and data still tended to be only partially integrated, and theoretical statements on archaeological methodology and prehistorical research only gave lip service to the integration and implementation of ecological concepts. Moreover, few project directors had the background, or made an effort, to understand the full range of what collaborating scientists might contribute.[36] These problems are only exacerbated by the underlying "disciplinary" philosophy at key granting agencies. (Ellwyn Stoddard addresses the problem of funding interdisciplinary research elsewhere, in the context of research on U.S./Mexico borderlands.)[37]

None of these problems is unique to archaeology. Geographers have despaired of being brought in only for "expert" technical advice and finding their work borrowed only for technical support. They are discouraged when they are mistaken for technicians who can just sketch in a regional description or give hard facts about physical environment or background.[38] In archaeological projects disciplinary collaborators complain they are not always given access to digested site data and emerging patterns, nor are they given incentive to apply their own particular experience to the resolution of issues requiring interdisciplinary input. Yet, at the same time, collaborating scientists share part of the blame, since they often fail to identify with the overriding goals of a project. The result has been a large collection of "multidisciplinary" site reports, not "interdisciplinary" problem-solving. All too often excavation directors and readers must do the synthesizing themselves.

Inevitably borrowing invites speculation about the metaphorical nature of interdisciplinarity. Metaphors may be didactic or illustrative devices, models, paradigms, or root images that generate new models.[39] Some metaphors are heuristic, whereas others constitute new meaning, similar to the way theory-constitutive metaphors drawn from computer science, information theory and related disciplines have functioned in cognitive psychology.[40] Borrowing is metaphoric in several ways. Theories and models from other disciplines may sensitize scholars to questions not usually asked in their own fields, or they may help interpret and explain, whether that means a framework for integrating diverse elements or hypothetical answers that cannot be obtained from existing disciplinary resources. When a research area is incomplete, borrowing may facilitate an inductive open-endedness. It may function as a probe, "facilitating understanding and enlightenment."[41] Or, it may provide insight into another system of observational categories and meanings, juxtaposing the familiar with the unfamiliar while exposing similarities and differences between the literal use of the borrowing and a new area.[42]

Borrowers have been called translators, clarifiers who interpret one discipline to those in another. The act of translation, George Steiner points out, entails a "hermeneutic motion," a fourfold act of the elicitation and transfer of meaning. It begins with an *initiative trust.* All understanding is an act of trust that derives from phenomenological assumptions about the coherence of the world, meaning in semantic systems, and the validity of analogy and parallel. Trust is followed by aggression, by an *incursive and extractive* act that suggests comprehension is the appropriation of another entity: "The translator invades, extracts, and brings home." The third act is *incorporative,* as the newly acquired, imported meaning or form is assimilated and placed, an act that may result in a dislocation or relocation of the original. It creates a dialectic of embodiment that may render translators lame. Just as "the inhaled voice of the foreign text" has choked the original voice of a textual translator, borrowers have been overwhelmed by what is being borrowed—thereby distracting them from issues in their own fields. Yet, the movement may be in quite another direction, distorting the original and creating a new entity that depends only metaphorically on the original—thereby distracting them from issues in the field from which the borrowing is extracted. The fourth stage of translation is one of *compensation,* of exchange and restored parity. It is the enactment of a reciprocity that restores balance while enhancing and even enlarging the stature of the original. This transfer raises the entire question of the meaning of meaning in time, suggesting the image of a mirror that not only reflects but also generates light. Because the original gains from "the orders of diverse relationship and distance established between itself and the translations," the reciprocity is dialectic.[43]

Borrowing creates a similar dialectic, in this case between the comprehension of existing knowledge and the creation of new knowledge. Although there are no standards for excellence in borrowing, or for that matter interdisciplinary work in general, Stephen Schneider's criteria for excellence in interdisciplinary research are highly appropriate. Excellence is not to be measured solely in terms of disciplinary originality but, instead, three criteria that acknowledge the importance of disciplinary accuracy while allowing the creation of new meaning: disciplinary clarity, the clarity of cross-disciplinary communications, and the utilization and combination of existing knowledge to help solve a problem or to raise or advance knowledge about a new issue.[44] Ultimately, then, the quality of borrowing depends upon the quality of both disciplinary and interdisciplinary communication, on a fuller reciprocity of "text" and translator.

6 The Critique of Limitation

We are confronted with insurmountable
opportunities.

—Pogo (Walt Kelley)

DAVID RIESMAN once suggested attacks on disciplinary boundaries have
become so widespread they are now part of the "standard repertory of
criticism from outside and inside American higher education."[1] These attacks rarely emanate from a well-developed theory of interdisciplinarity,
nor are they usually followed by critical analysis of the relationship between disciplinarity and interdisciplinarity. As a result, there is no real
literature on the subject, only a scattering of bits and pieces across the
archipelago. Yet when added up, these bits and pieces reveal a great deal
about how interdisciplinarity functions as a critique of disciplinary limitations. Although the critique is widespread, some of the richest examples
are in ethnic, women's, and area studies.

Ethnic and Women's Studies

Sarah Hoagland was mindful of limitations when, on behalf of
women's studies, she criticized "gross omissions and distortions" in the
form and content of traditional disciplines.[2] Likewise, Annette Kolodny's
propositions for a feminist literary criticism challenged prevailing approaches on the grounds of both methodological convenience and
philosophical validity. Feminist criticism was not only a new way of thinking about old material but an assault on "that dog-eared myth of intellectual neutrality."[3] Interdisciplinarity was seen as a way to push the disciplines,
not just nudge them along. It was a catalyst for moving past bias, distortion, and insularity.

By its very nature, the argument for interdisciplinarity in ethnic and
women's studies has been pluralistic. It rests, first of all, on a traditional
claim for seeing the whole instead of just the disciplinary parts. A wider
perspective would merge limited, specialized concerns and identify interrelationships.[4] In addition, there is a need for more accurate, self-defined

epistemologies. Because black studies is "disciplined" by the centrality of racism in American life, Ronald Walters explained, it is centered on "the discipline of the 'unity and the order of Blackness.'"[5] Likewise, Russell Thornton explained, American Indian studies must be allowed to define and build its own intellectual traditions, based not on the differentiated social and political systems of white culture but on the holistic "undifferentiated systems" of native American cultures. That has meant focusing on oral traditions, treaties and treaty rights, tribal government, forms of organization, group persistence, and American Indian epistemology.[6] It has also meant avoiding being classified as the study of "just another minority."

Although there is no shared philosophy of interdisciplinarity in the "studies," Arthur Kroker articulated a perspective that is shared implicity. Writing in the context of Canadian studies, Kroker distinguished *vacant interdisciplinarity,* which mechanically applies the bland "integrons" of normalization, from *critical interdisciplinarity.* Critical interdisciplinarity would entail a "collective deliberation on public problems" and the "negative presence" of "repressed memories of the Canadian historical experience." It would constitute a critical reinvention of Canadian discourse, a revision of the bourgeois episteme in favor of a method and style of scholarship that is simultaneously "*public, discursive* and *archaeological.*" The ultimate goal is a regeneration of method and reappraisal of the "public responsibilities of genuinely Canadian inquiry." Critical interdisciplinarity is based on a new social relation of intellectuality, a vigorous pluralism that requires "an active migration beyond the disciplines to a critical encounter with different perspectives on the Canadian situation."[7] For Kroker the interdisciplinarian is not only a Foucaldian archaeologist attempting to recover lost discourse but a scholar who fosters a new style of knowing, a new mode of intellectual discourse based on "rediscovery" and "rethinking," "resocialization" and "reintellectualization." Thus interdisciplinarity signifies a new way of knowing.

Interdisciplinarity has also been justified in terms of an instrumental alignment of knowledge and action, suggesting a new logic of inquiry and new standards for judging scholarly work. There is a job to be done. Women's studies was conceived as "a vehicle for change and expression." Raising consciousness was deemed an interdisciplinary process because a philosophy of knowledge attentive to "the forms and functions of power" cuts across disciplines.[8] Black studies was introduced in direct response to a "mandate for change" and group problem-solving skills.[9] Hence, there were arguments for black studies being defined by pluralistic praxis rather than by grand theory or the prevailing paradigms of sociology, economics, or political science. It has been important not only to research distortions and omissions in the disciplines but also to produce models of service for the black community.[10] Analysis was considered a purposeful activity; black studies a corrective, descriptive, and prescriptive field of knowledge.[11] With action as the "guiding criterion for formal knowledge," the model for a black studies scholar became a medical scientist, a doctor who brings pure and applied knowledge into closer relationship in order to improve life in the black community.[12] Likewise, American Indian studies developed along the lines of not only native American culture and social science but also applied dimensions, such as Indian education, social work, health care, and other native American problems and conditions. American Indian studies focused on teaching and service for deliberate reasons.

Attacks on the knowledge/action dichotomy are by no means confined to interdisciplinary discourse. They are part of a widespread critique of dualism in the West.[13] Dualistic thinking has created what Sinclair Goodlad calls a "drift to purity and fixing,"[14] a disposition to dissociate pure thought from action. In raising the question of whether feminist criticism is a threat to scientific objectivity, Elizabeth Fee cautioned that the very concept of objectivity has created "a hierarchy of distances within science, a series of dichotomies and silences" that drive a wedge between knowledge and its social uses.[15] Couched in these terms, interdisciplinarity has been conceived as a means of reuniting action and thought, though there are different views on the ideal balance. Some believe modern problems are so profound, so urgent, that research and teaching must be devoted exclusively to their solution. Others argue, more moderately, that problem-solving teams, research centers, and interdisciplinary programs should be accorded greater prestige in the academy. The internal status hierarchy that prizes knowing over doing should be altered. Still others contend this has happened all along, that the dichotomy between pure and applied knowledge does not actually exist. It is an ideal informed by tradition and the prestige of high-level theory, an abstraction that assumes disciplines are theory-centered and society's problems will fall inevitably outside the scope of pure disciplinary study.

What actually happens is an intermixing of values. There are many devices and criteria—historical, geographic, social, economic, psychological, and political—by which circumstances are differentiated and classified.[16] The pragmatic and theoretical claims, Robert Merton points out, are "partly independent of each other, authentically coinciding on occasion, turning up severally, and sometimes being altogether groundless."[17] Hence, the most extensive debates in women's studies continue to address the relationship of women's studies to the feminist movement and "the integration of activist and academic goals inside as well as outside the classroom." By necessity this requires a "balancing act" in the National Women's Studies Association.[18] In black studies there is also disagreement about how much importance should be attached to endogenous versus exogenous concerns, a conflict illustrated vividly by the Saunders Redding/Imamu Amiri Baraka debate on the black revolution in American studies.[19]

In his 1980 presidential address to the Association for Asian Studies, Benjamin I. Schwartz spoke to another related issue: "The questions that confront us at this point are: What is a theoretician, and what is a gatherer of facts? What is a theory and what is a fact? Anyone familiar with current literature in the philosophy of science will be aware that these are not simple questions. At one extreme one can find the view that there are no such things as bare statements of facts. In the words of Karl Popper, 'all observations are theory-impregnated.'"[20]

Facts archaeologically uncovered from silence or suppression were not "bare" facts but the substance of new theories that exposed the partiality of conventional axioms and received truths. The charges of intellectual solipsism and cultural ethnocentrism coming from ethnic and minority studies were not unrelated to the spreading attack on ethnocentrism in area studies. In all of these fields, there was a broad post-World War II critique of the way disciplinary and cultural knowledge has been circumscribed by authoritative categories and specious dichotomies. The interdisciplinary critique was, therefore, a disciplinary, and epistemological, *and* a cultural critique.

Area Studies

Sustained U.S. interest in distant parts of the modern world dates from the nineteenth century,[21] though area studies gained momentum as one "minor enterprise in the war effort,"[22] a crash program designed to supply information about foreign cultures during World War II.[23] At first areas presenting the "most immediate problems" to the United States were emphasized — namely, the Asian-Pacific theater of war and the Soviet Union. After 1945 area studies expanded to cover the whole of the non-Western world and even "marginal parts" of the West, though in Latin American studies the Spanish and Portuguese were emphasized over the indigenous heritage. Later on area programs also developed in some British and continental European universities, in Canada, Australia, and New Zealand. Although Europeans did have an edge in the amount of knowledge about areas they once ruled, that knowledge was often slanted in favor of official policies and, consequently, was often confined by colonialist pigeonholes.[24] Recently the Western monopoly on studies of the non-Western world has been broken by work being done in Japan, India, Singapore, Ghana, and other Asian and African countries.

From the start, area researchers were keenly aware of the need to move past disciplinary boundaries. In the 1950s, in Bulletin 63 of the Social

Science Research Council (SSRC), Julian Stewart spoke of four objectives: providing knowledge of practical value, giving students and scholars an awareness of cultural relativity, providing an understanding of social and cultural wholes within areas, and furthering the development of a universal social science. The term *integration* had no fixed or stable meaning. It tended to depend on the problem at hand, though for research purposes the area unit was conceived as a sociocultural system or whole. At the first SSRC national conference on study of world areas, Herring and Parsons implied that an area "whole" is similar to a biological organism, though they acknowledged important differences between biological organisms and social systems. In addition, they suggested the study of an area might well entail the kind of disciplinary cooperation characteristic of medical research.[25] In the end, however, the dream of a universal social science never materialized, and many research teams wound up functioning in more "multidisciplinary" than "interdisciplinary" fashion. Nevertheless, the interdisciplinary objectives of area studies did have an impact on the way inquiry was conducted.[26]

Attempts to do interdisciplinary work in distant locations create a compounded marginality. Area specialists are, as Lucian Pye put it, "lonely but visible."[27] They are isolated by geographical distance, the need for mastery of a second language, and an ethnographic model that demands years in the field. Requiring disciplinary, linguistic, cultural, and interdisciplinary skills, they face the demand for dual, triple, even quadruple competence. Moreover, though disciplinarians working in a particular geographical area may be united by a common devotion to that area, area scholars are not necessarily united by a common focus or design. Geographical and disciplinary parochialism have inhibited not only the infusion of new ideas from fellow disciplinarians but also cross-fertilization and comparative analysis from other area specialists.[28] In addition, there are unique problems of communication. It can be quite difficult to stay in touch with research done in developing countries, where books and papers may be distributed in limited numbers through official channels. Foreign scholars may also face resentment by local academics, particularly when they or their predecessors have "mined and exported" work to the West.[29]

Political science provides a good example of these problems, especially the subfields of political modernization and development.[30] In the 1960s, when the first generation of nationalist leaders in developing countries were stressing goals of change and modernization, they often denied details of their own cultural heritage. In this circumstance it was easy for political scientists with little historical knowledge of various cultures to analyze contemporary problems of development. In countries accentuating plans for development, academics who were generalists in matters of development were often preferred to foreign scholars with deep knowledge of indigenous languages and cultural traits. However, as disillusionment about rapid development spread among the leaders and intellectuals of developing countries, many foreign scholars were resented, especially those involved in empirical work. In many cases there was a reversal in attitudes that left foreign researchers denounced for their ignorance of local languages and cultural patterns.

There were, in addition, problems of scholarly integrity. Skepticism about statements by nonregional specialists and scholars lacking prerequisite credentials created a "what-can-he-possibly-know-about-the-*real*-Gabon syndrome." It worked to discourage and postpone comparative research. Area specialization could also act as a "refuge for mediocrity," especially when there was a lack of appropriate forums for scholarly discourse. African geographical studies, for example, could often be done without critical evaluation by other non-Africanist geographers. If necessary, one could shift audiences whenever convenient. Other disciplinary specialists in the same region could be viewed as lacking the necessary background and skills of, say, a geographer, and other geographers could be dismissed for not knowing enough about the "real Gabon." Such "academic broken field running" exists in the disciplines as well, but, Edward Soja found, it seemed to reach a higher pitch in area studies.[31]

Area studies were also plagued by the skewed distribution of disciplines from one area to another. Unfortunately, the underlying conditions have tended to be "self-perpetuating."[32] As a general rule, specialists tended to be underrepresented in the social sciences and applied disciplines most relevant to public policy. A humanistic imbalance arose, in part, because language and history were already organized along geographical divisions. Hence, with the exception of anthropology, they were the ones that could muster critical masses of personnel for programs of non-Western studies. Oriental studies developed along the pattern of the classical humanities,[33] and, in Islamic studies, a long-standing dependence on philological and chronological methods narrowed the range of topics, discouraging the use of other disciplinary methods.[34] The Orient that was studied in the West was largely a "textual universe" of books and manuscripts, with a traditional focus on the classical period of a given language or society.[35] East Asian studies, in contrast, tended to be dominated by historians,[36] though in 1948 modern historians and social scientists interested in China and Japan founded the Far Eastern Association out of dissatisfaction with the American Oriental Society, which had emphasized the classical Sinological tradition.

Area studies were also caught in a further imbalance, between factual knowledge of alien countries, chiefly of the "humanistic" kind, and the ability to solve general theoretical problems in macropolitics, many of them initially generated in area studies.[37] When area studies were developing, problems of a general-theoretical nature were ill defined in political science. The voids were filled with empirical work. Although that helped counteract disciplinary parochialism it also created a certain reputation for area specialists. Chalmers Johnson likened the role of an area specialist in a discipline to a "supplier of raw materials, rather like a Bantu miner, chipping away at the cliff face of a South African mine, who is supposed to ship the unrefined ore off to the master goldsmiths living elsewhere — in this case, to 'generalists,' or 'theorists,' or 'comparativists' toiling away at New Haven, Cambridge, Ann Arbor, or the Stanford 'think tank,' where the data will be processed."[38] This tended to foster what Chauncy Harris called "a complete separation of levels of discourse between detailed work within a country — say, the study of the utilization of a particular dam — and global generalizations from abroad."[39] The gap between theory and detail as levels of discourse is, of course, a problem within individual disciplines, but it is compounded in interdisciplinary research.

The problem was also noted in other areas. Ethnic, women's, and area studies were all accused of a preoccupation with data and facts. Yet the stark theory/data dichotomy projected an overly severe image of data hackers, since the new empirical work both challenged and reinvigorated existing theory. The picture is not a simple diptych with data gatherers on one panel and theory builders on the opposite panel. Johnson defied the dichotomy in a rather apt analogy: "rather like the Third World itself, a good many nationalizations are going on." The theorists were not sending back very good theories to the field, and some of the commodity suppliers were going into manufacturing for themselves.[40] Speaking from his experience in Latin American studies, Kalman Silvert also defied the theory/data dichotomy in an economic analogy — the trickle theory in economics. The trickle theory is based on the assumption that a well-primed pump will continue to shower some water on everybody. However, the trickle theory breaks down, in part, because unequal power distributions often prevent the flow from permeating the entire society: "Analogously, the flow of data from 'areas' to the disciplinary mills and out to the 'areas' dries up because the mill is unable to process the raw material; it cannot convert 'information' into 'data' without changing its own nature, without grappling with the fact that area studies came into existence because of the very ethnocentric limitations of the disciplines. Political science is a weak sister. Areas studies are her crutch."[41]

Some of the tension generated by the presumption of a neat division of theorists in the discipline and data collectors in area studies eased as area specialists became more methodologically sophisticated and disciplinary specialists more knowledgeable about particular areas. Furthermore, for a time the non-Western world attracted the attention of leading theorists in most of the social science disciplines. When disillusionment arose over rapid development, area specialists generally had the most convincing explanation for why "the deeper character" of politics in Asia and Africa inhibited the emulation of Western development. Consequently, relationships changed. At first it was the area specialist who sought skills and concepts from the disciplines. As increasing numbers of area specialists were able to combine advanced theories, sophisticated methods, and cultural knowledge in their research, the presumed division between theorists and low-status data collectors was challenged. Then, as area specialists made gains as social scientists, they "shifted their tack." Increasingly they questioned the general utility of concepts developed for the study of Western societies and, more particularly, American politics. As the discipline of political science expanded, area specialists discovered that, rather than stranding them permanently at the margins of the field, the discipline had reached out to incorporate their areas of interest. Ultimately, their status within the profession changed as a result.[42]

By the 1970s the initial tensions had receded. In the aftermath, however, there were new concerns about objectivity and ideology in the social sciences, new problems related to the politicizing of research. The relationship to discipline has been blurred further by the problem of scholars asserting their roles as social scientists—thereby drawing closer to discipline—while questioning the very propriety of describing the social sciences as objective and value neutral—thereby moving in another, quite opposite direction. In the earlier debates, area studies were singled out because of the difficulty of achieving exacting standards in uncongenial settings. In the later debates, there have been far-reaching questions related to basic philosophical values and assumptions that apply equally to disciplinary and interdisciplinary work.[43] Thus, the original confrontation eased as area specialists became more skilled in social science methods and disciplinary specialists became more experienced in foreign research. Yet, a new crisis emerged as the paradigms of political science were challenged from new sources. The crisis was by no means restricted to political science.

There have been attacks on all sides. The "studies" have attacked the disciplines for ethnocentrism, racism, sexism, uncritical scientism, positivism, and "paradigmatic fossilization."[44] The "studies," in turn, have been attacked for lack of objectivity. Their loyalty to discipline and country has been questioned, their work judged short on rigor, long on relativism, empiricism, description, and idiosyncrasy. Nevertheless, there has been movement on both sides, demonstrating the productive tension that can operate between disciplinarity and interdisciplinarity. Although the structure of knowledge and training has not changed dramatically in the academic disciplines and the track records of organized programs are marked by attrition, the "studies" have raised questions that go to the very foundations of the humanities and social sciences, questions about the need for a wider perspective, for synthesis, a more purposeful relationship between the university and the community, and a reflexive scholarship. Lucian Pye once described the confrontation between discipline and area studies as a "quiet but fundamental struggle," one that has affected the self-identities of aspiring scholars, the organizing and hiring of faculties, and the design, funding, and execution of research.[45] In varying degrees, the description applies to all the "studies."

Political science versus area studies? The question, Alfred Meyer suggests, is rather like asking a student to choose between zoology, on the one hand, and the study of spiders, elephants, or frogs, on the other. If there is a lack of communication between general zoologists and specialists on frogs, elephants, or spiders, neither can expect to learn much from each other. Without communication neither the species specialists nor the generalists can be entirely competent.[46] To picture the relationship between disciplinarity and interdisciplinarity as a "double impasse,"[47] as a fixed choice between one or the other, is to oversimply the creative interplay that has produced changes in the nature of both disciplinarity and interdisciplinarity.

7 The Disciplinary Paradox

We learn to swim by swimming.

—Chairman Mao

DEFINING disciplinarity is no less important than defining interdisciplinarity. The term *discipline* signifies the tools, methods, procedures, exempla, concepts, and theories that account coherently for a set of objects or subjects.[1] Over time they are shaped and reshaped by external contingencies and internal intellectual demands. In this manner a discipline comes to organize and concentrate experience[2] into a particular "world view."[3] Taken together, related claims within a specific material field put limits on the kinds of questions practitioners ask about their material, the methods and concepts they use, the answers they believe, and their criteria for truth and validity.[4] There is, in short, a certain particularity about the images of reality in a given discipline.

Adequate though this definition may be, it fails to account for differences that affect the relationship between disciplinarity and interdisciplinarity. There are, first of all, different degrees of formality and organization. R. D. Whitley has distinguished *restricted sciences* that are highly specific in subject and mathematical precision from *configurational sciences,* such as social and life sciences.[5] Richard Rose distinguished *consensual* from *nonconsensual fields,*[6] and Thompson et al. contrasted *highly codified fields* (mathematics and the natural sciences) to *less codified fields* (humanities and to a lesser extent the social sciences).[7] Likewise, Lodahl and Gordon distinguished *high-paradigm fields* such as physics and chemistry from *low-paradigm fields* such as sociology and political science.[8] Going one step further, Stephen Toulmin distinguished *compact disciplines* (the better-established physical and biological sciences) from both *would-be disciplines* (the behavioral sciences) and *nondisciplinary activities* (ethics, philosophy, and activities that would be considered IDR projects).[9] Archie Baum also distinguished *narrow specialism,* which concentrates on the division of functions, from *broad specialism,* which is open to their interdependence.[10]

In addition to formality, the scope of a discipline should also be taken into account. Physics, chemistry, and anthropology are sometimes considered "federated disciplines" because of their size and number of independent subdivisions. Even the smaller field of climatology has been called a "confederation of many little sciences" because of its special subdivisions of dendrochronology (the study of tree rings) and palynology (pollen grains); sedimentology (riverbeds) and stratigraphy (lake bottoms); pedology (soils) and glaciology (ice); lichenometry (algae and fungi) and phenology (the study of recurrent phenomena such as harvests and migrations), in addition to historical climatology.[11] Certain subfields, including the powerful interfield theories of the natural sciences,[12] may even bear the hallmarks of disciplinary organization, including their own professional associations, journals, and programs of graduate study. Cytology, for example, has grown considerably since the end of the nineteenth century, with special cytology societies and institutions serving its needs. Although cytology may not be taxonomically classed as a discipline, it does function sociologically as one. With lines so heterogeneous and subspecialties so well defined, it becomes difficult to determine if the recipient of a Ph.D. in arctic biology from the University of Alaska is really practicing the same discipline as a holder of a degree in mathematical biology from Chicago or the holder of a degree in radiation biology from Rochester.[13] Indeed, an embryologist and a geneticist may be more alike than two chemists in terms of their knowledge, interests, and techniques.[14]

Disciplines also have different degrees of receptivity, and they definitely have different growth patterns. Some develop without "definitional closure," and almost all disciplines have periods of definitional competition.[15] Disciplines with well-established vocational fields will tend to be eclectic rather than purist in their epistemological conception of themselves,[16] and certain disciplines in the social sciences and engineering center forthrightly upon questions of practice, fostering relations with other disciplines that impinge on the same social and technological problems. Other disciplines have also been open from their origin. From its beginnings experimental psychology borrowed from physics, physiology, and mathematics. The necessity of borrowing was so compelling it was not considered interdisciplinary: "It was simply the thing to do," Muzafer and Carolyn Sherif reported, "not a matter to be argued about."[17]

The problem of definition is further compounded by the continuing rhetorical opposition of disciplinarity and interdisciplinarity, an oversimplified dichotomy that obscures the more subtle interactions that do take place. There is also a related tendency to link disciplinarity strictly with analytical skills and interdisciplinarity with synthetic skills, when, in fact, there are different degrees of analysis and synthesis in each. Synthesis as pattern recognition at axiomatic and conceptual levels is an "innate process" in all disciplines,[18] and the relationship between synthesis and analysis is a recurrent topic within interdisciplinary discourse. The stark picture of disciplinarity as the product of arbitrary forces only adds to the confusion. In actuality disciplinary separations, as Wolf Lepenies showed with history and anthropology, are shaped by a range of factors.[19] Ultimately disciplinarity and interdisciplinarity are not only relative to each other but also time-bound in character.[20]

The oppositions and the dichotomies have created a paradox, an implied impossibility of being both disciplinary and interdisciplinary. This paradox has two parts. The first pertains to the role of disciplinarity. It is embodied in what may be called nondisciplinary and disciplinary positions within the discourse. The nondisciplinary position is more scornful of the disciplines. Visible in the call to overturn disciplinary hegemony, it has figured in propositions of "transdisciplinarity," revisionist theories of "critical interdisciplinarity," and the "integrative"/"interdisciplinary" distinction that emerged in education and the social sciences. The disciplinary position holds that disciplinary work is essential to good interdisciplinary work. It is important not only to have a disciplinary home[21] but also to have a grounding in cognate disciplines: to recognize that disciplines are the fundamental tools for interdisciplinary work, the source of instrumental and conceptual material for problem-solving, the base for integration, and the substance for metacritical reflection. It is in this sense that Delkeskamp[22] and Messmer,[23] in their separate ways, speak of a "disciplined interdisciplinarity" that moves outward from mastery of disciplinary tools.

The first part of the paradox — the need for disciplines — leads to the second part — the role of disciplinary behavior and structure in interdisciplinary work. Kenneth Boulding has addressed the problem for general systems theory. One might expect philosophers would have a place for general systems. Yet they were "hostile," judging it "an amateur threat to professional interest." Necessarily then, to gain respect and a place, general systems is confronted with a dilemma: unless general systems itself becomes a discipline, and an intellectual species, "the other species in the intellectual ecosystem are likely to regard it more as a virus that threatens them than as a food to sustain them." Yet there is a price. Boulding already sees a loss of generality in the identification of general systems with systems science and, especially, with large-scale computer modeling. This could threaten its philosophical growing edges, even though systems science has a great deal of validity as a discipline. The only choice might be to practice both disciplinarity and interdisciplinarity. There might be "a niche" for general systems, a "kind of quasi-masonic order, a quasi-secret society, among those who have to be good little disciplinary boys and girls outside the lodge in order to survive, but who have a hankering for a larger view, a broader perspective than can be found in single departments or disciplines." That would recognize the importance of *discipline* as a process of detecting error and distinguishing good work from bad, while, at the same time, demonstrating that discipline is inadequate if it is "too self-contained and too much closed to information from the outside."[24]

Unfortunately, "discipline" is too often confused with "department" and the competition for resources within the academy. Yet "discipline" also signifies something else, a stable epistemic community and agreement upon what constitutes excellence in a field. When tied to this meaning, disciplinarity has an undeniably positive value. When tied to the danger of prematurely settling on a paradigm or excluding certain dimensions of a problem, it has a negative value in the discourse. "Discipline" then becomes a threat to the invention that gave rise to interdisciplinarity in the first place. Interdisciplinarians who criticize disciplinarians for sacrificing openness must come to terms with that prospect themselves. Trying to maintain "discipline" in the midst of "epistemological polytheism"[25] can be very difficult, but, Boulding cautioned, the great danger of interdisciplinarity is that "it easily becomes the undisciplined if there is no organized payoff for the constant critical selection of its ideas, theories and data."[26]

Multimodality

In thinking about the "disciplinary" nature of an interdisciplinary field, it is important to bear in mind several caveats. To begin with, though scholars in many of these fields trace their core ideas and problems back several centuries, most organized efforts are relatively new and still in a developmental state. Questions of scope and content are not yet fully answered, and defining interrelationships with pertinent professions and disciplines is, very often, an uncompleted task. Disciplinary loyalties have also created a tendency for both researchers and teachers to move in and out of interdisciplinary problem communities, making it difficult to reach organizational and intellectual "critical mass," or, expressed another way, to ever get to Sjölander's Stage 10. Furthermore, while such fields tend to rely on the familiar disciplinary forums of communication, the complexity of their problem domains usually precludes becoming an isolable discipline. Moreover, the "burden of comprehension" increases as the topical agenda expands.[27] As a result, it is not always clear whether such fields are becoming disciplines, professions, or general branches of the humanities, social sciences, or natural sciences. Finally, they may be disciplinable only in certain limited respects, because they embody multivalent dimensions that are the province of more than one group of specialists. The questions that lie at the heart of these fields are liable to be more complex and more changeable than those that dominate a normal discipline. Their underlying protean quality also means that criteria for judging conceptual novelties will be less well defined and less likely to rest on a set of consensually determined ideals.[28] As a result their "multimodality" is evident at all stages, from their evolution to the point of defining standards.

Immunopharmacology provides a good example of the network of shared needs that promote the evolution of a new interdisciplinary area.[29] Its two parent fields, immunology and pharmacology, had their origins in other disciplines, in bacteriology and chemistry-physiology. The overlap between pharmacology and immunology has existed for some time. Research of "an immunopharmacological nature" was conducted early in the century by Paul Erhlich, then strong links were established in the early 1900s with the search for specificity of treatment and the resulting specific receptor concept. Later some of Erhlich's contemporaries applied the receptor theory more widely, and in the 1940s structural chemical approaches to immunological specificity were founded in the classic serological work of Landsteiner. Other links were also being forged, though the emergence of an immunopharmacological subspecialty was dependent on the fuller development of both parent fields. Immunology itself was rather slow to achieve the status of a separate field. Until the 1930s it was treated as an appendage of bacteriology and was confined, therefore, to immediate practical applications such as vaccines, skin tests, diagnostic antisera, blood groups, and allergic reactions. In this respect it resembled other applied sciences pursued without regard for their deep theoretical foundations. Its status changed, however, as chemists, zoologists, and geneticists started building an entirely new conceptual structure for immunology.

Immunopharmacology is more than just the study of drugs on the immune system. It is also concerned with selective chemical control of the immune response in disease states and possible immunological modifications of drug activity, including biotransformation in the treatment of overdoses and optimal clinical utilization of agents with low therapeutic indices. On a pragmatic level, the clinical and therapeutic potential of immunopharmacology is assured in the areas of organ transplantation, cancer, rheumatic and arthritic diseases, and disorders involving allergic or autoimmune mechanisms. However, the growth of immunopharmacology has been thwarted by a tendency among some to define the field narrowly. Its further development will depend on both immunologists and pharmacologists gaining a more sophisticated awareness of each other's work and the development of a common vocabulary shared by a growing nucleus of biomedical researchers. In addition, they will need to apply the principles and new techniques of chemistry and physics in order to gain a better understanding of selective chemical manipulations of the complex immune system.

These problems are not unique to immunopharmacology. The history of the family, to cite another example, is a new interdisciplinary field that is broadly interpreted and therefore has undefined boundaries. Its evolution was the result of not only internal changes in outlook and methodology but also external forces, including crises related to the conflict between generations, the rebellion of youth, the changing status of women, and growing concern about the future of the family. Because of its breadth and complexity, the history of the family is frequently confused with what might be considered some of its parts. It has been identified, for example, with "psychohistory," even though some aspects of the history of the family have not involved psychological interpretations.[30]

Popular culture and American studies have also experienced a similar de facto identification with some of their parts, though perhaps the best-known example is the phenomenon of the "two social psychologies." One is based on a sociological concern for structured aspects of social interaction, the other on a psychological concern for motivation, cognition, and other interindividual processes in addition to a more narrowly defined experimental method.[31] This split was reflected in a restructuring of the *Journal of Personality and Social Psychology* in order to provide three independently edited sections. It also surfaced in the establishment of semiautonomous sections for personality and social psychologists within the Division of Personality and Social Psychology of the American Psychological Association.[32] There is, in short, what Thomas Blank calls "a dichotomy on the basis of disciplinary identification."[33]

The problem of fields being defined by one of their parts raises the issue of reciprocal responsibility in what Ronald Grele has called a "community of interest." Grele illustrated the concept with the example of oral testimony, another area that has emerged from several forces: developments in its parent disciplines, linguistics and anthropology; possibilities for interaction among the subdisciplines of psycholinguistics, sociolinguistics, ethnohistory, and ethnomethodology; as well as a new awareness of the voice as a medium through which information is conveyed in older, more traditional disciplines and in the newer areas of oral history, English as a second language, and the linguistic study of poetics. Other forces also encouraged the study of people face to face in the field, including the academic revolution of the 1960s and a declining job market. Although the disciplines and subdisciplines of oral testimony have not merged into a single, formal discipline, their interpenetration is becoming more obvious, and Grele himself has outlined a framework for incorporating the disciplines of the field. In order for fully integrated work to take place, it is important that all field workers learn what kinds of information other investigators need and then familiarize themselves with the technical needs of workers in other disciplines. In collectively producing materials usable by the widest range of investigators, they will be assuming a certain liability for other disciplinary and subspecialist interests.[34] They will be assuming the "burden of comprehension" across their shared domains.

Janice Lauer has considered these issues in the context of another new area, the study of written discourse.[35] The majority of its theorists are members of English departments who are investigating the causes of increasing illiteracy and developing "new rhetorics" to account for the processes and pedagogy of written discourse, especially discourse ignored by literary studies. From the start their work has had a "multidisciplinary cast." They see the field not as a *tabula rasa* but as a place for building on relevant work and investigative methods in other fields. They have been led into foreign domains by questions about the nature of the writing process and interactions among the writer, reader, subject, and text, in addition to speculations about the epistemic potential of writing and its implications for improving powers of inquiry. Pursuing these questions, they have moved into classical rhetoric, transformation and tagmemic linguistics, semiotics and speech-act theory while making psychological studies of creativity, problem-solving, and cognitive development. In addition, the philosophical work of Gadamer, Johnstone, Perelman, Toulmin, Polanyi, and Kuhn has furnished theories that help them deal with the problem domain defined by dissonance between their responsibility for composition and the inadequacy of current understanding and training. In the process they have used several different modes of inquiry, including historical studies, theoretical research, linguistic analysis, hermeneutic studies, and empirical work.

This kind of "multimodality" has its benefits and its risks. The vastness and density of the problem domain have what Lauer calls a certain "subtle seduction." Multimodality helps researchers avoid nearsightedness and cultivates a "fruitful reciprocity among modes": "Historical studies have kept the field from reinventing the wheel; theoretical work provides guidance and hypotheses for empirical research, which, in turn, offers one kind of test or validation of theory. Hermeneutical and linguistic studies buttress and act as heuristics for theory development." Furthermore, connected as they are to praxis in the classroom, practitioners enjoy a constructive interplay between empirical and theoretical modes. Yet there are problems. The "burden of comprehension" demands knowledge of not only what is borrowed from another field but also its context, history, and status in that field. Like their counterparts in other interdisciplinary areas, researchers in the area of written discourse are necessarily involved in a form of continuing education. They must also define adequate training for students in the field and negotiate that training with English departments. In the process, they encounter the competition for proportion that pervades interdisciplinary research and education.

Not unexpectedly, multimodality often winds up being attacked on the grounds of both eclecticism and lack of rigor. Ethnography is a good example of a field that has faced both charges as it moves into a "niche" once dominated by deductive research paradigms. Critics concede ethnography is useful for "anecdotal data" to "flesh out" the statistical results of a survey but consider it to be, on the whole, "exploratory," conferring a kind of second-class citizenship on the field. Many of them believe ethnography is untrustworthy because it lacks explicit hypotheses, sampling designs, statistical plans of analysis, and a priori explicitness and control. "The centrality of emergence," Michael Agar explains, "grates against traditional linear models of social research that move from hypothesis through data collection and end with analysis."[36] Ethnography, however, is different from other kinds of research because it is concerned with the multidimensional world of experience that constitutes social reality for an informant and the fundamental process of learning that social reality. To lose "openness" to other fields, that fundamental willingness to explore and to "learn," would be for ethnographers and others to approximate different research traditions.[37] The danger in ethnography, as in other interdisciplinary fields, is falling back on strictly disciplinary standards for evaluation because alternative standards are not readily available. Still, the question remains: What would constitute an adequate set of standards? The formalization of a least a portion of ethnographic data, Agar suggests, may lie in the direction of taking the ethnographic statement as a hypothesis or, perhaps, rendering what the ethnographer does more explicit, then specifying procedures from which the ethnographic statement was derived.

Rendering the work being done in interdisciplinary fields more explicit is, in fact, the most urgent need in current scholarship. There are very few substantive accounts of individual fields. As a step toward compiling such histories, and thereby coming to understand the "disciplined" nature of those fields, we can compare what has happened in three important examples—urban affairs, environmental studies, and American studies.

Three Case Studies

Urban affairs programs were stimulated by three major factors: social pressure, in the form of increased public concern about poverty, racism, and environmental deterioration; criticism of the structure of higher education, including the university's relationship to the community; and financial support. From 1959 to 1974, the Ford Foundation distributed $36 million in the area of urban affairs, guided by the expectation of urban extension services patterned after agricultural services. Universities, especially those with interdisciplinary urban programs, came to be regarded as "ready-assembled Cape Canaverals capable of channeling the new technologies to cities through applied research and expert advice to public officials."[38] By the 1980s, however, things had changed.

The economic and social support characteristic of the 1960s began subsiding in the 1970s, at the same time new approaches to municipal management prompted research on productivity and the training of professional urban administrators with fiscal management skills. Unfortunately these changes occurred before a standarized set of conceptual and functional orientations had emerged. As a result, "urban affairs" has become an umbrella term for a variety of programs differing in size, disciplinary mix, administrative arrangements, intellectual commitments, and research and service opportunities. Although the urban focus of many established disciplines expanded after World War II, no single discipline came to organize its inquiry and mode of applying knowledge in ways that made it the logical vehicle for academic response to urban crises of the 1960s. Moreover, in the first decade of urban affairs programs, experimentation with teaching methods, applying academic skills to community problem-solving, political activism, and creating interdisciplinary units were more important than discovering "an appropriate niche" in university bureaucracies or building effective communication and achieving consensus on the content and boundaries of the field. Consequently, when the innovations budgeted in the 1960s were cut back the potential for synthesis had yet to be fulfilled.

There are several important analogies between urban affairs and environmental studies. Environmental studies emerged from what Lynton Caldwell calls a "misfit between perceived need, experience, information and the prevailing configuration of knowledge embodied in the disciplinary organization of academia."[39] During the late 1960s and early 1970s, environmental studies began appearing in colleges and universities in large numbers. In some cases "environmental" was simply added to the title of existing programs, though new programs and curricula were also developed. In the late 1960s, almost no one openly opposed programs of environmental studies, though the programs were often dependent on the "acquiescence" of established disciplines. As a result, environmental-related aspects of disciplines and professions formed an eclectic curriculum, rather than coalescing into a discrete and coherent field with its own integrative theory. Then, when financial support declined, the field was vulnerable to retrenchment and "effectively contained by the disciplines from further excursions into their territories." In the 1980s there was also an additional factor, a pullback in environmental concern within the society at large. This retrenchment occurred for a variety of ideological and economic reasons, including the argument for focusing on "real" people-oriented issues such as poverty, racism, and war. As support dwindled in both the public and private sectors, there was an apparent "disengagement" from the commitment to environmental quality that had risen so rapidly in the late 1960s. By the 1980s several universities were scrutinizing their long-established environmental and natural resource-related programs, even though public support for environmental protection still continues and efforts to repeal or weaken the environmental legislation of the two preceding decades have generally failed.

American studies has also experienced changes in expectation. Once called the oldest interdiscipline, American studies evolved out of English and history departments. From approximately 1950 to 1975, the scholarly pillars of the field were intellectual history and literary criticism, both concentrated on the products of a small group of thinkers and writers. Though a school of thought concentrated on myth and symbol did emerge, it was later judged a "false start," a premature settling upon a single paradigm. The framing concepts of tradition, style, myth, and culture had acted as "filters," "choices of focus and highlighting" that guided thinking along nationalist, consensus lines of thought, away from the comparative mode and attention to internal differences that might have developed through such categories as "class," "ethnicity," "institutions," "social structure," or even the categories of formal philosophy.[40] Optimism over a "coming of age" grew with the anticipated evolution of an integrative paradigm for the study of American culture, but optimism ultimately faded with the recognition that there was a rich multidisciplinary accumulation but no real synthesis.

By the 1970s American studies stood charged with elitism and a narrow, old-fashioned "high" culture bias.[41] Once described as "six disciplines in search of a methodology,[42] it was now pronounced in a "state of arrested development."[43] "Mere interdisciplinarity," David Marcell suggested, had not been enough to assure that American studies would do adequate justice to the rich pluralism of the culture.[44] Moreover, the anticipated merging of social scientific and humanistic perspectives had not, and still has not, taken place. There is still hope for a new synthesis that can incorporate literary criticism, intellectual history, popular culture, urban anthropology, oral history, and ethnic and minority perspectives. However, the plurality of interests housed under the "American Studies tent"[45] remains diverse in nature; and some parts, including ethnic and minority studies, have laid claim to their own agendas. Thus the problem of an "interdisciplinary" American studies remains unsolved.

A significant part of the debate has centered on what might constitute the "interdisciplinary approach." Robert Spiller contends there have been two principal approaches to the problem of defining and implementing American studies: the synthetic and the holistic. The two have appeared separately, sometimes in collaboration and sometimes in rivalry. The *synthetic* has been the more general and influential of the two and is related to other post–World War II movements in general education, area studies, and interdepartmental programs. It is the "Humpty Dumpty" technique of putting together fragmented pieces. In education it often meant retaining a departmental major at the upper level, marked by subject-matter concentrations that do not constitute a new discipline. In research it was successful to the extent that scholars interested in the study of American culture could work either individually or collectively out of their specialities. The result was undeniably positive: academics were reeducated to the concept of an indigenous American culture at a time when particular aspects of the cultural whole were being separated from colonial and traditional modes of thinking. The American Studies Association and the journal *American Quarterly* reflected the synthetic approach in bringing together scholars from different disciplines and relating special interests to the whole by tying them to "manageable parts of other fields." The *holistic* has been a supplementary, alternative approach aimed at defining a method for studying American culture through experimentation, a gestalt for the definition of culture that would have a higher degree of integration than the synthetic approach.[46] There have been problems with both approaches. The synthetic approach has been attacked for being a multidisciplinary mix, the holistic approach for reductionism.

Clearly, the problem of finding an adequate "interdisciplinary" identity is common to all three fields. Each has been viewed as both a platform for sectoral interests and a new holistic basis for understanding human experience. Environmental studies and urban affairs have a special affinity in the prospect of constituting a new profession, yet all three confront a set of basic questions common to the interdisciplinary enterprise. What is the disciplinary basis of the field? What is the field's relationship to pertinent issues in society? Can the field become a discrete discipline? Will it ever achieve a genuine synthesis?

On the last and most difficult question, there is a sense of failure in all three fields. It is explained, in part, by the continued lack of incentives in universities for long-term interdisciplinary work, especially by junior faculty. Urban affairs in particular has suffered from the traditional favoring of academic publication over nonpublishable research and community service. Financial pressures have also discouraged collaboration and reinforced disciplinary boundaries in structuring academic programs and making tenure and promotion decisions. Furthermore, urban affairs has not made significant progress as an autonomous generator of knowledge. It borrows virtually all of its concepts and theories and much of its data from other fields and disciplines. The limited scale of graduate programs has also made it difficult to generate knowledge on both an individual and a collective scale. In large institutions urban affairs has often been part of a sizable public affairs program and, therefore, must compete for demands on resources. As a result, urban affairs has fallen short of the threshold needed for sustained theoretical and empirical research. It has not reached a "critical mass," nor have sufficient opportunities for "horizontal interaction"— organizations, professional meetings, journals, informal research communication networks, and student flow across programs—developed among the various individuals engaged in the teaching and research of urban affairs.

Reflecting on the situation in environmental studies, Caldwell found the coordinated program of "multidisciplinary" studies has been the most common arrangement because it is the least disruptive. Yet even this arrangement depends upon cooperation from the disciplines and does not readily lend itself to new insights on environmental relationships or reveal gaps in scientific knowledge that handicap the formulation of sound environmental policies. Still, it is a logical first step. Ultimately, here and elsewhere, the question of becoming a discipline depends very much on what one means by "discipline." "Environment" does not fit into the conventional disciplinary mold because of its scope and diversity. Certain aspects of "environment" have also become the objects of professional and technical training and practice. Given the breadth of the field, it is not likely there can be an "all-purpose profession" of environmentalism. Achievement of interdisciplinary synthesis, in Caldwell's view, remains an unfulfilled objective that will depend on a more thorough and basic reorientation of the total structure of education. Others share his view of the general prospect for synthesis, based on their belief that even the most successful ad hoc structures are only transitory solutions that await a complete rethinking of our most basic assumptions about how knowledge is structured and transmitted.

In urban affairs, Rich and Warren concluded, it will take a long-term investment in conceptual growth or in sustained communication among colleagues, students, and practitioners. Should interdisciplinarity emerge, they suspect, it will probably take the form of a "tentative and shifting coalescence of concepts" that evolves from the coexistence and competition of perspectives, rather than a cumulative linear development of new explanatory knowledge. Adopting an applied problem focus on, say, housing or transportation will not automatically lead to integration without an effort being made to establish an "urban affairs" language capable of translating diverse inputs into common terms. Intensive follow-up and long-term frames for applied research will also be necessary, despite the short turn-arounds and discontinuities endemic to such research. Locating "an intellectual center of gravity" will also be crucial, since urban affairs has come to encompass descriptive, pragmatic, theoretical, and normative dimensions without tending to their interdependencies and complementarities.

Reflecting on the situation in American studies, Guenther Lenz drew several conclusions. To begin with, the earlier myth-symbol approach should not be dismissed but examined as part of a broad historical critique of the objectives of the field, a critique that would account for the interplay of criticism of ideology, scholarly disciplines, theoretical models, and practical work.[47] Critical analysis of the dimensions of historical criticism in American studies and the "rehistoricization" of sociology, historiography, and literary criticism have shown that turning to a conceptual or metatheoretical elaboration of philosophic problems is not sufficient by itself. Neither is an ahistorical reliance on paradigms and exemplars, nor is leaping ahead to interdisciplinary problems without understanding the history of the disciplines related to those problems. A variety of other strategies have also been suggested by other members of the American studies movement: devising a culture paradigm, adopting an ethnographic paradigm, building on a clearly defined "disciplinary matrix,"[48] continuing to ply an eclectic course, and taking a metatheoretical approach.[49] To these, Lenz replies the concept of a "theory" or "philosophy" of American studies must be separated from metatheoretical pursuits and the cooperation of various disciplines. In his view the search for a *"final, all-comprehensive, true* 'theory'" of American studies has to be given up. The unrealistic quality of the "'inter- and supradisciplinary' *einheitswissenschaft"*—a supradisciplinary science of culture—was an overly ambitious goal in the first place.

There are several general lessons to be drawn from the current history of interdisciplinary fields. Clearly the magnitude of achieving synthesis has been underestimated. Interdisciplinarity does not spontaneously emerge by putting an economist and a sociologist, or any other combination of specialists, in close proximity. Nor does an interdisciplinary field reach maturity in just a few decades. An interdisciplinary field constitutes a unique form of specialization. It is a selective integration within a spectrum of disciplines.[50] The idea of interdisciplinary specialization is not a new one. Donald Campbell, who conceived of narrow specialization in the interdisciplinary gaps left over from the proliferation of similar specialties, felt the best hope for a comprehensive social science or any other multiscience is in a continuous texture of overlapping, narrow specialties.[51] E. Michael Lipton has written of interdisciplinary "specialisms" in particular areas, for example, the body of hypotheses known as location theory in geography.[52] H. C. Brookfield also described a "viable interdisciplinary specialism" that developed in the Pacific Islands from 1950 to 1970, when anthropologists, economists, political scientists, prehistorians, and geographers explored the same set of problems at the level of small countries, small islands, and small societies.[53]

Although the ultimate unification of knowledge may still be an objective for some researchers, and the drive toward unified theory is readily apparent in the sciences, most interdisciplinary work is being done on a less comprehensive scale. Integrative frameworks are being built using a variety of strategies: the two Agar suggested (testing hypotheses and making the actual work of the researcher more explicit); working with one particular working paradigm or interactive framework;[54] devising a set of abstract hypotheses and testing them from a variety of perspectives;[55] determining the most effective repertoire of concepts and methods for the problems at hand;[56] settling upon a clearly defined "disciplinary matrix";[57] locating work at the level of a particular place or region (as in the *Annales* school of history);[58] and devising a shared conceptual terminology — a metalanguage.[59] Developing a metalanguage is integral to any interdisciplinary endeavor, though, as Gerhard Frey has demonstrated, there are ontological and metaphysical assumptions about any subjects and objects under study. Clarifying those assumptions is a fundamental part of the interdisciplinary process, no matter what overall strategy is employed. It is not possible to simply translate from one disciplinary language into another.[60]

The idea of "middle-range theory" has been linked on several occasions with the attempt to achieve synthesis, by Hershberg, in urban social history, by Yanitsky, in urbanization,[61] and by Baker, in human population biology.[62] It is further implied in a far greater number of examples, including Tamara Hareven's exhortation to concentrate on building blocks before attempting to form general theories about the history of the family.[63] Sociologist Robert Merton used the concept of *theories of the middle range* in chiding social scientists for their errors of presumed omniscience. Writing in 1949, Merton argued that sociological hypotheses derived from a master conceptual scheme had proven unimpressive, a lament that parallels Lenz' skepticism about the search for a "suprawissenschaft." More modest, less imposing, but better-grounded theories of the middle range, Merton suggested, ought to be explored in lieu of extravagant claims for total systems of theory. He urged the solid preparatory work of theories applicable to limited ranges of data, such as class dynamics, conflicting group pressures, the flow of power, and the exercise of interpersonal influence. Later, on more solid ground, it would be more readily possible to perceive relationships among variables and to consolidate groups of special theories.[64]

Operations research[65] and materials science[66] have been proposed as prototypical interdisciplinary fields, but there is no master paradigm of what an interdisciplinary field ought to look like. Nor is there an interdisciplinary Esperanto. The nature of a given field must be determined in the context of the questions and problems which gave rise to that field.

PART III

The State of the Art

8 IDR: Problem-focused Research

LAWRENCE WHEELER tells an instructive tale.

Once upon a time a planning group was formed to design a house for an elephant. On the committee were an architect, an interior designer, an engineer, a sociologist, and a psychologist. The elephant was highly educated too . . . but he was not on the committee.

The five professionals met and elected the architect as their chairman. His firm was paying the engineer's salary, and the consulting fees of the other experts, which, of course, made him the natural leader of the group.

At their *fourth* meeting they agreed it was time to get at the essentials of their problem. The architect asked just two things: "How much money can the elephant spend?" and "What does the site look like?"

The engineer said that precast concrete was the ideal material for elephant houses, especially as his firm had a new computer just begging for a stress problem to run.

The psychologist and the sociologist whispered together and then one of them said, "How many elephants are going to live in this house?" . . . It turned out that *one* elephant was a psychological problem, but *two* or more were a sociological matter. The group finally agreed that though *one* elephant was buying the house, he might eventually marry and raise a family. Each consultant could, therefore, take a legitimate interest in the problem.

The interior designer asked, "What do elephants do when they're at home?"

"They lean against things," said the engineer. "We'll need strong walls."

"They eat a lot," said the psychologist. "You'll want a big dining room . . . and they like the color green."

"As a sociological matter," said the sociologist, "I can tell you that they mate standing up. You'll need high ceilings."

So they built the elephant his house. It had precast concrete walls, high ceilings, and a large dining area. It was painted green to remind him of the jungle. And it was completed for only 15% over the original estimate.

The elephant moved in. He always ate outdoors, so he used the dining room for a library . . . but it wasn't very cozy.

121

He never leaned against anything, because he had lived in circus tents for years, and knew that walls fall down when you lean on them.

The girl he married *hated* green, and so did he. They were *very* urban elephants.

And the sociologist was wrong too . . . they didn't stand up. So the high ceilings merely produced echoes that greatly annoyed the elephants. They moved out in less than six months.[1]

Wheeler's fable of elephant housing makes a fitting introduction to the topic of interdisciplinary problem-focused research (IDR), for it evokes so many of the problems encountered by teams of disciplinary experts working in government, industry, and academe. Problem-focused research is distinct from what is called "free" or "basic" research because it is "field induced." It is responsive to, and partly dependent upon, social needs. Although the relationship between theory and application varies from project to project, problem-focused research lies, on the whole, between the field of pure theoretical research, which emphasizes the pursuit of knowledge, and that of informed action, which emphasizes usefulness, efficiency, and practical results.[2]

The Apollo Space project, a systematic investigation of the ecology of Lake Tahoe, attempts to harness resources from the oceans, international efforts to increase rice productivity, engineering transportation studies: each is a representative example of IDR. Yet, each is unique. When it comes to IDR, there is a "contingency theory."[3] There are no widely accepted models, and the "recipe" approach is only valid to a limited extent because IDR is not a routine or "natural" procedure that begins with shared methodologies or theories.[4] Nevertheless, the growing literature on the subject contains a wealth of information about the most effective management of IDR.

Like the literatures on interdisciplinary health care and education, the literature on IDR is dominated by individual case studies rather than empirical research. The literature also has a clear North-American bias, tends to be atheoretical, and usually lacks cross-citation to the larger body of interdisciplinary scholarship. It has also tended to focus on academic settings, despite growing interest in IDR in the private sector and a contrasting emphasis on free-standing research institutes in other nations, such as France, China, and the Soviet Union.[5] The literature had its origin at mid-century, and by the mid-1980s there were specialists in the subject. A portion of the literature, which is dominated by journal publications, has also begun coalescing around a core of journals and practitioners.[6]

IDR is shaped by a complex set of variables,[7] ranging from structure and resources to the social and psychological dynamics of collaborative research. The *external conditions* for IDR include problem characteristics, incentives and rewards, resources, and institutional setting. The *internal conditions* include personnel matters, leadership, appropriate skills, project organization, and the setting for team dynamics. Within each of these categories, there may be considerable variations. There are, for example, differences in the size and higher administrative controls of a public or private university, a nonprofit corporation, an industrial setting, and a governmental setting. Projects also vary in management style, incentives and disincentives, technical complexity, sense of urgency, degrees of predictability and uncertainty, barriers to collaboration, time frame (1 year, 1–3 years, or longer), and financial scale (under $250,000; $250,000 to $1 million; over $1 million), in addition to relationships with funding agencies, problem agencies, and users/clients of the research. Finally, the team itself presents yet another set of variables, including group size, sex and age differences, differences of disciplinary status and intellectual style, the degree of openness and group interaction skills, ability to manage conflict, stability of membership, and general attitudes towards competition and comprehensiveness.

In a helpful chart, Epton, Payne, and Pearson have summarized the key issues arising from doing IDR in different organizational contexts (see Table 1).[8]

The Structure of IDR

IDR takes place in many settings, but the lowest organizational barriers occur when it takes place within one unit. The model for this is the organized research unit (ORU). Usually a center or institute, an ORU is an "opportunistic entity" within a larger disciplinary structure. In the 1960s federal legislation gave birth to several kinds of ORU's, including NASA space centers, water resource centers, and, later, regional education laboratories. A number of ORU's are de facto independent of the universities that gave birth to them, and Caltech's Jet Propulsion Laboratory is even larger than its "nominal parent," Caltech.[9] There have been several studies that provide a much fuller picture of the organization of research within ORU's, including the results of NSF-funded investigations at the University of Tennessee's Transportation Center;[10] Ikenberry and Friedman's now classic study of research institutes;[11] and Philip Birnbaum's analysis of data from a stratified sample of eighty-four interdisciplinary research projects, ranging from solid state catalysts, fusion power, and space exploration, to epilepsy, social indicators, and the electrical properties of bone.[12]

Cravens et al., at the Tennessee Transportation Center, found a wide range of organizational models being used within universities:

Table 1. Issues Arising from Doing Interdisciplinary Research in Different Organizational Contexts

Key Issues	Organizational Context				
	Small, University Based	Large, University Based (ORU)	Small, Industry Based	Large, Industry Based	Inter-organizational Problem Solving System
Number of Disciplines Involved	Small	Moderate	Moderate	Moderate-large	Large
Typical Problems	Pure	Pure→Applied	Applied→Pure	Applied and pure→Applied	Applied
Funding	Short-term & uncertain	Relatively certain	By contract & short-term	Relatively certain	Relatively certain but limited duration
Source of Problems to Be Solved	Found by team	Found by team (largely)	Given by environment	Found by team and given by environment	Given by environment
Structure of Organization	Flat	Hierarchical (selective decentralization)	Flat	Hierarchical (selective decentralization)	Flat
Main Source of Power/Influence	Expertise	Role in Organization (may be expert based)	Expertise and ownership of problem	Role in Organization (may be expert based)	Role in system (experts are advisers)
Leader's Involvement	Part-time	Full-time	Part-time	Full-time	Part-time, full-time and temporary
Member's Career Prospects	Uncertain	Relatively certain/predictable	Uncertain	Relatively certain/predictable	Almost irrelevant
Key Leadership Roles	Outside liaison	Outside liaison and coordination—management of interdependence	Outside liaison—resource acquisition	Management of interdependence—motivation and performance	Coordination communication
Dominant Values	Scientific/team based	Discipline based	Problem-solving/entrepreneurial	Managerial	Problem-focused: pragmatic
Work Contracted Out	Unlikely	A little	Quite a lot	Some	Quite a lot
Communication Problems	Few potentially: mainly scientific liaisons if funds	Internal and external	External and scientific liaison if funds low	Internal	Internal due to physical separation and variety of disciplines
Access to Scientific & Technical Resources	Good	Good	Not so good	Good if affordable	Good if affordable

- independent research laboratory or institute
- university-level research center
- interdisciplinary college or school
- matrix approach (inter-departmental/college unit reporting to multi-departmental college committee)
- project team or committee approach
- college/school research unit approach
- informal faculty group.

These models vary greatly in terms of autonomy and formality. Ikenberry and Friedman found that standard institutes — such as computer centers and materials research laboratories — have relatively stable goals and resources, a full managerial hierarchy, permanent professional staff, and the ability to invest in equipment and space. The more adaptive institutes they studied — water resource centers and centers for educational research and school service — occupied a middle ground in terms of flexibility. They had a "persistent instability," marked by continual redefinition of goals, terminations, and the securing and releasing of staff. Only a small nucleus of professionals had continuing ties. Shadow (Paper) institutes usually exist on a part-time basis, with a designated director but no staff, budget, central location, or visible accomplishments. Birnbaum, in turn, found that independent projects not affiliated with an institution or supported directly by a department constituted the most traditional form of interdisciplinary collaboration prior to the growth of specialized institutes within universities.

Universities have different ways of dealing with the presence of IDR on their campuses. Those with large programs, such as the University of Michigan, have turned to centralized monitoring and review of projects, fostering better administration and greater prestige for interdisciplinary work. Although general wisdom endorses the university research center as a highly favorable environment for IDR,[13] having an independent center does not guarantee success, despite the high number of integrating devices found in such organizations.[14] There are both advantages and disadvantages to the center concept. A center provides an institutional framework for dealing with complex problems that require a large pool of physical and human resources. By creating an interdisciplinary environment in a disciplinary context, a center facilitates the spillover of methods, instruments, techniques, and paradigms. It also enhances the social visibility of the university. Yet the disadvantages are equally clear. Not all universities can marshall the resources for such organizations, and centers suffer the vagaries of "soft money." Their quasi-departmental status may infer a second-class citizenship on researchers, a physical and academic marginality that splits faculty loyalties and compounds feelings of isolation. Also, centers may not be able to confer adequate professional rewards upon participants,[15] and may even take on certain disciplinary biases.

General wisdom also endorses a particular organizational approach known as the "matrix" structure, a program structure superimposed on an existing hierarchy. It is a flexible free form that allows for overlapping project activities onto a specialist/functional set of activities.[16] Matrix structure is particularly appropriate for IDR because it facilitates a balance of power while increasing information processing, intrateam communication, and decision-making through lateral channels. The value of matrix structure can be illustrated by the example of the Upjohn pharmaceutical firm.

In 1968 the functional departments of organic chemistry, pharmacology, biochemistry, microbiology, endocrinology, immunology, infectious diseases, virology, clinical pharmacology, and medical development were abolished. A large part of their memberships were reorganized around product research departments that were assigned responsibility for drug discovery and development for specific problems, including central nervous system diseases, infectious diseases, cardiovascular diseases, hypersensitivity diseases, diabetes and atherosclerosis, cancer, and fertility control. Each new product unit consisted of all the chemists, biologists, and physicians required to make, identify, and prove the therapeutic value of drugs in a given particular product/disease area. Still, even with the reorganization, functional areas such as pathology and toxicology, pharmacy, biostatistics, and analytical chemistry were retained in order to support drug finding and development projects. There was also a change in leadership styles. Prior to 1968 project managers had functioned largely as *coordinators,* keeping everyone informed about the status of projects and letting them know when their contributions were needed. After 1968 they conformed more closely to a *leadership* matrix, a structure in which leaders motivate teams to work on project goals while members work together as a cohesive group.[17] As a result of these changes, the company was better equipped to resolve conflicts surrounding projects under development and more rapidly assume preparation and execution of a development plan. In the pre-1968 coordination matrix, communications had tended to be cumbersome and delayed.[18]

The Dynamics of Teamwork

Obviously a team of scientists working on environmental pollution will encounter different technical problems than a NASA engineering team or a communications team at the Bell Laboratories. Nevertheless, they share common problems typical of collaborative research.[19] Although those problems are by no means unknown on disciplinary teams, they take on added magnitude in IDR.[20] Mitchell McCorcle notes two important differences between an interdisciplinary team and a more conventional, homogeneous group. To begin with, the interdisciplinary team is an open rather than a closed system. The team owes its very existence to an external agent who may make demands in an unpredictable sequence. It also has a more heterogeneous though interconnected membership, creating not only a rich diversity of experience and capabilities but also status conflicts and communication problems.[21] Interdisciplinary teams in this respect are status systems that reflect external hierarchies and disciplinary chauvinism. Research in social psychology shows the status system of a team will tend to follow the status system of the world outside the team if there is no strong alternative organization, though even a strong organization cannot eliminate status ambiguity and clashes in career goals, professional styles, and epistemologies. Even natural scientists, who are generally better socialized for collaborative work, may be unprepared for the unique demands of IDR.

Case studies suggest teams can expect problems with both the illusion of consensus and the reality of open status conflict. In the early stages of collaboration, a team might arrive at premature agreement for the sake of amity. Yet this "illusion of friendship"[22] may prove costly, for it can inhibit the development of a common working vocabulary and concepts. In their anxiety about easing tensions, groups may avoid the very complexity on which ultimate success may depend. Too often team members think they are speaking the same language when they are really not.[23] In her study of working relationships among psychologists, psychiatrists, and sociologists on mental-health projects, Margaret Barron Luszki found members paid a price for congeniality. By staying at the level of phenomena, they reduced the number of creative problem-solving conflicts that would have promoted the development of high-level, systematic concepts. Members of a team might agree on common terms in order to avoid semantic difficulties but did so prematurely, ignoring the depth of their differences and jeopardizing work at larger stages. They might build a system of concepts around the term "aggression" but, when they began to analyze the data, would discover the only consensus was that it was a "nice word."[24]

Status conflicts occur for a variety of reasons. A team may be dominated by a prestigious person or discipline, inhibiting role negotiation, delaying communal work, and also creating an uncritical social and cognitive dependence. Luszki found that disciplines imported to help with a project tended to be in subordinate power positions and initiating disciplines tended to be in a primary position. Individuals are also affected by images of the relative maturity and prestige of certain disciplines.[25] Teamwork has been compromised by the disdain scientists have for engineers, mathematicians for physicists, pure scientists for applied scientists, physical scientists for social scientists and humanists, and vice versa. In a study of members of an alcoholism rehabilitation organization, Fry and Miller also found a related problem. Rehabilitation counselors were in a privileged position on teams because, as state employees, they had the right to authorize payment for services to patients. Consequently patients were clients of the state department of rehabilitation and therefore technically patients of the rehabilitation counselor.[26]

Because status is a major factor in team dynamics, status concordance has been an important topic in the literature. The theory of status concordance holds that organizational success is related to matched and equal ranks among members' age, sex, academic rank, highest degree obtained, and discipline.[27] Although there is a widespread belief that status concordance contributes to the success of a team,[28] Gillespie and Birnbaum discovered that it tends to facilitate effective coordination during the preproposal more than latter stages of a project. Concordance of academic rank and highest degree were positively associated with performance, though in projects over two years of age *discordance* was associated with performance, suggesting a persistent reliance on status concordance may tend to diminish interdisciplinary effectiveness. Older, higher-ranking professionals with higher academic degrees will tend to be effective administrators in the early stages of a project though, over time, administrators from less prestigious, less influential disciplines are more closely associated with higher performance. These findings affirm the value of high concordance levels for defining tasks, allocating resources, and guiding communications in the early stages of a project.

Failing to consider the common problems of IDR work may create additional problems, including different assessments of the interdisciplinary problem, premature solutions, and simplistic conclusions. Unstable team membership, unwillingness to take risks, and fidelity to the "lone-scholar" model have also proven counterproductive. In the absence of a shared understanding, members will very likely maintain their "expert" roles. Then, when challenged, they may withdraw to orthodox viewpoints, abandoning part of the accepted group goals. This conservative retreat is a "regressive return to categorization."[29] Veterans of IDR believe time and commonality are the keys to lessening these problems. It takes time to form working relationships based on clarifying differences, defining subobjectives, and creating a common language. The prospect of forming those relationships can be enhanced by early training in group interaction skills.

Stone speaks of young teams as secondary groups, older teams as primary groups. Although they are ideal types, Stone's definitions constitute a useful model of team development. Secondary group relations are basically self-protective of the individual, who tends to think in terms of "I" rather than "we." Primary group relations reflect the team's dedication to a common task and shared cognitive framework. Operating out of its new corporate identity,[30] a primary group comes to constitute a new epistemic community. Though problems can result, Holling and Chambers have suggested that a certain percentage of uncommitted individuals can be the target for "managed hostility," crystallizing an *esprit* on the part of the rest of the group.[31]

There are several theories about which factors produce the most successful teams. McCorcle discovered the most successful projects have a high percentage of tenured faculty.[32] Size is also a major factor. It is not unusual for 50 or more individuals to flow through some groups before a handful of individuals "settle out."[33] One study of technology assessments pointed toward five (plus or minus two) members as a desirable number.[34] Swanson contended the most successful interdisciplinary projects at academic institutions appear to be those with external funding and representation from no more than four or five disciplines.[35] Similarly, White recommended the interdisciplinary team should be small, with probably no more than eight or nine people and a balance of disciplinary perspectives.[36] Stankiewicz concluded academic research teams tend to reach optimum size at about five to six people.

Based on overall measures, small groups with stable membership appear to be the most integrative, though large groups with stable memberships have had positive results. Cohesion tends to fall dramatically in large groups that are poorly organized, though leaders with more than fourteen years of experience have successfully maintained productivity in large groups.[37] When given enough time to work together effectively, larger projects with a stable, highly educated work force and a clear division of labor with centralized policy-making can work successfully.[38] However, larger groups will have more difficulty achieving integration. They are more difficult to coordinate, and responsibility is more difficult to allocate. Large size can also inhibit creativity and provoke a tendency to work at the level of the "smallest common denominator."[39]

Although there are many organizational models and communication patterns, Rossini and his colleagues observed four models of social and intellectual organization:

1. *Common group learning*: a group-bounded process in which the final report is a common intellectual property. De-emphasis of individual expertise tends to limit the technical sophistication of the study and decrease the depth of disciplinary analyses.
2. *Modeling*: a process in which a formal model is the key integrative device, whether constructed by the team or imported from outside. Modeling favors empirical analysis.
3. *Negotiation among experts*: a process that focuses on the overlaps and linkages among separate draft reports. It may, however, lean towards multidisciplinary rather than interdisciplinary integration.

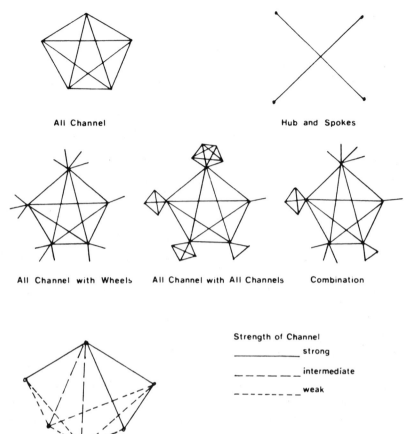

All Channel

Hub and Spokes

All Channel with Wheels

All Channel with All Channels

Combination

Strength of Channel
_____ strong
_ _ _ _ _ _ intermediate
_ _ _ _ _ _ _ weak

*Figure 7. A Communication Profile
In One Successful Study*

4. *Integration by a leader:* an efficient method for simple tasks in small groups, based on dividing and allocating parts of the problem according to members' expertise and using a "hubs and spokes" communication pattern. The multidisciplinary tendency is also present.

On IDR teams, they concluded, there are two ideal types of communication patterns: the *all channel pattern* of communication between all pairs of core team members and the *hub and spokes pattern* of links between team leaders and each team member.[40] (See Figure 7.)

Leaders and Managers

Identified as a good "ringmaster," a "bridge specialist," "gatekeeper," "boundary agent," "ombudsman," "polymath," "dynamo," "metascientist," "specialist/generalist," and a "strong entrepreneur," an IDR manager may be attracted by the prospect of wider recognition, financial support, or the opportunity to work on applied problems. Solving such problems, however, requires a considerable array of skills. Listing the qualities of an ideal IDR leader, Walter Baer once suggested, is rather like "combining the résumés of Aristotle and Alexander,"[41] though the following hypothetical job description demonstrates what the job requires:

- status as an established and respected person (with tenure in a university setting);
- previous interdisciplinary experience and some disciplinary/technological competence appropriate to team or project goals;
- sensitivity towards different paradigms and disciplinary epistemologies;
- a commitment to problem-solving;
- managerial skills for assembling and keeping personnel on schedule, redirecting personnel if necessary, getting to the core of project goals, serving as a liaison between team personnel and funding agencies, setting and monitoring performance standards, and performing public relations work with other units of the university and external agencies/society;
- group interaction skills for developing cooperation and participation, managing conflict, communicating among all parties, and balancing personnel against task factors; and
- enormous energy and patience.

Barth and Manners have conceptualized the IDR manager's role in graphic form.[42] (See Figure 8.)

The concept of a "bridge scientist" is a good model of the IDR leader. On a multidisciplinary team, a bridge scientist will tend to emphasize problems of language, translating the formulation of a research problem from one monodisciplinary perspective into another. On an interdisciplinary team, the bridge scientist's role extends beyond terminological conflicts to paradigmatic conflicts and different evaluational standards. Drawing on a study of the Stanford Research Institutes (SRI), Michael Anbar concluded there are four types of people who become bridge scientists:

1. Professionals who are strongly grounded in a particular discipline and, having found satisfaction in terms of scientific curiosity and peer recognition, have become adventurers.
2. Professionals who are strongly grounded in a particular discipline and might like to stay in it, but feel *forced* to get involved in other

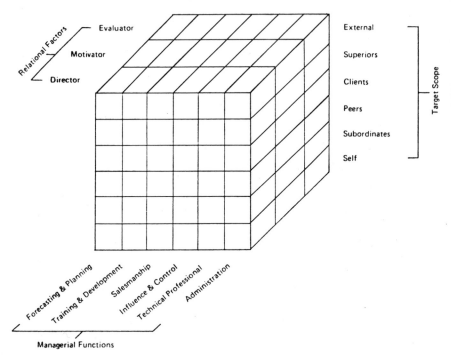

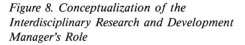

Figure 8. Conceptualization of the Interdisciplinary Research and Development Manager's Role

disciplines because their own discipline is becoming obsolete and nonmarketable.

3. People with superficial training in one or more disciplines who now find they can get work and ultimately recognition as generalists.
4. People who have moved into managerial, sales or other essential bridge positions, but have not been prepared to fulfill a bridge role.

The most active, creative bridge scientists will tend to be those in the first category, since they tend to look at the world from a wider perspective while remaining rooted in one or two fields of specialization. People in the second category are less enthusiastic. Those in the third category are better used in organization and marketing than project generation and management, and those in the fourth category, because of their reluctance and lack of skills, may tend to become "the most serious obstacles in interdisciplinary research."[43]

Just as the organizational needs of a project may change over time, a leader's style may also change. Birnbaum divides leadership styles into two groups: initiating behavior (with emphasis on tasks, authority, control, and structure) and consideration behavior (with emphasis on the social needs of the team, relationships among team members, and a democratic decision process). In projects less than four years old, leaders who exhibit both initiating and consideration behaviors will encourage mutual trust and support.[44] In older projects task-oriented behavior is more important to ensure coordination among members who become increasingly independent as they develop expertise and a sense of security.[45] Differing perceptions of urgency and predictability may also suggest the need for alternative leadership styles. Pearson, et al. contend a decisive leader who delegates authority is called for in an urgent project. In a less urgent project, the leader can be more supportive, given the availability of time and the possibility of resource-sharing. A leader must also be sensitive to changes in the team's sense of confidence.[46]

Finding these specialist/generalists is difficult enough, but accommodating their professional needs can be even more challenging. To that end Alpert proposed that such leaders enjoy a new kind of position, the *"all-university professor without tenure."* This position would be subject to periodic review on perhaps a seven-year basis.[47] Similarly, Rossi suggested the rank of research professor, and Nilles, et al. proposed the rank of research professor, comparable to regular professorial rank.[48] After one or two terms of office, an interim appointment in an academic department might be possible but only if the department would have the person. That's a big catch. Admirable though the idea is, and its acceptability is proved by the number of mission-oriented laboratory directors who have done just that, it still duplicates departmental logic not only in allowing a department to judge the person but also in choosing seven years as an interim period. These proposals only underscore the importance of choosing leaders who are sufficiently established to risk time out of their disciplinary mainstreams. If they are to be involved in IDR for a long time, leaders and members alike may find it desirable, as some have, to take disciplinary "leaves of absence" to update their skills.

The Life Cycle of IDR

When it comes to describing and predicting the life cycle of an IDR project, there are two caveats. First, since the needs of a project vary over time, strategies may differ from stage to stage. Second, popular wisdom alone does not suffice. Rossini and colleagues, for example, made the unexpected finding that greater intellectual distance among core members may result in a more integrated output, and there can be a more integrated output with a lower proportion of "systems" people. Diversity might actually increase awareness of taking steps towards integration, even though it is commonly believed that diversity inhibits collaboration.[49] In a different study, Birnbaum concluded that research managers will have problems if they blithely assume the universal merit of clearly defined tasks, integrated efforts, reduced turnover, open discussion of disagreements, and self-evaluations. Different outputs — the production of books and articles versus the production of technical reports versus the performance of patent activities — demand different structural and processual conditions.[50] Still, the literature does reveal a general picture of the IDR life cycle.

There are three major phases: planning, implementing, and concluding.

Planning

There is an old Dutch proverb: "Goed begonnen is half gewonnen." Starting off the right way is already half the result.[51] Tending to the preconditions for IDR will enhance the prospects considerably. The planning stage is an unstable period that may last several years. Often criticized as a "wallowing" period because of the length of start-up time, it is an essential kind of wallowing that will, as Harvey Gold put it, prevent wallowing later on.[52] Time and seed money are of the utmost importance. Adequate resources must be assembled, even if that requires extra time and travel to funding agencies and remote locations. Internal and external funding, sufficient space, and common facilities should be established and released time and rewards negotiated. In addition, organizers should line up potential consultants and extra-team liaisons while also making a comprehensive list of all knowledge needs. In technology assessments, there should be adequate, appropriate bridging mechanisms between interdisciplinary projects and appropriate constituencies both inside and outside the university. The use of common facilities cannot be overemphasized. Some veterans of IDR have suggested that vertical separation in a building inhibits communication more than horizontal separation. One U.S. education group even claimed the failure of their interdisciplinary endeavor was 30% due to a slow elevator linking up the various floors on which the different disciplines were housed.[53] The ideal arrangement, White suggests, is a suite with individual offices opening into a conference or lounge area.[54]

It is also essential to focus on definition and clarification in the early stages of a project. Tasks must be clearly defined[55] and interdisciplinary objectives clarified. Seed money can be used to support preliminary activities by exploratory teams, who should scrutinize coherent models, traditions, and support literatures, as well as competing projects. This is, in addition, the time for tending to managerial needs by establishing an independent "matrix" structure for the project (preferably highly placed in the university or industrial structure) and effective controls for accounting, information gathering, and subsystemic relations. If a university lacks such a system, a package system might be rented, though a centralized office makes it easier to monitor funding, disseminate and update information, identify administrative and faculty needs, monitor resources, and encourage disciplinary bridges. Balancing hard and soft money at this stage will provide long-term stability and allow for returning allocations back to departments as a form of disciplinary compensation. Projects without contingency money will not be able to make adjustments later on. Some thought should also be given to building in patronage options, such as aiding graduate students, helping other departments bring in speakers, and participating in programs with other departments.[56]

Implementing

Effective management and the evolution of a "secondary group" style are essential in the middle stage. The "interdisciplinary fallacy"[57] of assuming a direct and unambiguous relationship between two different objects must be constantly guarded against by steadily clarifying connections among participating disciplines, assuming the burden of comprehension for whatever is borrowed from other disciplines, and identifying basic cognitive maps. Through reciprocal learning, team members come to know each other's basic theoretical formulations and methods, building a "common denominator."[58] Emery Reeves suggests posting maps of the research mission and the domains of team members, so that disputes can be aired.[59] As a general rule, encouraging open discussion of disagreements rather than smoothing them over is a good idea, even if it means slowing down temporarily.

If the project is large, an active coordinating body will be essential and, again, flexibility will be aided by setting up contingency money in the planning stages. Both a large bureaucratic system and a special "bridging" person can be effective ways of "bleeding off" tensions in the status dynamics of a team.[60] Physically dispersed members can also use electronic mail and telecommunication to stay in touch with each another and their consultants. It is also a good idea for a leader to check on the flow of communications and members' perceptions of their own interdisciplinarity.

A number of concrete strategies have proved quite helpful in this middle stage. Iteration of the project and any reports and publications will help members review and refocus their work, whether iteration is done strictly on an internal basis or also involves external parties. When faced with a stalemate, participants can write separate statements to illuminate their individual positions, define disagreements, and expose potential bases for agreement. Regular reports, periodic reviews, continual documentation, and internal and external seminars also encourage an integrative focus, as do established techniques such as scenario and Delphi methods. So do common data-gathering analysis, common equipment and procedures, and joint publications, working papers, presentations, patent work, continuing education, and participation in legislative work. In all of these activities, it can be helpful to involve the user/client. It also helps to include lower-status members on the agenda in order to increase their participation.[61] Though the success of a particular technique will always tend to depend on the dynamics of a particular group, Kendall and Mackintosh have schematized techniques for handling common problems in a 34 by 29 matrix that identifies 63 variables and 265 possible interactions. (See Figure 9.) The techniques may be used in various combinations.[62]

Concluding

The concluding stage is the least understood part of the process. It remains, as Lowell Hattery put it, an "unsolved problem in R&D management."[63] There are no widely accepted criteria for evaluating collaborative work,[64] and prevailing disciplinary standards are often inappropriate. Conventional productivity measures such as the number of publications and citations do not readily apply in many IDR projects, since they are characterized by fewer individual publications, more collective authorships outside mainstream disciplinary publications, and such mission-directed measures of success as reciprocal learning, group problem-solving, and implementation of results in a social/technological context rather than an academic context. Furthermore, peer group evaluation is difficult to achieve,[65] and longer start-up times mean long periods when there are no tangible results outside of reciprocal learning.

This is the time for finding a permanent home for activities that are to continue and shifting personnel to different budgets. Project managers who were flexible in the earlier stages of a project will be better able to shift directions at this stage. Plans should also be settled for evaluating the project.[66] Though there are no established models for evaluating IDR, Peston's questions for the *ex ante* evaluation of interdisciplinary research provide a useful framework for evaluating the process of integration itself:

1. Does the project, formulated in interdisciplinary terms, show a recognition of the existing contribution made by the separate disciplines?
2. Is the interdisciplinarity genuine in the sense that the problems are formulated in terms which enable the different disciplines to get together rather than compete with one another?
3. Is the method of data acquisition likely to be helpful to all the relevant disciplines or is it biased in a particular direction?

Figure 9. Problems/Techniques Interaction Matrix

Techniques (columns):
1. GENERAL SYSTEM THEORY
2. ORGANIZATION THEORY
3. DECISION THEORY
4. EXPECTED UTILITY MODEL
5. BAYES' THEOREM
6. CYBERNETICS (integrating language)
7. SYSTEM SIMULATION (modeling)
8. SYSTEM ANALYSIS
9. PROBLEM ANALYSIS
10. CRITICAL PATH ANALYSIS
11. PERT
12. SYSTEMATIC DESIGN
13. MULTIDISCIPLINARY MODEL
14. INTERDISCIPLINARY MODEL
15. CYBERNETIC APPROACH TO GROUP DYNAMICS
16. PSYCHIATRIC APPROACH TO GROUP DYNAMICS
17. DEFERRAL OF JUDGMENT
18. EMPATHIC LISTENING
19. GROUP CONTACT
20. CHALLENGE CONFRONTATION
21. SYMBIOTIC COHESIVE FORCES
22. BRAINSTORMING
23. SYNECTICS
24. DIRECT REWARD FOR INTEGRATIVE BEHAVIOR
25. TRAINING BRIDGE PERSONNEL
26. TRAINING FULL-TIME COORDINATOR
27. INTEGRATED RESEARCH PROPOSAL
28. GROUP - ADMIN - FUNDING AGENCY CONTRACT
29. RECORDING INTRA - GROUP TRANSACTIONS
30. COMMON DATA ANALYSIS OR EXPERIMENTAL FORMAT
31. OUTSIDE STEERING COMMITTEE
32. COGNITIVE CONTACT

Problems (rows) — techniques marked with ● by column number:

Problem	Marked Technique Columns
PARADIGM CONFLICTS	1, 5, 17, 19, 20, 24, 30
PERSONALITY CONFLICTS	3, 4, 8, 9, 17, 18, 19, 20, 21, 22, 31
PRECISION	7, 31
COMMUNICATION	1, 2, 5, 6, 7, 9, 12, 13, 14, 15, 16, 17, 19, 24, 25, 26, 27, 29, 30, 31
SCHEDULING	9, 10, 14, 31
BALANCE	2, 6, 9, 12, 22, 24, 25
PERSONAL COMMITMENT	2, 9, 15, 16, 17, 19, 21, 24, 25, 26, 27
AMBIGUITY OF GOALS	8, 9, 12, 14, 19, 20
DIFFERENTIAL ASSESSMENT OF GOALS	8, 9, 12, 14, 19, 20
PROSPECT FOR APPLICATION	1, 2, 9, 15, 31
TEAM LEADERSHIP	12, 13, 19, 24, 25
ASSUMPTION OF PUBLIC ATTITUDES	3, 4, 7, 9, 21
DIFFERENTIAL ASSESSMENT OF PROBLEM	8, 9, 13, 15, 16
LACK OF SYSTEM PERCEPTION	1, 2, 6, 8, 9, 12, 14, 19, 32
AVOIDANCE OF COMPLEXITY	1, 2, 3, 4, 6, 7, 8, 9, 12, 15, 16, 21, 22, 24, 30
ISOLATION OF PROFESSIONAL DOMAINS	1, 2, 6, 7, 8, 9, 15, 16, 19, 21, 22, 24, 30
DIFFERENTIAL ENVIRONMENTAL ATTITUDE	16
APPOINTMENT OF COORDINATOR	12, 13, 19, 24
TIME ALLOTTED FOR GROUP MANAGEMENT	8, 9, 10, 12, 13, 19, 24
UNIVERSITY'S LIAISON FUNCTION	29, 31
INDIRECT REWARD FOR GROUP RESEARCH	24, 25, 26, 27
LACK OF TIME FOR COLLABORATION	12, 24, 25, 26, 27
COGNITION OF COORDINATOR'S ROLE	12, 13, 16, 24, 25, 26
SELECTION OF TEAM MEMBERS	8, 12, 13, 19, 24
GROUP ORGANIZATION	1, 2, 3, 4, 5, 6, 8, 9, 12, 13, 21, 22, 24, 28, 29, 30
DEGREE OF INTRA-ACTION IN TEAM	2, 5, 6, 8, 9, 12, 13, 14, 15, 16, 17, 18, 19, 20, 21, 22, 24, 28, 29, 30, 31, 32
COMPREHENSIVENESS OF TEAM	1, 2, 6, 8, 12, 16
DIFFERENTIAL PERCEPTION OF ROLES	8, 9, 13, 14, 19, 20, 21, 22, 24, 25
DEFENSE AND ATTACK IN TEAM INTRA-ACTION	3, 4, 7, 9, 12, 13, 17, 18, 19, 20, 21
AFFECTIVE COMPLEXITY	1, 2, 7, 9, 12, 13, 14
INSECURITY	17, 18, 19, 22, 24, 25, 32
SUPPRESSION OF EMOTIVE ASPECTS	16, 17, 18, 19
COGNITIVE DISSONANCE (percept inconsist.)	1, 16, 17, 18, 19, 27
ACCEPTANCE OF MANAGEMENT TECHNIQUES	32

Figure 9. Problems/Techniques Interaction Matrix

4. Does the interdisciplinarity enhance the possibility of hypothesis testing or does it obscure it?

5. What difference will the results of the research make to the policy decisions that will eventually be taken?[67]

The track record of IDR is mixed. Robert Cutler, of the NSF, found it "growing but barely surviving at a majority of publicly funded universities."[68] The tension between problem-focused ORU's and fundamental research in universities has led to the concept of "buffer institutions," organizations that might lessen the marginality of IDR personnel. Frank Press, former director of the President's Office of Science and Technology Policy, suggested in 1975 that the government designate certain university science departments as "national research centers."[69] Likewise, Osmond T. Fundingsland, of the U.S. General Accounting Office, suggested interdisciplinary research institutes be established at selected universities for basic and applied research in specified areas of national interest. Rustum Roy has also proposed a permanent organizational framework accommodating both discipline-oriented and mission-oriented entities within all major research universities. Roy envisioned the entire science and engineering activity of a university, particularly at the graduate level, being organized *primarily* around a dozen permanent mission-oriented interdisciplinary labs, with a *secondary* interlaboratory structure focused on each of the main degree programs and departments.

Countries with more centralized governmental involvement in research have enjoyed the kind of centrality that Press, Fundingsland, and Roy envisioned. Early in the 1970s, the Federal Republic of Germany established a new academic research support program called "Sonderforschungsbereiche" (special research areas), enabling more timely and effective responses to the changing character of research.[70] By 1981 a total of DM 41,500 million was being spent on R&D, with DM 22,500 million contributed by industry and DM 19,000 million from the Federal and Lander governments. Then, in November of 1982, the Christian-Liberal government introduced a reorientation in research policy to optimize resources for work in such areas as energy, aerospace research, electronics, and communication.[71] Now, in the late 1980s, there is widespread hope that the new NSF multidisciplinary engineering centers will play a similar role in maximizing IDR in the United States.

Gerald Holton has suggested a principle that would make science more coherent: "Try to be a scientist first, a specialist second."[72] It is a wise prescription, especially for IDR. However, the organization of research along disciplinary lines will continue to undermine interdisciplinary research in universities, reinforcing social, political, and intellectual obstacles to collaborative work.[73] Most problem-focused research in universities continues to function as an adhocracy. Nevertheless, the growth of IDR since mid-century and the expanding body of knowledge on the subject indicate that traditional structures have diversified in important ways. It also affirms the exogenous shift articulated in the new OECD formulation of interdisciplinarity and a growing belief that "disciplinary depth" is essential to good interdisciplinary research.[74] IDR has been a significant phenomenon in managing change and complexity, for it acts as a check and a clarification of disciplinary knowledge, at the same time it expands the current repertoire of problem-solving skills.

9 Interdisciplinary Care

At first glance it might seem reasonable to assume
that gathering several disciplines around the patient
might provide adequate opportunity to explore the
problem and plan a therapeutic course. However,
a successful and functional interdisciplinary team
is never the byproduct of a series of serendipitous
events.

—Donald W. Day

THE current health-care system is organized primarily along disciplinary lines. However, health problems are no more purely biological than their solutions are purely medical, social, psychological, pharmaceutical, or therapeutic. At a time when the system is confronted increasingly by problems of chronicity, resources and priorities are still being allocated, quite often, in terms of acute illness. Patients are sliced into body systems and problems categorized by disease entities.[1] For all its obvious value in advancing knowledge, the proliferation of specialties has also created problems of fragmented care, mislabeling and misdiagnosis, therapeutic uncertainty, and poor distribution of personnel, resources, and information. To cope with these problems, a variety of interdisciplinary approaches[2] and integrated care units have been developed. There is also a growing literature on the subject that covers a wide range of issues, from the treatment of disease and management of social and medical problems to current research, educational models, and the interdisciplinary nature of new areas. Like the literature on IDR, it too is dominated by descriptive case studies rather than empirical research and comparative studies.

At a theoretical level, interdisciplinary care is linked with the "biosocial" or "biopsychosocial" model of health care, a scientific model that tries to incorporate missing dimensions of the more hierarchical "biomedical model" with a comprehensive integrative, flexible approach.[3] Based on a systems approach, the biopsychosocial model incorporates scientific/analytic factors as well as psychological, social, and ethical factors. For this reason the terms *holistic* and *humanistic* have been used synonymously with *integrative* and *interdisciplinary* health care; and though the phrase *whole client* has become a bit trite through overuse, it remains the underlying concept of integrated health care. Integrated teamwork, which lies at the core of interdisciplinary health care, is holistic in three respects. The human being is considered an interacting, integrated whole, and, correspondingly, treatment must be dynamic and fluid to keep pace with changes in clients and their needs. Finally, the health-care team itself constitutes an interacting partnership of professionals who treat the client as a whole.[4]

There is an ontological premise at the heart of the biopsychosocial model and the accompanying argument for interdisciplinary care. It is the contention that reality, at any given time, is likely to be only a cross section of perceptions. Therefore, in the logic of the argument, an interdisciplinary team with a comprehensive outlook probably has a greater chance of gaining a sense of the "objective reality" of a patient. In the area of developmental disabilities, to illustrate, the reality of a child's problems would be distorted if viewed from only one of several relevant specialities: that of developmental pediatrics (incorporating medical, organic, and biological perspectives), clinical psychology (drawing on intrapsychic, psychosocial, psychometric, and psychiatric social work), psychiatric social work (considering social systems, sociometrics, and interpersonal factors), or special education (emphasizing learning process and educational factors).[5]

Teamwork

Good interdisciplinary care depends on good teamwork. For some, teamwork is a disruption of proper procedures. For others, it is the only way of dealing with complicated health problems. Samuel Pruzansky likens the difficulties faced by patients with complex problems to erecting a skyscraper: "Consider what might happen if there were no architect, no blueprint, and no construction foreman to supervise and coordinate the work of the various crafts." An interdisciplinary team can provide the missing coordination, though it differs both conceptually and operationally from a surgical team or a football team, on which every team player has a specific, circumscribed role subordinate to a team captain.[6] An interdisciplinary health-care team is a collaborative unit that uses a client- or task-centered approach.[7] By synthesizing their knowledge and experience, the members become, in effect, a problem-solving "community of scientific peers."[8] Teams range from strictly ad hoc, private referrals and partnerships to well-organized groups in large treatment centers. The effectiveness of any given team is to a large extent a function of the individuals comprising its membership. Most teams will be heterogeneous in size, setting, formality, and stability, in addition to such factors as sex, age, intelligence, dominance, authoritarianism, social sensitivity, and special skills.[9] Lawrence Fox contends the amount of "interdisciplinaryness" is often a reflection of the hierarchy of team members and the priorities they have established.[10]

Teamwork has several advantages. It facilitates greater accuracy in assessment, classification, placement, and communication, thereby encouraging modesty and reducing arbitrariness.[11] It also encourages timely referrals, while providing specialized consultative services and offering resources for developing innovative programs and evaluating existing ones. There are, in addition, several positive byproducts of teamwork, including the generation of useful data bases, rational treatment plans for the future, and increased patient/client advocacy.[12] Yet there are also a number of common problems. Individuals do not always have sufficient time for collaborative work, and most of them lack training in group dynamics. There are also problems with overlapping roles, territorial and status conflicts, increased time demands, and unsystematic data collection and analysis. There can, in addition, be a tendency for certain disciplines to dominate the process, and the entire effort may be plagued by insufficient funding and inadequate logistics.

Teamwork can be confusing to not only the patient but also team members, since it tends to blur professional boundaries. For this reason continual communication is essential, especially as reciprocal learning begins to take place. On a craniofacial team, to illustrate, a dentist may begin anticipating questions that a speech pathologist would raise. This kind of sensitivity is obviously integral to teamwork, but it can cause problems. If the dentist's information about speech pathology is too superficial, it can be misleading. Likewise, the speech pathologist may make assumptions about the surgeon's choice of surgical procedures in lieu of general physical management of a patient. The dentist, the speech pathologist, and all team members need to know what they don't know as much as what they do know, for there is often a fine line between understanding the responsibilities of a teammate and usurping them.[13]

University-affiliated facilities (UAFs) have played a vital role in the promotion and delivery of interdisciplinary health care. They have a special appeal for the patient. Rather than having to shuttle back and forth between different physicians, surgeons, and paramedical specialists, a patient can go to one facility for integrated care. As a result, accounts of individual UAFs appear frequently in the literature.[14] One of the largest such facilities in North America is the Center for Craniofacial Anomalies at the University of Illinois in Chicago. In its history the center has grown from a Cleft Palate Center and Training Program, established in 1949, to a division within the College of Medicine housing a data base and basic scientific laboratories supported on a contractual basis. It was inevitable that the original mission of the center would broaden, because children with clefts may have associated problems affecting the head. To build excellence the center looked beyond its own institution for personnel and laboratory resources, eventually developing a consortium of collaborating institutions that mobilized regional resources while providing optimal care at the lowest possible cost. This arrangement facilitated a "catch basin of referrals," insuring cash flow to sustain operations and curbing institutional chauvinism through a wider network of contacts and resources.

The center did not win ready acceptance, since it did not fit the established pattern of medical education.[15] In time, though, the center's reputation grew and its clinics became popular electives. Nursing students valued the center because it was the only comprehensive health care service available to them. Medical students with an interest in family practice gravitated there because of its comprehensive services and contacts with relevant social agencies involved in long-term care. The exact number and composition of teams varies, reflecting each team's unique historical origins, funding patterns, and patient flow characteristics. Whatever the context — problem-focused research, health-care, or education — interdisciplinary teams, like individual people, have personalities.[16] Some teams at the center have had only one plastic or otologic surgeon; others had several members representing the services of different institutions. In each case, though, it was important that a team include members of some medical and paramedical disciplines who could frame habilitative care in a global perspective. Pediatric medicine and the psychosocial nursing professions tended to be cast in this role because of their traditional experience in doing just that.

Status problems can be especially troublesome for health care teams. If a highly regarded, better-paid professional — say, a physician or a lawyer — is teamed with social, psychological, and rehabilitation workers, there may be marked differences in the way they value their time and each other, let alone what they are actually paid. Status has also been a factor in the choice of team leader.[17] Studies have shown that higher-status individuals tend to receive more communication, are better liked, and give less communication that is judged "irrelevant" by other members.[18] Schlesinger contended a cardiologist should chair a rehabilitation team for patients recuperating from acute myocardial infarction, since the responsibilities are so great.[19] Likewise, pediatricians typically assume the leadership role on teams dealing with developmental disabilities because of their status.[20] Others disagree with the strictly hierarchical approach to leadership, arguing the physician is not necessarily the best choice of team manager. One New Zealand–based team used a social worker instead of a physician as team coordinator because the rest of the team believed the social worker had the most appropriate personality, experience, objectivity, and, most important, the time to perform coordinating chores. Physicians, they cautioned, often lack the necessary time and coordinating skills. If physicians do act as coordinators, the difference between their roles as physician and as coordinator must be clearly defined and recognized.[21]

Because status is such a prominent variable in teamwork, status conflicts have been a prominent concern in the literature. One particular example, drawn from a general hospital setting, provides a revealing look at how both status hierarchies and conflicts in disciplinary world views can affect the attempt to deliver integrated care. In order to alleviate problems created by reliance on a disciplinary structure and the haphazard nature of consultation services, an integrated psychosocial consultation service was organized at a 352-bed university-affiliated veterans hospital in San Francisco.[22] When a psychiatrist interested in consultation was appointed, requests for service increased. To improve communication, the liaison psychiatrist instituted a weekly consultation conference open to all services. As their discussions shifted from a clinical focus to the common goals and problems of participating disciplines, members of the conference began to see the wisdom of an integrated service. They believed from the start that professionals should work together as equals. However, in trying to turn their belief into practice, they made several interesting discoveries. When they considered, for example, how to designate primary consultants, a major difference in time frames became apparent. Psychiatrists and nurses, it turned out, were influenced by the medical model of immediate response, whereas psychologists and social service personnel thought more in terms of long-term problem-solving approaches. Also, when the psychology staff suggested adding a research dimension, the clinically oriented staff objected, contending it might compromise patient care.

They were able to get past these differences by steadily clarifying their views and focusing on the working styles, roles, and needs of the participants. This kind of clarification and role negotiation helps individuals assess what they need from not only each other but also from patients/clients and representatives of various institutions. Making a comprehensive list of all needs and then ranking them has helped some teams to see areas of commonality and disagreement more clearly.[23] After gathering information, the team can interpret their findings, including diagnoses made at different periods of time. Because of their recurring attempts to clarify differences, the San Francisco team was able to move past stereotyped responses to a more flexible system. Ultimately they were able to begin a new program with a new liaison committee, composed of a senior staff member from psychiatry, psychology, nursing, and social services.

The new program brought several changes on the four pilot wards.

Under the new system, both head nurses and house officers could initiate requests for psychosocial consultation. For each consultation request, a primary consultant from any of the four disciplines was named responsible for a given patient. Each of the primary consultants, in turn, kept similar records and gave copies to the liaison committee. Although this system had obvious advantages, several problems emerged. One of them involved the nursing staff, who were reluctant to use their new prerogative to initiate requests for medical consultation. They feared rebuke if their requests were deemed inappropriate. The medical staff, in turn, questioned whether complex diagnostic issues could be handled by someone without a medical background, even though many requests for help dealt with the patient's social rather than strictly medical background. (Elsewhere, in the context of caring for critically ill newborns, Thomas Murray has commented on the relationship between medical hierarchies and the role of nurses.[24])

As the system evolved and became more familiar, these problems tended to subside. Head nurses relied less frequently on contacts with the liaison team nurse and began initiating more consultation requests. Cryptic demands, such as "Psychotic?" or "Please evaluate," were replaced by more thoughtful formulations of problems, and the general emphasis shifted from dumping and crisis management to preventive involvement. Several interdisciplinary, open-group meetings were also held to deal with not only the consultation process but also medical status examinations and the writing of reports. In addition, members of the liaison team assumed peer review functions, providing feedback about the consultation process and record-keeping. In evaluating their experience, the group found medical status traditions had proven hardest to breach. Consultants from other professions were often misperceived as physicians, and nurses generally tended to underestimate their own clinical skills. Persistent support of the nurses' preventive function and discussion of significant position papers on the extended role of the nurse fostered their increased involvement on the psychosocial team. Social service personnel were particularly responsive to improved communication, since it promoted greater rapport with outside consultants, more immediate and complete collaboration, and greater recognition of their own psychotherapy skills. Psychologists, in turn, gained knowledge of the organic contributions of psychopathology and the complexities of a hospital community. Members of the psychiatry staff even began to reexamine their long-accepted practice of mental status testing and diagnostic labeling. Finally, a new consultation theory seminar also emerged, and, as students were exposed to the team model, there was a shift to an interdisciplinary teaching pattern.

The Integration of Services

Adding new services to existing teams is perhaps the major theme in the literature on interdisciplinary care. In many cases they are undervalued and previously neglected services. The common denominator in the thousands of case studies that populate the literature is improved communication among the newly affiliated practitioners. At Marianjoy Rehabilitation Hospital (Illinois), two changes were made: one to address communication problems and the other to integrate a previously neglected specialty. Members of clinical departments at Marianjoy were having several problems that are commonly encountered in staff meetings: excessive amounts of time were being spent on the meetings, reports were being issued in professional jargon, physical restoration was being overemphasized at the expense of psychosocial-spiritual aspects, and excessive energy was being spent on treating the chart for the sake of third-party payers.[25] After several months of investigating these problems, Marianjoy adopted the "Patient Evaluation Conference System" (PECS), originally developed by Drs. Harvey and Jellinek of the University of Wisconsin. The system called for having each disciplinary participant complete an appropriate worksheet on a patient's current status, inpatient goals, and short-term (14-day) objectives. Next, data-entry personnel collected the worksheets, transcribed them onto a master worksheet, and entered them into a computer data base in order to get a plot profile, which was then printed and converted into a transparency. At a subsequent meeting, the group was able to use the transparency to formulate a treatment plan. Later, the plot profile was shared with the patient and entered into the patient's permanent medical record.

The new system had several advantages. It was now possible to report functional items in a common language accessible to all therapists and third-party payers. There was also increased awareness of psychosocial aspects, and a "sensitive gain scale" was used to track small changes and distinguish dependent from independent status in a patient's functional performance. In addition, computerized staffing procedures and program evaluation facilitated feedback. Besides adopting the system, Marianjoy also added an element missing from the original PECS, pastoral care. The integration of pastoral care into the staffing system at Marianjoy produced not only greater accountability for pastoral care services but also improved understanding of what chaplains do and why it is important. Chaplains, in turn, had a heightened sense of goal completion, and pastoral care units of fifteen minutes each were now formally delineated on the daily management report and the patient's bill, even though there was not a designated fee for those services.

The new procedures at Marianjoy bring to mind Holm and McCarthy's list of "do's and dont's" for increasing integration in staff meetings and conferences. It is important that conflicting views be aired and controversies settled. The person in charge should be the case manager, someone who is familiar with the situation and able to facilitate the exchange of information. There are also additional tips: knowing everyone's identity and professional affiliation, providing information in written form, listing all the problems for discussion, and making sure everyone is heard in order to encourage broad participation. There are, in turn, steps to avoid. They include letting someone just read a report, going around the table haphazardly rather than logically, getting bogged down on a minor issue or irrelevant topic, and allowing a guest or team member to monopolize the discussion. Demanding or refusing compromise can also be damaging. If a social worker knows a child is in a situation where he or she is exposed to abuse, then remedial school placement may have to wait until the social situation is changed. In a different instance, therapists and physicians may advocate intensive physical therapy for a child who also has a severe communication disorder at the same time a psychologist and speech pathologist may advocate handling the problem in a specialized remedial program. Instead of setting priorities that separate these needs, the team might try to find a program that can provide both needs.[26]

Integrating services on rounds has also been a means of achieving interdisciplinary care, one that not only benefits the patient but also provides a form of continuing education for the care givers. For participants in the residency program at the University of Washington's Department of Family Medicine, the first change came when they added a discussion of ambulatory patient problems presented to the resident on call the previous night.[27] The first additional health-care professional to join morning rounds was the medical social worker, who provided physicians with a better understanding of the psychosocial aspects of a patient's problems, the effect those problems were having on the family as a whole, and knowledge of appropriate community resources. When the program became involved in a formal interdisciplinary project in July 1976, the services of a clinical pharmacist were added. The pharmacist contributed expertise in drug education, assessment, and cost effectiveness. Nurses were the next to join. A registered nurse joined rounds once or twice a week on a rotating basis, providing physicians with knowledge of any previously identified relationships between a patient and the center. The nurse also linked hospital medical staff with a patient's regular primary physician. After adding a nurse, the group then recognized their need for greater knowledge about new developments, so they invited a member of the hospital library staff to join them on a weekly basis. They gained ready access to reprints and increased knowledge about recently published references. Previous links with the dietary staff also led to their inviting a member of that staff on a weekly basis to provide expertise on nutritional management both during and after a patient's hospital stay.

Team members agreed that management of patients improved and the educational program expanded as a result of integrated rounds. Initially the residents were apprehensive, fearing dilution of their responsibilities. Yet after the experience they concluded their knowledge had increased and their understanding of other professional roles expanded. Other health-care professionals felt equally enriched. The medical social worker gained a better understanding of the relationship between her skills and the physician's role in providing health care. The clinical pharmacist gained clinical skills and a much better understanding of the pathophysiology and natural history of diseases as they affect the use of pharmaceutical agents. The librarian improved her judgment in selecting appropriate materials and became more familiar with professional jargon. And, finally, the nutritionist was able to see dietary problems and make plans in a more global context.

The integration of pharmacy services is a particularly good example of the extent to which continuing education is part of the interdisciplinary process. Clinical pharmacists have not been included very often on teams. In facilities for developmentally disabled individuals, to take one example, pharmacy services have been limited traditionally to three functions: (1) procurement or stocking, (2) repackaging or formulation and packaging of the drug, and (3) dispensing and accounting for drug usage. This kind of tangential "operational pharmacy" does not necessarily serve clients as well as "clinical pharmacy," a system that allows the pharmacist to evaluate drug actions, dosages, behaviors, and symptoms. In a behaviorally oriented system with built-in feedback to both medical and psychological staff, drug manipulation can be coordinated through data analysis over a period of time. In the process physicians gain a more systematic accounting for dosages, target behaviors, and symptoms. Psychologists also gain additional information that can be correlated with behavioral data as a reliability check.[28]

This kind of comprehensive system was used to advantage at the Muskegon Regional Center for Developmental Disabilities (Michigan). When a 39-year-old female was transferred from another developmental disabilities center, she was diagnosed as being mentally retarded. In evaluating her history, the pharmacist found long-term, heavy, and uninterrupted use of antipsychotic medication. After reviewing drug and laboratory histories, the pharmacist suggested her aggressive behavior might be the result of drug-induced toxicity known as "tardive dyskinesia." It is marked by extraneous body movements and limb-shaking behaviors. When the health-care team concurred with the pharmacist's recommendation of gradual reduction in dosages, the patient was withdrawn from antipsychotic medication over a three-month period. During that time data were collected on her behavior and then summarized each week by the pharmacist, for use by the physician and interdisciplinary team. In addition to controlled withdrawal of medication, there was also an extensive behavior modification program designed to reduce aggression. As a result of these coordinated efforts, the woman's unmanageable, aggressive behavior was reduced from almost daily to occasional occurrence, the shaking subsided, and her motor skills improved. After a three-year period, she was no longer exhibiting physical aggression and was released to a group home.[29]

A similar improvement was observed at the Coldwater Regional Center for Development Disabilities (Michigan), where data-based interdisciplinary reviews of medication led to reduction in the use of drugs and relative size of doses. The center used interdisciplinary teams attached to three programs, though the pharmacist was a common member on each team. Each team met once a month to discuss the behavior of each resident receiving a neuroleptic (antipsychotic) drug. They found several advantages to relying upon interdisciplinary meetings designed to help monitor drug use, not the least of which was economical use of time in meetings. Physicians were not dependent solely on the written reports of whichever staff might be available at the time of drug reviews. The system also further reduced the risk of serious side effects and provided a legal safeguard against litigation for failure to monitor drug usage and excessive or improper dosages.[30]

Two additional examples, one in Maryland and the other in Utah, demonstrate the multiple roles that a single member of a team can play. The University of Maryland's Center for the Study of Pharmacy and Therapeutics in the Elderly evolved from a university task force on interdisciplinary care of the elderly. By working with the university's Center for Aging, the schools of dentistry, law, medicine, nursing, pharmacy, and social work and community planning were able to plan a variety of activities in the areas of research, education, and service. By choosing the nearby John L. Deaton Medical Center for a facility, they could provide space for each participating discipline. Dentistry had the largest space and proved to be the most popular service offered. Clinical pharmacy services provided an extensive range of services: in order of effort, they were chronic care management, reviews of drug profiles, taking of drug histories, home visits, and formal therapeutic consultations. Each time a change was made in a patient's drug profile, the pharmacist reviewed it. The pharmacist also conducted regular reviews on a weekly basis, took drug histories on a referral basis, offered formal consultations on intermittent acute problems such as adverse drug reactions, selected drugs of choice for acute problems or the monitoring of drug therapy, and answered questions about particular drugs and therapeutic problems. In addition, the pharmacist participated in interdisciplinary care on an ongoing basis by collaborating with other team members and referring patients to other care providers.[31]

A similar pattern of education emerged when a clinical pharmacist became a member of a rural care facility in Vernal, Utah. Established in mid-1975, the Vernal Family Health Center was monitored from the main campus of the University of Utah by an Interdisciplinary Primary Care Committee from the Health Sciences Center. Among its several objectives, the site team wanted to train physicians, medical students, nurse clinicians, clinical pharmacists, graduate students in social work, and Medex (experienced medical personnel trained to be physicians' assistants) in an interdisciplinary rural primary care setting. Since none of the team members had prior training in teamwork, workshops were used to present core concepts. Although the role of the clinical pharmacist was not defined at the outset, the pharmacist became a key member of the team.

The original goal of obtaining medication histories and monitoring all drug therapy proved impractical, since approximately 1,400 patients a month were seen at the Vernal Family Health Center. Since routine and acute problems did not necessarily call for medication histories, patients were referred to the clinical pharmacist for a medication history only if they had a chronic disease or took four or more prescription drugs. Instead of monitoring all drug therapies, the pharmacist developed a formulary of therapeutic agents for routine and acute problems. The pharmacist also followed up on care of patients with chronic diseases such as congestive heart failure, hypertension, seizure disorders, and diabetes mellitus. Follow-up consisted of taking a history, performing simple physical assessment, ordering routine lab tests, and making therapeutic decisions or alterations within the limits of protocols established by the team. Unresponsive patients were referred to the physician. For particular kinds of patients — those with psychosocial problems such as alcoholism, depression, enuresis — the pharmacist worked with the social worker and, where appropriate, referred patients to other members of the team.[32]

Clearly, successful teamwork is not a matter of serendipity or some mysterious jelling of personalities. It is a matter of hard work. Like IDR, it is also a continuous process that may change as new and different needs are identified. It depends in large part upon tending to two major issues: the communication process and the cultivation of skills that are fundamental to interdisciplinary work. Practitioners must be able to acquire, evaluate, and use information acquired from a variety of sources. They must be able to judge which disciplines are appropriate to a particular problem and be able to cooperate with fellow team members. Finally, where appropriate, they must also be able to make referrals and offer educational services.[33]

Education and Training

Training for integrative care draws on a variety of methods ranging from traditional lectures, colloquia, and case conferences[34] to innovative curricula organized around organ modules, clinical and ambulatory settings,[35] the integration of behavioral sciences and clinical practice, and the study of specific diseases.[36] There are also programs with a humanistic, ethical focus,[37] and it is possible to receive training in teamwork[38] and a variety of pertinent skills, such as groups dynamics, conflict resolution, problem-solving, decision-making, interpersonal relations, and interpersonal, group and organizational communications.

These methods have been incorporated into four major models of integrative education in the health sciences.[39] The *traditional model* is found in some form in almost all health science teaching centers. It is usually a "multidisciplinary" content course or subject taught in a single-discipline lecture, with discussion of topics such as epidemiology and legal medicine. The *common-interest model* is being used increasingly in health science centers. Described as a "nondisciplinary" topical approach, it focuses on various aspects of health care delivery, financing of health care, moral and ethical problems, and anatomy. Relying mostly on lectures, discussions, and seminars, the common-interest model may also include core courses in the behavioral or physical sciences. The *case presentation model* is a passive patient-centered activity that relates some element of academic study to an actual patient. Relying on the clinical-case conference, this model focuses on topics oriented towards disease, social history, and rehabilitation of the patient, highlighting cases that demonstrate principles of comprehensive care. In the *health team model,* students from several disciplines take joint responsibility for a task in either *research teams* or *patient care teams*. Research teams study a particular problem, such as a community attitude survey, through independent or guided study of research methods. Patient care teams are responsible for comprehensive care in clinical work, with on- or off-campus clinical conferences. These conferences may have a *professional orientation,* in a setting where the focus is on cooperation among designated disciplines, or a *patient orientation,* in a setting where a patient's needs determine the relevant disciplines. Students are usually concerned about such topics as role definition, interdisciplinary communication, integrated patient care, and non-institutional patient care.

Many programs have a special commitment to outreach, and certain medical faculties have made far-reaching innovations by basing their training programs on local health needs, including Newcastle University (Australia), McMaster University (Canada), Negev University (Israel), the State University of Limburg, Maastricht (Netherlands), and Metropolitan Autonomous University (Mexico).[40] New Mexico State University has also pioneered a model for incorporating sociocultural skills in a Mexican-American context,[41] and, at other institutions, field trips have been used.[42] In addition, the Department of Pediatrics at the University of Helsinki's Children's Hospital has used house calls as an important part of training. The department cooperated with the Helsinki Swedish School of Nursing, the Swedish School of Social Work and Local Administration, and a district hospital in southern Finland to provide a decentralized, interdisciplinary opportunity for medical, nursing, and social work students to study a holistic approach to families with chronically ill children.[43]

Community-based programs occur in both rural and urban areas. The Upper Peninsula Medical Education Program (Michigan) was established in 1973, and is designed to train primary-care physicians for practice in rural, underserved areas.[44] It is connected with Michigan State University's College of Human Medicine, and its program is based on a four-year ambulatory outpatient experience in a family practice office away from the central campus. All basic and clinical sciences are learned in the field. Similarly, there is a program in Minnesota that uses on-site, experiential education as an alternative to didactic programs in academic settings. The Community-University Health Care Center (CUHCC) serves a high-risk, medically-underserved inner-city population in south Minneapolis. In order to provide both comprehensive health care and training, the program developed several teams that deal with health assessment, common health concerns, sharing resources, and facilitating referrals. The training program itself focused on group problem-solving, decision-making techniques, readings, visits to service agencies, and interviews with both professionals and paraprofessionals. Graduates of the program have cited interaction with patients and colleagues as one of its key strengths, in addition to gaining knowledge about interdisciplinary teams. They feel the system provides more optimal care and more appropriate treatment plans for patients.[45]

The barriers to integrated care are not only intellectual and psychological but also physical. In one particular case, practitioners who wanted to work together literally tore down the wall separating their offices. In the early 1950s, when Dr. Richard Layton began a group medical practice in a small town in eastern Washington,[46] Layton and his three partners shared part of their building with a dentist. At first the arrangement was purely financial. Soon, however, they discovered a majority of their patients had problems requiring mutual care. So, after a year, they began practicing jointly and eventually cut a door between the medical and dental units. When Layton left private practice in 1974 to become director of the Providence Family Medical Center and Residency Program at the University of Washington, he built upon this experience by developing a joint training program for family physicians and dentists. Rather than simply increasing the number of lectures and didactic sessions, Layton and his colleagues wanted to train dental and medical residents in a clinical unit. Clinical and ambulatory settings have proved powerful settings for interdisciplinary training, since students often see problems that cannot necessarily be isolated.

When the program was finally instituted, faculty were able to move into a model dental unit in space contiguous to the Family Medical Center. Four family practice residents and one dental resident spent the first four weeks of their first year working together in the model unit. In addition to taking over the practices of graduating residents, they spent at least one half-day working with, and doing the job of, every faculty employee in the center, a technique used by interdisciplinary training programs to foster empathy and increased knowledge. The dental resident went on to spend a month in anesthesiology and then worked in the model dental unit for four days a week, with one day free for seminars and classes at the University of Washington Dental School. The dental resident also shared night-time and weekend emergency calls with the university's general practice dentistry residents and was expected to attend a weekly didactic program with the family practice residents. In addition, a dental resident might also undertake special projects and was available for in-house hospital consultations requiring a dental opinion. When necessary, the emergency room also referred possible jaw fracture patients for consultation and X-rays.

The Providence program was unique in that students arrived at the center already trained as a team, ready to work with the Providence team. Moreover, grant support enabled the program to obtain the full-time services of a medical social worker, a nurse practitioner, and a clinical pharmacist, facilitating cooperation among the schools of dentistry, nursing, medical pharmacy, and social work. In preparing for the program, staff members discovered a relatively recent expansion of general practice dental residencies, so they surveyed the prevalence of integrated medical/dental care. Of the 285 family medicine residency programs they contacted in the fall of 1976, 90% responded. Only 30 of the 285 replied affirmatively when asked if they were involved with dentistry in any way. Only 15 reported any coordinated dental program in their units, and none of the 15 were similar to the integrated unit at Providence. In May 1977, in fact, the American Dental Association confirmed there were no other integrated family medicine and general practice dentistry residencies operating in the country at the time.

Several indicators of success are apparent in these examples. Commonality is the major factor, not only common learning and goals but also logistics and, where possible, a common data system. The Providence program relied on a common waiting room, reception area, billing office, and record-keeping, making it possible to handle increased loads. The billing system was also integrated through a common form that could be coded into the Providence Medical Center computer. Charts for each family were still kept in a family folder, but the folder now included dental records and progress notes, as well as problem-lists and medication pages to be used by both family practice and dental residents. Another important factor is making a conscious effort to achieve integration. An interdisciplinary training program developed at the Pittsburgh Child Guidance Center provides a good example of how this can be accomplished.

In line with its commitment to helping deal with child abuse and neglect,[47] the center designed a project that focused, in part, on perceiving abuse as an interdisciplinary problem and understanding interdisciplinary methods of managing abuse. The project began with an assessment of all local training courses in the area, including courses provided by educational, legal, and social agencies. To ensure that each group was heterogeneous, the trainees were drawn from several different social and community agency networks. To help them project organizers provided factual information from articles and government pamphlets, then structured opportunities for group dynamics, sociodrama, case presentation and analysis, extensive group discussion, and an integrative presentation of child abuse cases. The roles and problems of various agencies were also clarified and the interdisciplinary collaborative process examined. The value of the interdisciplinary collaboration was reinforced by several activities: assessment of relationships in the family, examination of the role of crisis as a precipitator of abuse, and clarification of the necessity of support systems. The culminating event of the training program included a "multidisciplinary evaluation" of a single case, the design of a "multidisciplinary treatment plan," and discussion of continuing integrative activity on behalf of children. This project only underscores the importance of a steady focus on the underlying process of care and training, not just particular techniques and approaches.

Beyond the practical problems presented by teamwork, there are several ethical and philosophical considerations. There is, to begin with, the matter of the patient. A team should be not only problem-centered but also patient-centered, educating patients to the process and making them, in effect, fully qualified members of the team.[48] Yet, the more parties who are involved, the wider information is spread. The growing dissemination of information about patients through computers, joint committees, and teams raises questions about confidentiality. There are, to be sure, recognized standards of conduct for transmitting information between professionals, but they can differ from profession to profession. Problems also arise when qualitatively different kinds of data are used. This stems, in part, from prevailing status hierarchies, which hold "scientific" medical data higher than other kinds of "softer" data from the behavioral fields.

Derek Pheby has expressed concern about information that circulates between professionals of different disciplines, often in a secondhand manner. In a case conference dealing with child abuse, for example, only a minority of those present may have direct personal knowledge of the child or its family. The consensus that ultimately emerges may rest upon a medical pronouncement about a behavioral phenomenon that is not basically "scientific" or falsifiable. This may lead to inappropriate labeling of the family. Information may also be credited on the basis of expectation, without regard for situational factors. Nonmedical personnel may also interpret data incorrectly, though, at the same time, physicians may draw inaccurate conclusions from reports of teachers or social workers.[49] There is a clear danger of imparting a seal of authority to data that a physician includes from other professionals. At the same time, as the example of the San Francisco veterans hospital demonstrated so clearly, professional status hierarchies may lead medical personnel to discount the perspectives of nonmedical personnel.

Finally, there are ethical issues associated with how power is distributed on a team and how responsibility is shared. Even though teamwork is based on the premise that no particular part of a diagnosis or treatment program is sacrosanct,[50] individual responsibility is not abrogated by the team process.[51] Furthermore, though integrated care has a great potential for eliminating the "fishbowl effect" of narrow vision,[52] its effectiveness will depend very much on more thorough education at both the pre-professional and professional levels. If educational programs were structured to reveal and explore differences between disciplines, different treatment approaches for similar problems could be compared and evaluated.[53] Both interdisciplinary training and care have the potential for promoting greater knowledge[54] by creating a broader and more realistic perspective on the needs of patients and clients,[55] especially when there is a system of comprehensive planning and coordinated use of data. This kind of care, however, makes greater demands on all the participants because it represents an alternative epistemology to the dominant mode of health-care delivery.

10 IDS: Interdisciplinary Education

Interdisciplinarity is far more than a relatively
recent addition to educational jargon. It is a mode
of thought which, at all societal and academic
levels, ultimately purports to enable one to
synthesize ever-increasing amounts of discernable
and subliminal input.

— Tamara Swora and James L. Morrison

SOMEBODY once claimed the only thing connecting the classes in many schools is the plumbing. Popular though the sentiment may be, it is not an accurate description of higher education today, for, despite the dominance of disciplinary structures, interdisciplinary studies (IDS) are in evidence. William Mayville spoke of three types of IDS: *revolutionary* programs, which dispense with the traditional disciplinary apparatus; *professional* programs, which are committed to training specialists and use integrated approaches to acquaint students with the broader dimensions of their professional fields; and *programmatic* curricula, which seek to broaden the cultural and intellectual frameworks of students.[1] Flexner and Hauser categorized programs into three paradigms exemplified by Columbia University's programs in general education at the graduate and professional levels, Newark State College's two-year individualized general education curriculum, and Pennsylvania State University's problem-oriented interdisciplinary graduate program in the humanities.[2] At present there are six kinds of interdisciplinary curricula worldwide:
- interdisciplinary universities
- four-year undergraduate programs
- core curricula and clustered courses
- individual courses
- independent studies
- graduate and professional studies

Any attempt to define IDS is plagued from the start by an institutional particularity about academic goals, student needs, pedagogical philosophies, administrative policies, disciplinary contexts, integrative approaches, and attitudes towards interdisciplinarity. Moreover, some names — such as Evergreen, Ramapo, Sussex, Green Bay, Santa Cruz — have become part of the folklore of innovation in higher education. They keep popping up again and again, sometimes well after the original programs have been revised and always at the expense of other, lesser-known, but equally important, models. Still, by looking at a representative sample of programs, it is possible to construct a picture of IDS in the most recent era, spanning the late 1960s through the 1980s.

Interdisciplinary Universities

The place to begin is with the boldest of the experiments, the universities founded on interdisciplinary principles. They were "telic" institutions in the sense Grant and Riesman used the term to describe institutions that pointed towards a different conception of education.[3] Opened in 1961, the University of Sussex[4] was the first of seven new British universities and one of the first comprehensive attempts to redefine relations between academic subject areas.[5] Its founders sought to destroy the antithesis between "general" and "specialized" education by combining specialization in one discipline with common work across disciplines. The Sussex experiment was followed by other institutions founded on similar principles, including the Universty of East Anglia (Britain) in 1962, the University of Wisconsin, Green Bay (United States) chartered in 1965, Griffith University (Australia) in 1971, University Center Roskilde (Denmark) in 1972, the University of Tromso (Norway) opened in 1972, and the University of Tsukuba (Japan) also opened in 1972.

Green Bay was described as an institution that challenged "the sanctity of individual disciplines and professions."[6] The emphasis on themes and field study made Green Bay the model for a number of other universities. Griffith was conceived as an alternative to the more traditional University of Queensland, and, likewise, University Center of Roskilde was founded to relieve the 500-year-old University of Copenhagen of some of its students, in addition to providing a setting for interdisciplinarity and other pedagogical alternatives. Tromso was also designed to cope with increasing numbers of students while serving regional needs and facilitating the development of integrative teaching and research. The seventh of these examples, Tsukuba, was opened as a "spearhead of renewal" for higher education in Japan. A future-oriented, problem-solving university similar in some ways to Green Bay, Tsukuba was to be an "open university" in the fullest sense, fostering education and research activities that would reach not only across the disciplines but out into the wider society.

The prevailing academic structure in these universities was the multi-subject school. At Sussex each school brought together a number of related subjects, increasing cooperation and permitting the development of special "combined" and "contextual" courses that provided an integrative framework.[7] These courses made it possible to focus on interrelationships among the social science disciplines, to examine Westernization and modernization, to concentrate on basic concepts and methods of scientific reasoning, and to abandon traditional distinctions in order to study such subjects as control engineering and materials. When the University of East Anglia was founded a year later, it too was divided into fairly large schools instead of departments, including schools of English, American, and European studies. There was also a school of development studies, and faculty established a comprehensive school of biological sciences, combining plant physiology, zoology, biochemistry, and biophysics.[8] At Griffith University, modeled in part on the examples of East Anglia and the Open University in Britain, a student's curriculum consisted of a coherent set of units within a school. Students were taught to master intrinsic components and problems of particular themes focused, quite often, on complex problems of contemporary culture.

Two of these universities offered particularly intriguing approaches to the question of specialization. Green Bay[9] was organized around four colleges based on environmental themes rather than disciplines; the curriculum itself was based on nine problem-centered concentrations that could be pursued in the four theme colleges. To develop a concentration, a student selected a problem, then tried to solve it through studies in several concentrations. Interdisciplinary or disciplinary competence could be achieved by selecting one of three choices for majors and minors: an *environmental problem* that constituted a required concentration or major, an option or co-major in a *discipline or field of knowledge,* or an optional concentration in a *professional application.*

At University Center of Roskilde,[10] where education was based on the concept of group work and projects, students started out in a two-year "basis," then moved into a one-and-a-half to three-year "superstructure." Students in "basis" selected a field of study, then became members of a "house," a unit composed of undergraduates and teachers who selected common themes each term. The "superstructure" differed, in that students selected their own particular studies and then chose problems that would help them satisfy the requirements in selected subjects. In this sense the "superstructure" was divided into disciplines, each strictly defined by "modules" consisting of the curricula for one term at a time. Yet the house structure still continued to facilitate an "ambience of interdisciplinarity" as students explored their themes from different angles. Two students pursuing Danish and sociology as their subjects combined the demands of one of the Danish modules and one of the sociology modules in a project

on the culture of narcissism. Most students completed their degrees in two
subjects, using various possibilities in alternate terms.

There was never a uniform degree of integration at any one of these
universities. At Griffith some schools fit content to meet broad themes,
but other schools wound up sacrificing broad themes to disciplinary content. There were also varying degrees of commitment to the foundation-
year program,[11] and, by the mid-1980s, Griffith was facing internal pressures
that might cause a regression to disciplinary modes and retreat of the interdisciplinary mission to just the foundation year.[12] Like the other universities, Griffith changed as new staff were recruited and informal groups
of discipline-oriented academics emerged. Like the University of Tromso,
Griffith also found the most important and prestigious reference groups
for faculty are often scholarly associations and journals that are largely
disciplinary in character. These reference groups, in Don Anderson's view,
have proved the source of the most powerful regressive pressures on interdisciplinary experiments in Australia.

Griffith has not been the only interdisciplinary experiment in Australia,
and the differences are instructive. The Australian National University in
Canberra had a multidisciplinary unit composed of representatives from
sociology, social psychology, economics, and politics. They had a common problem focus and borrowed methodologies from different disciplines.
There were also formal collaborations, but, as the contexts changed, the
experiment ended. When the parent institution was hit by funding cuts
in the 1970s, the innovative unit was the first "fat" to be trimmed, a familiar
story in higher education. Resources were "cannibalized," and some staff
argued that disciplinarity had existed all along. In contrast, a new medical
school at Newcastle has been more successful. The beneficiary of careful
advanced planning and legislative protection, it is organized along functional "school" lines rather than traditional departments of physiology,
anatomy, biochemistry, and clinical sciences.

None of these institutions remains the same as it was on founding day.
At Green Bay, disciplinary majors and interdisciplinary minors were added
to the original structure of interdisciplinary majors and disciplinary minors.
This change has been called a response to "'real-world' pressures." Incom-
ing students still tend to identify more readily with traditional disciplinary
designations.[13] In the late 1970s, a four-year, all-university seminar program in liberal education was also replaced by a new set of all-university
requirements featuring a more structured program of nine hours each in
the humanities, natural sciences, and social sciences. This change has been
called "a compromise" between the forces of tradition and innovation.[14]
Even with these changes, however, interdisciplinarity has been reaffirmed
in keeping interdisciplinary concentrations as budgetary units and in des-
ignating interdisciplinary "majors," rather than just "concentrations." Here

and elsewhere there is evidence of a change in thinking not only about interdisciplinarity but also disciplinarity. Co-majoring in a discipline has always been an option at Green Bay, though traditionally the disciplines displayed a "low profile." Now disciplinarity is more fully recognized for what it offers. Suggesting earlier anxiety about disciplines reasserting their traditional dominance has now passed, authors of the Year 2000 report at Green Bay contended interdisciplinary programs must be built on a "foundation of strong curricula and faculty in the disciplines."[15]

At Roskilde the original system broke down in 1977 when the three faculties of humanities, natural sciences, and social sciences were dissolved in order to establish interfacultative departments. To illustrate, historians from various departments and faculties convened with some of the sociologists to establish the first interfaculty body, a department of history and social conditions. The new departments were to assume responsibility for relevant subjects in the superstructure (the French Department for French, and so on). However, there were so few people in each area that several disciplines wound up being represented in a department. As a result, some of the departments were "multidisciplinary," others more truly "interdisciplinary." The change did not win unanimous approval. Environmentalists wanted to keep their department interdisciplinary to correspond with their interdisciplinary subject. Historians and sociologists also wanted to work together in a common, multidisciplinary department crossing faculty borders. Consequently, permission was granted to give up the faculty structure.[16]

Beyond the visible breakdown of the system, Roskilde was also plagued by a more fundamental problem that has been apparent at Tsukuba and, in differing degrees, the other universities as well: a clash between the organization of interdisciplinary teaching and the organization of research. At Roskilde the initial goal of forming ad hoc interdisciplinary groups of teachers and researchers turned out to be politically unfeasible. Some departments functioned well, but others formed tight restrictions around promising interdisciplinary projects. Moreover, as the first students began appearing in the superstructure for disciplinary studies, faculty faced an annual negotiation of how many teachers should go to basis and how many remain in the superstructure. Currently there are more curricular and organizational changes going on and, as always, external pressure. In 1975, in fact, a threat of closure was defeated by only two votes in the Danish Parliament. Yet, despite the changes and pressures, a large portion of the research projects at RUC continue to be integrative in nature. They have included projects on working conditions in Danish breweries, Danish volunteers who fought in Germany on the Eastern Front during World War II, educational problems, and various aspects of new electronic technologies. Interdisciplinarity may not be the superior ideal at Roskilde, but it is highly valued, for it is conceived as politically and socially engaged work on problems that arise in contemporary society. Thus interdisciplinarity is not considered an asset in and of itself, but rather a consequence of the kind of problems in which faculty and students are engaged.

The University of Tsukuba is also based on a problem focus.[17] Located in Tsukuba City of Science and Technology, a new Japanese city planned and developed by the government, the university is at the center of an "academic metropolis" that facilitates cooperation among many of the more than fifty national research institutions located in the area. Undergraduate education at Tsukuba is set at the level of basic training in clustered disciplines. There are frequent "multidisciplinary" lectures, and it is possible to specialize. It is also possible to pursue master's and doctorate degrees. Interdisciplinarity at Tsukuba has been most apparent at the master's level, where there are problem-oriented studies in eight areas. Apart from the educational system, there are also twenty-six research institutes designed for carrying out large-scale advanced research. There have been problems of transfer when projects finish; but researchers find it advantageous to return to their individual fields, and the transfers do spread a spirit of interdisciplinarity throughout the entire university. By the mid-1980s research projects had been completed in the areas of national physical fitness, nuclear and solid state research, exercise prescription, Latin America, tropical agricultural resources, aging, and instinct.

At Tsukuba the term interdisciplinarity is often used for a somewhat heterogeneous mass of concepts. Geoscience professor Tadashi Sato saw three different levels of interdisciplinarity operating at Tsukuba: cooperation among highly advanced specialists who may work independently but come to see close relations at a basic level; the learning of neighboring disciplines in order to solve individual problems; and multidisciplinary courses that are already in some respect disciplinary. Tsukuba is hardly unique in lacking a single definition of interdisciplinarity. What makes the story of the interdisciplinary universities so important is the "proving" of the concept through experience. There was no agreement on what interdisciplinarity meant when they were founded, and, though there is still no single definition even today, it is clear that students, teachers, and researchers have learned a great deal about what is and is not possible. That lesson has been particularly apparent in the shifting attitudes towards disciplinarity at Green Bay and in the history of the University of Tromso, the northernmost university in the world and the most recent university in Norway.

At Tromso interdisciplinarity has been conceived primarily in terms of the problems of society,[18] though there are differences of definition. For some the term has implied the cooperation or representation of different disciplines in a "multidisciplinary" project. For others it has meant creating a new subject by merging common features of various related disciplines.

Interdisciplinarity is promoted in several ways: by research groups dealing with related topics, integrative degree courses, common teaching programs, and cooperation between particular institutes. In a 1981 assessment of the university, Karen Nossum Bie concluded that disciplinary fences had been kept lowest in medicine, social sciences, and fisheries. Those areas were designed to provide education that would qualify students to work in a number of fields rather than in one specialized area.

In *medicine,* teaching is organized along the "organ model," illuminating different medical phenomena and problems while incorporating sociological perspectives and providing courses for a higher degree in biochemistry and physiology. There are further breaks with tradition in the integration of preclinical and clinical parts of the course as well as the integration of theory and practical service. In *fisheries,* traditionally a specialized program in Norway, a "multidisciplinary" course of study unites separate areas from the biological sciences, chemistry, social sciences, and economics within two main areas of study, biological subjects and economic sociology. The bridge is technology. The fisheries institute also offers higher-degree courses to students from the institutes of social sciences and the pure and applied sciences. In the *social sciences,* a first-year course attempts to integrate various aspects of the individual social science disciplines into a common unit. During the second year, different research groups provide most of the teaching, emphasizing ongoing research at the institute and problems related to interdisciplinary research. Except for the separate units of history and philosophy, the social sciences are organized into research groups intended to cross boundaries.

Because cooperation across institute boundaries has proved more difficult than envisioned in the original design of the university, research groups have had a tendency to develop into more purely disciplinary units. One group, concerned with educational problems, consisted solely of educationists. A second group, working on ethnic questions, consisted primarily of anthropologists; and a third group, concerned with social policy, was oriented primarily towards sociology. In contrast, a fourth group working on planning and local society had a "multidisciplinary" composition, and there was a "multidisciplinary" group working on social policy. Yet even in the fourth group, the need to defend and promote the objectives of one's own discipline led psychologists to introduce a separate course in psychology, partly in frustration over lack of a disciplinary milieu and their inability to influence the orientation of the group to which they belonged, a group that moved in a sociological direction.

There also have been difficulties in constructing a common curriculum. Research groups took over more of the teaching than originally intended, at the expense of a common integrative curriculum. Some staff members also found individual disciplines a more fruitful starting point than interdisciplinarity. Although students in the social sciences did seem to have a wider orientation than their counterparts at other universities, some graduates claim they were forced to define themselves in disciplinary terms at the thesis stage. Even in the more cooperative areas of medicine and fisheries, where definition of disciplinary alliance was not required, staff remained on the whole "safety anchored" in their own disciplines. Thus interdisciplinary curricula at Tromso have been more prosperous *within* institute boundaries than *across* them, a trend observed in other interdisciplinary institutions.

Changes have also been made to accommodate "real world pressures." Because students transferring from Tromso to other universities had trouble gaining recognition of their integrative studies, the fourth and originally interdisciplinary year of study was replaced by another one-year subject that could be chosen from a list of reorganized subjects, bringing students' programs more in line with requirements elsewhere. Now students are able to move between the different institutes more readily than before and are better suited to compete for teaching jobs in the school system, an important need in the labor market of northern Norway. Some of these problems are considered "birth pains" that should ease with time. Others will not. The original hopes and goals, Bie concluded, were products of a particular time, a time of student revolt and support for reforms. At Tromso, as elsewhere, it is clear that staff members are not part of a single university community but also members of a broader national and international community with disciplinary standards on teaching and research.

Interdisciplinary Liberal Studies in the United States

Interdisciplinary liberal studies[19] span the entire curriculum, from foundation programs and core curricula, to integrative minors[20] and majors, graduate programs, and faculty seminars. Although no program is identical with another, they do share a number of common characteristics; and the trends apparent in four-year degree programs are often echoed on a smaller scale within core curricula, clustered courses, and even single courses.

The curriculum in most interdisciplinary degree programs is centered on issues of national experience, major ideas in Western culture, important social topics, and scientific issues that are regarded as socially and intellectually important. The courses themselves are usually organized around a particular subject: a theme, problem, topic, issue, region, cultural period, institution, figure, idea, or in some cases a given field of study. The usual procedure is to organize them around three clusters of disciplines: the social sciences, natural sciences, and humanities. In general, there are two types of courses:

- courses promoting breadth through exposure to a wide spectrum of knowledge, usually in essential surveys of "the best of" great ideas, books, or thinkers;
- courses examining disciplinary and interdisciplinary methods, concepts, and theories, either within different modes of inquiry or applied to particular problems and issues.

Although there is no hard and fast line between the two, the dominant pattern is to emphasize *addition* at the lower levels and *synthesis* at the upper level. Arguments for humanistic learning and the liberal arts are often justified on the grounds of enlarging a student's existing knowledge. Arguments for associating and synthesizing are aimed at what Charles Fethe calls "appreciating and binding together" the disparate elements of intellectual experience.[21] *Western civilization* and *humanities* have tended to be the mainstay of lower-level curricula, where "multidisciplinary" surveys of Western cultural history are often structured as a cross-departmental program organized around themes, periods, and styles. Sometimes regional studies are an added element, though cross-cultural studies are still the exception.

The opportunity to work on individualized projects is a common feature of many interdisciplinary programs, whether it is a shorter-term program guided by an adviser or group of advisers, such as the Independent Human Studies program at Schoolcraft College (Michigan), or a project integrated into a four-year program. The Paracollege at St. Olaf College (Minnesota)[22] was designed to offer individualized, integrative study in a program of seminars, academic tutorials, and a senior colloquium. Students work with tutor-advisers to plan their academic study, which culminates in a research or creative project that may parallel traditional majors or be original interdisciplinary work. The most unique feature of the Paracollege is the tutorial, modeled on the British system and based on topics issued by Paracollege tutors. Tutorials may be coupled with regular classes at St. Olaf and special Paracollege seminars and workshops.

The Paracollege example demonstrates how many interdisciplinary degree programs are integrated into the life of their parent institutions and, in fact, may serve several functions within those institutions. Paracollege students live with students from the general college, take general college classes, and must satisfy the same general proficiencies as other students. General college students, in turn, can take several seminars and workshops in the Paracollege or just transfer in for a one-semester Paraloop. Students wanting to transfer out of the program can receive a "translation" of Paracollege work into general college requirements. The Hutchins School of Liberal Studies at Sonoma State University (California), which was started in 1969 as a "cluster school"[23] response to pressures for change, serves as an alternative general-education program for lower-division students, a formal minor in integrative studies, and an integrative B.A. major in liberal studies. Likewise, The School of Interdisciplinary Studies at Miami University (Ohio),[24] known as Western College, is integrated into the larger university in the sense that students take a substantial part of their upper-level work outside the program itself, along with special Western College seminars and a senior project.

Like the interdisciplinary universities, undergraduate degree programs have also undergone changes since their founding. When the Paracollege was founded in 1969, students were attracted to it as an experimental college that could provide a more "relevant," "involving" education. A small number of faculty at St. Olaf also saw the Paracollege as a vehicle for constructive change. The largest and most articulate group of them supported integration in the Christian liberal arts tradition. Due in part to the demands of the program and in part to control of assignments by regular college departments, enrollment began declining after the first half-dozen years. With few exceptions, Paracollege faculty were new or marginal members of other departments assigned to the Paracollege for only a fraction of their loads. Their professional futures lay in their own departments, creating the problem of split loyalties experienced even by programs with resident faculties and some control over promotion and tenure decisions. Over time the Paracollege has been "drifting away" from its original distinctive character towards a more traditional format, a move that was partially responsible for halting the enrollment drain. The original general education examinations are still on the books but are no longer required and rarely given. In the 1980s Paracollege faculty have been putting a lot of effort into seminars that resemble courses. Even so, the seminars still differ from conventional classes, though they now reflect what George Helling calls more of a "difference in degree" than a "difference in kind."

In many of these programs, there is also an increasing effort to help students balance specialization and integration. This reflects not only "market" pressures but also the same deepened appreciation of the role of disciplinarity reflected in the history of the interdisciplinary universities. Students at Miami University's Western College plan their academic work in a "Statement of Educational Objectives" (SEO) and, upon graduation, have a brief description of their individualized concentrations included on their transcripts. Students enrolled in New College at the University of Alabama develop a "depth study" of their own design within the context of a problem-focused curriculum that includes interdisciplinary seminars in the humanities, social sciences, and natural sciences. The "depth-study" involves drawing up a learning contract and an area of concentration that may or may not resemble a traditional major.[25] At Mt. Ida Senior College (Massachusetts), students blend general and specialized education by not only balancing the amount of hours spent in those areas but also synthesizing their experiences in senior seminars and a senior project.[26]

Ultimately it is synthesis that distinguishes "disciplinary" and "multidisciplinary" education from "interdisciplinary" education. Synthesis is achieved in a variety of ways, though the most common methods are core seminars, individualized study, workshops, colloquia, projects, and theses. In some schools special courses have been developed for the purpose of synthesizing knowledge in not only interdisciplinary degree programs but also the general curriculum. The College of Liberal Arts at Willamette University (Oregon) has offered courses such as "Integration and Use of Knowledge," and University of Maryland faculty developed two upper-level integrative courses that use any appropriate subject matter to introduce students to the epistemological bases, modes of discourse, standards of truth, and value assumptions of academic disciplines. Faculty in the University Studies/Weekend College Program at Wayne State University devised a suite of upper-level courses on the nature of knowledge that are taken in conjunction with either a yearlong senior seminar or senior essay/project. One of the most intriguing institution-wide approaches is the Tier II Synthesis. Developed for all Ohio University (Athens) seniors, it is the final integrative stage in a comprehensive general education program. It stresses the development of a capacity for synthesis, defined as bringing together two or more disciplines to yield patterns or corresponding ideas. Even though many faculty believe students are not intellectually equipped for interdisciplinary study until they have completed basic and even intermediate studies, there is, in fact, a strong argument for synthesis at lower levels. The Inquiry Program at the University of Massachusetts (Amherst) is a two-year alternative to a portion of traditional general education requirements. It begins with an "Inquiry into Education" seminar, continues with three "Modes of Inquiry" seminars (one each in the natural sciences, social sciences, and humanities and arts), and ends with an "Integrative Seminar." Classwork is supported by individual tutorial sessions, and students maintain portfolios that include contracts and documents for each semester.

In all of these programs, one question inevitably arises: what can students do with an interdisciplinary degree? Graduates of the Hutchins School have gone on to advanced study in a variety of fields, including law, theology, art, play writing, anthropology, American studies, social work, psychology, communication, education, and library sciences. A number of them are also teaching and working in such areas as ranching, management, printing, film editing, and television. Although students often worry about having a harder time getting into graduate or professional school or a job of choice, their track record is generally quite good. In a recent class of 48 Paracollege graduates, 25 percent went on to graduate and professional school, 8 percent became teachers, and 34 percent went into business and industry.[27] Graduates of the Paracollege have also gone on to law and medicine, the other social and helping professions, editing and printing, teaching, research, insurance, and the Peace Corps. Of the 1980 graduating class at Western College, 30 percent entered graduate school, 9 percent law school, 6 percent medical school, and 30 percent found jobs in social services, business, government, and education. An additional 25 percent took temporary jobs with plans to go to school later on.[28] Other interdisciplinary degree programs report similar patterns of career and graduate placement.

Within shorter-term programs such as core and clustered curricula, interdisciplinarity often serves as an alternative to general education programs that merely shuffle the standard distribution requirements. Integrated core curricula vary in length from a single first-year course to a cluster of courses to a sequence extending across all four years of the undergraduate experience. At Alaska Pacific University, where interdisciplinarity is regarded as "the cornerstone of the very philosophy of the institution," the four-year core is structured around the four basic environments of life: the natural environment (for freshmen), the social environment (sophomores), the individual environment (juniors), and the spiritual environment (seniors). At Shimer College (Illinois),[29] a four-year liberal arts college based on small classes and a "great books" curriculum modeled on the University of Chicago, students move from "associative generalizations" at the basic level to a more rigorous study of interrelationships among the modes and methods of inquiry in various disciplines and, ultimately, synthesis. Each course is team-taught to facilitate an interrelated view of the political, social, economic, artistic, scientific, and ideological aspects of an age. At St. Joseph's College (Indiana),[30] students move from centering on the self to Western, then global and cosmic civilization. Each semester of the core curriculum evolves out of a "consensus statement" among the faculty assigned to a part of the core, though there are five dominant themes running through the entire ten-course sequence: self-knowledge, history, science, cross-cultural studies, and synthesis. In the final seminar, students are asked to move from a purely theoretical perspective to considering the policy-making activities. Thus synthesis occurs at both the theoretical level of principles and the practical level of values. The ultimate goal at St. Joseph's is a personal synthesis of what it means to be a human and a Christian in this world.

Clustered courses have also played an important role in attempts to combat fragmentation in community and junior college curricula,[31] especially in the social sciences and humanities.[32] Lacking the kind of "house" structure available at Roskilde or the communal living experience available at Western College, where students not only move through the curriculum together but can live in the same building that houses classes, many colleges use clustered courses to provide a sense of *community,* an "esprit de corps" that may be the only common experience at the undergraduate level. Los Medanos College (California)[33] offers a three-tiered general education program featuring interdisciplinary courses focused on social and humanistic issues. The first tier is more encyclopedic in nature, whereas the remaining tiers focus on integrating concepts and establishing the process of ethical decision-making.[34]

The same sense of commonality is also fostered in four-year colleges and universities. At Ohio Dominican College, the freshman core in liberal studies provides a common foundation spanning twenty centuries in two semesters, taught by core faculty drawn from a variety of disciplines.[35] The University of Southern California's freshman-level "Thematic Option" in general education offers a common experience in team-taught courses,[36] and the Colloquium Program at Dominican College (Califiornia) is an alternative to a traditional humanities program.[37] A colloquium is a cluster of courses integrated through a seminar and set of intellectual problems common to the courses, which are based on either disciplines or historical figures. Because the readings and discussions are shared by an entire class of students, the program generates a cross-campus "reference base" of ideas and basic concepts. It also promotes dialogue between faculty in different disciplines, liberally educating the faculty by exposing them to seminal literature and significant films.[38] The same kind of common discourse has been fostered by the "great books" curricula at St. John's (Maryland), Shimer College, the University of Chicago, and other institutions imitating the Chicago model. It can also occur within individual courses. Ault and Rutman, for instance, noted increased faculty interaction when using economics as a problem-solving tool in an undergraduate business course.[39]

There are intriguing parallels between the Dominican Colloquium and one of the most imaginative approaches to integration in general education, the Federated Learning Communities (FLC) at the State University of New York, Stony Brook. Existing courses are "federated" around a particular theme and then coordinated with the university's distribution requirements, allowing students who discontinue the program to retain credit. In addition, the FLC programs are frequently coordinated with departmental programs, so that students can build up credit for their majors.[40] Like the faculty at Dominican, Stony Brook faculty chose to federate already existing courses, to build a new academic community on routine activities rather than risking the isolation and marginalization that can plague autonomous programs. To ensure integration, the FLCs rely on core "Program Seminars" focused on the relationship between separate disciplines and the central theme. The seminars are taught by special teaching professionals who are conceived as interpreters, mediators, community builders, role models, and a valuable source of feedback for teachers.

A number of schools imitate the Federated Learning Community model, and a variety of similar devices have been used by other programs. The program of Integrated Studies in the Humanities at the University of Missouri–Kansas City clusters courses from different departments around a common topic. In each cluster students explore how different disciplines complement, and contrast with, each other. California Lutheran College has also experimented with a device called the "loop sequence." Each loop consists of a sequence of two traditional courses and a third bridging course. All instructors and students enrolled in the two regular courses are involved in the bridge course. Faculty have developed several loop sequences, including a thematic sequence on peace and justice, which includes English, religion, and sociology, and a major sequence involving macroeconomics, international business, and English.[41]

An additional word should be said about graduate study. Interdisciplinarity is not a prominent part of graduate education, dominated as it is by training for specialists. Nevertheless, interdisciplinary graduate study is available in a variety of areas. Some of them, in fact, are quite well known, including programs in the humanities (at Florida State University and Pennsylvania State University), American studies (the Universities of Minnesota and Michigan), the history of consciousness (the University of California, Santa Cruz), liberal studies (Georgetown University), and in a variety of areas based on ongoing faculty research (the University of Chicago and Columbia University). A number of universities also have special institutes for interdisciplinary study, and instruction takes place within professional schools and problem-focused research centers. Finally, there are individualized interdisciplinary programs in a number of universities, though many have more of a "paper" life than an actual existence. In general practice interdisciplinary graduate programs tend to be more "multidisciplinary" than "interdisciplinary," and students are usually expected to demonstrate competence in designated subjects, especially at the Ph.D. level. There is also a tendency to rely on existing disciplinary courses and "voluntary" programs that depend on student initiation.[42]

One of the more prominent areas of interdisciplinary graduate study has been that of liberal studies. Graduate liberal studies began over thirty years ago with a summer program at Wesleyan University in Middletown, Connecticut; it was designed to complement and enhance liberal arts education for teachers. The most common means of achieving an "interdisciplinary" synthesis is the core seminar, and many such seminars have been added to what were technically "multidisciplinary" programs. The arts faculties at Texas Tech University, for example, strengthened their masters program by adding one new course in each of the participating arts and an interdisciplinary seminar on timely issues in the arts.[43] At Arizona State University, the Master of Arts in the Humanities, an individualized, integrated study in two or more departments, was revised in the early 1980s to include newly developed seminars on integrative methodology and a course called "Cultural Synthesis." This course, along with two other courses on aesthetics and the Renaissance, came to constitute the core of the newly structured Master of Arts in the Humanities.[44] At The University of Texas, Dallas, faculty in the master of arts program turned to two topic-based seminars that vary from semester to semester. In addition to taking disciplinary courses, students are also introduced to the methods, terminology, and purposes of several disciplines and learn to look at topics from several disciplinary perspectives.

The program at Dallas also culminates in a capstone seminar. Originally a thesis or project was required, but students often ended up lacking the background to complete a thesis, a common problem in interdisciplinary graduate programs. Thesis advisers may demand more thorough specialization than a student possesses, a project may be too superficial, or faculty members may simply be unwilling to work on interdisciplinary projects with students lacking traditional expertise. The capstone seminar attempts to solve that problem by requiring students to do a lengthy research paper on an interdisciplinary topic, using the methodologies and materials of more than one discipline and demonstrating their interrelationship. Before selecting their topics, students must read a number of articles on interdisciplinarity and attempt to synthesize the knowledge they have gained over thirty hours of graduate course work. Echoing many of their undergraduate counterparts, seminar organizers contend that a discussion of interdisciplinary theory is more appropriate at the end of the program, when students can reflect on what they have studied and the connections among different kinds of knowledge.[45]

These are not unusual examples. Most graduate programs in liberal studies rely on one or more required or "core" courses that are interdisciplinary in nature. At Johns Hopkins and the New School for Social Research (New York), the core is a seminar series based on the history of ideas. The University of Southern California uses a sequence of specifically designed courses, the University of Maine at Orono relies on core seminars, and Kean College (New Jersey) employs both introductory and advanced interdisciplinary seminars. At Loyola College (Baltimore), the core is centered on three themes, with one course required in each theme; and at Boston's Metropolitan College, the core consists of six required interdisciplinary seminars exploring the humanities and the natural and social sciences. At Johns Hopkins and the New School for Social Research, the core is a set of seminars on the history of ideas. The Master of Arts in Liberal Studies at Georgetown University relies on all three integrative devices: theme-based courses, a culminating essay, and a culminating seminar.

In several additional cases, the basis for interdisciplinary study at the graduate level has been ongoing faculty research. The University of Chicago, an institution long devoted to fostering interdisciplinary discourse,[46] began offering graduate research workshops in the 1980s. Of varying organization and requirements, these workshops are offered by small groups of faculty from one or more related disciplines. They enable faculty to share their interests with both students and other faculty.[47] During the 1985–86 academic year, workshops were offered in areas ranging from area, religious, and cultural studies, to issues in education, literature, social history, and the sciences. Like the University of Chicago, Columbia University has also had a long-standing institutional commitment to interdisciplinarity. Through a rich series of programs, it has fostered general and interdisciplinary education at the graduate and professional levels. These programs are not simply preliminary steps towards monodisciplinary competence but substantial, problem-focused investigations of value questions and human options implicit in various fields, with historical and cross-cultural reflections on contemporary problems. In this respect they offer liberal education for faculty and students alike. They have included, in the past, seminars on professional issues, programs, and conferences in a variety of academic areas, plus seminars on the role of the humanities. The Columbia program is a good model for other universities, since it does not require fundamental changes in the organizational structure of the institution and has worked well within existing structures.[48]

The Interdisciplinary Graduate Program in the Humanities at Penn State (IGPH) provides an additional example of faculty development in conjunction with an academic program. The IGPH evolved in 1970 when a group of faculty were exploring the possibilities for interdisciplinary discourse in the humanities and social sciences.[49] Their goal was not to create a new field but to help students and scholars become "better disciplinarians."[50] Thus, interdisciplinarity at IGPH, as at Roskilde, is not pursued as an end in itself but as a means of facilitating problem-oriented research and discourse. This program has also changed since its origin. Since the early eighties, the emphasis has shifted from courses to interdisciplinary seminars for faculty and graduate students, focused on the humanities and social sciences. Each year three to five seminars are offered, and in 1988 there were thirty students engaged in interdisciplinary research.[51]

In a 1979 evaluation of the IGPH program, Flexner and Hauser drew several conclusions that can be extended to other programs. Although there were few interdisciplinary courses at the graduate level prior to the inception of IGPH, by 1979 there were fifty new courses, and a number of them have been incorporated into permanent university offerings. Prior to IGPH, only one department required a minor of its Ph.D. candidates. Now, however, there are strong minor requirements in a majority of departments in the college. There is also evidence that interdisciplinary discourse at the university, once confined primarily to the undergraduate level, has expanded. Prior to the inception of the program, people interested in graduate-level "transdisciplinary discourse" tended to gravitate to programs such as American Studies, Latin American Studies, or Medieval Studies. At the urging of IGPH, some of these undergraduate options began petitioning for graduate status. There has also been a visible increase in the number of students requesting special committees to serve as ad hoc departments for guiding their graduate work. Ultimately one of the most important results of the program has been a change in the way that students are exposed to subjects in regular programs, as IGPH courses have been internalized into those departments. These kinds of changes, even when they do not result in a major restructuring of departments at a given university, do have a genuine impact on the nature of interdisciplinary discourse at the university.

Interdisciplinary Concentrations

It is possible to pursue interdisciplinary concentrations or majors in a wide variety of fields, including cybernetic systems, human services, international studies, communications, psychobiology, humanities, urban studies, multicultural education, regional and ethnic studies, border studies, environmental studies, human ecology, human development, and a variety of career and professional interests. There is no sharp dividing line between liberal education and interdisciplinary concentrations because the interdisciplinary approach is often a way of making training more "liberal" in both scope and substance. Before looking closely at several individual programs, it would be useful to take a brief look at three typical areas: women's studies, American studies, and science, technology, and society.

In all three cases, there is no single definition of interdisciplinarity or single format. Concentrations may be housed under an umbrella organization, stand as independent units, or operate as minor or major programs of study within a single department or group of departments. Also, like the lower-level curricula of many interdisciplinary degree programs, interdisciplinary concentrations often serve a variety of purposes. The University of Alabama's program in women's studies, for instance, may be used for electives, partial fulfillment of humanities requirements, an undergraduate minor or major, an undergraduate concentration with a major in American studies, an undergraduate depth study, or as credit for continuing education units. Interdisciplinary concentrations also introduce students to different departments and may utilize several kinds of courses. At the University of Oklahoma, introductory courses in women's studies constitute a "sample"; other courses in the program formally bridge two disciplines (such as psychology and sociology of the family), and the senior seminar is an overtly integrative experience. In most programs definitions of interdisciplinarity are intrinsically linked with feminist philosophy. Hence they often incorporate a critique of the disciplines for their exclusion of women, and their claims of universality. The program at West Virginia University reflects a widely held belief that women's studies is interdisciplinary because feminist scholarship demands a careful revision of received knowledge in every discipline.

There are also similarities and differences in American studies programs. At Bowling Green State University (Ohio), the American studies major is a college and department-wide program. At Brandeis University (Massachusetts), it is a department that functions as an integrative catalyst, drawing on data from more than one discipline and approaching broad questions about periods, regions, themes, or institutions. At California State University at Fullerton, the Department of American Studies is housed within the School of Humanities and Social Sciences. In addition to teaching American studies, the faculty also teach general education. Programs at the University of Iowa, the University of Michigan, and the University of California, Davis are based on the interdisciplinary study of culture. The program at Iowa State University originally emphasized history, literature, art, and ideas, but, like American studies itself, the program has moved towards social science, popular culture, and attention to ethnic, regional, and other subcultures. Although some of these programs borrow faculty from other departments, well-established programs have their own core faculty and a full roster of degrees.

One of the growing areas is that of science, technology, and society. Here too programs serve a variety of goals: providing general education, extending liberal education into the realm of science, and offering a new interdisciplinary field centered on values and problem solving. The faculty at Worcester Polytechnic Institute (Massachusetts) revised their traditional curriculum to demonstrate, in part, that science education is a critical part of liberal education. The Science, Technology, and Society Program at Clark University (Massachusetts), which offers degrees in environmental affairs as well as technology assessment and risk analysis, is oriented towards problem-solving and aligned with ongoing research. At Northwestern University (Illinois), the Integrated Science Program is an undergraduate degree program that stresses principles common to the natural sciences and mathematics. Penn State's Science, Technology, and Society Program is an integrative general education minor that arose in response to student protests against the social irrelevance of higher education and the faculty's determination to achieve a unified worldview. Stanford University's Values, Technology, and Society Program provides an undergraduate major and an A.B. or B.S with honors. It combines scientific and technical studies with the study of cultural and social context while serving as a forum for interdisciplinary exchange among faculty.

A variety of other courses also center on science-related issues and topics. They include more specialized courses, such as a course on the frontiers between theoretical physics and biology (developed in 1974 in the physics department at the University of Toronto),[52] and "Physics, History, and Society," a course centered on the implicit assumptions underlying history and physics (developed at Iowa State University).[53] There are also broader programs, including Portland State University's (Oregon) six-term "Science and Humanities" sequence on interrelationships over six historical periods and, perhaps the best known program, the NEH-supported NEXA Science-Humanities convergence at San Francisco State University. In the early 1970s, a small curriculum of interdisciplinary courses was designed to focus on three figures: Newton, Darwin, and Einstein. Eventually the curriculum was expanded to include courses that combined the history of ideas and the history of science. An alternative to conventional general education courses, the NEXA program emphasizes both the distinctiveness and interrelationships of disciplines across the natural and social sciences as well as arts and humanities. The program also gave birth to a faculty seminar and a series of public events that appeared under the generic title of the California Symposium on Science and Human Values.[54]

A number of additional degree programs illustrate in greater detail the actual structure of interdisciplinary concentrations: the Program in Social Ecology at the University of California, Irvine, the Human Development and Social Relations Program at Earlham College (Indiana), the Department of Human Development at California State University at Hayward, the Honors Mathematical Models in the Social Sciences Program at Northwestern University (Illinois), and the TEMA Ph.D. program at the University of Linköping (Sweden).

The Program in Social Ecology at the University of California, Irvine, started in 1970, offers integrative study of a wide range of recurring social and environmental problems.[55] The program is based on social ecology, a growing multidisciplinary field centered on the concept of the human being as a biological organism in a cultural-physical environment. The faculty at Irvine emphasize direct interaction between the intellectual life of the university and recurring problems of social and physical environments. They make use of community lecturers, and a number of them are involved in interventions aimed at improving the way individuals, institutions, and communities function. As a result, field study is an important part of the upper-division requirements. "It is axiomatic in the Program," Arnold

Binder explains, "that learning must be applicable to the community and the community must serve as an auxiliary source of educational enrichment."[56]

The undergraduate curriculum is organized around four components: a principles and methods cluster and three problem-based subareas focused on environmental analysis, criminal justice, and social behavior. At the graduate level, the emphasis is on theory and research that hold implications for policy and social action. The approach is primarily empirical, and, similar to the TEMA Ph.D. program at Linköping, collaborative research with faculty members is an important aspect of the program. Students in the undergraduate program do not major in a particular subarea; rather, they develop a degree of competence in each of them. An applied ecology major, for example, receives the same basic science training that a biological science major does and then uses that training in environmentally based courses within the Social Ecology Program. During the final year, students can specialize in areas of their choice. "Specialization" tracks are a recent innovation, comparable to changes made in the social science institute at the University of Tromso. The specialization tracks give students more recognizable backgrounds for graduate school and employment by combining courses in ways that fit more traditional labels. Similar to Western College, the area of specialization is also noted on a student's transcript. Students may choose from psychology and social behavior; criminology, criminal justice, and legal studies; and environmental health and planning. Even with specialization tracks, however, there is still an ecological, problem-based orientation to a large problem-focused field.

Like the program at Irvine, the Human Development and Social Relations Program (HDSR) at Earlham uses field study and discussions of the relationship between theory and application.[57] In the HDSR interdisciplinary study, human values, career choice, and career preparation are intrinsically linked, and "interdisciplinary" study means not only integrating more than one disciplinary perspective but also raising value questions and epistemological issues.[58] Faculty from sociology/anthropology, psychology, philosophy, and education cooperate in offering the program as individuals and as teams. The heart of the program is a core sequence that begins with a two-term sequence in psychology and social anthropology. This sequence introduces students to the idea of an academic department, major theoretical paradigms, methodological strategies, and bodies of empirical data in disciplines related to particular problem areas. Students also take workshops to help build personal skills and consider ideal models of human development and sociocultural systems in preparation for examining the actual state of persons and systems.

In the upper-class major, students take at least two advanced seminars in either psychology or sociology/anthropology in order to deepen their understanding of a discipline or content area and to align their choices with individual interests, career goals, or plans for graduate study. Although ethical and value questions are discussed throughout the curriculum, they constitute the central focus of a team-taught course called "Social Science and Human Values," where students can relate classroom and field experiences to future career problems and issues.[59] The program culminates in a senior seminar that also provides an integrative opportunity to bridge academic study and career objectives. After completing core courses, students take a term of supervised field study in Earlham's off-campus programs (such as the Philadelphia Urban Studies Program or the SICE Japan Program) or in a variety of other settings in the community. Though field studies are tailored to individual interests, they also emphasize human development, institutional structures, and cultural forces. Other schools have also taken integrative approaches to field experience. The Interdisciplinary Studies Program at Bennett College (North Carolina), for example, uses not only fieldwork and externships in the local community but also group work, simulations, projects, and a unique workshop, "Synergistic Strategies," emphasizing intellectual skills and interrelations in both contemporary and historical knowledge.

Bridging theory and practice is also a major concern in the Department of Human Development at California State University, Hayward. The program, designed and implemented in 1970, brings a diversity of disciplinary perspectives to the study of human development through concentration on questions of personality, social organization, and epistemology.[60] Interdisciplinarity is conceived primarily as an educational tool for studying human development. Through the juxtaposition of conflicting materials—for example, behavioral/phenomenological approaches—students break down their naïve vision of the whole into contradictory components seen from different disciplines. Then they begin restructuring their own epistemologies with the help of fellow students and faculty.[61]

Although the program is complex, it has five essential components: (1) an *initial meeting,* where students identify their educational needs and possibilities of meeting them within the program; (2) *lower-division courses,* which prepare students for a core sequence and specialty area; (3) *junior-level core,* which consists of a series of twelve complementary and contrasting modular courses representing different approaches to human development; (4) faculty-monitored *small-group meetings,* where students evaluate their participation and the program as a whole, supported by *faculty symposia,* which help them clarify relevant issues from different perspectives; and (5) a *senior thesis* and *senior project,* including a seminar for the study of self-development and group projects for small groups of students working on an issue of human development. One of the most intensive components of the program is at step 4, the double course sequence taken with, or sometimes after, the modular series. Each small group identifies the developmental objectives of its members and then supplements group work with symposia centered on case studies. The groups generally move from a more-structured toward a less-structured method, crossing academic, professional, personal, and intellectual lines.

The Honors Mathematical Models in the Social Sciences Program at Northwestern University is quite different from the three previous examples. The program, a unique interdisciplinary concentration developed in the 1970s under a grant from the National Science Foundation, addresses a clear need for mathematical, statistical, and computer skills in the social sciences. It is limited to a small number of students who have high mathematical aptitude and a strong interest in social problems and issues. Students can earn a double major by completing the Mathematical Models Program and a departmental major in one of the social science disciplines. During their first two years, students take coordinated sequences of courses in the social sciences and mathematics. The social science core emphasizes individual and group behavior, social structures and processes, and policy analysis. This study is related to the mathematics sequence as students encounter methods of optimization, stochastics, decision theory, game theory, dynamics, and statistics. Integration is promoted by both the alignment of courses and an empirical-theoretical orientation that stresses the historical context in which various models and methods have developed. Faculty believe the "symbiotic dependence" generated by simultaneous teaching of the social sciences and mathematics offers a unique approach to teaching mathematics. In senior seminar students may conduct research and write a paper on either a discipline-oriented or an interdisciplinary topic. In doing so they can take advantage of campus centers for urban affairs, transportation, mathematical studies in economics and management science, and statistics and probability. They are also encouraged to use their 10–12 elective courses to round out their education in the liberal arts tradition. Finally, there is also a biweekly noncredit colloquium for students, faculty, and visitors interested in the exchange of ideas on major topics in the social sciences.

Once again the question of what students can do with their degrees arises. Graduates of Northwestern's program in mathematics and the social sciences find their preparation useful for graduate study in social and managerial sciences as well as private- and public-sector careers requiring both quantitative skills and a social science background that equips them to deal with modeling, planning, and policy analysis of economic, social, demographic, and political issues. The combination of analytic and social science training also makes them strong candidates for legal and management studies. Graduates of the program at Hayward have gone on to a variety of fields, including health, education, and welfare, in addition to personnel work, business, and research.

There is a strong orientation towards service among graduates of Earlham's Human Development and Social Relations Program, exemplifying the school's Quaker roots. Graduates are working in not only the traditional helping professions, such as counseling and social work, but also community relations, early childhood education, industrial personnel work, medicine and health services, the ministry, and international agencies. Some of them have also gone into the fields of television and business management. At Irvine the undergraduate program in social ecology is aimed at three kinds of students: those going into various governmental agencies and industrial departments; those going on to professional specialization (administration, law, public health, social welfare, psychology, sociology, criminology, and urban planning) or graduate study (e.g., psychology, sociology, and biology); and those wanting to become more effective and knowledgeable citizens, regardless of their major and ultimate career objectives. Some graduates have found their study useful for careers in management and personnel, and it also provides a good background for students seeking jobs in planning departments, mental health settings, educational institutions, and a variety of community and governmental agencies. Holders of the master's degree have assumed positions in governmental and private agencies, as well as areas of planning, mental health and welfare, and probation and parole. Holders of the Ph.D. have gone into teaching and research, as well as private and governmental agencies appropriate to their training.

The University of Linköping's Tema Ph.D. program, proposed in the late 1970s, is the result of a new organization of research[62] based on broad problem areas.[63] The program derives its name from the Swedish word for *theme* (*Tema*), and is based on work in four themes: (1) technology and social change, (2) water in environment and society, (3) health and society, and (4) communication. Students complete coursework designed, in part, to provide common knowledge relevant to a particular theme. By using two levels of generality—the four main themes and related subthemes or research programs—it has been possible to implement both long-term and short-term planning of research appropriate to each of the current four themes.

Although the program has its problems, among them its relative youth, it has produced some important lessons echoed in the experience of graduate liberal studies. The overall goal at Tema is to balance competence and integration. Being competent in a theme means being able to surmount narrow boundaries in an attempt to achieve integrative theories and explanations.[64] Yet, at the same time, there is strong commitment to assuming a disciplinary "burden of comprehension." Interdisciplinarity at Tema is manifested in the choice of problems. It is not practiced for its own sake but represents "solely the general ambition to achieve systematic and fundamental scientific co-operation."[65]

When asked what specific interdisciplinary methodologies have evolved at Linköping, most faculty replied that such methodologies are still evolving, though statistical methodology and advanced decision theoretic models play an important integrative role, and there are theoretical and methodological explorations of theme work. Students who were surveyed seemed to stick close to an individual adviser in a particular discipline and, in the words of recent evaluators of the program, do not seem to be "budding polymaths." Still, particularly in the Technology and Change Tema, there is a feeling that students should strive to become exemplars of "a new interdisciplinary breed," a goal that can best be accomplished, faculty felt, by dealing intelligently with broad problems while fulfilling minimum standards in disciplines represented in student theses. There is no governing interdisciplinary theory, and staff do not feel it necessary to go through the "transdisciplinary" phase and form new disciplines. Interdisciplinarity seems to have been achieved in a number of projects and seminars of the Communication Tema, though, in the other three themes, it was still considered an "emergent possibility" in the early 1980s. People were generally more comfortable characterizing themselves as "multidisciplinary."[66]

There is both pessimism and optimism about interdisciplinary education in the late 1980s. The flexibility and economic largess that sped innovation in the 1960s and 1970s have now faded. Moreover, then as now, interdisciplinary programs have been limited in three major ways: by the lack of a long-standing tradition for interdisciplinary education, by the power of disciplinary and departmental boundaries, and by the influence of conditions outside the university.[67] Reflecting on the OECD's 1984 international assessment of interdisciplinarity, Stanley Bailis found a "disquieting" tone to the institutional track record of IDS. The evidence is widespread: the dismantling of one of the Australian experiments, the pull of disciplinary career patterns, modifications along departmental and subject lines, and the gradual reduction of institutional commitments to interdisciplinarity. The experiments of the 1960s and early 1970s have not supplanted the disciplines, and their "instrumental" orientation has directed attention from the broader "synoptic" concerns of interdisciplinary work.[68]

At the same time, in compiling a 1986 directory of undergraduate interdisciplinary programs in the United States, William H. Newell found evidence of a widely touted renaissance of IDS. Newell found that undergraduate interdisciplinary programs are not only numerous but span all four years of the curriculum and forty-nine of the fifty states. While good programs do exist at prestigious institutions such as Brown, Kenyon, M.I.T., Stanford, and Vassar, most of the programs today are in state universities and community colleges. Moreover, the majority of the 235 programs included in Newell's directory are of relatively recent vintage, and they are dominated by general education reform, followed by humanities and honors programs. Consequently, the interdisciplinary renaissance in the United States is linked strongly with the desire to revitalize the core of the liberal arts. Newell also found an independently rooted though equally strong representation in women's studies programs.

The chronological trends are particularly revealing. Over 80 percent of the interdisciplinary general education programs included in the directory were started after 1971, and the pace is accelerating. Interdisciplinary programs in the humanities and fine arts tend to spread out more evenly across the decades, reaching back to the 1950s and even earlier. Interdisciplinary honors have survived in comparable numbers from the 1960s and 1970s, though the pace has tripled in the 1980s. In all three areas — general education, humanities, and honors — the programs are spread across all levels of institutions, though church-related schools are more likely to start humanities programs than other types of interdisciplinary programs. In general, interdisciplinary undergraduate programs started before the 1960s have survived to the late 1980s primarily in larger institutions, particularly those with national draw and many graduate students. Programs started in the 1960s and early 1970s have been most likely to survive in state institutions. Programs started in the 1980s tend to come disproportionately from small, private institutions though not, as a general rule, from the most prestigious schools. Based on his findings, Newell concluded that IDS today tends to be more "renovative rather than radical," fostering not only coherence but also excellence in the form of higher-order intellectual skills of synthesis or integration.[69] Newell's findings parallel the observed pattern of revisions in interdisciplinary programs that are more than one decade old.

Reflecting on the experience of telic institutions, Martin Trow drew several relevant lessons. "Telic" institutions and programs have had a certain life cycle. Motivated by their commitment to a distinctive mission, their founding faculty were charged with the zeal of a "secular religion." Resources were often abundant, recruitment of staff and students selective, and problems handled communally. However, as time passed, so did the "euphoria of creation." Work became "increasingly exhausting" and "decreasingly exhilerating." Routines came to be viewed with hostility and, by the third and fourth years, the loss of extra resources, structural difficulties, internal conflicts, and pressure to move from *ad hoc* status to permanent budget lines were causing serious problems, tantamount to a "loss of Eden." The start-up years came to be viewed as the Golden Age in the mythology of such institutions. Trow concluded that programs of interdisciplinary study can be critics of the disciplines, because disciplines may not always be the best way of organizing study. However, they should not be their enemies. Many programs that abused their hosts, while claiming unique and almost "ethereal virtues," have failed.[70] Reflecting on the Australian experience, Don Anderson concluded that it is important to pay careful attention to individual career development patterns and to make sure programs are not in direct competition for funds with traditional departments. Anderson also found that projects can be sustained more readily when they are focused on concrete objectives, rather than general idealized mission statements.

Every interdisciplinary course, like every problem-focused research project and every attempt to deliver interdisciplinary care, begins anew, because each attempt at synthesis involves the specific characteristics and techniques of the fields being examined.[71] Nevertheless, in the last two decades, a rich and sizeable body of knowledge on how to teach and administer interdisciplinary programs has emerged. There are resources for every stage of IDS, from writing proposals, to designing, delivering, and evaluating programs. This information applies to not only new programs but also the modification of existing ones.[72] Unfortunately, that knowledge is woefully underused. The challenge in the remaining decade of the twentieth century is to make more systematic and productive use of the abundant resources that have emerged in the last two decades.

Conclusion:
The Integrative Core

A way of seeing is also a way of not seeing.

—Kenneth Burke

WHAT may be said, in a way of conclusion, about a concept that is so vast, so complex, and so various? There are two final questions to address. What are the characteristics of an interdisciplinary individual? And, what is the nature of the interdisciplinary process?

The Interdisciplinary Individual

Research on career patterns supports the widely held belief that senior faculty are the most likely and perhaps the best suited for interdisciplinary activities. They are the ones who can risk time out of the disciplinary mainstream, and they are the ones who often need new challenges.[1] With increasing numbers of over-tenured departments searching for career-development alternatives, this argument has even greater appeal today.[2] It is certainly true that many senior faculty have experienced the same "resurgence of energy" Patricia Spacks reported from a National Humanities Institute designed to stimulate integrative teaching and research.[3] Senior people, however, are not always the most likely or necessarily the best participants, despite the continuing lack of incentives and rewards for junior faculty. The University of Utah's integrative Liberal Education program originated in a belief that the broad experience and perspective of its senior faculty would make them the mainstay of the curriculum. Yet, in actuality, the courses are dominated by younger scholars who value the creative possibilities.[4] Even so, they are not alone. Faculty tend to come from all parts of the academic life cycle: as young assistant professors, associate professors, and full professors. Some of them even come to the program more than once.[5]

Certain character traits have also been associated with interdisciplinary

182

individuals, among them reliability, flexibility, patience, resilience, sensitivity to others, risk-taking, a thick skin, and a preference for diversity and new social roles. The tendency to follow problems across disciplinary boundaries is, in fact, seen as a normal characteristic of highly active researchers,[6] though Mario Bunge distinguishes "adventurers" from "adventurous scientific minds."[7] The ideal person for interdisciplinary work, Forrest Armstrong suggested, would probably be someone with a high degree of ego strength, a tolerance for ambiguity, considerable initiative and assertiveness, a broad education, and a sense of dissatisfaction with monodisciplinary constraints.[8]

Some scholars have linked these traits with specific behavioral types. Given the "ill-defined" nature of so many interdisciplinary problems, Irvin White suggested people who tend toward Taylor's category of *divergent thinkers* are probably more likely to find interdisciplinary research enjoyable than *convergent thinkers*.[9] Correspondingly, Margaret Mead suggested "analogic" thinkers may be more successful at handling integrative tasks than "digital" thinkers, who may be too narrow to deal with cross-cutting issues.[10] Swora and Morrison, in turn, believe the best-suited faculty are "academic intellectuals," the term Jencks and Reisman used for people interested in questions of personal and societal importance. Accountable to a wider audience, academic intellectuals may have experience with concepts and problems outside academe.[11]

Certain abilities have also been associated with interdisciplinary individuals: not only the general capacity to look at things from different perspectives but also the skills of differentiating, comparing, contrasting, relating, clarifying, reconciling, and synthesizing. Since interdisciplinarians are often put in new situations, they must also know how to learn. They need to know what information to ask for and how to acquire a working knowledge of the language, concepts, information, and analytical skills pertinent to a given problem, process, or phenomenon. We would know more about how individuals use these skills if there were more accounts of how interdisciplinarians actually work. Unfortunately there are very few accounts, and there is only one publication that deals directly with the issue of measuring individual participation on interdisciplinary teams.[12] There are three approaches that may be taken. The first is to consult the few explicit "interdisciplinary autobiographies" that do exist. The second is to look at autobiographies and biographies in general, including the Alfred P. Sloan Foundation series, which brought to light the working lives of such individuals as Freeman Dyson (*Disturbing the Universe*), Lewis Thomas (*The Youngest Science: Notes of a Medicine Watcher*), Salvador Luria (*A Slot Machine, A Broken Test Tube*), Peter Medawar (*Advice to a Young Scientist*), Hendrick Casimir (*Haphazard Reality: Half a Century of Science*), and Jerome Bruner (*In Search of Mind: Essays in Autobiography*).[13] The third way is to glean insights from the actual work of interdisciplinarians, even though such work is rarely self-reflective of methodology.

Though it is a rather slim genre, the interdisciplinary autobiographies and biographies that have been published demonstrate the value of compiling and studying narratives of actual interdisciplinary work. They temper abstract theory in the forge of experience, as the complex actuality of doing interdisciplinary work is brought in alongside theory. Neither is sufficient by itself. Thomas Murray drew this conclusion in considering his own interdisciplinary nature. His awareness of the importance of interdisciplinary work began with a social psychology experiment he conducted in graduate school, an experience that showed him there were moral and ethical dimensions that were largely ignored in the design of the experiment itself. Later, in his doctoral dissertation, he turned to the problem of how people attribute responsibility, an investigation that led him into semantics, moral philosophy, and jurisprudence. Eventually he worked in two interdisciplinary institutes, and is now concerned about the problem of seriously ill newborns, a medical problem that is surrounded by a host of social, legal, and moral issues. In order to deal with the ethical issues involved in the care of newborns, he and others have reached beyond the boundaries of moral philosophy into the fields of economics, sociology, and health policy. Reflecting on his own experience, Murray emphasized the overriding importance of reading and working with others.[14]

The same lesson became clear to Dorothy Swaine Thomas. Thomas, whose interests spanned sociology, economics, and anthropology, studied at Barnard College in the early 1920s, when sociology was an insignificant appendage to the economics department. She was able to study economics, sociology, and statistics, and was also intrigued by the empiricism of anthropology as taught by Franz Boas. As a result, her first published works drew on history of science, cultural anthropology, economics, sociology, and statistics. After a period of study at the London School of Economics and the completion of a Ph.D. on social aspects of English business cycles, Thomas then spent a strictly disciplinary year as a statistical assistant at the Federal Reserve Bank of New York. This was followed by collaborative research with William Thomas, work that culminated in 1928 with the publication of *The Child in America*. Using the situational approach, they incorporated firsthand examination and systematic critiques of practical behavioral programs with existing psychiatric, psychological, physiological, and sociological knowledge. Next Thomas turned to populational studies in Sweden, where she found a setting conducive to integrative analysis of the relationships between economic development and sociodemographic change. Later, after her work in Sweden, she turned to a study of Japanese American evacuation and resettlement. By the time Thomas joined the University of Pennsylvania in 1948, associating for the first time with a department of sociology, she had become so thoroughly conditioned to interdisciplinary research that she found herself involved in two new projects: one on technological change and social adjustment, the other on the shifts and redistribution of population and economic resources. Reflecting on her career, Thomas realized the importance of learning from, and working with, particular kinds of individuals. She had also found it unprofitable to make arbitrary separations: to separate economics from the strictly behavioral disciplines relevant to the problems that interested her, or to neglect the realities of economic structure, differentials, and development. In addition, she had found it profitable to take occasional and sometimes lengthy "'disciplinary' leaves of absence" in order to fill in gaps in her training and technique.[15]

The collaboration between Karl Llewellyn and E. Adamson Hoebel is a noteworthy demonstration of two quite fundamental lessons in the Thomas and Murray autobiographies: working with particular kinds of people and being open to other possible explanations. Their relationship began in 1933 and continued intermittently until Llewellyn's death in 1962. Llewellyn was one of Hobel's advisers in early studies of law-ways of the Comanches and Shoshones. Later they worked together on a well-known study of the Cheyennes and, in 1943, began a joint investigation of the law-ways of some of the Keresan Puebloes of New Mexico. While he was a postgraduate student at Columbia, Hoebel encountered skepticism about his plan to study the law of the Plains Indians. Skeptics argued those societies lacked anything resembling law "properly so called." Franz Boas suggested Hoebel contact Karl Llewellyn at Columbia Law School. Known primarily as a commerical lawyer, Llewellyn had no training in anthropology. However, he had been influenced by Sumner and Keller while he was an undergraduate and, while he was at Yale Law School, by Arthur Corbin, who, like Sumner, emphasized the influence of folkways and mores and the cultural dependence of law. After graduating from Yale in 1918, Llewellyn continued to read generally in anthropology and sociology.

Llewellyn suggested Hoebel sidestep the question of whether or not the Comanches have "law" by focusing on the institutions and techniques for settling disputes. Thus Hoebel came to focus on how actual disputes were settled rather than considering what the rules were or were not said to be. Under Llewellyn's supervision, he pursued these interests in his doctoral thesis on the law-ways of the Comanche. Generalizing about how "the lawyer" or "the anthropologist" would behave in a collaborative situation is dangerous in this or any other case, since there is no single model of either disciplinarian. In examining this particular collaboration, William Twining concluded that compatible personalities, common interests, and a common vocabulary were essential for successful interdisciplinary work. Both men were interested in jurisprudential questions, and both favored the closer integration of the social sciences. They also had a common interest in the dynamics and functioning of institutions focused on human behavior. Moreover, they were temperamentally well suited to each other and mutually appreciative of the beauty of Cheyenne culture.

At the same time, there was a productive complimentarity to their relationship. Llewellyn excelled at devising new approaches more than applying them systematically, whereas Hoebel was an excellent field-worker. It was, Twining explained, "a meeting of realistic jurisprudence and functional anthropology." Llewellyn's "legal realism" was more in harmony with the intellectual traditions of social anthropology than a narrower legal concern for rules. He revolted against the narrow, rule-oriented tradition, and was also a highly imaginative and intuitive person, in fact a prolific writer of lyric verse. At the same time, he identified with practitioners of law and was concerned with contemporary problems of law in the United States. Llewellyn was, in an important sense, more of an anthropologist than a lawyer, though his approach to the Pueblos was more "lawyerlike" than his approach to the Cheyennes.[16]

Conducting analyses of actual interdisciplinary work, as Twining's study of the Llewellyn/Hoebel collaboration demonstrates, is a potentially fruitful endeavor. Yet it is also a complex task. Putting them into any kind of ad hoc typology is highly problematic, given their varied nature and the sheer length of any list of candidates.[17] Many names have been proposed, from Plato, Dante, da Vinci, Petrarch, Kant, Hegel, and Freud to Hannah Arendt, Robert Brady, Harrison Brown, Sebastian de Grazia, Erich Kahler, Ferdinand Lundberg, Richard L. Maier, Jose Ferrater Mora, W. Warren Wagar, Ian Watt, Marjorie Hope Nicholson, Kenneth Burke, Norman O. Brown, Kenneth Boulding, Robert Darnton, Hayden White, Douglas Hofstadter, and Fernand Braudel. Nevertheless, the Philosophy Network of the Association for Integrative Studies once undertook the study of selected works and, in the process, gained greater insight into the integrative scholarship of several individuals, notably Edward Said (*Orientalism*), Robert Bellah and his co-authors (*Habits of the Heart*), James Weaver and Kenneth Jameson (*Economic Development: Competing Paradigms*), Ernst Pawel (*The Nightmare of Reason: A Life of Franz Kafka*), and James Boyd White (*Heracles' Bow: Essays in the Rhetoric and Poetics of the Law*).

What do these individuals have in common? They all fit Winthrop's description of the "broad-gauge scholar." They are interested in problems of wide latitude and complexity. Interdisciplinary "collators," Henry Winthrop suggests, are likely to be especially gifted in exercising the *hermeneutical function,* the ability to use interpretation in addressing problems, processes, and phenomena. Winthrop believes many social problems lead inevitably to methods of "intellectual correlation" because they do not lend themselves to neat experimental designs: they include "meaningful-causal analysis," the methods of philosophical anthropologists, methods of phenomenological analysis, and the broad, synthetic approaches discussed by Oliver Resier[18] and exemplified by Chardin.[19] The common objective is to "screen all the disciplines and winnow out" synoptic considerations germane to an over-all viewpoint. This process will frequently be carried out with specialists, even though the generalists' questions will extend across social, spiritual, and intellectual implications.[20]

Not unexpectedly, broad-gauge works may provoke considerable reaction because they are plural in nature. Robert Darnton's book *The Great Cat Massacre* grew out of an introductory course on the history of *mentalites* which became, in turn, a seminar on history and anthropology. It is an investigation of ways of thinking of eighteenth-century France, a work of what is called ethnographic history. Michael Messmer has described the work of Hayden White, Raymond Williams, and Edward Said as "exemplary instances of boundary-violating critiques of conventional knowledge." White's *Metahistory: The Historical Imagination in Nineteenth-Century Europe*[21] has been called "an embodiment of a radically interdisciplinary method."[22] In examining the rhetorical strategies, linguistic protocols, and grammatical deep structures of historical discourse, White has called into question not only the separation of history and philosophy of history but also history and literature. He has drawn upon the techniques of history and the work of literary critics such as Kenneth Burke, Northrop Frye, and the French structuralists. Some critics thought the book dangerous, "brilliant but unsound," with gestures toward the "currently conventional." A large part of their apprehension came from not knowing how to classify such works. The work of Raymond Williams, to cite another example, has been variously classified as cultural history, historical semantics, history of ideas, social criticism, literary history, and sociology. In *The Country and the City,* Williams examined the structures of feeling in the English past through a reading of English literature, grounding the study in the persistence of and changes in older forms of social life. Williams has drawn upon not only the literary critics' tools but also the nuances of social change.[23]

These works share a common objective, that of opening up new and wider perspectives. To the extent they have done this, they have reinvigorated a number of fields. Fernand Braudel has uncovered a number of what he termed "parahistoric languages" — demography, goods, costumes, lodging, technology, money — usually kept separate from each other and developing in the margins of history. Braudel's work was prompted by the conviction that scholars who consider economy a homogenous reality ignore the "shadowy zone" of material civilization that exists below the sunlit world of market economy. He found that the coexistence of upper- and lower-level forces — between economic civilization and material civilization — produced an illuminating dialectic for the historian, making it possible to define the fuller context in which preindustrial economics operated. To accomplish this, Braudel relied on a tripartite framework that was widely comparative in both time and space.[24]

Edward Said has been described as methodologically eclectic by some reviewers. Just as Hayden White attempted to invigorate history, Said, in his book *Beginnings,* sought to reinvigorate literary criticism using critical methods developed in France and moving into the larger ideas that give shape to texts. Said's *Orientalism* is an "archaeological" demonstration of the ways in which texts not only create knowledge but also the reality they appear to describe.[25] "Orientalism," Said argued, is a network of interests brought to bear upon "the Orient." It is an idea that has a history and a tradition of thought, imagery, and vocabulary that give it a certain reality and presence in the West. Ultimately "Orientalism" became "a system of knowledge about the Orient" that is lodged in a multidisciplinary distribution of geopolitical awareness within aesthetic, scholarly, economic, sociological, historical, and philological texts.[26] Said's perspective is both historical and "anthropological" as he moves from text to text, genre to genre, and from period to period, demonstrating how philology, lexicography, history, biology, political and economic theory, novel writing, lyric poetry, journalism, and travel writing have been used in ways that cannot be understood if discipline is isolated from discipline, or interpretation from history and political purpose. It is an epistemological critique that begins to deconstruct the institutional, cultural, and disciplinary instruments that link the incorporative practice of world history with partial knowledge like Orientalism, on the one hand, and, on the other hand, the continued "Western" hegemony of the non-European, peripheral world. It is, moreover, the same recognition of a "plurality of terrains, multiple experiences, and different constituencies"[27] that propelled ethnic, minority, and area studies.

The Integrative Process

The question of the interdisciplinary individual leads inevitably to the question of interdisciplinarity itself. Interdisciplinarity is neither a subject matter nor a body of content. It is a process for achieving an integrative synthesis, a process that usually begins with a problem, question, topic, or issue. Individuals must work to overcome problems created by differences in disciplinary language and world view. Although there is no absolute linear progression, there are a number of different steps in the process.[28]

   1a. *defining* the problem [question, topic, issue];
     b. *determining* all knowledge needs, including appropriate disciplin-

ary representatives and consultants, as well as relevant models, traditions, and literatures;

c. *developing* an integrative framework and appropriate questions to be investigated;

2a. *specifying* particular studies to be undertaken;

b. *engaging* in "role negotiation" (in teamwork);

c. *gathering* all current knowledge and *searching* for new information;

d. *resolving* disciplinary conflicts by working toward a common vocabulary (and focusing on reciprocal learning in teamwork);

e. *building and maintaining* communication through integrative techniques;

3a. *collating* all contributions and *evaluating* their adequacy, relevancy, and adaptability;

b. *integrating* the individual pieces to determine a pattern of mutual relatedness and relevancy;

c. *confirming or disconfirming* the proposed solution [answer]; and

d. *deciding* about future management or disposition of the task/ project/patient/curriculum.

The process is aided by a variety of integrative techniques. Though many of them apply directly to teamwork, they can also be adapted by individuals.[29]

•regular meetings
•internal and external presentations
•joint organizing and planning
•internal and external seminars

•periodic reports and reviews
•joint presentations, papers, and publications

•joint legislative work
•joint continuing education
•common data
•common data gathering and analysis
•common data reporting forms
•common teaching rounds and staff meetings

•joint patent work

•common equipment
•common facilities
•common objective(s)

•articulating differences among team members
•training in group interaction skills
•building interdependence in

•involving the client/user/ patient/student
•performing iterations

•using established techniques

analysis of a common object/objective

• focusing on a "common enemy" or "target" (a common concern that will dominate over individual differences)

(scenario, Delphi, etc.)

• having informal gatherings
• using telecommunication for dispersed members

Of these different techniques, iteration and role clarification have proved especially useful. Iteration allows authors to become readers and critics by going over each other's work in order to achieve a coherent, common assessment. To facilitate interaction, a project director or team leader can act as synthesizer. Role negotiation[30] and role clarification[31] allow team members to assess what they need and expect from each other while clarifying differences in methodology and ideology. Members of interdisciplinary teams are, in effect, translating specialized knowledge into a "synthetic product," acting as filters for each other, consulting experts, and the ultimate recipients of their work, whether they are students, patients, clients, or other scholars. In many ways, Koepp-Baker suggests, a team is like a "polygamous marriage." The association is launched by the announcement of intentions, an engagement, considerable publicity, a honeymoon, and, finally, the long haul, which is inevitably threatened by the onset of ennui.[32] Making it through the long haul depends in no small part on identifying several factors: where difficulties lie, where and by whom goals are clarified and roles defined, what the levels of communication are inside and outside the group, how the group builds and maintains its identity and sense of purpose, what its capacity for change is, and how and by whom points are assessed and achievements measured.[33]

Both Irvin White and James Sharp have described integrative strategies in problem-focused research. White reported on quality-control measures used to ensure a synthetic product in technology assessments of oil and gas operations on the U.S. outer continental shelf. The work involved an interdisciplinary team from the natural and social sciences as well as engineering. To promote integration, assignments were rotated among team members, who then conducted internal reviews. They also performed numerous rewrites. Both internal and external reviews were helpful in resolving communication problems. After several internal iterations, the team members involved outside consultants, an oversight committee, and representatives of various parties of interest. By relying on this system of reviews, the core research team was able to produce papers that formed the basis of an "interdisciplinary" rather than "multidisciplinary" report.[34]

Sharp believes fragmentation can be avoided by consigning all pertinent data to a computer and then assigning the appraisal, synthesis, and interpretation of that data to a combination of system generalists and disciplinary specialists. This procedure depends on a continuous process of appraising and interpreting the collective knowledge of all co-investigators. In addition to sending feedback to the disciplines, participants can test data for consistency and then organize the results into a program database that can be merged. It is, in addition, possible to develop peer group consensus on the data as well as types of conclusions that can be supported from data, plus the range of valid applications and selection of visual displays and tabulations of data. Using iterative judgment and reformulating hypotheses also plays an important role in interpretation, as does an "old-fashioned naturalist," Sharp adds, or a generalist who can appraise data in relation to system behavior.[35]

Organizing frameworks and controlling questions have also played a vital role in the process of integration, not only in problem-oriented projects, such as coping with increased carbon dioxide levels in the atmosphere and ecosystem research,[36] but also in interdisciplinary education. From his experience as director of a large-scale project concerned with human effects on Lake Tahoe (Nevada), James McEvoy concluded that it is vital to have a framework that can be used to help make conceptual sense of data, especially in large projects with many subsystemic relations. A framework permits the conceptual integration of diverse metrics and data. In quite a different context, an undergraduate course "Approaches to Value in a Technological Culture," instructors ensured integration in three ways: by establishing controlling questions for the course, by asking that the controlling questions be answered relative to three areas of a dialectical framework, and by actually devoting a segment of the course to synthesis. Their dialectical framework enabled students to integrate material from separate disciplines (literature, the arts, philosophy, and popular culture) around a *thesis* (a positive approach to technology), an *antithesis* (a negative approach), and finally a *synthesis* (a position that accounted for technology as an integral part of human nature).[37] Each of these examples underscores Thomas Maher's contention that dealing openly with the *idea* of integration is crucial not only for achieving the immediate objectives of a given project or course but also for attaining a heightened sense of the meaning of interdisciplinary work.[38]

Models of the Process

Though there is, and can be, no single model of the interdisciplinary process, there are two rather useful depictions that have wide applicability. In describing an interdisciplinary model of general education, Hursh, Hass, and Moore have diagramed the process for interdisciplinary study of a given problem.[39] (See Figure 10.) It is based on two levels. The *first level is one of clarification,* focused on developing an understanding of both the salient concepts and skills to be used in evaluating those concepts. "Power," to illustrate, is a concept relevant to virtually all the social sciences, each with its own definitions. By contrasting the ambiguities and assumptions of those definitions, students can practice the skill of clarification and then build higher-order constructions to accommodate discrepancies. They can gather a list of disciplinary definitions of "power," then construct a composite meaning consistent with the disciplines under consideration.

The *second level is one of resolution,* focused on a more thorough integration of the different perspectives identified by definitions of "salient concepts" in the participating disciplines. Students can challenge their conclusions by combining inputs from more than one discipline and working towards a more comprehensive understanding of the problem at hand.

Writing in the context of bioethics, Maurice deWachter has conceptualized the interdisciplinary process in a more complex model.[40] Bioethics, deWachter explained, does not substitute for the competencies and responsibilities of traditional disciplines. Rather, it confirms and sometimes reinforces the autonomy of other disciplines, putting them into wider perspective, adding new tasks and responsibilities to previous ones. DeWachter's model is based on using methodical epochè, a philosophical technique for the temporary suspension of all known methods. Its purpose is to achieve an interdisciplinary way of stating a global question. Ideally, there are five phases in the interdisciplinary process:

1. accepting methodical epochè by having all disciplines abstain from approaching the topic along lines of their own monodisciplinary methods;
2. trying to formulate in an interdisciplinary way the global question, acknowledging all aspects as well as the total network;
3. translating the global question into the specific language of each participating discipline;
4. constantly checking the answer to this translated question by checking for its relevance in answering the global question; and
5. agreeing upon a global answer that must not be produced by any one particular discipline but rather integrating all particular answers.

This ideal model may be pictured as shown in Figure 11.

This is, however, a idealized model. Realistically speaking, the best chance of succeeding lies in starting at the level of the third phase of idealized interdisciplinarity and then trying to work back to the original epochè. (See Figure 12.)

When planning to implement integrative techniques or follow any model or description of the interdisciplinary process, it is wise to remember

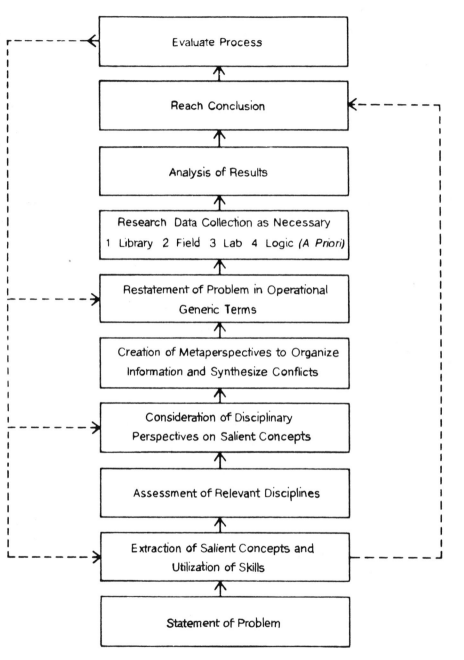

*Figure 10. Process for Interdisciplinary
Study of a Given Problem*

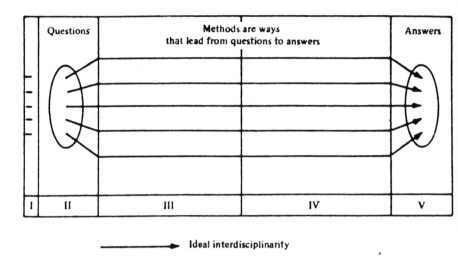

Ideal interdisciplinarity

Figure 11

Sjölander's cautionary tale of the ten stages in an interdisciplinary venture. Failing to tend to the integrative process may leave participants stranded at any of several stages. Interdisciplinary work is sometimes attacked for lacking rigor. However, rigor is not diminished but shifted to what Rivers Singleton, Jr., calls a "core sense of interdisciplinary rigor" that transcends boundaries to address a particular problem or question by using the most pertinent resources in a continuously integrative manner.[41] This is, in many respects, a dialectical process. The original meaning of dialectic is discourse between two or more speakers who express two or more positions or opinions. Walter Davis suggests dialectic is *the* interdisciplinary method, since interdisciplinarity is achieved when disciplinary differences are stated, clarified, and then resolved in order to produce a synthesis.[42] David Halliburton speaks of a dialectical relationship between fixed and fluid elements of the curriculum,[43] and Jonathan Broido has demonstrated how the dialectical approach can be a practical methodological heuristic for overcoming "disciplinary entrenchment" in problem-oriented work. The instrumentalities of different disciplines are compared and their dependence and independence mapped. Misunderstandings, animosities, and competitions are not glossed over or mitigated by this democratic approach. Instead, they are taken seriously as attempts are made to spell out what the differences mean and their possible consequences. Both the price of reductionism and the interdisciplinary strength of a given disciplinary framework become clearer in the process, at the same time that

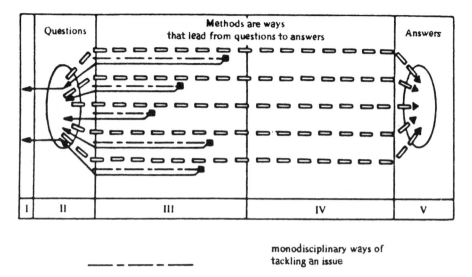

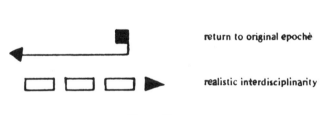

Figure 12

possibilities for exporting and importing disciplinary methods and terminology become more apparent.[44] The very skills that Broido considers fundamental to this process, that William H. Newell regards as central to an
"integrative habit of mind"[45] and Henry Winthrop believes exemplify a
broad gauge scholar," are, in fact, fundamental to the dialectical process.

Epilogue: Interdisciplinary Futures

There is much that we know, but there is also much to do in order
to reach a fuller understanding of interdisciplinarity. Five of these tasks
are of utmost importance:

1. Compiling narratives in order to understand how interdisciplinary
   work is actually done by individuals and teams, including the work
   done within projects, organizations, institutions, conferences, and
   journals.

2. Conducting empirical studies of current interdisciplinary research, teaching, and practice in order to broaden the data base on which general observations are drawn and theories constructed.

3. Writing histories of particular fields, problem areas, and patterns of relations among disciplines, in order to understand the "local" nature of interdisciplinarity.

4. Disclosing the "concealed reality" of interdisciplinarity, in order to have more accurate knowledge of both its nature and consequence.

5. Exploring the connections among creativity, problem solving, and the interdisciplinary process.

These investigations will be aided considerably by an expanding rhetoric of inquiry. Rhetoric of inquiry is itself a new interdisciplinary field concerned with language and argument in both scholarship and public affairs. By analyzing the logics that operate in different fields, scholars in a variety of areas have been able to reveal their underlying practices and assumptions to both disciplinary and wider audiences,[46] enhancing the prospects for interdisciplinary discourse.

Interdisciplinarity has been variously defined in this century: as a methodology, a concept, a process, a way of thinking, a philosophy, and a reflexive ideology. It has been linked with attempts to expose the dangers of fragmentation, to reestablish old connections, to explore emerging relations, and to create new subjects adequate to handle our practical and conceptual needs. Cutting across all these theories is one recurring idea. Interdisciplinarity is a means of solving problems and answering questions that cannot be satisfactorily addressed using single methods or approaches. Whether the context is a short-range instrumentality or a long-range reconceptualization of epistemology, the concept represents an important attempt to define and establish common ground.

Notes

Introduction

1. Bedrick Baumann, *Imaginative Participation: The Career of an Organizing Concept in a Multidisciplinary Context* (The Hague: Martinus Nijhoff, 1975), p. 15.
2. Clifford Geertz, "Blurred Genres: The Refiguration of Social Thought," *American Scholar,* 49, No. 2 (1980), 165–79.
3. Quentin Skinner, ed., *The Return of Grand Theory in the Human Sciences* (Cambridge: Cambridge Univ. Press, 1985).
4. Stephen Toulmin, *The Return to Cosmology* (Berkeley: Univ. of California Press, 1982).
5. Robert W. Kates, quoted in Karen J. Winkler, "Interdisciplinary Research," *Chronicle of Higher Education,* 7 Oct. 1987, p. 15.
6. Georges Gusdorf uses this phrase in "Project for Interdisciplinary Research," *Diogenes,* 42 (Summer 1963), 127.
7. A remark reported in *Interdisciplinarity: Papers Presented at the Society for Research into Higher Education, European Symposium on Interdisciplinary Courses in European Education, 13 September 1975.* ERIC ED 165 512.
8. Personal conversation with Joseph Kockelmans, Professor of Philosophy, The Pennsylvania State University, 20 June 1983.
9. James L. Kinneavy, *A Theory of Discourse: The Aims of Discourse* (New York: Norton, 1971), p. 30.
10. David Hollinger, "Historians and the Discourse of Intellectuals," in *New Directions in American Intellectual History,* ed. John Higham and Paul K. Conkin (Baltimore: Johns Hopkins Univ. Press, 1979), p. 43.
11. Roger Westcott used the term "intellectually homeless" in "The Plight of the Interdisciplinarian," *Academy Notes* [Academy of Independent Scholars] 2 (Apr. 1982), 4.

Chapter 1

1. R. R. Bolgar, *The Classical Heritage and Its Beneficiaries* (Cambridge: Cambridge Univ. Press, 1954), p. 31.
2. Paul Goodman, *The Community of Scholars* (New York: Random House, 1962), p. 20.

3. Georges Gusdorf, "Past, Present, and Future in Interdisciplinary Research," *International Social Science Journal,* 29 No. 4 (1977), 580–81.

4. Bolgar, pp. 164–65, 230–31.

5. Hastings Rashdall, *The Universities of Europe in the Middle Ages* (Oxford: Clarendon, 1936), I, 6–7.

6. A.B. Cobban, *The Medieval Universities: Their Development and Organization* (London: Methuen, 1977), p. 8.

7. Wolfram Swoboda, "Disciplines and Interdisciplinarity: A Historical Perspective," in *Interdisciplinarity and Higher Education,* ed. Joseph J. Kockelmans (University Park: Pennsylvania State Univ. Press, 1979), p. 57.

8. D.C. Philips, "Organicism and Biology," in *Holistic Thought in the Social Sciences* (Palo Alto: Stanford Univ. Press, 1976), pp. 21–29.

9. Wilhelm Vosskamp, "From Scientific Specialization to the Dialogue between the Disciplines," *Issues in Integrative Studies,* 4 (1986), 19–20.

10. Norman Birnbaum, "The Arbitrary Disciplines," *Change, The Magazine of Higher Learning,* July/Aug. 1969, p. 11.

11. Swoboda, p. 59.

12. Hans Flexner, "The Curriculum, the Disciplines, and Interdisciplinarity in Higher Education," in *Interdisciplinarity and Higher Education,* pp. 105–06.

13. I thank Thomas Benson for pointing this out.

14. Theodore Hershberg, "The New Urban History: Toward an Interdisciplinary Theory of the City," in *Philadelphia: Work, Space, Family, and Group Experience in the Nineteenth Century,* ed. Theodore Hershberg (New York: Oxford, 1981), p. 23.

15. Vosskamp, pp. 21–22.

16. Vosskamp, p. 7.

17. Nicholas Rescher, *Cognitive Systematization: A Systems-Theoretic Approach to a Coherentist Theory of Knowledge* (Oxford: Basil Blackwell, 1979).

18. Alastair M. Taylor uses this metaphor in "Education and the Search for Order," *Main Currents in Modern Thought,* 27 No. 4 (1971), 129.

19. Gerald Holton uses this second metaphor; see Karen J. Winkler "Interdisciplinary Research," *Chronicle of Higher Education,* 7 Oct. 1987, p. 14.

20. Rustum Roy, "Interdisciplinary Science on Campus: The Elusive Dream," in *Interdisciplinarity and Higher Education,"* p. 162.

21. Flexner, pp. 106–07.

22. William Mayville, "Educational Models and Interdisciplinarity," *Interdisciplinarity: The Mutable Paradigm* (Washington, D.C.: American Association of Higher Education, 1978), pp. 25–26. AAHE-ERIC Higher Education Research Report No. 9.

23. Phillips, pp. 49–55, 107–14.

24. Ernest L. Boyer, "The Quest for Common Learning," in *Common Learning: A Carnegie Colloquium on General Education* (Washington, D.C.: Carnegie Foundation for the Advancement of Teaching, 1981), p. 4.

25. Rae Carlson, "What's Social about Social Psychology? Where's the Person in Personality Research?," *Journal of Personality and Social Psychology,* 47 No. 6 (1984), 1309.

26. M. Landau, H. Proshansky, and W. H. Ittelson, "The Interdisciplinary Approach and the Concept of Behavioral Science," in *Decisions, Values and Groups,* ed. Norman F. Washburne (New York: Pergamon Press, 1962) II, 11–12.

27. See Panos D. Bardis, "Science and the Religious Absolute," in *The Search for Absolute Values in a Changing World* (New York: The International Cultural Foundation Press, 1978), II, 1162.

28. Gerard Radnitzky, *Anglo-Saxon Schools of Metascience* (Sweden: Akademiforlaget Goteborg, 1968), p. 78. Contemporary Schools of Metascience, Vol. I.

29. Otto Neurath, "Unified Science as Encyclopedic Integration," *International Encyclopedia of Unified Science: Foundations of the Unity of Science* (Chicago: Univ. of Chicago Press, 1938), I, 20–22, 26 n.1.

30. Nelson Bingham suggested this term.

31. Landau, Proshanky, and Ittelson, pp. 8, 15–16.

32. Landau, Proshanky, and Ittelson, pp. 15, 17.

33. Robert Joseph Connole, *A Study of the Concept of Integration in Present-Day Curriculum Making.* (Washington, D.C.: Catholic University of America, 1937), p. 15.

34. John D. McNeil, *Curriculum: A Comprehensive Introduction* (Boston: Little, Brown, 1985), pp. 326–28.

35. See also Edward A. Ciccorico, "'Integration' in the Curriculum," *Main Currents in Modern Thought,* 27 (Nov./Dec. 1970), 60–61.

36. Alastair Taylor, "Integrative Principles and the Educational Process," *Main Currents in Modern Thought,* 25 (May/June 1969), 130.

37. Richard Pring, "Curriculum Integration," *Proceedings of the Philosophy of Education Society of Great Britain,* 5 No. 2, Supplementary Issue (July 1971), 184.

38. See *Interdisciplinarity,* a study undertaken by Geoffrey Squires with Helen Simons, Malcolm Parlett, and Tony Becher (London: Nuffield Foundation, 1979), pp. 42–47. I thank Tony Becher for supplying me with a copy.

39. Birnbaum. p. 14.

40. Ronald Gross, "Columbia's University Seminars: Creating a Community of Scholars," *Change, The Magazine of Higher Learning,* 14 No. 2 (1982), p. 43.

41. William H. Berquist, "Curricular Practice," *Developing the College Curriculum: A Handbook for Faculty and Administrators,* ed. Arthur Chickering et al. (Washington, D.C.: Council for the Advancement of Small Colleges, 1977), p. 87.

42. Boyer, p. 7.

43. Birnbaum, p. 14.

44. Raymond C. Miller, "Varieties of Interdisciplinary Approaches in the Social Sciences: A 1981 Overview," *Issues in Integrative Studies,* 1 (1982), 25.

45. See Jean Piaget, "The Epistemology of Interdisciplinary Relationships," in *Interdisciplinarity: Problems of Teaching and Research in Universities* (Paris: OECD, 1972), pp. 127–39.

46. E. Laszlo and H. Margenau, "The Emergence of Integrative Concepts in Contemporary Science," *Philosophy of Science,* 39 No. 2 (1972), 252–59.

47. Anatol Rapoport, "General Systems Theory: A Bridge between the Cultures," *General Systems Yearbook* 23 (1978), p. 155.

48. Stanley Bailis, "Against and for Holism: A Review and Rejoinder," *Issues in Integrative Studies,* 3 (1984/85), 24.

49. Diana Crane, *Invisible Colleges: Diffusion of Knowledge in Scientific Communities* (Chicago: Univ. of Chicago Press, 1972), pp. 109–10.

50. James H. Stone, "Integration in the Humanities: Perspectives and Prospects," *Main Currents in Modern Thought,* 26 No. 1 (1969), 17.

51. Fernand Braudel, *On History,* trans. Sarah Matthews (Chicago: Univ. of Chicago Press, 1980), p. 17.

52. Georg G. Iggers and Harold T. Parker, eds., *International Handbook of Historical Studies: Contemporary Research and Theory* (Westport, Conn.: Greenwood Press, 1979), pp. 5–6, 10.

53. See Shepard B. Clough, "A Half-Century in Economic History: Autobiographical Reflections," *Journal of Economic History,* 30 (Mar. 1970), 4–17.

54. John Higham, *History: Professional Scholarship in America* (New York: Harper and Row, 1965), pp. 138–39.

55. On the humanities, see Nancy Anne Cluck, "Reflections on the Interdisciplinary Approaches to the Humanities," *Liberal Education,* 66 No. 1 (1980), 67–77.

56. Clifford Geertz, "Blurred Genres: The Refiguration of Social Thought," *American Scholar,* 49 No. 2 (1980), 165–79.

57. Richard Harvey Brown, *A Poetic for Sociology* (Cambridge: Cambridge University Press, 1977) and *Society as Text* (Chicago: University of Chicago Press, 1987).

58. Hayden White, *Metahistory: The Historical Imagination in Nineteenth Century Europe* (Baltimore: Johns Hopkins Univ. Press, 1973).

59. James Boyd White, *The Legal Imagination: Studies in the Nature of Legal Thought and Expression* (Boston: Little, Brown, 1973).

60. See Beth A. Casey, "The Quiet Revolution: The Transformation and Reintegration of the Humanities," *Issues in Integrative Studies,* 4 (1986), 71–92.

61. See Jost Hermand and Evelyn Torton Beck, *Interpretive Synthesis: The Task of Literary Scholarship* (New York: Frederick Ungar, 1968), especially "The Voices of Methodological Reintegration," pp. 146–57.

62. See Harry Slochower, "Kenneth Burke's Philosophy of Symbolic Action," *University Review,* 8 (Winter 1941), 119–23.

63. Cited in Karen J. Winkler, "Interdisciplinary Research: How Big a Challenge to Traditional Fields?," *Chronicle of Higher Education,* 7 Oct. 1987, p. A15.

64. Winkler, p. A14.

65. See D.A. Conway, "Operational Research: Interdisciplinarity and Higher Education," in *Interdisciplinarity* (Surrey: Society for Research into Higher Education, 1977). ERIC 165 512.

66. John Walsh, "Social Studies in Science: Society Crosses Disciplinary Lines," *Science,* 18 Nov. 1977, pp. 706–07.

67. John H. Berthel, "Twentieth Century Scholarship and the Research Library: A Marriage of Convenience," *University of Tennessee Library Lectures,* 20 (1969), 25–27.

68. Steve Heims, "Encounter of Behavioral Sciences with New Machine-Organism Analogies in the 1940's," *Journal of the History of the Behavioral Sciences,* 11 No. 4 (1975), 368–73.

69. Jan Vlachy, "Interdisciplinary Approaches in Physics: The Concepts," *Czechoslovakian Journal of Physics,* B32 No. 11 (1982), 1312.

70. See Jagdish Mehra, "Quantum Mechanics and the Explanation of Life," *American Scientist,* 61 No. 6 (1973), 722–28.

71. Roy, p. 163.

72. Gerald Holton, quoted in Winkler, p. A14.

73. Anthony R. Michaelis, "Interdisciplinary Creativity," in *The Search for Absolute Values in a Changing World,* II, 1099.

74. See Preston Cloud, "Beyond Plate Techtonics," *American Scientist,* 68 No. 4 (1980), 382.

75. Mark E. Kann, "The Political Culture of Interdisciplinary Explanation," *Humanities in Society,* 2 No. 3 (1979), 188–89.

76. David A. Hollinger, "T.S. Kuhn's Theory of Science and Its Implications for History," in *Paradigms and Revolutions: Applications and Appraisals of Thomas Kuhn's Philosophy of Science,* ed. Gary Gutting (Notre Dame: University of Notre Dame Press, 1980), p. 195.

77. Cited by Alan L. Porter, "Interdisciplinary Research: Current Experiences in Policy and Performance," *Interdisciplinary Science Reviews,* 8 No. 2 (1983), 158.

78. Dale L. Wolfle, "Interdisciplinary Research as a Form of Research" *Journal of the Society of Research Administrators,* 13 (Fall 1981), 5.

79. See Martha Garrett Russell, "Introduction and Overview," in *Enabling Interdisciplinary Research: Perspectives from Agriculture, Forestry, and Home Economics,* ed.

Martha Garrett Russell (St. Paul: University of Minnesota Agricultural Experiment Station, 1982). Misc. Publication 19.

80. Randolph Barker, "Farming Systems Research: Interdisciplinary Response to Problems," in *Enabling Interdisciplinary Research,* p. 101.

81. B. Saxberg, W.T. Newell, and Brian Mar, "The Integration of Interdisciplinary Research with the Organization of the University," in *Interdisciplinary Research Groups,* ed. Richard T. Barth and Rudy Steck (Vancouver, B.C.: International Research Group on Interdisciplinary Programs, 1979), p. 229.

82. Graham Toft and R. Tomlinson Sparrow, "University Interdisciplinary Engineering Centers: New Directions — Persistent Organizational Problems." Paper presented at the Third International Conference on Interdisciplinary Research, Seattle, Washington, 1 Aug. 1984.

83. Arthur D. Little, Inc., *Into the Information Age: A Perspective for Federal Action on Information* (Chicago: American Library Association, 1978), p. 10.

84. Kann, pp. 188–89.

85. Roy, p. 163.

86. Noted in Anne S. Williams et al. "Impacts of Large Recreational Development upon Semi-Primitive Environment," in *Guidelines for Conducting Interdisciplinary Applied Research in a University Setting* (Bozeman: Montana State Univ. Press, 1976).

87. Nancy Lindas, "Conclusions from the American Society for Public Administration's Assessment of Four Interdisciplinary Management Projects," in *Interdisciplinary Research Groups,* p. 279.

88. Remark made by Don Anderson at the OECD conference "Interdisciplinarity Revisited" in Linköping, Sweden, 5 Oct. 1984.

89. Remark made at the OECD conference "Interdisciplinarity Revisited" in Linköping, Sweden, 3 Oct. 1984.

90. Descriptive brochure issued prior to the conference on "Interdisciplinarity Revisited" in Linköping, Sweden, 3–5 Oct. 1984.

91. Gerald Grant and David Riesman, *The Perpetual Dream: Reform and Experiment in the American College* (Chicago: Univ. of Chicago Press, 1978), p. 15.

92. See accounts of many NEH-funded programs in the spring 1979 issue of *Liberal Education.*

93. Guy Michaud, "General Conclusions," in *Interdisciplinarity: Problems of Teaching and Research in Universities,* p. 281.

94. Hans Schütze, of the OECD, used this term in his introductory remarks at the OECD conference on "Interdisciplinarity Revisited" in Linköping, Sweden, 3 Oct. 1984.

95. "'Communities Have Problems, Universities Have Departments,'" in *The University and the Community: The Problems of Changing Relationships* (Paris: Organization for Economic Cooperation and Development, 1982), p. 130.

96. This phrase is from Richard McKeon, "Philosophy and Action," *Ethics,* 62 No. 2 (1952), 575.

97. Hans Klette, "Discussion," in *Interdisciplinarity* (London: Society for Research into Higher Education, 1977), p. 13.

98. Stephen Toulmin, "From Form to Function: Philosophy and History of Science in the 1950's and Now," *Daedalus,* Summer 1977, 160.

99. Quoted in Winkler, p. A15.

100. D.E. Chubin, A.L. Porter, and F.A. Rossini, "Interdisciplinarity: How Do We Know Thee? — A Bibliographic Essay," in *Interdisciplinary Analysis and Research* (Mt. Airy, Md.: Lomond, 1986), pp. 427–29.

101. Georges Papadopoulos, "Concluding Remarks," in *Inter-Disciplinarity Revisited* (Stockholm: OECD, SNBU, and Linköping University, 1985), pp. 206–08.

102. Remarks from a paper by Harry Hermanns, of the University of Kassel (West

Germany), at a conference on "Inter-Disciplinarity Revisited," in Linköping, Sweden, 4 Oct. 1984.

Chapter 2

1. Guy Berger, "Opinions and Facts," in *Interdisciplinarity: Problems of Teaching and Research in Universities* (Paris: Organization for Economic Cooperation and Development, 1972), p. 23.

2. Remark by Keith Clayton at the OECD-sponsored conference "Inter-Disciplinarity Revisited," in Linköping, Sweden, 4 Oct. 1984.

3. Berger, pp. 37–38.

4. See Corinna Delkeskamp, "Interdisciplinarity: A Critical Appraisal," in *Knowledge, Value, and Belief,* ed. H.T. Englehardt and D. Callahan (Hastings-on-Hudson: The Hastings Center, 1977), pp. 324–54.

5. *Interdisciplinarity: Problems of Teaching and Research in Universities,* pp. 44–47.

6. Ernest Lynton used these terms in "Interdisciplinarity: Rationales and Criteria of Assessment," in *Inter-Disciplinarity Revisited: Re-Assessing the Concept in Light of Institutional Experience,* ed. Lennart Levin and Ingemar Lind (Stockholm: OECD, SNBUC, Linköping University, 1985), 137–52. Recognizing parallels between my own definitions of "conceptual" and "instrumental" interdisciplinarity, Lynton and I then joined in presenting a paper on "Imaging the Whole: From Instrumental to Synoptic Definitions of Interdisciplinarity" at the seventh annual meeting of the Association for Integrative Studies at Eastern Kentucky University, 19 Oct. 1985.

7. See especially the multivolume series by Robert Hermann under the general title of *Interdisciplinary Mathematics* (Brookline, Mass.: Mathematical Science Press), beginning with Vol. I in 1973.

8. See Janusz Kacprzyk, *Multistage Decision-Making under Fuzziness: Theory and Application* (Rheinland: Verlag TUB, 1983).

9. See Peter Bøgh Andersen and Arne Kjaer, "Artificial Intelligence and Self-Management," *Journal of Pragmatics,* 6 No. 3/4 (1982), 321–55.

10. For a rich use of the interview, see Robert Bellah et al., *Habits of the Heart: Individualism and Commitment in American Life.* (Berkeley: Univ. of California Press, 1985).

11. Fernand Braudel "Communication and Social Mathematics," in *On History,* trans. Sarah Matthews (Chicago: Univ. of Chicago Press, 1980), pp. 38–47.

12. I.J. Spalding, "Laser Applications," *Physics Bulletin,* 35 No. 10 (1984), 425–27.

13. Charles J. Lumsden and L.E.H. Trainor, "Nonequilibrium Ensembles of Self-Organizing Systems: A Simulation Study," *Canadian Journal of Physics,* 57 No. 1 (1979), 23–38.

14. T. Dreyfus, "Introducing Shock Waves: An Interdisciplinary Approach," *Helvetica Physica Acta,* 52 No. 5–6 (1979), 680.

15. See, for example, Rolf Schulmeister's view in *Interdisciplinarity. Papers Presented at the SRHE European Symposium on Interdisciplinary Courses in European Education* (Surrey: Society for Research into Higher Education, 1977), pp. 54–55. ERIC ED 165 512.

16. Lynton, p. 143.

17. Giovanni Gozzer, "Interdisciplinarity: A Concept Still Unclear," *Prospects, Quarterly Review of Education,* 12 No. 3 (1982), 281.

18. On the latter, see especially Durganand Sinha, "Social Psychologist's Stance in a Developing Country," *Indian Journal of Psychology,* 50 Pt. 2 (1975), 91–107.

19. D.E. Chubin, A. L. Porter, and F. Rossini, "'Citation Classics' Analysis: An Approach to Characterizing Interdisciplinary Research," *Journal of the American Society for Information Science,* 35 No. 6 (1984), 360.

20. Physics Survey Committee of the National Research Council, *Physics in Perspective* (Washington, D.C.: National Academy of Sciences, 1972), p. 67.

21. Solomon H. Snyder, "Neurosciences: An Integrative Discipline," *Science,* 21 Sept. 1984, pp. 1255–57.

22. See also Frederick Rossini et al., "Crossdisciplinarity in the Biomedical Sciences: A Preliminary Analysis of Anatomy," in *Managing Interdisciplinary Research,* ed. S.R. Epton, R.L. Payne, and A.W. Pearson (London: Wiley and Sons, 1984), p. 182.

23. Cited in Karen J. Winkler, "Interdisciplinary Research: How Big a Challenge to Traditional Fields," *Chronicle of Higher Education,* 7 Oct. 1987, p. A14.

24. William Sturtevant, "Anthropology, History, and Ethnohistory," *Ethnohistory,* 13 No. 1–2 (1966), 1.

25. Berger, p. 44.

26. See Robert Dubin, "Contiguous Problem Analysis: An Approach to Systematic Theories about Social Organization," in *Interdisciplinary Relationships in the Social Sciences* (Chicago: Aldine, 1969), pp. 65–76.

27. Frederick L. Holmes, "The History of Biochemistry: A Review of the Literature of the Field," in *Biochemistry Collections: A Cross-Disciplinary Survey of the Literature,* ed. Bernard S. Schlesinger (New York: Haworth, 1982), p. 13.

28. Paul-Emile Pilet, "The Multidisciplinary Aspects of Biology: Basic and Applied Research," *Scientia,* 74 No. 116 (1981), 634.

29. "Preface," in *Interdisciplinarity: Problems of Teaching and Research in Universities,* p. 41.

30. Remark by Keith Clayton at the OECD-sponsored conference on "Inter-Disciplinarity Revisited" in Linköping, Sweden, 4 Oct. 1984.

31. Berger, p. 41.

32. Neal Mucklow, "Grounds for Grouping Disciplines," *Journal of Philosophy of Education,* 14 No. 2 (1980), 225–37.

33. Winkler, p. A14.

34. Gary E. Schwartz and Stephen M. Weiss, "Yale Conference on Behavioral Medicine: A Proposed Definition and Statement of Goals," *Journal of Behavioral Medicine,* 1 No. 1 (1978), 4.

35. Wolf Lepenies, "History and Anthropology: A Historical Appraisal of the Current Contact between the Disciplines," *Social Science Information,* 15 No. 213 (1976), 302.

36. Winkler, p. A14.

37. *Physics in Perspective,* pp. 283–84, 290–91.

38. *Physics in Perspective,* p. 67.

39. J.T. Lemon, "Study of the Urban Past: Approaches by Geographers," *Canadian Historical Association: Historical Papers* (1973), 179–90.

40. Ronald J. Grele, "A Surmisable Variety: Interdisciplinarity and Oral Testimony," *American Quarterly,* 27 (Aug. 1975), 276.

41. Jeroom Vercruysee, "Why the Enlightenment: An Introduction," *Arizona Quarterly,* 31 No. 2 (1975), 104–05.

42. Harold W. Proshansky, "An Environmental Psychologist's Perspective on the Interdisciplinary Approach in Psychology," in *Cognition, Social Behavior, and the Environment,* ed. John H. Harvey (Hillsdale, N.J.: Lawrence Erlbaum, 1981), p. 4.

43. Shinichi Ichimura, "Interdisciplinary Research and Area Studies," *Journal of Southeast Asian Studies,* 6 (Sept. 1975), 112.

44. Norman Dinges, "Interdisciplinary Collaboration in Cross-Cultural Social Science Research," in *Research in Culture Learning: Language and Conceptual Studies,* ed. Michael P. Hamnett and Richard W. Brislin (Honolulu: East-West Center, Univ. of Hawaii Press, 1980), p. 166.

45. See Lawrence R. Murphy, "Social Science Research in the Middle East: The American University in Cairo, Egypt," *Journal of the History of the Behavioral Sciences,* 15 No. 2 (1979), 115–27.

46. John Adams, "The Analysis of Rural Indian Economy: Economics and Anthropology," *Man in India,* 52 No. 1 (1972), 1–20; Michael Lipton, "Interdisciplinary Studies in Less Developed Countries," *Journal of Development Studies,* 7 (Oct. 1970), 5–18; a reply to Lipton by M.P. Moore, "The Logic of Interdisciplinary Studies," *Journal of Development Studies,* 11 (Oct. 1974), 98–106.

47. Robert S. Chen, "Interdisciplinary Research and Integration: The Case of CO_2 and the Climate," *Climatic Change,* 3 No. 4 (1981), 429–47. See also Richard A. Warrick and William E. Riebsame, "Societal Response to CO_2-Induced Climate Change: Opportunities for Research," *Climatic Change,* 3 No. 4 (1981), 392.

48. P.J. Perry, "Agricultural History: A Geographer's Critique," *Agricultural History,* 4 No. 2 (1972), 261.

49. John J. Mannion, "Multidisciplinary Dimensions in Material History," *Material History Bulletin,* 8 (1979), 21.

50. Remark made at the Third International Conference on Interdisciplinary Research in Seattle, Washington, 3 Aug. 1984.

51. John G. Reid, "'The Beginnings of the Maritimes': A Reappraisal," *American Review of Canadian Studies,* 9 No. 1 (1979), 41–43.

52. References for these and other fields are in the bibliography.

53. Talcott Parsons, "Theory in the Humanities and Sociology," *Daedalus,* Spring 1970, 507–08.

54. Quoted in Winkler, p. A14.

55. Donald Levine makes this point in "Reflections from an Interdisciplinary Milieu," *Forum for Liberal Education,* 8 No. 4 (1986), 2–4.

56. Personal correspondence from Minor Meyers, provost and dean of Faculty at Hobart and William Smith Colleges, 27 July 1984.

57. Levine, p. 2.

58. Frederick E. Peterson, "Exploring the Relationships between Academic Disciplines: A Fresh Perspective at the Smithsonian," *Teachers College Record,* 82 No. 2 (1980), 314–15.

59. Ignacy Malecki, "Twenty Five Years of the Institute of Fundamental Technical Research, Polish Academy of Sciences," *Review of The Polish Academy of Sciences,* 23 No. 2 (1978), 83–90.

60. Jerrod Meinwald et al., "Chemical Ecology: Studies from East Africa," *Science,* 17 Mar. 1978, pp. 1167–73.

61. G.S. Khush and W.R. Coffman, "Genetic Evaluation and Utilization (GEU) Program," *Theoretical and Applied Genetics,* 51 (1977), 97–110.

62. J. Hillis Miller, quoted in Winkler, p. A15.

63. Diana Crane, *Invisible Colleges: Diffusion of Knowledge in Scientific Communities* (Chicago: Univ. of Chicago Press, 1972), p. 35.

64. Stephen Toulmin, *Human Understanding: The Collective Use and Evolution of Concepts* (Princeton: Princeton Univ. Press, 1972), p. 366.

65. See John Lankford, "The Writing of American History in the 1960s: A Critical Bibliography of Materials of Interest to Sociologists," *Sociological Quarterly,* 14 (Winter 1973), 99–126.

66. Peter W. Mullen, "Editorial. An Immunopharmacology Journal: Reflections on Its Interdisciplinary and Historical Context," *International Journal of Immunopharmacology,* 1 No. 1 (1979), 1–4.

67. R.B. Roller, "Thermoset and Coatings Technology: The Challenge of Interdisciplinary Chemistry," *Polymer Engineering and Science,* 19 No. 10 (1979), 1–4.

68. G. Milazzo, "Bioelectrochemistry and Ioenergetics: An Interdisciplinary Survey," *Bioelectrochemistry and Bioenergetics,* 8 (1981), 513; listed as a section of *Journal of Electroanalytical Chemistry,* 128 No. 4 (1981).

69. "Editorial," *Cell Calcium,* 1 (Jan. 1980), 1–5.

70. Schwartz and Weiss, pp. 10–11.

71. Harold C. Urschel, Jr., "Interdisciplinary University without Walls," *Chest,* 75 No. 4 (1979), 495–599.

72. "Scholarly Disciplines: Breaking Out," *New York Times,* 25 Apr. 1986, p. A18–19.

73. Raymond C. Miller, "Varieties of Interdisciplinary Approaches in the Social Sciences," *Issues in Integrative Studies,* 1 (1982), 15.

74. Charles Adams used these phrases in "The Inquiry Program at the University of Massachusetts-Amherst," *Association for Integrative Studies Newsletter,* 6 No. 4 (1984), 6.

75. A phrase used by Russell Hardin, quoted in Winkler, p. A15.

76. Bryce Crawford, "The Support of Interdisciplinary and Transdisciplinary Programs." Paper presented to the ninth annual meeting of the Council of Graduate Schools in the United States. Washington, D.C., 5 Dec. 1969. ERIC ED 035 364.

77. György Darvas, "Paradox of Interdisciplinarity." Paper presented at the sixteenth meeting of the International Congress of the History of Science in Bucharest, Rumania, 1981.

78. Noted in Gerald Studdert-Kennedy, *Evidence and Explanation in Social Science: An Interdisciplinary Approach* (London: Routledge and Kegan Paul, 1975), p. 2.

79. Richard Gelwick, "Truly Interdisciplinary Study and 'Commitment in Relativism,'" *Soundings,* 66 No. 4 (1983), p. 423.

80. Stanley Bailis, "Review of *Interdisciplinarity Revisited," Association for Integrative Studies Newsletter,* 8 No. 1 (1986), 9.

81. Clifford Geertz, "Blurred Genres: The Refiguration of Social Thought," *American Scholar,* 49 No. 2 (1980), 165–66.

82. Susan R. Suleiman uses these terms in "Introduction: Varieties of Audience-Oriented Criticism," in *The Reader in the Text,* ed. Susan R. Suleiman and Inge Crossman (Princeton: Princeton Univ. Press, 1980), p. 3.

Chapter 3

1. Guy Berger, "Opinions and Facts," in *Interdisciplinarity: Problems of Teaching and Research in Universities* (Paris: Organization for Economic Cooperation and Development, 1972), p. 71.

2. Kenneth Burke, *Language as Symbolic Action: Essays on Life, Literature, and Method* (Berkeley: Univ. of California Press, 1966), pp. 45–46, 49.

3. Guy Michaud and C.C. Abt, from "Introduction," in *Interdisciplinarity: Problems of Teaching and Research in Universities,* p. 25.

4. Erich Jantsch, "Towards Interdisciplinarity and Transdisciplinarity in Education and Innovation," in *Interdisciplinarity: Problems of Teaching and Research in Universities,* pp. 106–07.

5. Raymond C. Miller, "Varieties of Interdisciplinary Approaches in the Social Sciences: A 1981 Overview," *Issues in Integrative Studies,* 1 (1982), 9.

6. Jean Piaget, "The Epistemology of Interdisciplinary Relationships," in *Interdisciplinarity: Problems of Teaching and Research in Universities,* 136–37.

7. Nancy Anne Cluck, "Interdisciplinary Approaches to the Humanities," *Liberal Education,* 66 No. 1 (1980), 68.

8. Desna W. Hansen, "New Directions in General Education," *Journal of General Education,* 33 (Winter 1982), 24.

9. Heinz Heckhausen, "Discipline and Interdisciplinarity," in *Interdisciplinarity: Problems of Teaching and Research in Universities,* p. 87.

10. See Benjamin D. Paul, "Teaching Cultural Anthropology in Schools of Public Health," in *The Teaching of Anthropology* (Berkeley: Univ. of California Press, 1963), pp. 504–05.

11. Forrest H. Armstrong, "Faculty Development through Interdisciplinarity," *JGE: The Journal of General Education,* 32 No. 11 (1980), 53–54.

12. William C. Sturtevant, "Anthropology, History, and Ethnohistory," *Ethnohistory,* 13 No. 1–2 (1966), 3.

13. Paul W. Wilderson, "Archaeology and the American Historian: An Interdisciplinary Challenge," *American Quarterly,* 27 (May 1972), 115, 118–19.

14. See M.I. Finley, "Archaeology and History," *Daedalus,* 100 No. 1 (1971), 168–86.

15. Joseph J. Kockelmans, "Why Interdisciplinarity?," in *Interdisciplinarity and Higher Education* (University Park: Pennsylvania State Univ. Press, 1979), p. 131.

16. Daniel Alpert, "The Role and Structure of Interdisciplinary and Multidisciplinary Research Centers." Address at the ninth annual meeting of the Council of Graduate Schools, Washington, D.C., 4–6 Dec. 1969, p. 2. ERIC ED 035 363.

17. See "Multidisciplinary, Interdisciplinary: What Is the Difference?," in *Managing Interdisciplinary Research,* ed. S.R. Epton, R.L. Payne, and A.W. Pearson (Chichester: John Wiley, 1983), pp. 3–9.

18. Pierre de Bie, "Introduction" to section on "Multidisciplinary Problem-Focused Research," *International Social Science Journal,* 20 No. 2 (1968), 204.

19. John M. Barnes, "Regional Coordination of Scientists' Initiatives in Interdisciplinary Research," in *Enabling Interdisciplinary Research,* ed. Martha Garrett Russell (St. Paul: Agricultural Experiment Station, University of Minnesota, 1982), pp. 135–37.

20. See Lillian Hoddeson, "The Discovery of the Point-Contact Transistor," *Historical Studies in the Physical Sciences,* 12 No. 1 (1981), 41–76.

21. See B. Wilpert, "Managing Interdisciplinarity with Internationality," in *Interdisciplinary Research Groups,* ed. R.T. Barth and R. Steck (Vancouver: International Research Group on Interdisciplinary Programs, 1979), pp. 168–79.

22. See E.J. Alagoa, "The Inter-Disciplinary Approach to African History in Nigeria," *Présence Africaine,* 94 (1975), 173–74, 182–83.

23. Terrence J. McDonald, "Comment," *Journal of Urban History,* 8 No. 4 (1984), 454.

24. See Theodore Hershberg, "Prologue," *Philadelphia, Work, Space, Family, and Group Experience in the Nineteenth Century: Essays toward an Interdisciplinary History of the City* (New York: Oxford Univ. Press, 1981) pp. vi–viii.

25. Hershberg, p. viii.

26. See J.M. Sharp, "A Method for Peer Group Appraisal and Interpretation of Data Developed in Interdisciplinary Research Programmes," in *Managing Interdisciplinary Research,* pp. 211–19.

27. Hershberg, p. viii.

28. Allen Pred, review of *Philadelphia. Work, Space, Family, and Group Experience in the Nineteenth Century,*" *American Historical Review,* 87 No. 11 (1982), 268–69.

29. David A. Bella and Kenneth J. Williamson, "Diagnosis of Chronic Impacts of Estuarine Dredging," *Journal of Environmental Systems,* 9 No. 4 (1979–80), 290.

30. Information is from J. Barmark and G. Wallen, "Interaction of Cognitive and Social Factors in Steering a Large Interdisciplinary Project," in *Interdisciplinary Research Groups,* pp. 180–90.

31. Hakan Törnebohm, Report on "Researcher Roles and the Organization of Interdisciplinary Groups: R&D for Higher Education." Stockholm, Research and Development Unit of the Swedish National Board of Universities and Colleges, 1980. ERIC ED 201 235.

32. Barmark and Wallen, pp. 180–90.

33. Berger, p. 25.

34. Piaget, p. 130.

35. Alpert, p. 3.

36. Georges Gusdorf, "Project for Interdisciplinary Research," *Diogenes,* 42 (Summer 1963), 119–42.

37. See Richard B. Schwartz, "Contextual Criticism and the Question of Pedagogy," *Eighteenth Century Life,* 5 No. 3 (1979), 95–100.

38. See David Sheehan, "Pope and Palladio, Hogarth and Fielding: Kinds of Disciplines in Interdisciplinary Studies," *Eighteenth Century Life,* 5 No. 3 (1979), 77–78.

39. Heckhausen, pp. 83–89.

40. Marcel Boisot, "Discipline and Interdisciplinarity," *Interdisciplinarity: Problems of Teaching and Research in Universities,* 89–97.

41. Claudia Huerkamp et al., "Criteria of Interdisciplinarity," in *Center for Interdisciplinary Research: The Univerisity of Bielefeld: Annual Report 1978 and Supplement 1979-1981* (Bielefeld: Center for Interdisciplinary Research, 1981, Supplement to the 1978 Edition), pp. 23–24.

42. Hansen, p. 24.

43. See Daniel Rigney and Donna Barnes, "Patterns of Interdisciplinary Citation in the Social Sciences," *Social Science Quarterly,* 61 No. 1 (1980), 126.

44. Miller, pp. 20–22.

45. Susan Magery, "Women's Studies in Australia: Towards Trans-disciplinary Learning," *Journal of Educational Thought,* 17 No. 2 (1983), 167.

46. William Eckhardt, "Changing Concerns in Peace Research and Education," *Bulletin of Peace Proposals,* 3 (1974), 280.

47. Magorah Maruyama, "Paradigmatology and Its Application to Cross-Disciplinary, Cross-Professional, and Cross-Cultural Communication," *Dialectica,* 28 No. 3–4 (1974), 191.

48. Richard M. Coe, "The Rhetoric of Paradox," in *A Symposium on Rhetoric,* ed. W.E. Tanner, J.D. Bishop, and T.S. Kobler (Denton: Texas Women's Univ. Press, 1976), p. 4.

49. Maruyama, p. 141.

50. Paul T. Baker, "Human Population Biology: A Viable Transdisciplinary Science," *Human Biology,* 54 No. 2 (1982), 203–20.

51. Eckhardt. pp. 280–83.

52. Joseph B. Casagrande, "The Relations of Anthropology with the Social Sciences," in *The Teaching of Anthropology,* p. 461.

53. Erich Jantsch, *Interdisciplinarity: Problems of Teaching and Research in Universities,* p. 106.

54. B. Wilpert, p. 171.

55. Henry A. Regier, *A Balanced Science of Renewable Resources with Particular Reference to Fisheries* (Seattle: Univ. of Washington Press, 1978).

56. Erich Jantsch, "Towards Interdisciplinarity and Transdisciplinarity in Education and Innovation," in *Interdisciplinarity: Problems of Teaching and Research in Universities,* p. 104.

57. Erich Jantsch, "Interdisciplinarity: Dreams and Reality," *Prospects,* 10 No. 3 (1980), 305.

58. Information is from V.A. Holm and R.E. McCarthy, "Interdisciplinary Child Development Team: Team Issues and Training in Interdisciplinariness," in *Early Intervention: A Team Approach,* ed. K.E. Allen, V.A. Holm and S. Schieferbusch (Baltimore: University Park Press, 1978), pp. 102–03.

59. Stephen W. Stile and F. Ann Olson, "The Transdisciplinary Model: An Alternative

Approach for Meeting the Needs of Children in Early Childhood Education Programs for the Handicapped" (Las Cruces: New Mexico State University, 1980). ERIC ED 189 803.

60. Information and charts are from R. Wasniowski, "Futures Research as a Framework for Transdisciplinary Research," in *Managing Interdisciplinary Research,* p. 228–35.

61. Information is from Sverre Sjölander, "Long-Term and Short-Term Interdisciplinary Work: Difficulties, Pitfalls, and Built-In Failures," in *Inter-Disciplinarity Revisited,* ed. Lennart Levin and Ingemar Lind (Stockholm: OECD, SNBUC, Linköping University, 1985), pp. 85–101.

62. See Ernest Lynton, "Interdisciplinarity: Rationales and Criteria of Assessment," in *Inter-Disciplinarity Revisited,* pp. 137–52.

Chapter 4

1. Oscar Handlin, "The Search for the Factual in History," in *The Search for Absolute Values in a Changing World* (New York: International Cultural Foundation Press, 1978), 2, 1247.

2. The last expression is used by Stanley Milgram in "Interdisciplinary Thinking and the Small World Problem," in *Interdisciplinary Relationships in the Social Sciences,* ed. Muzfer and Carolyn Sherif (Chicago: Aldine, 1969), p. 119.

3. Renée Friedman used this expression at the Third International Conference on Interdisciplinary Research in Seattle, Wash., 2 Aug. 1984.

4. Norman Birnbaum, "The Arbitrary Disciplines," *Change: The Magazine of Higher Learning,* July/Aug. 1969, 12.

5. Robert Dubin, "Contiguous Problem Analysis: An Approach to Systematic Theories about Social Organization," in *Interdisciplinary Relationships in the Social Sciences,* p. 68.

6. Rustum Roy, "Interdisciplinary Science on Campus," in *Interdisciplinarity in Higher Education,* ed. Joseph Kockelmans (University Park: Pennsylvania State Univ. Press, 1979), p. 162.

7. B.J. James, "Niche Defense among Learned Gentlemen," *Human Organization,* 30 (Fall 1971), 224.

8. Marvin Mikesell, "The Borderlands of Geography as a Social Science," in *Interdisciplinary Relationships in the Social Sciences,* p. 237.

9. Ernest L. Boyer, "The Quest for Common Learning," in *Common Learning: A Carnegie Colloquium on General Education* (Washington, D.C.: Carnegie Foundation, 1981), p. 18.

10. Used by Alvin Gouldner in *The Coming Crisis of Western Sociology* (New York: Basic Books, 1979), and Rustum Roy, p. 168.

11. David Riesman, "The Scholar at the Border: Staying Put and Moving Around inside the American University," *Columbia Forum,* Spring 1974, 26.

12. J.R. Royce, "Toward a Theory of Man: A Multi-Disciplinary, Multi-Systems, Multi-Dimensional Approach," in *The Search for Absolute Values in a Changing World,* p. 1124.

13. Donald Campbell, "Ethnocentrism of Disciplines and the Fish-Scale Model of Omniscience," in *Interdisciplinary Relationships in the Social Sciences,* p. 137.

14. Forrest Armstrong in "Faculty Development through Interdisciplinarity," *JGE: The Journal of General Education,* 32 No. 1 (1980), 55.

15. Veronica Strong-Boag, "'You be sure to tell it like it is': The Recovery of Canada's Past," *Journal of Canadian Studies,* 15 No. 3–4 (1981), 217.

16. Jerry G. Gaff and Robert C. Wilson, "Faculty Cultures and Interdisciplinary Studies," *Journal of Higher Education,* 42 No. 3 (1971), 199.

17. Rustum Roy, p. 168.

18. George J. Gumerman and David A. Phillips, Jr., "Archaeology beyond Anthropology," *American Antiquity,* 43 No. 2 (1978), 186.

19. M. Landau, H. Proshansky, and W.H. Ittelson, "The Interdisciplinary Approach and the Concept of Behavioral Science," in *Decisions, Values, and Groups,* ed. Norman Washburne (New York: Pergamon Press, 1960), II, p. 11.

20. Wilhelm Sturmer, "Interdisciplinary Paleontology," *Interdisciplinary Science Reviews,* 9 No. 2 (1984), 132.

21. Dawn Wallace, "Finding the Common Ground," *English Journal,* 69 No. 2 (1980), 37.

22. Kenneth E. Boulding, "Peace Research," *International Social Science Journal,* 29 No. 4 (1977), 605.

23. John Lankford, "The Writing of American History in the 1960s: A Critical Bibliography of Materials of Interest to Sociologists," *Sociological Quarterly,* 14 (Winter 1973), 126.

24. A. King and J. Brownell, *The Curriculum and the Disciplines of Knowledge* (New York: J. Wiley, 1966), pp. 144–46.

25. Commission on the Humanities, *The Humanities in American Life* (Berkeley: Univ. of California Press, 1980), p. 76.

26. L. Jackson Newell and Karen I. Spear, "New Dimensions for Academic Careers: Rediscovering Intrinsic Satisfactions," *Liberal Education,* 69 No. 2 (1983), 115.

27. Pierre Duguet, "Approach to the Problems," in *Interdisciplinarity: Problems of Teaching and Research in Universities* (Paris: Organization for Economic Cooperation and Development, 1972), p. 3.

28. Heinz Heckhausen, "Disciplines and Interdisciplinarity," in *Interdisciplinarity: Problems of Teaching and Research in Universities,* p. 87.

29. Joseph J. Kockelmans, "Why Interdisciplinarity?," *Interdisciplinarity and Higher Education,* p. 135.

30. Noted in Lowell H. Hattery, "Interdisciplinary Research Management," in *Interdisciplinary Research Groups,* ed. Richard R. Barth and Rudy Steck (Vancouver: International Research Groups on Interdisciplinary Programs, 1979), p. 22.

31. John Higham, *Writing American History: Essays on Modern Scholarship* (Bloomington: Indiana Univ. Press, 1970), p. 28.

32. Geoffrey Squires, "Discussion," in *Interdisciplinarity. Papers Presented at the SRHE Symposium on Interdisciplinary Courses in European Education, 13 September 1975,* p. 9 ERIC ED 165 512.

33. Fernand Braudel, *On History,* trans. Sarah Matthews (Chicago: University of Chicago Press, 1980), p. 26.

34. Robert L. Scott, "Personal and Institutional Problems Encountered in Being Interdisciplinary," in *Interdisciplinarity and Higher Education,* p. 312.

35. George Lakoff and Mark Johnson, *Metaphors We Live By* (Chicago: Univ. of Chicago Press, 1980), p. 4.

36. Joan Dyste Lind, "Confusion, Conflict—Cooperation?," *Improving College and University Teaching,* 30 No. 1 (1982), 17.

37. Muzafer and Carolyn Sherif, "Interdisciplinary Coordination as a Validity Check: Retrospect and Prospects," in *Interdisciplinary Relationships in the Social Sciences,* p. 8.

38. Dubin, p. 67.

39. Murray Wax, "Myth and Interrelationship in Social Sciences: Illustrated through Anthropology and Sociology," in *Interdisciplinary Relationships in the Social Sciences,* pp. 86–87.

40. Andre Lichnerowicz, "Mathematic and Transdisciplinarity," in *Interdisciplinarity: Problems of Teaching and Research in Universities,* p. 121.

41. Muzafer Sherif, "Crossdisciplinary Coordination in the Social Sciences," in *Interdisciplinary Relationships in the Social Sciences,* p. 8.

42. Arthur H. Scouten, "The Limitations of the Interdisciplinary Approach," *Eighteenth-Century Life,* 5 No. 3 (1979), 107.

43. J.H. Lesher, "An Interdisciplinary Course on Classical Athens," *Teaching Philosophy,* 5 No. 3 (1982), 203.

44. Norwood Russell Hanson, *Perception and Discovery: An Introduction to Scientific Inquiry,* ed. Willard Humphreys (San Francisco: Freeman, Cooper, 1969).

45. Daniel Rich and Robert Warren, "The Intellectual Future of Urban Affairs: Theoretical, Normative, and Organizational Options," *Social Science Journal,* 17 No. 2 (1980), 63.

46. John G. Reid, "'The Beginnings of the Maritimes': A Reappraisal," *American Review of Canadian Studies,* 9 No. 1 (1979), 41.

47. Edward Joseph Shoben, Jr., "General and Liberal Education: Problems of Person and Purpose," *Perspectives. Journal of the Association of General and Liberal Education,* 4 (Spring 1972), 8.

48. Scott, p. 319.

49. Guy Berger as quoted by Guy Michaud in "General Conclusions," in *Interdisciplinarity: Problems of Teaching and Research in Universities,* p. 287.

50. Kockelmans, quoting one kind of argument in "Why Interdisciplinarity?," p. 149.

51. Lichnerowicz, p. 122.

52. William J. McGuire, "Theory-Oriented Research in Natural Settings: The Best of Both Worlds in Social Psychology," in *Interdisciplinary Relationships in the Social Sciences,* p. 22.

53. Campbell, p. 339.

54. John Deely, *Introducing Semiotics: Its History and Doctrine* (Bloomington: Indiana Univ. Press, 1980), p. xvi.

55. Wayne C. Booth, "Mere Rhetoric, Rhetoric, and the Search for Common Learning," in *Common Learning,* p. 37.

56. Milgram, p. 103.

57. Lichnerowicz, p. 122.

58. Nevitt Sanford, "The Human Problems Institute and General Education," *Daedalus,* Summer 1965, pp. 646–47.

59. C.C. Abt, from an OECD document, "One Description and One Ideal Model and Implications for University Organisation for General, Professional, and Lifelong Education and Research" (Note by the Secretariat), p. 6.

60. Lewis Thomas, "The Natural World," in *Common Learning,* p. 112.

61. M. Gordon Wolman, "Interdisciplinary Education: A Continuing Experiment," *Science,* 25 Nov. 1977, p. 804.

62. Vincent Kavaloski, "Interdisciplinary Education and Humanistic Aspiration," in *Interdisciplinarity and Higher Education,* p. 229.

63. Asa Briggs and Guy Michaud, "Perspectives: Context and Challenge," in *Interdisciplinarity: Problems of Teaching and Research,* p. 191.

64. Joseph Kockelmans, "Why Interdisciplinarity?," in *Interdisciplinarity and Higher Education,* p. 146.

65. A.J. Meadows, "Diffusion of Information across the Sciences," *Interdisciplinary Science Reviews,* 1 (Sept. 1976), 259.

66. Landau, Proshanky, and Ittelson use the phrase "vertical pillars of knowledge," p. 16.

67. S. Aronoff, "Interdisciplinary Scholarship." Address to the Ninth Annual Meeting of the Council of Graduate Schools, 5 Dec. 1969. ERIC ED 035 365.

68. Campbell, pp. 329–31.

69. Lucien W. Pye, "The Confrontation between Discipline and Area Studies," in *Political Science and Area Studies: Rivals or Partners?,* ed. Lucien W. Pye (Bloomington: Indiana Univ. Press, 1979), p. 20.

70. Gene Wise, "Some Elementary Axioms for an American Culture Studies," *Prospects,* 4 (Winter 1978), 517–47.

71. John Adams, "The Analysis of Rural Indian Economy: Economics and Anthropology," *Man in India,* 52 No. 1 (1972), 3.

72. Emil Hadač et al., "Complex Interdisciplinary Investigation of Landscape," *Landscape Planning,* 4 (1977), 338.

73. Wise, 539.

74. Julian Huxley, "Science and Synthesis," in *Science and Synthesis* (New York: Springer-Verlag, 1967), p. 32.

75. Les Humphreys, "Interdisciplinarity: A Selected Bibliography for Users," p. 3. ERIC ED 115 536.

75. Huxley, p. 32.

77. B.M. Kedrov, "Integration and Differentiation in the Modern Sciences: General Evolution of Scientific Knowledge," in *Science and Synthesis,* p. 72.

Chapter 5

1. Clive Dewey, "Annals of Rural Punjab," *Modern Asian Studies,* 10 No. 1 (1976), 131.

2. Gerard Studdert-Kennedy, *Evidence and Explanation in Social Science: An Interdisciplinary Approach* (London: Routledge & Kegan Paul, 1975), p. 217.

3. Archie J. Baum, "Interdisciplinology: The Science of Interdisciplinary Research," *Nature and System,* 2 No. 1 (1980), 29.

4. Physics Survey Committee, *Physics in Perspective* (Washington, D.C.: National Academy of Sciences, 1972), pp. 67, 112, 285.

5. Thurstan Shaw comments on relations between archaeology and the sciences in "In Praise of Interdisciplinary Archaeology," *Interdisciplinary Science Reviews,* 2 No. 2 (1977), 92–93.

6. James Kinneavy, *A Theory of Discourse* (New York: Norton, 1980), p. 144.

7. Muzafer and Carolyn Sherif, "Interdisciplinary Coordination as a Validity Check," in *Interdisciplinary Relationships in the Social Sciences,* ed. Muzafer and Carolyn W. Sherif (Chicago: Aldine, 1969), p. xii.

8. Samuel P. Huntington, "The Change to Change: Modernization, Development, and Politics," *Comparative Politics,* 3 No. 3 (1971), 305.

9. Emil Hadač et al., "Complex Interdisciplinary Investigation of Landscape," *Landscape Planning,* 4 (1977), 339.

10. James Austin makes this point in "On the Trail of Serendipity," in *Chase, Chance, and Creativity: The Lucky Art of Novelty* (New York: Columbia Univ. Press, 1978), pp. 66–71.

11. Jack Lee Mahan, Jr., discusses this aspect of interdisciplinarity in "Toward Transdisciplinary Inquiry in the Humane Sciences," Diss., United States International University, San Diego, 1970.

12. Michael Schiffer, "Some Issues in the Philosophy of Archaeology," *American Antiquity,* 46 No. 4 (1981), 899–908.

13. Philip Abrams, "History, Sociology, Historical Sociology," *Past and Present,* 87 (May 1980), 4.

14. Huntington, p. 305.

15. Marvin Mikesell, "The Borderlands of Geography as a Social Science," in *Interdisciplinary Relationships in the Social Sciences,* p. 233.

16. See David J. Hufford, "Psychology, Psychoanalysis, and Folklore," *Southern Folklore Quarterly,* 38 (Sept. 1974), 187–97.

17. M. Palmer, L. Stern, and C. Gaile, *The Interdisciplinary Study of Politics* (New York: Harper and Row, 1974), 12.

18. Theodore K. Rabb, "The Historian and the Climatologist," *Journal of Interdisciplinary History,* 10 No. 4 (1980), 834.

19. This is an extension of problems cited by Leon Pomerance, "The Need for Guidelines in Interdisciplinary Meetings," *American Journal of Archaeology,* 75 No. 4 (1971), 429.

20. Janice M. Lauer used this term in "Studies of Written Discourse: Dappled Discipline." Address to the Rhetoric Society of America at the thirty-fourth meeting of the Conference on College Composition and Communication in Detroit, Mich., 17 Mar. 1983.

21. Andrew B. Appleby, "Disease, Diet, and History," *Journal of Interdisciplinary History,* 8 No. 4 (1978), 729.

22. Earl Pomerance, "The Need for Guidelines in Interdisciplinary Meetings," *American Journal of Archaeology,* 75 No. 4 (1971), 429.

23. See Marilyn Robinson Waldman, "Islamic Studies: A New Orientalism?," *Journal of Interdisciplinary History,* 8 No. 3 (1978), 545–62.

24. "Fryxell Award for Interdisciplinary Research," *American Antiquity,* 45 No. 2 (1980), 229–30.

25. "1983 Fryxell Award for Interdisciplinary Research," *American Antiquity,* 48 No. 3 (1983), 453.

26. "Fryxell Award for Interdisciplinary Research," *American Antiquity,* 45 No. 4 (1980), 660–61.

27. George J. Gumerman and David A. Phillips, Jr., "Archaeology beyond Anthropology," *American Antiquity,* 43 No. 2 (1978), 186–87.

28. The following discussion is from Schiffer, pp. 899–908; see also Paul S. Martin, "The Revolution in Archaeology," *American Antiquity,* 36 (1971), 1–8.

29. Gumerman and Phillips, Jr., p. 184.

30. The following summary is from Schiffer, pp. 901–04.

31. Karl W. Butzer, "The Ecological Approach to Archaeology: Are We Really Trying?," *American Antiquity,* 40 No. 1 (1975), 106–16.

32. Robert E. Rhoades, "Archaeological Use and Abuse of Ecological Concepts and Studies: The Ecotone Example," *American Antiquity,* 43 No. 4 (1978), 608.

33. Gumerman and Phillips, pp. 186–87.

34. See Douglas M. Davy, "Borrowed Concepts, A Comment on Rhoades," *American Antiquity,* 45 No. 2 (1980), 346–49; and the reply by Rhoades and David A. Phillips, Jr. on 349–50.

35. Robert Rhoades makes this point.

36. Butzer, pp. 106–16.

37. Ellwyn R. Stoddard, "Multidisciplinary Research Funding: A 'Catch 22' Enigma," *American Sociologist,* 17 Nov. 1982, 210–16.

38. Robert Minshull, "Functions of Geography in American Studies," *Journal of American Studies,* 7 No. 3 (1973), 268.

39. Richard Harvey Brown, *A Poetic for Sociology: Toward a Logic of Discovery for the Human Sciences* (Cambridge: Cambridge Univ. Press, 1977), p. 78.

40. Richard Boyd discusses theory constitutive metaphors in "Metaphor and Theory Change: What Is 'Metaphor' a Metaphor for," in *Metaphor and Thought,* ed. Andrew Ortony (Cambridge: Cambridge Univ. Press, 1979), pp. 356–408.

41. Arthur Porter, "The Expansion of Transdisciplinary Studies," *Transactions of the Royal Society of Canada,* Ser. 4 (1973), II, 14.

42. Hugh G. Petrie explores this idea in "Do You See What I See? The Epistemology of Interdisciplinary Inquiry," *Educational Research,* 5 No. 2 (1976), 9–15.

43. George Steiner, *After Babel: Aspects of Language and Translation* (London: Oxford Univ. Press, 1975), pp. 296–301.

44. See Stephen N. Schneider, "Climate Change and the World Predicament: A Case Study for Interdisciplinary Research," *Climatic Change,* 1 (1977), 21–43.

Chapter 6

1. David Riesman, "The Scholar at the Border: Staying Put and Moving Around inside the American University," *Columbia Forum,* Spring 1974, p. 26.

2. Sarah Hoagland, "On the Reeducation of Sophie," in *Women's Studies: An Interdisciplinary Collection,* ed. Kathleen O'Connor Blumhagen and Walter Johnson (Westport, Conn.: Greenwood, 1978), p. 17.

3. Annette Kolodny, "Dancing through the Minefield: Some Observations on the Theory, Practice, and Politics of a Feminist Literary Criticism," *Feminist Studies,* 6 (Spring 1980), 8.

4. Ellen Bonaparth, "Evaluating Women's Studies: Academic Theory and Practice," in *Women' Studies: An Interdisciplinary Collection,* p. 23.

5. Ronald Walters, "The Discipline of Black Studies," *Negro Educational Review,* 21 No. 4 (1970), 144.

6. Russell Thornton, "American Indian Studies as an Academic Discipline," *Journal of Ethnic Studies,* 5 (Fall 1977), 10–13.

7. Arthur Kroker, "Migration across the Disciplines," *Journal of Canadian Studies,* 15 (Fall 1980), 3.

8. Marilyn Salzman-Webb, "Feminist Studies: Frill or Necessity," *Female Studies V,* ed. Rae Lee Siporin (Pittsburgh: Know, 1972), p. 67.

9. Carlene Young, "The Struggle and Dream of Black Studies," *Journal of Negro Education,* 53 No. 3 (1984), 369.

10. Carlos A. Brossard, "Classifying Black Studies Programs," *Journal of Negro Education,* 53 No. 3 (1984), 279–91. See especially the citations in n.6.

11. Philip T.K. Daniel, "Theory Building in Black Studies," *Black Scholar,* 12 No. 3 (1981), 34.

12. Maurice Jackson, "Toward a Sociology of Black Studies," *Journal of Black Studies,"* 1 (Dec. 1970), 134–35.

13. See Rob Walker, "Holistic Knowledge and the Politics of Fragmentation." Speech delivered at the symposium "An Image of the Whole: Knowledge and Curriculum in an Age of Fragmentation." ERIC ED 153 817.

14. Sinclair Goodlad, "What Is an Academic Discipline," in *Cooperation and Choice in Higher Education,* ed. Roy Cox (London: University of London, 1979), p. 12. ERIC ED 181 836.

15. Elizabeth Fee, "Is Feminism a Threat to Scientific Objectivity?," *International Journal of Women's Studies,* 4 No. 4 (1981), 384.

16. Richard M. McKeon, "Philosophy and Action," *Ethics,* 62 No. 2 (1952), 80.

17. Robert S. Merton, "Social Problems and Sociological Theory," reprinted in *Social Research and the Practicing Professions,* ed. Aaron Rosenblatt and Thomas F. Gieryn (Cambridge: Abt Books, 1982), p. 45.

18. Marilyn Boxer, "For and about Women: The Theory and Practice of Women's Studies in the United States," *Signs,* 7 No. 3 (1982), 674–75.

19. See Saunders Redding, "The Black Revolution in American Studies," and Imamu Amiri Baraka's "Reply" in *American Studies International,* 17 No. 4 (1979), 8–21.

20. Benjamin I. Schwartz, "Presidential Address: Area Studies as a Critical Discipline," *Journal of Asian Studies,* 40 (Nov. 1980), 18.

21. See "The Historical Setting," in *Beyond Growth: The Next Stage in Language and Area Studies,* ed. Richard Lambert et al. (Washington, D.C.: Association of American Universities, 1984), pp. 2–4.

22. Schwartz, p. 15.

23. For a comprehensive history, see Robert A. McCaughey, *International Studies and Academic Enterprise: A Chapter in the Enclosure of American Learning* (New York: Columbia Univ. Press, 1984).

24. C.A. Fisher, "The Contribution of Geography to Foreign Area Studies: The Case of Southeast Asia," in *Geographers Abroad: Essays on the Problems and Prospects of Research in Foreign Areas,* ed. Marvin Mikesell (Chicago: Univ. of Chicago Press, 1973), pp. 185–86.

25. Julian H. Steward, *Area Research: Theory and Practice* (New York: Social Science Research Council, 1950), pp. 2, 95–96, 126, 151. Bull. 63.

26. Harry Eckstein, "A Critique of Area Studies from a West European Perspective," in *Political Science and Area Studies: Rivals or Partners?,* ed. Lucian Pye (Bloomington: Indiana Univ. Press, 1975), p. 202.

27. Lucian Pye, "The Confrontation between Discipline and Area Studies," in *Political Science and Area Studies,* p. 10.

28. See Edward W. Soja, "African Geographical Studies and Comparative Regional Development," in *Geographers Abroad,* pp. 167.

29. Hanna Pananek, "Women in South and Southeast Asia: Issues and Research," *Signs,* 1 No. 1 (1975), 202–03.

30. This discussion is from Lucian Pye, "The Confrontation between Discipline and Area Studies," 14–15.

31. Soja, p. 167.

32. *Beyond Growth,* pp. 101–15.

33. Fisher, p. 188.

34. See Marilyn Robinson Waldman, "Islamic Studies: A New Orientalism?," *Journal of Interdisciplinary History,* 8 No. 3 (1978), 545–62.

35. Edward Said, *Orientalism* (New York: Pantheon, 1978), p. 52.

36. Chalmers Johnson, "Political Science and East Asian Studies," in *Political Science and Area Studies,* p. 80.

37. Harry Eckstein, "A Critique of Area Studies from a West European Perspective," in *Political Science and Area Studies,* 215.

38. Johnson, p. 81.

39. Chauncy D. Harris, "Geographic Studies of the Soviet Union: Some Reflections," in *Geographers Abroad,* p. 14.

40. Johnson, p. 81.

41. Kalman H. Silvert, "Politics and the Study of Latin America," in *Political Science and Area Studies,* p. 155.

42. Pye, p. 20.

43. Pye, p. 18.

44. Edward Said uses this phrase in "Orientalism Reconsidered," *Cultural Critique,* 1 (Fall 1985), 94.

45. Pye, p. 3.

46. Alfred G. Meyer, "Political Science and Area Studies," in *Political Science versus Area Studies,* p. 101.

47. See Yves Bertrand's discussion of this problem in "Disciplinarité ou Inter-disciplinarité?," *Journal of Canadian Studies,* 15 No. 3 (1980), especially 21–24.

Chapter 7

1. See definitions of disciplinarity and interdisciplinarity in *Interdisciplinarity: Problems of Teaching and Research in Universities* (Paris: Organization for Economic Cooperation and Development, 1972), especially pp. 75–139.

2. See Sinclair Goodlad, "What Is an Academic Discipline?," in *Cooperation and Choice in Higher Education,* ed. Roy Cox (London: University of London, 1979). ERIC ED 181 836.

3. Raymond C. Miller, "Varieties of Interdisciplinary Approaches in the Social Sciences," *Issues in Integrative Studies,* 1 (1982), 6.

4. Stanley Bailis, "The Social Sciences in American Studies: An Integrative Conception," *American Quarterly,* 2 No. 3 (1974), 204.

5. R.D. Whitley, "The Organization of Scientific Work in 'Configurational' and 'Restricted' Sciences," *International Journal of Sociology,* 8 No. 1–2 (1978), 95–112.

6. Richard Rose, "Disciplined Research and Undisciplined Problems," *International Social Science Journal,* 28 No. 1 (1976), 106–07.

7. J.D. Thompson, R.W. Hawkes, and R.W. Avery, "Truth Strategies and University Organization," *Educational Administration Quarterly,* 5 (Spring 1969), 5.

8. See a pertinent discussion of the Lodahl/Gordon scheme in Mark E. Thompson and David A. Brewster, "Faculty Behavior in Low Paradigm versus High Paradigm Disciplines: A Case Study," *Research in Higher Education,* 8 (1978), 169–75.

9. Stephen Toulmin, "The Variety of Rational Enterprises," in *Human Understanding* (Princeton: Princeton Univ. Press, 1972), pp. 364–411.

10. Archie J. Baum, *The Specialist: His Philosophy, His Disease, His Cure* (Delhi: Macmillan Company of India, 1977), 27.

11. David Hackett Fisher, "Climate and History: Priorities for Research," in *Climate and History: Studies in Interdisciplinary History,* ed. Robert I. Rotberg and Theodore K. Rabb (Princeton: Princeton Univ. Press, 1981), 241.

12. Lindley Darden and Nancy Maull, "Interfield Theories," *Philosophy of Science,* 44 (1977), 43–64.

13. Wolfram Swoboda, "Disciplines and Interdisciplinarity: A Historical Perspective," in *Interdisciplinarity and Higher Education,* ed. Joseph J. Kockelmans (University Park: Pennsylvania State Univ. Press, 1979), p. 53.

14. Dael L. Wolfle, "Interdisciplinary Research as a Form of Research," *Journal of the Society of Research Administrators,* Fall 1981, p. 5.

15. Daniel Rich and Robert Warren, "The Intellectual Future of Urban Affairs: Theoretical, Normative, and Organizational Options," *Social Science Journal,* 17 No. 2 (1980), 59–60.

16. Heinz Heckhausen, "Discipline and Interdisciplinarity," in *Interdisciplinarity: Problems of Teaching and Research in Universities,* pp. 83–99.

17. Muzafer and Carolyn Sherif, "Preface," *Interdisciplinary Relationships in the Social Sciences,* ed. Muzafer Sherif and Carolyn Sherif (Chicago: Aldine, 1969), p. xii.

18. Arthur Porter, "The Expansion of Transdisciplinary Studies," *Transactions of the Royal Society of Canada,* Ser. 4. II (1973), 12.

19. Wolf Lepenies, "History and Anthropology: A Historical Appraisal of the Current Contact between the Disciplines," *Social Science Information,* 15 No. 213 (1976), 287–306.

20. Daya Krishna, "Culture," *International Social Science Journal,* 29 No. 4 (1977), 652.

21. David Riesman, "The Scholar at the Border: Staying Put and Moving Around inside the American University," *Columbia Forum,* Spring 1974, p. 29.

22. Corinna Delkeskamp, "Interdisciplinarity: A Critical Appraisal," in *Knowledge, Value, and Belief,* ed. H.T. Engelhardt and D. Callahan (Hastings-on-Hudson: Hastings Center, 1977), p. 330.

23. Michael W. Messmer, "The Vogue of the Interdisciplinary," *Centennial Review,* 12 No. 4 (1978), 474.

24. Kenneth Boulding, "The Future of General Systems," in *Interdisciplinary Teaching,* ed. Alvin M. White (San Francisco: Jossey Bass, 1981), p. 33.

25. Georges Gusdorf used this phrase in "Past, Present, and Future in Interdisciplinary Research," *International Social Science Journal,* 29 No. 4 (1977), 580-99.

26. Kenneth E. Boulding, "Peace Research," *International Social Science Journal,* 29 No. 4 (1977), 604.

27. See a discussion of this problem in David Webber and Roger Lotchin, "The New Chicano Urban History," *History Teacher,* 16 No. 2 (1983), 223-47.

28. Stephen Toulmin makes these points in describing "non-disciplinary activities" in *Human Understanding: The Collective Use and Evolution of Concepts* (Princeton: Princeton Univ. Press, 1972), p. 396.

29. Information is from Peter W. Mullen, "Editorial: An Immunopharmacology Journal: Reflections on its Interdisciplinary and Historical Context," *International Journal of Immunopharmacology,* 1 No. 1 (1979), 1-4.

30. Tamara K. Hareven, "The History of the Family as an Interdisciplinary Field," *Journal of Interdisciplinary History,* 2 No. 2 (1971), 399-400.

31. R. Boutilier, J.C. Roed, and A.C. Svendsen, "Crises in the Two Social Psychologies: A Critical Comparison," *Social Psychology Quarterly,* 13 No. 1 (1980), 5-17.

32. Rae Carlson, "What's Social about Social Psychology? Where's the Person in Personality Research?," *Journal of Personality and Social Psychology,* 47 No. 6 (1984), 1304.

33. See Thomas O. Blank, "Two Social Psychologies: Is Segregation Inevitable or Acceptable?," *Personality and Social Psychology Bulletin,* 4 No. 4 (1978), 553-56; see also David W. Wilson and Robert B. Schafer, "Is Social Psychology Interdisciplinary," *Personality and Social Psychology Bulletin,* 4 No. 4 (1978), 548.

34. See Ronald J. Grele, "A Surmisable Variety: Interdisciplinarity and Oral Testimony," *American Quarterly,* 27 (Aug. 1975), 275-95.

35. Janice Lauer, "Studies of Written Discourse: Dappled Discipline." Address to the Rhetoric Society of America, at the 34th meeting of the Conference on College Composition and Communication in Detroit, Mich., 17 Mar. 1983.

36. Michael H. Agar, "Toward an Ethnographic Language," *American Anthropologist,* 84 (Dec. 1982), 781.

37. Michael Agar, "Getting Better Quality Stuff: Methodological Competition in an Interdisciplinary Niche," *Urban Life,* 9 No. 1 (1980), 34-36, 49.

38. Information is from Daniel Rich and Robert Warren, "The Intellectual Future of Urban Affairs: Theoretical, Normative, and Organizational Options," *Social Science Journal,* 17 No. 2 (1980), 53-66.

39. Information is from Lynton K. Caldwell, "Environmental Studies: Discipline or Metadiscipline?," *Environmental Professional,* 5 (1983), 247-59.

40. Fred Matthews, "Polemical Palefaces and Genteel Redskins: The Debate over American Culture and the Origins of the American Studies Movement," *American Quarterly,* 35 No. 5 (1983), 545.

41. Robert Sklar, "The Problem of an American Studies 'Philosophy': A Bibliography of New Directions," *American Quarterly,"* 27 No. 3 (1973), 245-46.

42. Henry Wasser, "Principled Opportunism and American Studies," in *American*

Studies in Transition, ed. Marshall W. Fishwick (Philadelphia: Univ. of Pennsylvania Press, 1964), 166.

43. Leo Marx, "Comment [on C. Vann Woodward's J. Franklin Jameson Lecture, 'The Aging of America,']" *American Historical Review,* 82 (1977), 599.

44. David Marcell, "Characteristically American: Another Perspective on American Studies," *Centennial Review,* 21 No. 4 (1977), 388–400.

45. David W. Marcell, "Recent Trends in American Studies in the United States," *American Studies: An International Newsletter,* 8 No. 1 (1970), 9.

46. Robert E. Spiller, "Unity and Diversity in the Study of American Culture: The American Studies Association in Perspective," *American Quarterly,* 25 No. 5 (1973), 614–17.

47. See Guenther H. Lenz, "American Studies – Beyond the Crisis?: Recent Redefinitions and the Meaning of Theory, History, and Practical Criticism," *Prospects,* 7 (1982), 53–113.

48. J. Mechling, R. Merideth, and D. Wilson use this term in "American Culture Studies: The Discipline and the Curriculum," *American Quarterly,* 25 No. 4 (1973), 368.

49. See especially Stanley Bailis, "The Social Sciences in American Studies: An Integrative Conception," *American Quarterly,* 26 (1974), 202–24.

50. Norman Dinges uses this phrase in "Interdisciplinary Collaboration in Cross-Cultural Social Science Research," *Research in Culture Learning: Language and Conceptual Studies,* ed. Michael P. Hamnett and Richard W. Brislin (Hawaii: East-West Center, 1980), 171.

51. Donald T. Campbell, "Ethnocentrism of Disciplines and the Fish-Scale Model of Omniscience," in *Interdisciplinary Relationships in the Social Sciences,* p. 328.

52. E. Michael Lipton, "Interdisciplinary Studies in Less Developed Countries," *Journal of Development Studies,* 7 No. 1 (1970), 15.

53. H.C. Brookfield, "The Pacific Realm," in *Geographers Abroad: Essays on the Problems and Prospects of Research in Foreign Areas,* ed. Marvin Mikesell (Chicago: Univ. of Chicago Press, 1979), 75, 80–81, 91.

54. For an example see Abraham Wandersman, "A Framework of Participation in Community Organizations," *Journal of Applied Behavioral Science,* 17 No. 1 (1981), 27–53.

55. Michael Woolf, "Victorian Studies: An Interdisciplinary Essay," *Victorian Studies,* 8 No. 1 (1964), 59–70.

56. Gene Wise, "Some Elementary Axioms for an American Culture Studies," *Prospects,* 4 (Winter 1978), 517–47.

57. See Mechling, Merideth, and Wilson.

58. See a similar argument by P.J. Perry, "Agricultural History: A Geographer's Critique," *Agricultural History,* 4 No. 2 (1972), 259–67.

59. S. Nilsson, "Aerobiology: Its International and Interdisciplinary Significance," *Scandinavian Journal of Respiratory Diseases,* 102 (1978 Supplementum), 115–18; see also Emil Hadač, "Complex Interdisciplinary Investigation of Landscape," *Landscape Planning,* 4 (1977), 333–48.

60. Gerhard Frey, "Methodological Problems of Interdisciplinary Discussions," *RATIO,* 15 No. 2 (1973), 161–82.

61. Oleg Yanitsky, "Toward an Eco-City: Problems of Integrating Knowledge with Practice," *International Social Science Journal,* 34 No. 3 (1982), 472.

62. Paul T. Baker, "Human Population Biology: A Viable Interdisciplinary Science," *Human Biology,* 54 (May 1982), 203–20.

63. Hareven, pp. 399–414.

64. Robert Merton, *Social Theory and Social Structure* (Glencoe, Illinois: The Free Press, 1957), revised and enlarged edition, p. 9.

65. See Mohammed Allal Sinaceur, "What Is Interdisciplinarity?," *International Social Science Journal,* 29 (1977), 571–79; see also D. A. Conway, "Operational Research: Interdisciplinarity and Higher Education," *Interdisciplinarity. Papers Presented at the European*

Symposium on Interdisciplinary Courses in European Education (Surrey: Society for Research into Higher Education, 1977), 18. ERIC ED 165 512.

66. See Rustum Roy, "Interdisciplinary Science on Campus: The Elusive Dream" in *Interdisciplinarity and Higher Education,* 161-96.

Chapter 8

1. From Lawrence Wheeler and Ewing Miller, "MultiDisciplinary Approach to Planning." Paper presented at Council of Education Facilities Planners 47th Annual Conference in Oklahoma City, Okla., 6 Oct. 1970. ERIC ED 044 814.

2. Pierre de Bie uses this term in "Introduction" to the section on "Multidisciplinary Problem-Focused Research," *International Social Science Journal,* 20 No. 2 (1968), 193-95.

3. Graham S. Toft and F. Tomlinson Sparrow, "University Interdisciplinary Engineering Centers," *Managing High Technology: An Interdisciplinary Perspective,* ed. B. Mar, W.T. Newell, and B.O. Saxberg (Amsterdam: North-Holland, 1985), p. 93.

4. C. Richard Schuller, "Three Synergistic Preconditions for Interdisciplinary Research," in *The Interdisciplinary Management of Research and Development in a Global Economy,* ed P. Birnbaum, F.A. Rossini, and D. Baldwin. Forthcoming.

5. J.T. Klein and A.L. Porter, "Preconditions for Interdisciplinary Research," in *International Research Management: Studies in Interdisciplinary Methods,* ed. Philip H. Birnbaum, Frederick A. Rossini, and Donald Baldwin (New York: Oxford University Press: 1990).

6. D.E. Chubin, A.L. Porter, & F.A. Rossini, "Interdisciplinarity: How Do We Know Thee? – A Bibliographic Essay," in *Interdisciplinary Analysis and Research,* ed. D.E. Chubin et al. (Mt. Airy: Lomond, 1986), pp. 427-34.

7. See Philip H. Birnbaum, "Predictors of Long-Term Research Performance," in *Managing Interdisciplinary Research,* ed. E.P. Epton, R.L. Payne, and A.W. Pearson (Chichester: John Wiley & Sons, 1983), p. 47.

8. From S.R. Epton. R.L. Payne, & A.W. Pearson, "Contextual Issues in Managing Cross-Disciplinary Research," in *Managing High Technology,* p. 211.

9. Albert Teich, "Trends in the Organization of Academic Research: The Role of ORU's and Full-time Researchers," in *Interdisciplinary Research Groups,* ed. R.T. Barth and R. Steck (Vancouver: International Group on Interdisciplinary Programs, 1979), pp. 242, 252.

10. See especially D.W. Cravens, K.W. Heathington, & R.A. Mundy, "Organizing for Interdisciplinary Research in a University Setting," *Journal of the Society of Research Administrators,* 3:1 (Summer 1976), in addition to reports filed at the University of Tennessee Transportation Center, 1977, by same authors.

11. S. Ikenberry and R. Friedman, *Beyond Academic Departments* (San Francisco: Jossey-Bass, 1972), 34-37.

12. Philip Birnbaum, "Academic Contexts of Interdisciplinary Research," *Educational Administration Quarterly,* 14 (Spring 1978), 84-85.

13. See Peter H. Rossi, "Researchers, Scholars, and Policy Makers: The Politics of Large Scale Research," *Daedalus,* 4 (Fall 1964), 1142-61.

14. Birnbaum (1978), p. 94.

15. See R.S. Friedman and R.C. Friedman, "Organized Research Units in Academe Revisited," *Managing High Technology,* pp. 75-91.

16. A.W. Pearson, R.L. Payne, H.P. Gunz, "Communication, Coordination, and Leadership in Interdisciplinary Research," in *Interdisciplinary Research Groups,* p. 114.

17. See the distinction between leadership and coordination matrices in Pearson, Payne, and Gunz, p. 114.

18. J.C. Stucki, "A Goal-Oriented Pharmaceutical Research and Development Organization: An Eleven year Experience," in *Interdisciplinary Research Groups,* pp. 90–91.

19. See a model for analysis: Manual London and W. Bruce Walsh, "The Development and Application of a Model of Long-Term Group Process for the Study of Interdisciplinary Teams." Abstract in *Catalogue of Selected Documents in Psychology,* 5 (1975), 188.

20. On the differences see S.E. Gold and H.J. Gold, "Some Elements of a Model to Improve Productivity of Interdisciplinary Groups," in *Managing Interdisciplinary Research,* pp. 86–101.

21. Mitchell McCorcle, "Critical Issues in the Functioning of Interdisciplinary Groups," *Small Group Behavior,* 13 (Aug. 1982), 296.

22. Anthony R. Stone, "The Interdisciplinary Research Team," *Journal of Applied Behavioral Science,* 5 (July 1969), 359.

23. Irvin L. White, "Interdisciplinarity," in *Perspectives on Technology Assessment,* ed. Sherry R. Arnstein and Alexander Christakis (Washington, D.C.: Academy for State and Local Governments, 1975), p. 385.

24. Margaret Barron Luszki, *Interdisciplinary Team Research: Methods and Problems* (New York: New York Univ. Press, 1958), pp. 150–51.

25. Luszki (1958), pp. 150–51.

26. Lincoln J. Fry, and Jon P. Miller, "The Impact of Interdisciplinary Teams on Organizational Relationships," *Sociological Quarterly,* 15 (Summer 1974), 423.

27. D. Gillespie and Philip Birnbaum, "Status Concordance, Coordination, and Success in Interdisciplinary Research Teams," *Human Relations,* 33 No. 1 (1980), 106.

28. William T. Newell, "Guidelines for Applied Interdisciplinary Research in the University." Seattle: Graduate School of Business Administration, University of Washington, 1980, p. 29. Report on NSF Grant NM44380.

29. W. Caudill and B. Roberts, "Pitfalls in the Organization of Interdisciplinary Research," *Human Organization,* 10 (Winter 1951), 14.

30. A. Stone, "The Interdisciplinary Research Team," *Applied Behavioral Science,* 5 (1969), 354–55.

31. Cited in Stephen Kendall and E.E. Mackintosh, *Management Problems of Polydisciplinary Environmental Projects in the University Setting* (Guelph, Ont.: University of Guelph Centre for Resources Development, May 1978), p. 10. Publication No. 86; also listed as UNESCO MAB Report 13.

32. McCorcle, p. 303.

33. B.W. Mar, W.T. Newell, and B.O. Saxberg, "Interdisciplinary Research in the University Setting," *Environmental Science and Technology,* 10 No. 7 (1976), 651.

34. D.E. Chubin et al., "Experimental Technology Assessment: Explorations in Processes of Interdisciplinary Team Research," *Technological Forecasting and Social Change,* 15 (1979), 87–94.

35. E.R. Swanson, "Working with Other Disciplines," in *Enabling Interdisciplinary Research,* ed. Martha G. Russell (St. Paul: Agricultural Experiment Station, University of Minnesota, 1982), p. 22. Miscellaneous Publication 19.

36. White, p. 385.

37. R. Stankiewicz, "The Effects of Leadership on the Relationship Between the Size of Research Groups and Their Performance," *R&D Management,* 9 (1979), 207–12.

38. Philip Birnbaum, "Assessment of Alternative Management Forms in Academic Interdisciplinary Research Projects," *Management Science,* 24 No. 3 (1977), 281–83.

39. A term used by D. Bents and W. Horsmann, "Determination of the Research of

Compter-Based Technologies for Urban Traffic Systems," in *Interdisciplinary Research Groups,* p. 197.

40. F.A. Rossini et. al., "Interdisciplinary Integration within Technology Assessments," *Knowledge: Creation, Diffusion, Utilization,* 2 No. 4 (1981), 515.

41. Walter S. Baer, "Interdisciplinary Policy Research in Independent Research Centers," *IEEE Transactions on Engineering Management,* 23 (May 1976), 3.

42. R.T. Barth and G.E. Manners, Jr., "Some Behavioral, Managerial, and Research Perspectives on the Organization and Management of Interdisciplinary Research: An Overview," in *Interdisciplinary Research Groups,* p. 52.

43. Michael Anbar, "The 'Bridge Scientist' and His Role," *Research/Development,* July 1973, p. 33.

44. See Philip Birnbaum, "A Theory of Academic Interdisciplinary Research Performance," *Management Science,* 25 (Mar. 1979), 231–42.

45. William R. MacDonald, *The Management of Interdisciplinary Research Teams: A Literature Review.* Report for the Department of the Environment and the Department of Agriculture (Edmonton, Alberta, January 1982), p. 112.

46. Pearson et al., p. 112.

47. Daniel Alpert, "The Role and Structure of Interdisciplinary and Multidisciplinary Research Centers." Address to the ninth annual meeting of the Council of Graduate Schools, 1969. ERIC ED 035 363.

48. A.Z. Kaprielian and J.M. Nilles, "Improvement of Interdisciplinary Research Management at Universities," in *Background Material and Summary Report.* Los Angeles: University of Southern California, 1977. A reprint of two 1974 reports on NSF/RMI grant NM-39528, p. 19 (Background section).

49. Rossini et al., pp. 503–28.

50. See Philip H. Birnbaum, "Integration and Specialization in Academic Research," *Academy of Management Journal,* 24 No. 3 (1981), 487–503.

51. Cited by Maurice deWachter, "Interdisciplinary Bioethics: But Where Do We Start?," *Journal of Medicine and Philosophy,* 7 (1982), 276.

52. Remark made at the Third International Conference on Interdisciplinary Research, 2 Aug. 1984.

53. Noted by Guy Berger, "Opinions and Facts," in *Interdisciplinarity: Problems of Teaching and Research in Universities* (Paris: Organization for Economic Cooperation and Development, 1972), p. 57.

54. White, p. 384.

55. See Warren G. Bennis, "Some Barriers to Teamwork in Social Research," *Social Problems,* 3 No. 4 (1956), 234.

56. White, p. 382.

57. deWachter, p. 279.

58. Caudill and Roberts, p. 13.

59. Reeves made this suggestion at the Third International Conference on Interdisciplinary Research in Seattle, Wash., 2 Aug. 1984.

60. Ronald Kruse et al., "Interdisciplinary Research Teams as Status Systems." Paper presented at the American Society for Engineering Education meeting, Ft. Collins. Colo. 16–19 June 1975. ERIC ED 118 450.

61. McCorcle, p. 308.

62. Kendall and Mackintosh, pp. 33a, 34.

63. Lowell Hattery, "Interdisciplinary Research Management: Research Needs and Opportunities," in *Interdisciplinary Research Groups,* p. 22.

64. For one proposal see Donald B. Bailey, "Measuring Individual Participation on the Interdisciplinary Team," *American Journal of Mental Deficiency,* 88 No. 3 (1983), 247–54.

65. See Martha G. Russell, "Peer Review in Interdisciplinary Research: Flexibility and Responsiveness," in *Managing Interdisciplinary Research,* pp. 184–202; J. M. Sharp, "A Method for Peer Group Appraisal and Interpretation of Data Developed in Interdisciplinary Research Programs," in *Managing Interdisciplinary Research,* pp. 211–19.

66. See Martha Garrett Russell, "Evaluating Interdisciplinary Research," in *Managing Interdisciplinary Research,* pp. 167–74.

67. M. Peston, "Some Thoughts on Evaluating Interdisciplinary Research," *Higher Education Review,* Spring 1978, 55–60.

68. R. Cutler, "A Policy Perspective on Interdisciplinary Research in U.S. Universities," in *Interdisciplinary Research Groups,* p. 307.

69. Cited in Cutler, p. 308.

70. Cited in Cutler, p. 309.

71. See also Heinz Riesenhuber, "Interdisciplinary Cooperation between Industry and Government in the FRG," *Interdisciplinary Science Reviews,* 8 No. 2 (1983), 102–04.

72. Gerald Holton, "Niels Bohr and the Integrity of Science," *American Scientist,* 74 No. 3 (1986), 237–43.

73. Theodore Hershberg, "Epilogue: Sustaining Interdisciplinary Research," in *Philadelphia, Work, Space, Family, and Group Experience in the Nineteenth Century,* ed. Theodore Hershberg (Oxford: Oxford Univ. Press, 1981), pp. 492–495.

74. Paul E. Waibel, "Improving Interdisciplinary Research Management to Help Faculty Scientists," in *Enabling Interdisciplinary Research,* p. 70.

Chapter 9

1. Wlibert E. Fordyce, "On Interdisciplinary Peers," *Archives of Physical and Medical Rehabilitation,* 62 (Feb. 1981), 51–53.

2. See S.Z. Nagi, "Teamwork in Health Care in the United States: A Sociological Perspective," *Milbank Memorial Fund Quarterly,* 53 (1975), 75–91.

3. George L. Engel, "The Clinical Application of the Biopsychosocial Model," *American Journal of Psychiatry,* 137 No. 5 (1980), 535–44.

4. F.A. Whitehouse, "Teamwork: A Democracy of Professions," *Exceptional Children,* 18 (1951), 45–46.

5. Anthony D. Udziela et al., "The Psychologist on the Multidisciplinary Developmental Disabilities Team," *Professional Psychologist,* 13 No. 6 (1982), 782.

6. Samuel Pruzansky, "Center for Craniofacial Anomalies: Spin-offs for Medical Education and Delivery of Health Care," *Otolaryngologic Clinics of North America,* 14 No. 4 (1981), 778.

7. Alex J. Ducanis and Anne K. Golin, *The Interdisciplinary Health Care Team: A Handbook* (Germantown, Md.: Aspen Systems Corporation, 1979), pp. 5–7. See especially the bibliography on teamwork.

8. Donald Day, "Perspectives on Care: The Interdisciplinary Team Approach," *Otolaryngologic Clinics of North America,* 14 No. 4 (1981), 771.

9. Ducanis and Golin, pp. 126–29, 134–37.

10. Lawrence A. Fox, "Dentistry," in *Interdisciplinary Approaches to Human Services,* ed. Peter J. Valletutti and Florence Christopolos (Baltimore: University Park Press, 1977), p. 64.

11. Herbert Koepp-Baker, "The Craniofacial Team," in *Communicative Disorders Related to Cleft Lip and Palate,* ed. Kenneth R. Bzoch (Boston: Little, Brown, 1979), p. 54.

12. Hughlett L. Morris, "The Structure and Function of Interdisciplinary Health Teams," in *Dentistry in the Interdisciplinary Treatment of Genetic Diseases,* ed. Carlos F. Salinas and Ronald J. Jorgenson (New York: Alan R. Liss, 1980), p. 109.

13. Morris, pp. 109–10.

14. See especially Jay Rotberg et al., "Status of Interagency Cooperation between Interdisciplinary Clinics or Hospitals and the Public Schools," *Child Psychiatry and Human Development,* 12 No. 3 (1982), 153–59.

15. Pruzansky, p. 779.

16. Vanja A. Holm, "Interdisciplinary Child Development Team: Team Issues and Training in Interdisciplinariness," *Early Intervention: A Team Approach* (Baltimore: University Park Press, 1978), p. 104.

17. See A.W. Parker, *The Team Approach to Primary Health Care.* (Berkeley: California University Extension, 1972). Neighborhood Health Center Seminar Program. Cited in Ducanis and Golin, p. 124.

18. Cited in Ducanis and Golin, pp. 122–23.

19. Z. Schelsinger, "An Interdisciplinary Approach to Cardiac Rehabilitation," *Heart and Lung,* 12 No. 4 (1983), 336–37.

20. Anthony D. Udziela et al., "The Psychologist on the Multidisciplinary Development Disabilities Team," *Professional Psychology,* 13 No. 6 (1982), 782–88.

21. Robert Logan and Maxine McKendry, "The Multi-Disciplinary Team: A Different Approach to Patient Management," *New Zealand Medical Journal,* 95 (1982), 883–84.

22. Information is from Nancy B. Kaltreider et al., "The Integration of Psychosocial Care in a General Hospital," *International Journal of Psychiatry in Medicine,* 5 No. 2 (1974), 125–34.

23. See Peter J. Valletutti and Florence Christopolos, "Interdisciplinary Approaches to Human Services: An Introduction and Overview" in *Interdisciplinary Approaches to Human Services,* pp. 1–11.

24. Thomas H. Murray, "Confessions of an Unconscious Interdisciplinarian," *Issues in Integrative Studies,* 4 (1986), 57–69.

25. Rodger F. Accardi, "Pastoral Communication." Paper presented at the 1982 American Congress of Rehabilitation Medicine. Abstract in *Archives of Physical Medicine and Rehabilitation,* 64 No. 10 (1983), 508.

26. Vanja Holm and E.E. McCarthy, "Interdisciplinary Child Developmental Team," in *Early Intervention: A Team Approach,* ed. K. Allen, A. Holm, and S. Schieferbusch (Baltimore: University Park Press, 1978), p. 108–09.

27. Information is from John A. Lincoln and Merril N. Werblun, "Interdisciplinary Family Practice Rounds," *Journal of Family Practice,* 6 No. 4 (1978), 889–91.

28. Nellis B. VanKrevelen and Eric R. Harvey, "Integrating Clinical Pharmacy Services into the Interdisciplinary Team Structure," *Mental Retardation,* 20 No. 2 (1982), 64.

29. VanKrevelen and Harvey, 64–68.

30. Donald G. Ferguson et al., "Effects of Data-Based Interdisciplinary Medication Reviews on the Prevalence and Pattern of Neuroleptic Drug Use with Institutionalized Mentally Retarded Persons," *Education and Training for the Mentally Retarded,* 17 No. 2 (1982), 103–08.

31. Robert Beardsley et al., "The Interdisciplinary Approach," *American Pharmacy,* n.s. 211 No. 11 (1981), 54–55.

32. L.L. Hart et al., "The Clinical Pharmacist on an Interdisciplinary Primary Health-Care Team," *Drug Intelligence and Clinical Pharmacy,* 13 No. 7–8 (1979), 414–19.

33. "Beyond the Ordinary: The Preparation of Professionals to Educate Severely and Profoundly Handicapped Persons toward the Development of Standards and Criteria." From the American Association for the Education of the Severely/Profoundly Handicapped, 1977, ERIC ED 182 873.

34. For a discussion of these approaches in the context of care of the elderly, see Beardsley, 670–80.

35. David M. Scott et al., "The Development and Evaluation of an Interdisciplinary Health Training Program: A Pharmacy Perspective," *American Journal of Pharmaceutical Education,* 47 No. 1 (1983), 42–48.

36. See an account of the University of Hacettepe (Turkey) in *The University and the Community: The Problems of Changing Relationships* (Paris: OECD, 1982), 133–35; see also D.E. Benor, "Interdisciplinary Integration in Medical Education: Theory and Method," *Medical Education,* 16 (1982), 355–61. (With an account of the Ben-Gurion University of the Negev faculty of Health Sciences.)

37. Robert C. Cassidy et al., "Teaching Biophysics-Ethical Medicine in a Family-Practice Clerkship," *Journal of Medical Education,* 58 no. 10 (1983), 782.

38. Ducanis and Golin, p. 159; see also P.A. Bottom et al., "Curriculum Development for Interdisciplinary Health Team Education," *Alabama Journal of Medical Sciences,* 15 No. 1 (1978), 98–100.

39. Tom Connelly, Jr.. Appendix 6: "Interdisciplinary References III: A Reference Document for Those Contemplating Interdisciplinary Educational Programs in the Health Sciences." Proceedings of the Workshop on Interdisciplinary Education—Kentucky January Prototype, Lexington College of Allied Health Professions, Lexington, Ky., 17 Apr. 1975, 1–3, 6. ERIC ED 129 134.

40. "Changes in Interdisciplinary Content," in *The University and the Community: The Problems of Changing Relationships,* pp. 131–33.

41. See Richard R. DeBlassie and Juan N. Franco, "An Interdisciplinary Graduate Program for Mexican-American Researchers-Evaluators," *American Journal of Orthopsychiatry,* 51 No. 4 (1981), 730–33.

42. E.T. Molnar and D. Armstead, "Students and Children Learning from Each Other during a Paediatric Field Trip Program," *Journal of Medical Education,* 8 (1977), 866.

43. Carina Wallgren-Pettersson et al., "Interdisciplinary Teaching of Community Paediatrics," *Medical Education,* 16 (1982), 290–95.

44. See Paul T. Werner et al., "Ambulatory Family Practice Experience as the Primary and Integrating Clinical Concept in a Four-Year Undergraduate Curriculum," *Journal of Family Practice,* 7 No. 2 (1978), 325–32.

45. Scott et al., pp. 42–48.

46. Richard H. Layton and Mark M. Schubert, "Integrated Residency Training in Family Medicine and General Practice Dentistry," *Journal of Family Practice,* 7 No. 2 (1978) 333–36.

47. Information is from Elizabeth Elmer, "Child Abuse Training: A Community-Based Interdisciplinary Program," *Community Mental Health Journal,* 14 No. 3 (1978), 179–89.

48. Maurice deWachter, "Interdisciplinary Teamwork," *Journal of Medical Ethics,* June 1976, 53–57; S.C. Blumenthal, "Effects of an Interdisciplinary Team Approach to the Treatment of Asthma on Patient Compliance," *American Review of Respiratory Disease,* Supplement 121 No. 4, Pt. 2 (1980), 210.

49. Derek F.H. Pheby, "Changing Practice on Confidentiality: A Cause for Concern," *Journal of Medical Ethics,* 8 No. 1 (1982), 13–14, 17.

50. Deane L. Critchley and Irving N. Berlin make this point in "Day Treatment of Young Psychotic Children and Their Parents: Interdisciplinary Issues and Problems," *Child Psychiatry and Human Development,* 9 No. 4 (1979), 229.

51. Ducanis and Golin, p. 169.

52. On this matter see W. Peter Geis et al., "An Integrated University Emergency Medicine-Trauma Program," *Journal of Trauma,* 22 No. 4 (1982), 295–302.

53. John Greden et al., "Interdisciplinary Differences on a General Hospital Psychiatry Unit," *General Hospital Psychiatry,* 1 No. 1 (1979), 91–97.

54. On this issue see J.T. Amsterdam, D.K. Wagner, and L. Rose, "Interdisciplinary

Training: Hospital Dental General Practice/Emergency Medicine," *Annals of Emergency Medicine,* 9 No. 6 (1980), 310–13.

55. On the matter of patient advocacy, see Walter W. Siggers, "The Role of the Psychologist in Advocacy for the Handicapped," *Professional Psychology,* 10 No. 1 (1979), 80–86.

Chapter 10

1. William Mayville, *Interdisciplinarity: The Mutuable Paradigm* (Washington, D.C.: American Association for Higher Education, 1978), p. 31. AAHE-ERIC Higher Education Research Report No. 9.

2. Hans Flexner and Gerard A. Hauser, "Interdisciplinary Programs in the United States, Some Paradigms," in *Interdisciplinarity and Higher Education,* ed. Joseph J. Kockelmans (University Park: Pennsylvania State Univ. Press, 1979), pp. 328–49.

3. Gerald Grant and David Riesman, *The Perpetual Dream: Reform and Experiment in the American College* (Chicago: Univ. of Chicago Press, 1978), p. 15.

4. I thank Tony Becher of the University of Sussex and Keith Clayton of the University of East Anglia for supplying information on the British universities.

5. George T. Potter, "The Promise of Interdisciplinarity and Its Problems," *Ramapo Papers,* 1 No. 3 (1977), 14–15.

6. See the account in "Experiences through Examples," *Interdisciplinarity: Problems of Teaching and Research in Universities* (Paris: OECD, 1972), pp. 242–46.

7. "Experiences through Examples," pp. 237–42.

8. Keith M. Clayton, "The University of East Anglia," *Inter-Disciplinarity Revisited* (Stockholm: OECD, SNBUC, Linköping University, 1985), pp. 189–96.

9. I thank Richard Logan and David Jowett for supplying information and corresponding with me about the University of Wisconsin at Green Bay. See also accounts in *Interdisciplinarity: Problems of Teaching and Research in Universities,* pp. 242–46; and Mayville, pp. 39–40.

10. I thank Soren Kjørup for providing me with information on RUC; see Soren Kjørup, "Roskilde Universitetscenter, Denmark," *Inter-Disciplinarity Revisited,* pp. 197–205.

11. Bob Ross, "New Universities: The Experience of a New Problem-Oriented University." Paper presented at the Society for Research into Higher Education conference in London (1978), p. 49.

12. See an account of the Australian experiments in Don Anderson, "Interdisciplinary Innovations in Traditional Contexts," *Inter-Disciplinarity Revisited,* pp. 181–88.

13. Personal correspondence from Richard D. Logan, 24 Apr. 1984.

14. Nathaniel Sheppard, Jr., "A Thematic Approach to Concerns of the Future," *Change, The Magazine of Higher Learning,* August 1978, p. 32.

15. "The Final Report of the Committee for the Year 2000, *The Academic Plan,*" University of Wisconsin–Green Bay document, p. 1. I thank David Jowett for supplying me with a copy of the report.

16. Personal correspondence from Soren Kjørup, 23 Oct. 1985.

17. See Tadashi Sato, "Interdisciplinary Research and Education in the University of Tsukuba," *Inter-Disciplinarity Revisited,* 153–67.

18. Information on Tromso comes from Karen Nossum Bie, *Creating a New University: The Establishment and Development of the University of Tromso* (Oslo: Institute for Studies in Research and Higher Education, 1981). I thank Sigmund Vangsnes for supplying a copy.

19. Examples not footnoted separately are drawn from the Association for Integrative Studies archive on undergraduate interdisciplinary education, housed at Miami University (Ohio) in the School of Interdisciplinary Studies.

20. For an intriguing proposal, see Frederick S. Weaver, "Inquiry, Interdisciplinary Study, and Minor Programs of Study," *Issues in Integrative Studies,* 4 (1986), 37–55.

21. Charles B. Fethe, "A Philosophical Model for Interdisciplinary Programs," *Liberal Education,* 59 No. 4 (1973), 491.

22. I thank George Helling and Wesley Brown for providing information and corresponding with me about the Paracollege.

23. On the subject of cluster schools, see David J. Davis, "The Cluster College Revisited: A Dream Falls on Hard Times," *College Teaching,* 33 No. 1 (1985), 15–20.

24. I thank William H. Newell for providing information on the Western College Program.

25. I thank Bernard J. Sloan for providing a comprehensive account of New College by correspondence, 14 Aug. 1984.

26. Information is from *The Senior College Division* catalogue, 26–27, and Bryan E. Carlson, "Rationale for the Development of Mount Ida Senior College," Jan. 1982.

27. Brochure, *The Paracollege: A Community for Individualized Education at St. Olaf College.*

28. Booklet, *A Look at Western: The School of Interdisciplinary Studies.*

29. I thank Shimer College business manager David B. Buchanan for supplying information on the college.

30. I thank John Nichols for supplying information.

31. See James C. Palmer, "Interdisciplinary Studies: An ERIC Review," *Community College Review,* 11 No. 1 (1983), 59–64.

32. See Deborah Crandall and Elizabeth Rinnander, "Interdisciplinary Humanities: Sources and Information," *New Directions for Community Colleges,* 12 (Winter 1975), 95–102.

33. I thank Sandra Acebo for supplying information.

34. "Los Medanos College: The Educational Plan."

35. "Ohio Dominican College: Relating Disciplines to Universal Themes," *The Forum for Liberal Education,* 8 No. 4 (1986), 10–11.

36. William Mayville discusses the program, pp. 48–51.

37. Barbara Bundy, "The One and the Many: A Colloquia Program in Humanities at Dominican College of San Raphael," *Liberal Education,* 65 No. 1 (1979), 33, 39–40, 43 n.7.

38. Malcolm L. Peel and Leo L. Nussbaum, "The Core Course Redivivus," *Liberal Education,* 60 No. 4 (1974), 478–88.

39. David Ault and Gilbert Rutman, "The Role of Economics in Interdisciplinary and Problem-Oriented Programs," *Journal of Economic Education,* 9 No. 2 (1978), 96–101.

40. "Federated Learning Communities . . . The Best of Both Worlds." Brochure distributed by State University of New York at Stony Brook.

41. Jerry Gaff, *General Education Today: A Critical Analysis of Controversies, Practices, and Reforms* (San Francisco: Jossey Bass, 1983), pp. 104–05.

42. Lin Foa, "The Integrated Humanities in Higher Education: A Survey," *Journal of Aesthetic Education,* 7 No. 3 (1973), 92–95.

43. See Thomas A. Langford, "A Model of Interdisciplinary Study in the Fine Arts," *Journal of Aesthetic Education,* 16 No. 3 (1982), 115–18.

44. Information is from Bettie Anne Boebler, "The Master of Arts in Humanities: Arizona State University," in *Integrated Studies: Challenges to the College Curriculum,* ed. Stephen H. Dill (Washington, D.C.: University Press of America, 1982).

45. Carolyn Galverstein, "Interdisciplinarity at the Graduate Level," *Perspectives: The Journal of the Association for General and Liberal Studies,* 11 No. 3 (1981), 20.

46. See especially Donald Levine, "The Physical Sciences among the Liberal." Paper presented at the Symposium on Undergraduate Education in Chemistry and Physics, University of Chicago, 18 Oct. 1985. I thank Stephen R. Loevy for providing me with recent information on graduate workshops at the University of Chicago.

47. Cited in "Report of the Commission on Graduate Education," *University of Chicago Record,* 16 No. 2.

48. Flexner and Hauser, pp. 331-35.

49. I thank Joseph Kockelmans for supplying me with information on the program.

50. Noted in an account of the program by Flexner and Hauser, p. 345.

51. Personal correspondence from Joseph Kockelmans, 1 Dec. 1987.

52. Charles J. Lumsden, L.E.H. Trainor, and M. Silverman, "Physical Theory in Biology: An Interdisciplinary Course," *American Journal of Physics,* 47 No. 4 (1979), 302-08.

53. Robert A. Leacock and Harold I. Sharlin, "The Nature of Physics and History: A Cross-disciplinary Inquiry," *American Journal of Physics,* 45 No. 2 (1977), 146-53.

54. Michael W. Gregory, "NEXA: The Science-Humanities Convergence Program at San Francisco State University," *Liberal Education,* 65 No. 1 (1979), 66-91.

55. I am indebted to Arnold Binder, of the Social Ecology faculty, who supplied information on the program.

56. Arnold Binder, "A New Context for Psychology: Social Ecology," *American Psychologist,* 27 No. 9 (1972), 904.

57. I thank faculty member Nelson Bingham for supplying information and checking this account.

58. Nelson Bingham, "Preparing Society's Servants," *The Earlhamite,* Summer 1983, p. 22.

59. Bingham, 21.

60. Final report on the program by Ivan Kovacs, project director for the Human Development Program, 15 July 1974, 1-2. I am indebted to Professor Kovacs, who supplied information about the program, talked with me in San Francisco on 27 October 1984, and solicited evaluations of an earlier account from former students of the program.

61. Personal correspondence from Ivan Kovacs, 8 Oct. 1985.

62. See Lennart Nordenfelt, "On the Notion of a Research Program," in *Inter-Disciplinarity Revisited,* pp. 70-84.

63. See a recent evaluation by T. Brock et al., *Interdisciplinary Research and Doctoral Training* (Stockholm: Swedish National Board of Universities and Colleges, 1986).

64. See Ulrik Lohm and Jan Lundqvist, "Competence and Orientation of a TEMA Doctor," *Inter-Disciplinarity Revisited,* pp. 62-69.

65. See Goran Graninger and Ingemar Lind, "The Faculty of Theme Research at Linköping University, Sweden: Concepts and Experiences," *Inter-Disciplinarity Revisited,* pp. 28-45.

66. Brock et al., pp. 31-46, 102.

67. Karen Nossum Bie made this point.

68. See Stanley Bailis, "Review of *Inter-Disciplinarity Revisited,*" *Association for Integrative Studies Newsletter,* 8 No. 1 (March 1986), 1, 8-9.

69. William H. Newell, "Interdisciplinary Studies are Alive and Well," *Association for Integrative Studies Newsletter,* 10 no. 1 (March 1988), 1, 6-8.

70. Martin Trow, "Interdisciplinary Studies as a Counterculture: Problems of Birth, Growth, and Survival," *Issues in Integrative Studies,* 3 (1984/85), 3, 14.

71. Charles B. Fethe, "A Philosophical Model for Interdisciplinary Programs," *Liberal Education,* 59 No. 4 (December 1973), 491.

72. See especially Thomas Maher, "Creating Connections: An Experiment in Interdisciplinary Education." The Report of a Project Sponsored by FIPSE and Wichita State University (1981-1984).

Conclusion

1. L. Jackson Newell and Karen I. Spear, "New Dimensions for Academic Careers: Rediscovering Intrinsic Satisfactions," *Liberal Education,* 69 No. 2 (1983), 113-14.

2. See, for example, Raymond L. Cravens, "The Battle over Turf," *Association of Governing Boards of Universities and Colleges,* 20 No. 2 (1978), 41-44. See also Armstrong, below.

3. Patricia Meyer Spacks, "Do Cats Eat Bats?" *Yale Review,* 67 No. 2 (1978), 315.

4. Newell and Spear, pp. 109-11.

5. Personal conversation with the program's dean, Jackson Newell, in San Francisco, 27 Oct. 1984.

6. Belver C. Griffith and Nicholas C. Mullins, "Coherent Social Groups in Scientific Change," *Science,* 15 Sept. 1972, p. 959.

7. Mario Bunge, "The Role of Forecast in Planning," *Theory and Decision,* 3 No. 3 (1973), 21.

8. Forrest Armstrong, "Faculty Development through Interdisciplinarity," *JGE: Journal of General Education,* 32 No. 1 (1980), 62-63.

9. Irvin L. White, "Interdisciplinarity," in *Perspectives on Technology Assessment,* ed. Sherry R. Arnstein and Alexander N. Christakis (Washington, D.C.: Academy for State and Local Governments, 1979), p. 384.

10. Margaret Mead, Discussant. "Can Research Institutions Accommodate Inter-disciplinary Researchers?" Symposium at the 143rd Annual Meeting of the American Associa-tion for the Advancement of Science, Denver, Colorado, 20-25 February 1977. Taped transcript available from the AAAS.

11. Tamara Swora and James L. Morrison, "Interdisciplinarity and Higher Educa-tion," *Journal of General Education,* 26 No. 1 (1974), 45-52.

12. See Donald B. Bailey et al., "Measuring Individual Participation on the Inter-disciplinary Team," *American Journal of Mental Deficiency,* 88 No. 3 (1983), 247-54.

13. I thank Stanley Bailis for pointing out the Sloan series to me.

14. Thomas H. Murray, "Confessions of an Unconscious Interdisciplinarian," *Issues in Integrative Studies,* 4 (1986), 57-69.

15. Dorothy Swaine Thomas, "Experiences in Interdisciplinary Research," *American Sociological Review,* 17 No. 6 (1952), 663-69.

16. William Twining, "Law and Anthropology: A Case Study in Interdisciplinary Col-laboration," *Law and Society Review,* 7 No. 4 (1973), 561-83.

17. Philip Lewin makes this point in considering the magnitude of this task.

18. Oliver L. Reiser, *The Integration of Human Knowledge* (Boston: Porter Sargent, 1958).

19. Pierre Teilhard de Chardin, *The Phenomenon of Man,* with an introduction by Julian Huxley (New York: Harper, 1961).

20. Henry Winthrop, "Methodological and Hermeneutic Functions in Interdisciplinary Education," *Educational Theory,* 14 (April 1964), 118-27.

21. Hayden White, *Metahistory: The Historical Imagination in Nineteenth Century Europe* (Baltimore: Johns Hopkins Univ. Press, 1973).

22. Carl A. Rubino, Review of *Metahistory* in *Modern Language Notes,* 91 (1976), 113.

23. See Michael W. Messmer, "Vogue of the Interdisciplinary," *Centennial Review,* 12 No. 4 (1978), 467-78.

24. Fernand Braudel, "Preface," *The Structure of Everday Life: The Limits of the Possi-ble,* translated and revised by Sian Reynolds (New York: Harper and Row, 1979), pp. 27-29.

25. Comment by Beth Casey on Edward Said's *Orientalism.* Manuscript circulated within the Philosophy Network of the Association of Integrative Studies.

26. Edward Said, *Orientalism* (New York: Pantheon, 1978).

27. Edward Said, "Orientalism Reconsidered," *Cultural Critique,* 1 (Fall 1985), 89–107.

28. Some of these items are from Winthrop, 118–27, and James McEvoy, "Multi- and Interdisciplinary Research: Problems of Initiation, Control, Integration, and Reward," *Policy Sciences,* 3 No. 2 (1972), 201–08.

29. Philip H. Birnbaum discusses some of these techniques in "Academic Contexts of Interdisciplinary Research," *Educational Administration Quarterly,* 14 (1978), 80–97.

30. Lincoln J. Fry and Jon P. Miller, "The Impact of Interdisciplinary Teams on Organizational Relationships," *Sociological Quarterly,* 15 (Summer 1974), 417–31.

31. Lynne Ackerman et al., "Role Clarification: A Procedure for Enhancing Interdisciplinary Collaboration on the Rehabilitation Team." Paper presented at the 60th annual session of the American Congress of Rehabilitation Medicine in Los Angeles, Calif., 1983.

32. Herbert Koepp-Baker, "The Craniofacial Team," *Communicative Disorders Related to Cleft Lip and Palate,* ed. Kenneth R. Bzosch (Boston: Little, Brown, 1979), p. 54.

33. R. Logan and M. McKendry, "The Multi-Disciplinary Team: A Different Approach to Patient Management," *New Zealand Medical Journal,* 95 No. 722 (1982), 884.

34. White, pp. 385–86.

35. J. M. Sharp, "A Method for Peer Group Appraisal and Interpretation of Data Developed in Interdisciplinary Research Programs," in *Managing Interdisciplinary Research,* ed. S.R. Epton, R.L. Payne, and A.W. Pearson (Chichester: John Wiley & Sons, 1984).

36. Robert S. Chen, "Interdisciplinary Research and Integration: The Case of CO_2 and Climate," *Climatic Change,* 3 No. 4 (1981), 429–47.

37. T. Klein and J. Nachbar, "In Search of Technology," *Science, Technology, and Society: Curriculum Newsletter of the Lehigh University STS Program,* 29 (1982), 1–9.

38. Thomas H. Maher, report: "Evaluation of Tier II Program at Ohio University," 1983–84, p. 10.

39. Barbara Hursh, Paul Haas, and Michael Moore, "An Interdisciplinary Model to Implement General Education," *Journal of Higher Education,* 54 (1983), 42–59.

40. Maurice deWachter, "Interdisciplinary Bioethics: But Where Do we Start? A Reflection on Epochè as Method," *Journal of Medicine and Philosophy* 7 (1982), 275–87.

41. Rivers Singleton, Jr., "Interdisciplinary Teaching with Humanists: Reflections of a Biological Scientist," *Perspectives in Biology and Medicine,* 26 No. 2 (1983), 304–14.

42. See Walter A. Davis, *The Act of Interpretation: A Critique of Literary Reason* (Chicago: Univ. of Chicago Press, 1978). See chapter 3, "Critical Theory and Philosophical Method."

43. David Halliburton, "Designing Curriculum," in *Developing the College Curriculum: A Handbook for Faculty and Administrators,* ed. Arthur Chickering et al., (Washington, D.C.: Council for the Advancement of Small Colleges, 1977), pp. 56, 63–64.

44. Jonathan Broido, "Reflections on Methodology," in *Interdisciplinarity and Higher Education,* ed. Joseph J. Kockelmans (University Park: Pennsylvania State Univ. Press, 1979), pp. 244–305.

45. William H. Newell, "The Role of Interdisciplinary Studies in the Liberal Education of the 1980's," *Liberal Education,* 69 No. 3 (1983), 245–46.

46. See, for example, *The Rhetoric of the Human Sciences,* ed. J. Nelson, A. Megill, and D. McCloskey (Madison: Univ. of Wisconsin Press, 1987).

Selected Bibliography

Introduction

This is a bibliography of primarily English-language references. It has two functions. It is intended, first of all, to be a foundation for reading. The most basic readings are collected in section 1 and in sections 2–7 are marked with asterisks. It is also intended to be a representative sample of a vast literature that extends well beyond this basic bibliography. There are literally thousands of additional references for sections 2–7 that may be obtained easily through data-base searching. Given the multitude of resources, I have offered a representative sample that indicates the breadth and variety of those resources. All documents and publications listed with an ERIC ED number are generally available in United States academic libraries and may be ordered in either microfiche or paper copy from the Educational Resources Information Center in Washington, D.C.

The bibliography is organized into seven sections:

1. Essential References:
   containing bibliographies, books, special issues, and additional essential references.
2. Problem-focused Research:
   including references on IDR, computers, engineering, general systems, the environment, and agriculture.
3. Interdisciplinary Care and Services.
4. Education.
5. The Humanities:
   including references on American studies, language and literature, linguistics, philosophy, and religion, with a separate section on history.
6. The Social Sciences:
   including references on economics, geography, law, political science, and general systems with a separate section on anthropology, archaeology, and ethnography, as well as one on psychology, sociology, and social psychology.
7. The Sciences:
   including references on the sciences and technology with a separate section on biology, chemistry, and physics, and another on mathematics.

Essential References

Bibliographies

Chubin, D. E., A. L. Porter, and F. A. Rossini. "Annotated Bibliography." In *Interdisciplinary Analysis and Research: Theory and Practice of Problem-Focused Research and Development,* ed. D. Chubin, A. Porter, F. Rossini, and T. Connolly. Mt. Airy: Lomond, 1986, pp. 441–70.

Cunningham, Frank, and Susan J. Wolfe. "Selected Bibliography." In *Integrated Studies: Challenges to the College Curriculum,* ed. Stephen Dill. Washington, D.C.: University Press of America, 1982, pp. 133–42.

Grandberg, A. "The Problem of Interdisciplinary: A Bibliography." Lund, Sweden: Research Policy Program, Lunds Universitet, 1975.

Humphreys, Les. "Interdisciplinarity: A Selected Bibliography for Users." 1975. ERIC ED 115 536.

Klein, Julie Thompson. "Interdisciplinary Literature." *Perspectives: The Journal of the Association for General and Liberal Studies.* 14 No. 3 (1984), 36–47. An expanded version is available as part of "The Interdisciplinary Concept: Past, Present and Future." In *Interdisciplinarity Revisited: Re-Assessing the Concept in the Light of Institutional Experience,* ed. Lennart Levin and Ingemar Lind. Stockholm: OECD/CERI, Swedish National Board of Universities and Colleges, Linköping University, 1985, pp. 123–36.

———. "Interdisciplinarity: A Bibliography." In *International Research Management: Studies in Interdisciplinarity Methods,* ed. Philip H. Birnbaum, Frederick A. Rossini, and Donald Baldwin. New York: Oxford University Press, 1990.

Mahan, Jack Lee. "Selected Bibliography." In "Toward Transdisciplinary Inquiry in the Humane Sciences." Diss. United States International University, San Diego, 1970, pp. 198–211.

Mayville, William V. "Bibliography." In *Interdisciplinarity: The Mutable Paradigm.* Washington, D.C.: American Association for Higher Education, 1978, pp. 63–72. AAHE-ERIC/Higher Education Research Report No. 9.

Palmer, James C. "Interdisciplinary Studies: An ERIC Review." *Community College Review,* 11 No. 1 (1983), 59–64.

"Relations Interdisciplinaires." *Social Science Information.* 7 No. 2 (1968); 8 No. 2 (1969); 10 No. 2 (1972), 14 No. 2 (1975).

Russell, Martha Garrett, and John Cornwell. "Selected Annotated Bibliography." In *Enabling Interdisciplinary Research: Perspectives from Agriculture, Forestry, and Home Economics,*

232

ed. Martha Garrett Russell. St. Paul: Agricultural Experiment Station, University of Minnesota, 1982, pp. 175–82.

"Selected Bibliography." In *Interdisciplinarity and Higher Education,* ed. Joseph J. Kocklemans. University Park: Pennsylvania State Univ. Press, 1979, pp. 361–64.

"Selected Bibliography, References in Interdisciplinary Social Science." Compiled by Faculty and Students of Social Science, with Raymond C. Miller. Interdisciplinary Studies, San Francisco State University, 1981.

Books

Barth, Richard T., and Rudy Steck, eds. *Interdisciplinary Research Groups: Their Management and Organization.* Vancouver, B.C.: International Research Group on Interdisciplinary Programs, 1979. Papers from the First International Conference on Interdisciplinary Research.

Bayerl, Elizabeth. *Interdisciplinary Studies in the Humanities: A Directory.* Metuchen, N.J.: Scarecrow Press, 1977.

Bechtel, W., ed. *Integrating Scientific Disciplines.* Dordrecht: Martinus Nijhoof, 1986.

Birnbaum, Philip H., Frederick A Rossini, and Donald Baldwin, eds. *International Research Management: Studies in Interdisciplinary Methods.* New York: Oxford University Press, 1990.

Blaschke, D. *Probleme Interdisziplinärer Forschung.* Wiesbaden: Franz Steiner Verlag, 1976. (In German)

Boyer, Ernest, ed. *Common Learning: A Carnegie Colloquium on General Education.* Washington, D.C.: Carnegie Foundation for the Advancement of Teaching, 1981.

Case Studies in Interdisciplinarity. London: Group for Research and Innovation in Higher Education, Nuffield Foundation. Printed by the University of York (England), 1975. Vol. 1: *Environmental Sciences and Engineering,* Sept. 1975. Vol. 2: *Science, Technology and Society,* Oct. 1975. Vol. 3: *Integrated Social Sciences,* Sept. 1975. Vol. 4: *National and International Studies,* Sept. 1975. Vol. 5: *Humanities and Cognitive Studies,* Sept. 1975.

Chubin, Daryl E., Alan L. Porter, Frederick A. Rossini, and Terry Connolly, eds. *Interdisciplinary Analysis and Research: Theory and Practice of Problem-Focused Research and Development.* Mt. Airy: Lomond, 1986.

Dill, Stephen H., ed. *Integrated Studies, Challenges to the College Curriculum.* Washington, D.C.: University Press of America, 1982.

Epton, S.R., R.L. Payne, and A.W. Pearson, ed. *Managing Interdisciplinary Research.* Chichester: John Wiley & Sons, 1983.

Holzhey, Helmut, ed. *Interdisciplinär: Philosophie Aktuell.* Basel: Schwabe, 1974. (In German)

Interdisciplinarity: A Report by the Group for Research and Innovation. Regents Park: Group for Research and Innovation, Nuffield Foundation, July 1975.

Interdisciplinarity. Papers presented at the Society for Research into Higher Education European Symposium on Interdisciplinary Courses in European Education held at City University, London, Sept. 1975. Surrey: Society for Research into Higher Education, University of Surrey, 1977. ERIC ED 165 512.

Interdisciplinarity: Problems of Teaching and Research in Universities. Paris: Organization for Economic Cooperation and Development, 1972.

Internationales Jahrbuch fur Interdisziplinäre Forschung. Ed. Richard Schwartz. Vol. I: *Wissenschaft als Interdisziplinäres Problem.* Berlin: de Gruyter, 1974. (In German)

Jurkovich, R., and J.H.P. Paelinck, eds. *Problems in Interdisciplinary Studies: Issues in Inter-*

disciplinary Studies, No. 2. Hampshire, Eng.: Gower, 1984. (Steering Committee in Interdisciplinary Studies, Erasmus University, Rotterdam)

Karpinski, Adam, and Marcel Samson. *Interdisciplinarité.* Montreal: International School Book Service, University of Quebec, 1972. (In French)

Kocka, Jurgen, ed. *Interdisziplinaritat: Praxis, Herausforderung. Ideologie.* Frankfurt: Suhrkamp, 1987. (In German)

Kockelmans, Joseph, ed. *Interdisciplinarity and Higher Education,* University Park: The Pennsylvania State Univ. Press, 1979.

Levin, Lennart, and Ingemar Lind, eds. *Inter-Disciplinarity Revisited: Re-Assessing the Concept in the Light of Institutional Experience.* Stockholm: Organization for Economic Cooperation and Development, Swedish National Board of Universities and Colleges, Linköping University, 1985.

Luszki, Margaret Barron. *Interdisciplinary Team Research: Methods and Problems.* Washington, D.C.: National Training Laboratories. Printed by New York Univ. Press, 1958. Number 3 in the Research Training Series.

Mar, B.W., W.T. Newell, and B.O. Saxberg, eds. *Managing High Technology: An Interdisciplinary Perspective.* Amsterdam: North Holland, 1985.

Margenau, Henry, ed. *Integrative Principles of Modern Thought.* New York: Gordon and Breach, 1972.

Mayville, William. *Interdisciplinarity: The Mutable Paradigm.* Washington, D.C.: American Association for Higher Education, 1978. AAHE/ERIC Higher Education Report No. 9.

Milicic, Vladimir. *Symposium on Interdisciplinary Aspects of Academic Disciplines.* Bellingham: Western Washington University, 1973.

Newell, William H., ed. and comp. *Interdisciplinary Undergraduate Programs: A Directory.* Oxford, Ohio: Association for Integrative Studies, 1986.

Palmade, Guy. *Interdisciplinarité et Idéologies.* Paris: Editions Anthropos, 1977. (In French)

Piaget, Jean. *Main Trends in Interdisciplinary Research.* New York: Harper and Row, 1973.

Russell, Martha Garrett, John M. Barnes, and John R. Cornwell, eds. *Enabling Interdisciplinary Research: Perspectives from Agriculture, Forestry and Home Economics.* St. Paul, Minnesota: Agricultural Experiment Station, University of Minnesota, 1982. Miscellaneous Publication No. 19.

——, eds. *Bridging Disciplinary Strengths.* St. Paul: Agricultural Experiment Station, University of Minnesota, 1986. Miscellaneous Publication No. 39.

Sherif, Muzafer, and Carolyn Sherif, eds. *Interdisciplinary Relationships in the Social Sciences.* Chicago: Aldine, 1969.

White, Alvin, ed. *Interdisciplinary Teaching.* San Francisco: Jossey Bass, 1981. New Directions for Teaching and Learning Series, No. 8.

Selected Special Issues and Sections

American Behavioral Scientist, Sept./Oct. 1976. Political Decision Making: Interdisciplinary Developments from a Microanalytic Perspective.

Change, The Magazine of Higher Learning (August 1978). Report on Teaching: 6. Interdisciplinary Studies. ERIC ED 157 461.

Current Issues in Higher Education, 2 (1981). Creating on Integrated Curriculum, The "Higher" in Higher Education. ERIC ED 213 324.

Eighteenth Century Life, 5 No. 3 (1979). Interdisciplinarity and Eighteenth-Century Studies.

The Forum for Liberal Education, 8 No. 4 (1986). Interdisciplinary Education.

German Quarterly, 62 No. 2 (Spring 1989). Germanistik as German Studies, Interdisciplinary Theories and Methods.

Improving College and University Teaching, 30 No. 1 (1982). Interdisciplinary Studies.

International Social Science Journal, 16 No. 4 (1964). Problems of Surveying the Social Sciences and Humanities.

International Social Science Journal, 20 (1968), 192–210. Multidisciplinary Problem-Focused Research.

International Social Science Journal, 29 No. 4 (1977), 571–670. Facets of Interdisciplinarity.

Journal of Canadian Studies, 15 (Fall 1980). Thoughts on Interdisciplinarity.

Liberal Education, Spring 1979. Interdisciplinary Education.

National Forum: The Phi Kappa Phi Journal, 69, No. 2 (Spring 1989).

New Literary History, 12 No. 1 (1980). Psychology and Literature: Some Contemporary Directions.

Policy Studies Journal, 2 No. 1 (1973). Interdisciplinary Approaches to Policy Studies.

R&D Management, 14 No. 2 (1984). Problem-Focused Research.

Social Science Information. Periodic Special Sections on Interdisciplinary Research.

Social Science Journal, 12/13 (Oct. 1975/Jan. 1976), 1–112. U.S.–Mexico Borderlands Studies.

Social Science Quarterly, 50 No. 1 (1969), 6–58. Some Convergences in History and Sociology.

Soundings, 54 No. 1 (1971), 82–123. Experimental Interdisciplinary Programs.

Soundings, 58 No. 2 (1975). Structuralism: An Interdisciplinary Study.

SRA, Journal of the Society of Research Administrators, Fall 1981. Management of Interdisciplinary Research.

Teacher's College Record, 73 No. 2 (1971). Curriculum: Interdisciplinary Insights.

Technological Forecasting and Social Change, 2 (1979). Problem-focused research.

Additional Essential References

Allan, Ann. "A Method for Determining Interdisciplinary Activities within a University." *Library Research,* 2 No. 1 (1980/81), 83–94.

Arnoff, S. "Interdisciplinary Scholarship." Address to the Ninth Annual Meeting of the Council of Graduate Schools in the United States. 5 Dec. 1969. ERIC ED 035 365.

Bahm, Archie J. "Interdisciplinology: The Science of Interdisciplinary Research." *Nature and System,* 2 No. 1 (1980), 29–35.

———. *The Specialist: His Philosophy, His Disease, His Cure.* Delhi: Macmillan Co. of India, 1977.

Bailey, M.J. "Selecting Materials for Interdisciplinary Programs." *Special Libraries,* 69 No. 12 (1978), 468–74.

Bailis, Stanley. "Against and for Holism: A Review and Rejoinder to D. C. Phillips." *Issues in Integrative Studies,* 3 (1984/85), 17–41.

Bateson, Gregory. "The Pattern Which Connects." In *Mind and Nature: A Necessary Unity.* New York: Dutton, 1979.

Beam, Robert D. "Fragmentation of Knowledge: An Obstacle to Its Full Utilization." In *The Optimum Utilization of Knowledge,* ed. Kenneth Boulding and Lawrence Senesh. Boulder: Westview, 1983, pp. 160–74.

Beckwith, Guy. "Interdisciplinarity and Dialectics: Integrative Concepts and Methods in Hegel's *Phenomenology of Spirit.*" *Issues in Integrative Studies,* 3 (1984/85), 91–101.

Berthel, John H. "Twentieth Century Scholarship and the Research Library: A Marriage of Convenience." *University of Tennessee Library Lectures,* 20 (1969), 15–31.

Binder, Arnold. "Criminology and Interdisciplinarity." *Issues in Integrative Studies,* 5 (1987), 41–67.

Birnbaum, Norman. "The Arbitrary Disciplines." *Change, The Magazine of Higher Learning,* July-Aug. 1969, pp. 10–21.

Blum, Mark E. "Dialogue with Autobiography: Integrating through the Study of Personality." *Issues in Integrative Studies,* 2 (1983), 75–92.

Bohm, David. *Wholeness and the Implicate Order.* London: Routledge & Kegan Paul, 1980.

Boulding, Kenneth E. *The Image: Knowledge in Life and Society.* Ann Arbor: Univ. of Michigan Press, 1956.

Caldwell, Lynton K. "Environmental Studies: Discipline or Metadiscipline?" *Environmental Professional,* 5 (1983), 247–59.

Campbell, Donald. "Ethnocentrism of Disciplines and the Fish-Scale Model of Omniscience." in *Interdisciplinary Relationships in the Social Sciences,* ed. Muzafer and Carolyn Sherif. Chicago: Aldine, 1969, pp. 328–48.

Casey, Beth A. "The Quiet Revolution: The Transformation and Reintegration of the Humanities." *Issues in Integrative Studies,* 4 (1986), 71–92.

Cassell, Eric J. "How Does Interdisciplinary Work Get Done?" In *Knowledge, Value, and Belief,* ed. H.T. Englehardt and D. Callahan. New York: Hastings Center, 1977, pp. 355–61. Volume II of The Foundations of Ethics and Its Relationship to Science.

Chapman, Ian, and Farina Chummer. "The Funding of Interdisciplinary Research in Canada." *Journal of Canadian Studies* (Canada), 15 No. 3 (1980), 30–33.

Chen, Robert S. "Interdisciplinary Research and Integration: The Case of CO_2 and Climate." *Climatic Change,* 3 No. 4 (1981), 429–48.

Chubin, Daryl E., Alan Porter, and Frederick Rossini. "'Citation Classics' Analysis: An Approach to Characterizing Interdisciplinary Research." *Journal of the American Society for Information Science,* 35 No. 6 (1984), 360–68.

Cluck, Nancy Anne. "Reflections on the Interdisciplinary Approaches to the Humanities." *Liberal Education,* 66 No. 1 (1980), 67–77.

"'Communities Have Problems, Universities Have Departments.'" In *The University and the Community, The Problems of Changing Relationships.* Paris: Organization for Economic Cooperation and Development, 1982, pp. 127–31.

Conklin, Kenneth R. "The Integration of the Disciplines." *Educational Theory,* 16 (July 1966), 225–38.

Cotterell, Roger B.M. "Interdisciplinarity: The Expansion of Knowledge and the Design of Research." *Higher Education Review,* 11 (Summer 1979), 47–56.

Darden, Lindley, and Nancy Maull. "Interfield Theories." *Philosophy of Science,* 44 (March 1977), 43–64.

Darvas, György. "Paradox of Interdisciplinarity." Paper presented at the Sixteenth Meeting of the International Congress of the History of Science in Bucharest, Rumania, 1981.

DeBie, Pierre. "Introduction" to the special section on "Multidisciplinary Problem-Focused Research." *International Social Science Journal,* 20 No. 2 (1968), 192–210.

Delkeskamp, Corinna. "Interdisciplinarity: A Critical Appraisal." In *Knowledge, Value, and Belief,* ed. H.T. Englehardt, Jr., and D. Callahan. Hastings-on-Hudson: Hastings Center, 1977, pp. 324–354. Volume II of The Foundations of Ethics and Its Relationship to Science.

Derrida, Jacques. "The Principle of Reason: The University in the Eyes of Its Pupils," *Diacritics* (Fall 1983), Response Section, 3–20.

DeWachter, Maurice. "Interdisciplinary Bioethics: But Where Do We Start? A Reflection on Epochè as Method." *Journal of Medicine and Philosophy,* 7 No. 3 (1982), 275–87.

Dluhy, Milan J., and Kan Chen, eds. *Interdisciplinary Planning: A Perspective for the Future.* New Brunswick, N.J.: Transactions Books-Rutgers, 1978.

Dorn, Harold. "The Dialectics of Interdisciplinarity." *Humanities,* 8 No. 2 (1987), 30–33.

Doyal, Len. "Interdisciplinary Studies in Higher Education," *Universities Quarterly, Higher Education and Society,* 28 No. 4 (1974), 470–87.

Fethe, Charles B. "A Philosophical Model for Interdisciplinary Programs." *Liberal Education,* 59 No. 4 (1973), 490–97.

Frank, Roberta. "'Interdisciplinary': The First Half-Century." In *Words,* ed. E.G. Stanley and T.F. Hoad (Woodbridge, Suffolk: D.S. Brewer, 1988), 91–101; reprinted in *Items,* Newsletter of the Social Science Research Council, 42 No. 3 (Spring 1988), 72–78; also reprinted in *Issues of Integrative Studies,* 6 (1988).

Frey, Gerhard. "Methodological Problems of Interdisciplinary Discussions." *RATIO,* 15 No. 2 (1973), 161–82.

Fryxell, Roald. "The Interdisciplinary Dilemma: A Case for Flexibility in Academic Thought." Rock Island, Ill.: Augustana College Library, 1977. Occasional Paper No. 13. ERIC ED 146 102.

Gaff, Jerry G., and Robert C. Wilson. "Faculty Cultures and Interdisciplinary Studies." *Journal of Higher Education,* 42 No. 3 (1971), 186–201.

Garfield, E. "Discipline-Oriented Citation Indexes and Data Bases: Bridging the Interdisciplinary Gap Via Multidisciplinary Input." *Current Contents,* 1981 No. 3 (1981), 5–8.

Geertz, Clifford. "Blurred Genres: The Refiguration of Social Thought." *American Scholar,* 49 No. 2 (1980), 165–79.

Gelwick, Richard. "Truly Interdisciplinary Study and Commitment in Relativism." *Soundings,* 66 No. 4 (1983), 422–36.

Goodlad, Sinclair. "What Is an Academic Discipline?" In *Cooperation and Choice in Higher Education,* ed. Roy Cox, London: University of London, 1979. ERIC ED 181 836.

Gordon, M.D. "Language Barriers, Literature Usage and the Role of Reviews: An International and Interdisciplinary Study." *Journal of Information Science,* 3 No. 4 (1981), 185–89.

Gordon, William J. *Synectics.* New York: Macmillan, 1968.

Govan, James F. "Community Analysis in an Academic Environment." *Library Trends,* 24 (Jan. 1976), 541–56.

Gozzer, Giovanni. "Interdisciplinarity: A Concept Still Unclear." *Prospects: Quarterly Review of Education,* 12 No. 3 (1982), 281–92.

Grele, Ronald. "A Surmisable Variety: Interdisciplinarity and Oral Testimony." *American Quarterly,* 27 (Aug. 1975), 275–95.

Gusdorf, Georges. "Past, Present, and Future in Interdisciplinary Research." *International Social Science Journal,* 29 No. 4 (1977), 580–99.

———. "Project for Interdisciplinary Research." *Diogenes,* 42 (Summer 1963), 119–42.

Hagstrom, Warren O. "The Differentiation of Disciplines." In *The Scientific Community.* New York: Basic Books, 1965, pp. 222–26.

Hall, Stuart. "Cultural Studies and the Centre: Some Problematics and Problems." In *Culture, Media, Language,* ed. Stuart Hall et al. London: Hutchinson, 1984, 16–47.

Hanisch, Thor Einar, and Wolfgang Vollman, eds. *Interdisciplinarity in Higher Education.* Bucharest, Romania: European Centre for Higher Education, UNESCO-CEPES, 1983. ERIC ED 249 864. Proceedings from symposium on "Interdisciplinarity in Higher Education in Europe," held in Bucharest, 24–26 November 1981.

Hareven, Tamara. "The History of the Family as an Interdisciplinary Field." *Journal of Interdisciplinary History,* 2 No. 2 (1971), 339–414.

Harvey, John H., ed. *Cognition, Social Behavior, and the Environment.* Hillsdale, N.J.: Lawrence Erlbaum Associates, 1981. See especially Baruch Fischoff, "No Man Is a Discipline," pp. 579–83.

Hershberg, Theodore, ed. *Philadelphia, Work, Space, Family, and Group Experience in the Nineteenth Century: Essays toward an Interdisciplinary History of the City.* New York: Oxford Univ. Press, 1981.

Holton, Gerald. "Analysis and Synthesis as Methodological Themata." *Methodology and Science,* 10 (1977), pp. 3–33.

———. "On the Role of Themata in Scientific Thought." *Science,* 188 No. 4186 (1975), 328–34.

Huerkamp, Claudia, et al. "Criteria of Interdisciplinarity." In *Center for Interdisciplinary Research, the University of Bielefeld: Annual Report 1978 and Supplement 1979–1981.* Bielefeld: Center for Interdisciplinary Research, 1981 [Supplement to the 1978 edition], pp. 23–24. Note: also discussed in Vosskamp, below.

Ichimura, Shinichi. "Interdisciplinary Research and Area Studies." *Journal of Southeast Asian Studies* (Singapore), 6 No. 2 (1975), 112–20.

Jantsch, Erich. "Interdisciplinary and Transdisciplinary University: A Systems Approach to Education and Innovation." *Higher Education,* 1 (Feb. 1972), 7–37. See also *Ekistics,* 32 (1971), 430–37; and *Policy Sciences,* 1 (1970), 403–28.

———. "Interdisciplinarity: Dreams and Reality." *Prospects: Quarterly Review of Education,* 10 No. 3 (1980), 304–12.

Kallen, H.M. "The Meanings of Unity among the Sciences." In *Structure, Method, and Meaning. Essays in Honor of Henry M. Sheffer,* ed. Paul Henle, Horace Kellen, and Susanne Langer. New York: Liberal Arts Press, 1951.

Kann, Mark E. "The Political Culture of Interdisciplinary Explanation." *Humanities in Society,* 2 No. 3 (1979), 185–200.

Kermoade, Arthur L. "The Interdisciplinary Approach and Its Comparative Effectiveness." Seattle: University of Washington College of Education, 1972. ERIC ED 064 238.

Kim, Chai, and Neil A. Yerkey. "Impact of Other Disciplines on Information Retrieval and Librarianship." Paper presented at the midyear meeting of the American Society for Information Science. Pittsburgh, Pa. 14–17 May 1980. ERIC ED 191 467.

Klein, Julie Thompson. "The Dialectic and Rhetoric of Disciplinarity and Interdisciplinarity." *Issues in Integrative Studies,* 2 (1983), 35–74.

———. "The Evolution of a Body of Knowledge: Interdisciplinary Problem-Focused Research." *Knowledge: Creation, Diffusion, Utilization.* 7 No. 2 (1985), 117–42.

Kleiner, Elaine. "Interdisciplinary Theory and Ambiguous Form Perception." *Issues in Integrative Studies,* 3 (1984/85), 43–50.

Kocklemans, Joseph J. "Interdisciplinarity and the University: The Dream and the Reality." *Issues in Integrative Studies,* 4 (1986), 1–16.

Kroker, Arthur. "Migration across the Disciplines." *Journal of Canadian Studies,* 15 (Fall 1980), 3–10.

Landau, Martin, Harold Proshansky, and William Ittelson. "The Interdisciplinary Approach and the Concept of Behavioral Sciences." In *Decisions: Values and Groups,* ed. Norman F. Washburne. New York: Pergamon Press, 1962, pp. 7–25.

Laszlo, E., and H. Margenau. "The Emergence of Integrative Concepts in Contemporary Science." *Philosophy of Science,* 39 No. 2 (1972), 252–59.

Leary, Lewis Gaston, ed. *The Unity of Knowledge.* New York: Doubleday, 1955.

LePair, C. "Switching between Academic Disciplines in Universities in the Netherlands." *Scientometrics,* 2 (May 1980), 177–91.

Lipton, Michael. "Interdisciplinary Studies in Less Developed Countries." *Journal of Development Studies,* 7 No. 1 (1970), 5–18; See also reply by M.P. Moore, "The Logic of Interdisciplinary Studies." *Journal of Development Studies,* 11 No. 1 (1974), 98–106.

Luyten, Norbert A. "Interdisciplinarité: Un Imperatif de la Recherche Scientifique." *Civitas,* 29 (1973–74), 221–42.

McCorcle, Mitchell D. "Critical Issues in the Functioning of Interdisciplinary Groups." *Small Group Behavior,* 12 No. 3 (1982), 291–310.

McGrath, Earl J. "Interdisciplinary Studies: An Integration of Knowledge and Experience." *Change, The Magazine of Higher Learning,* 6 (Aug. 1978), 6–9. Report on Teaching Issue.

Mahan, Jack Lee, Jr. "Toward Transdisciplinary Inquiry in the Humane Sciences." Diss., United States International University. San Diego, 1970.

Maruyama, Magorah. "Paradigmatology and Its Application to Cross-Disciplinary, Cross-Professional, and Cross-Cultural Communication." *Dialectica,* 28 (1974), 135–56, 237–81.

————. "Philosophy as an Open Meta-Science of Interdisciplinary Cross-Induction." *Dialectica,* 16 No. 4 (1962), 361–84.

Mead, Margaret, Discussant. "Can Research Institutions Accommodate Interdisciplinary Researchers?" Symposium at the 143rd Annual Meeting of the American Association for the Advancement of Science. Denver, Colo., 20–25 February 1977. Taped transcript available from the AAAS.

Meadows, A.J. "Diffusion of Information across the Sciences." *Interdisciplinary Science Reviews,* 1 No. 3 (1976), 259–67.

Meeth, L. Richard. "Interdisciplinary Studies: a Matter of Definition." *Change Magazine,* 6 (Aug. 1978), 10.

Messmer, Michael W. "The Vogue of the Interdisciplinary." *Centennial Review,* 12 No. 4 (1978), 467–78.

Miller, Raymond C. "Varieties of Interdisciplinary Approaches in the Social Sciences." *Issues in Integrative Studies,* 1 (1982), 1–37.

Morrison, James L., and Tamara Swora. "Interdisciplinarity and Higher Education." *Journal of General Education,* 26 (Apr. 1974), 45–52.

Mucklow, Neale H. "Grounds for Grouping the Disciplines." *Journal of Philosophy of Education,* 14 No. 2 (1980), 226–37.

Murray, Thomas. "Confessions of an Unconscious Interdisciplinarian." *Issues in Integrative Studies,* 4 (1986), 57–70.

Nelson, J., A. Megill, and D. McCloskey, eds. *The Rhetoric of the Human Sciences.* Madison: Univ. of Wisconsin Press, 1987.

Nelson, N. "Issues in Funding and Evaluating Interdisciplinary Research." *Journal of Canadian Studies,* 15 No. 3 (1980), 25–29.

Neurath, Otto. "Unified Science as Encyclopedic Integration." In *International Encyclopedia of Unified Science: Foundations of the Unity of Science.* Vol. I, No. 1. Chicago: Univ. of Chicago Press, 1938.

Newell, William. "Interdisciplinary Studies Are Alive and Well." *Association for Integrative Studies Newsletter,* 10 No. 1 (1988), 1, 6–8.

Nyiri, Nicolas, and Rod Preece, eds. *Unity in Diversity: Proceedings of the Interdisciplinary Research Seminar at Wilfrid Laurier University.* Waterloo, Ont.: Wilfrid Laurier Univ. Press, 1977.

Palmer, Monte, Larry Stern, and Charles Gaile. *The Interdisciplinary Study of Politics.* New York: Harper and Row, 1974.

Peston, M. "Some Thoughts on Evaluating Interdisciplinary Research." *Higher Education Review,* 10 No. 2 (1978), 55–60.

Peterson, Frederick E. "Exploring the Relationships between Academic Disciplines: A Fresh Perspective at the Smithsonian." *Teacher's College Record,* 82 No. 2 (1980), 311–16.

Petrie, Hugh G. "Do You See What I See: The Epistemology of Interdisciplinary Inquiry." *Journal of Aesthetic Education,* 10 (Jan. 1976), 29–43.

Phenix, Philip. "Use of the Disciplines as Curriculum Content." *Educational Forum,* 26 (1962), 273–80.

Phillips, D.C. *Holistic Thought in the Social Sciences.* Stanford. Calif: Stanford Univ. Press, 1976.

Physics Survey Committee. *Physics in Perspective. V. I. Physics Survey Committee, National Research Council.* Washington, D.C.: National Academy of Sciences, 1975.

Pilet, Paul-Emile. "The Multidisciplinary Aspects of Biology: Basic and Applied Research." *Scientia,* 116 (1981), 629–31.

Porter, Arthur. "The Expansion of Transdisciplinary Studies." *Transactions of the Royal Society of Canada.* 11 (1973), 11–20.

Potter, George. The Promise of Interdisciplinarity and Its Problems." *Ramapo Papers,* 1 (1977), 1–23.

Pring, Richard. "Curriculum Integration." *Proceedings of the Philosophy of Education Society of Great Britain Supplementary Issue,* 5 No. 2 (1971), 170–200.

Pye, Lucian W., ed. *Political Science and Area Studies: Rivals or Partners?.* Bloomington: Indiana Univ. Press, 1975.

Radnitzky, Gerard. *Continental Schools of Metascience.* Goteborg: Akademiforlaget, 1968. Vol. 1: *Anglo-Saxon Schools of Metascience;* Vol. 2: *Continental Schools of Metascience.*

The Re-evaluation of Existing Values, 2 vols. New York: ICF Press, 1974.

Reiser, Oliver L. *The Integration of Human Knowledge.* Boston: Porter Sargent, 1958.

Rich, Daniel, and Robert Warren. "The Intellectual Future of Urban Affairs: Theoretical, Normative, and Organizational Options." *Social Science Journal,* 17 No. 2 (1980), 53–66.

Rickson, Roy E., and Sarah T. Rickson. "Problems and Prospects of Crossdisciplinary Research." *Rural Sociologist.* 2 (March 1982), 95–103.

Riesman, David. "The Scholar at the Border: Staying Put and Moving Around inside the American University." *Columbia Forum,* Spring 1974, pp. 26–31.

Rigney, Daniel, and Donna Barnes. "Patterns of Interdisciplinary Citation in the Social Sciences." *Social Science Quarterly,* 61 No. 1 (1980), 114–27.

Ripley, S.D. "Smithsonian: Interdisciplinary Institution 150 Years After Its Conception by Smithson, James." *Interdisciplinary Science Reviews,* 3 No. 2 (1978), 89–98.

Rose, Richard. "Disciplined Research and Undisciplined Problems." *International Social Science Journal,* 28 No. 1 (1976), 99–121.

Roy, Rustum. "Interdisciplinary Science on Campus: The Elusive Dream." *Chemical and Engineering News,* 29 August 1977, pp. 28–40. Also in *Interdisciplinarity and Higher Education.* University Park: The Pennsylvania State Univ. Press, 1979, pp. 161–96.

Salmon-Cox, Leslie, and Burkart Holzner. "Managing Multidisciplinarity: Building and Bridging Epistemologies in Educational R&D." Paper presented at the American Educational Research Association Annual Meeting in New York, 4–8 April 1977. ERIC ED 135 760.

Schiffer, Michael B. "Some Issues in the Philosophy of Archaeology." *American Antiquity,* 46 No. 4 (1981), 899–908.

Schneider, Stephen N. "Climate Change and the World Predicament: A Case Study for Interdisciplinary Research." *Climatic Change,* 1 (1977), 21–43.

"Scholarly Disciplines: Breaking Out." *New York Times,* 25 April 1986, A18–19.

Schwartz, Benjamin I. "Presidential Address: Area Studies as a Critical Discipline." *Journal of Asian Studies,* 40 No. 1 (1980), 15–25.

The Search for Absolute Values in a Changing World. 2 Vols. New York: International Cultural Foundation, 1978.

Shapiro, B.J., and J. Whaley. *Selection of Library Materials in Applied and Interdisciplinary Fields.* Chicago: American Library Association, 1987. Monograph.

Shin, Un-chol. "The Structure of Interdisciplinary Knowledge: A Polanyian View." *Issues in Integrative Studies,* 4 (1986), 93–104.

Sinaceur, Mohammed Allal. "What Is Interdisciplinarity?" *International Social Science Journal,* 29 No. 4 (1977), 571–79.

Skinner, Quentin, ed. *The Return of Grand Theory in the Human Sciences.* Cambridge: Cambridge Univ. Press, 1985.

Smith, Linda C. "Systematic Searching of Abstracts and Indexes in Interdisciplinary Areas." *Journal of the American Society for Information Science,* 25 (1974), 343–53.

Snyder, Solomon H. "Neurosciences: An Integrative Discipline." *Science,* 21 Sept. 1984, pp. 1255–57.

Spacks, Patricia Meyer. "Do Cats Eat Bats?" *Yale Review,* 67 No. 2 (1978), 307–20.

Stoddard, Ellwyn R. "Multidisciplinary Research Funding: A 'Catch-22' Enigma." *American Sociologist,* 17 (Nov. 1982), 210–16.

Stoddard, Ellwyn R., ed. "The Status of U.S.-Mexico Borderlands Studies: A Multidisciplinary Symposium." *Social Science Journal,* 12/13 (Oct. 1975/Jan. 1976), 1–112.

Sweet, Albert. "Intersubjective Reference." *Nature and System,* 2 (Mar. 1980), 21–28.

Tagliacozzo, Giorgio. "The Literature of Integrated Knowledge." *American Behavioral Scientist,* 4 No. 10 (1961), 3–11.

Taylor, Alastair M. "Integrative Principles and the Educational Process." *Main Currents in Modern Thought,* 25 No. 5 (1969), 126–33.

Tenopir, C. "Distribution of Citations in Databases in a Multidisciplinary Field." *Online Review* (Great Britain), 6 No. 5, (1982), 399–419.

Thom, Rene. "The Virtues and Dangers of Interdisciplinary Research." *Mathematical Intelligencer,* 7 No. 3 (1985), 31–34.

Thomas, Dorothy Swine. "Experiences in Interdisciplinary Research." *American Sociological Review,* 17 (Dec. 1952), 663–69.

Toulmin, Stephen. *The Return to Cosmology: Postmodern Science and the Theology of Nature.* Berkeley: Univ. of California Press, 1982.

———. "The Variety of Rational Enterprises." In *Human Understanding: The Collective Use and Evolution of Concepts.* Princeton: Princeton Univ. Press, 1972, pp. 359–411.

Tranoy, Knut Erik. *Wholes and Structures.* Copenhagen: Munksgaard, 1959.

Trent, John E. "Internationalization? Interdisciplinarity? Development? The Social Sciences from 1952–1977." *Social Science Information,* 17 No. 2 (1978), 337–42.

Twining, William. "Law and Anthropology: A Case Study in Inter-Disciplinary Collaboration." *Law and Society Review,* 7 No. 4 (1973), 561–84.

Van Bertalanffy, Ludwig. "An Essay on the Relativity of Categories." *General Systems* (Yearbook), 7 (1962), 71–83.

Vlachy, J. "Interdisciplinary Approaches in Physics: The Concepts." *Czechoslovakian Journal of Physics, Section B,* B32 No. 11 (1982), 1311–18.

———. "The Measures of Interdisciplinarity in Research." *Teorie a Metoda* (June 1971), 51–66.

———. "More Data on Interdisciplinarity." *Teorie a Metoda,* 3 (1971), 63–80.

Vosskamp, Wilhelm. "From Scientific Specialization to the Dialogue between the Disciplines." *Issues in Integrative Studies,* 4 (1986), 17–36.

Walker, Rob. "Holistic Knowledge and the Politics of Fragmentation." From "An Image of the Whole: Knowledge and Curriculum in an Age of Fragmentation." Proceedings of a Series of Symposia. Kingston (Ontario), Queen's University (February 1978). Available as ERIC ED 153 817.

Westcott, Roger W. "The Plight of the Interdisciplinarian." *Academy Notes* (Academy of Independent Scholars), April 1982, p. 4.

White, I.L. "Interdisciplinary Approach to Applied Policy Analysis." *Technological Forecasting and Social Change,* 2 (1979), 95–106.

———. "Interdisciplinarity." In *Perspectives on Technology Assessment.* Eds. S.R. Arnstein and A.N. Christakis. Jerusalem: Science and Technology Publishers, 1975, pp. 87–96.

White, James Boyd. "Intellectual Integration." *Issues in Integrative Studies,* 5 (1987), 1–18.

Winkler, Karen. "Interdisciplinary Research: How Big a Challenge to Traditional Fields?" *Chronicle of Higher Education,* 7 Oct. 1987, pp. A1, 14–15.

Winthrop, Henry. "Methodological and Hermeneutic Functions in Interdisciplinary Education." *Educational Theory,* 14 (Apr. 1964), 118–27.

Wise, Gene. "Some Elementary Axioms for an American Culture Studies." *Prospects, The Annual of American Cultural Studies,* 4 (Winter 1978), 517–47.
Wolff, Michael. "Victorian Study: An Interdisciplinary Essay." *Victorian Studies,* 8 No. 1 (1964), 59–70.

Note also: A unique series of papers by individuals who participated in Cornell University's Center for International Studies project for the Improvement of Undergraduate Education, with insight into their perceptions of working relationships. Presented at the annual meeting of the American Educational Research Association in Chicago, Illinois (April 1975):
David. B. Macklin. "Impacts on a Social Psychologist-Consultant." ERIC ED 107 677.
Alison Brown. "Impacts on an Intellectual Historian." ERIC ED 107 678.
Stephen C. Brock. "Impacts on an Educationist/Administrator." ERIC ED 107 679.
Steward Paine Whiton. "Impacts on an Educational Researcher." ERIC ED 107 680.

Problem-focused Research

Abestalo, Marja. "Interdisciplinarity in the Light of the Development of Science and the Actual Research Work." In *Sociology of Science and Research,* ed. J. Farkas. Budapest: Akademiai Kiado, 1979.

Allen, T. Harrell. "Cross Impact Analysis: A Technique for Managing Interdisciplinary Research." *SRA, Journal of the Society of Research Administrators,* 10 (Summer 1978), 11–18.

Allen, Thomas J., James M. Piepmeier, and S. Cooney. "The International Technological Gatekeeper." *Technology Review,* March 1971, pp. 37–43.

*Alpert, Daniel. "The Role and Structure of Interdisciplinary and Multidisciplinary Research Centers." Address to the Ninth Annual Meeting of the Council of Graduate Schools in the United States, Washington, D.C., 4–6 Dec. 1969. ERIC ED 035 363.

———. "University Research on Problems Posed by Society." Paper at the Annual Conference on Special Emerging Programs in Higher Education. St. Louis, Mo. 17 Oct. 1973. ERIC ED 083 002.

*Anbar, Michael. "The 'Bridge Scientist' and His Role." *Research/Development,* 24 (July 1973), 30–34.

Anderson, James. "Organizing for Interdisciplinary Team Research." *Hortscience.* 21 No. 1 (1977), 33–35.

Andrews, Frank M. "Motivation, Diversity, and the Performance of Research Units." In *Scientific Productivity: The Effectiveness of Research Groups in Six Countries,* ed. F.M. Andrews. Cambridge: Cambridge Univ. Press, 1979.

Armstrong, David L., Charles W. Laughlin, and George S. Ayers. "Adminstration of Interdisciplinary Activities." *Hortscience,* 12 No. 1 (1977), 35–36.

*Arnstein, Sherry R., and Alexander Christakis, eds. *Perspectives on Technology Assessment.* Washington, D.C.: Academy for State and Local Governments, 1975; Jerusalem: Science and Technology Publishers, 1977. See especially James B. Taylor, "Building an Interdisciplinary Team," and Irvin L. White, "Interdisciplinarity."

*"Background Material and Summary Report for a Workshop on the Management of Interdisciplinary Research, 9–10 July 1974." Prepared by the University of Southern California as Part of Grant No. NM-39528. NSF Research Management Improvement Program. Principal Investigator: Z.A. Kaprielian; Co-principal Investigator J.M. Nilles.

Baer, Walter S. "Interdisciplinary Policy Research in Independent Research Centers." *IEEE Transactions on Engineering Management,* 23 (May 1976), 74–78.

Baldwin, Donald R., and Barbara J. Faubian. "Interdisciplinary Research in the Academic Setting." *SRA, Journal of the Society of Research Administrators,* 6 (Spring 1975), 3–8.

Barker, W.T., et al. "Environmental Implications of Coal Development: An Interdisciplinary Research Team Approach." *North Dakota Farm Research,* 38 No. 1 (1980), 22–26.

*Barmark, Jan, and Goran Wallen. "The Development of an Interdisciplinary Project." In *The Social Process of Scientific Investigation,* ed. K.D. Knorr, R. Krohn, and R. Whitley. Dordrecht: D. Reidel, 1980, pp. 221–35. Vol. 4 of Sociology of the Sciences. See also "Interaction of Cognitive and Social Factors in Steering a Large Interdisciplinary Project." In *Interdisciplinary Research Groups,* ed. Richard T. Barth and Rudy Steck. Vancouver: Interdisciplinary Research Group on Interdisciplinary Programs, 1979, pp. 180–90.

*Barth, Richard T., and Rudy Steck, eds. *Interdisciplinary Research Groups: Their Management and Organization.* Vancouver: Interdisciplinary Research Group on Interdisciplinary Programs, 1979.

Bartlett, C.D.S. "Interdisciplinary Co-operation to Identify Innovations for Small Farmers: The Role of the Economist." *Agricultural Administration,* 13 No. 3 (1983), 123–35.

Bass, Lawrence W. *Management by Task Forces: A Manual on the Operation of Interdisciplinary Teams.* Mt. Airy, Md: Lomond, 1975. See especially "Categories of Interdisciplinary Activities," "Environment and Benefits of Interdisciplinary Teams," and "How to Start Task Force Systems" (Appendix).

Bawden, R.J. "A Perspective for Parasite Management." *Agriculture and Environment,* 4 No. 1 (1978), 43–56.

*Bella, D.A., and K.J. Williamson. "Conflicts in Interdisciplinary Research." *Journal of Environmental Systems,* 6 No. 2 (1976–77), 105–24.

*———. "Interdisciplinary Research and Environmental Management." *[American Society of Civil Engineers, Engineering Issues] Journal of Professional Activities,* 104 (July 1978), 193–202.

*———. "Diagnosis of Chronic Impacts of Estuarine Dredging." *Journal of Environmental Systems,* 9 No. 4 (1979–80), 289–311.

Bennis, Warren G. "Some Barriers to Teamwork in Social Research." *Social Problems,* 3 No. 4 (1956), 223–35.

*Benton, Douglas A. "Management and Effectiveness Measures for Interdisciplinary Research." *SRA, Journal of the Society of Research Administrators,* 6 (Spring 1975), 37–45.

Benton, D.A., et al. "Organization and Personnel Management for Effective Interdisciplinary Research Projects." Ft. Collins: Colorado State University, Feb. 1977. NTIS PB 271 796.

Bewersdorff, A., ed. *Materials Science in Space: Proceedings of the Topical Meeting of the COSPAR Interdisciplinary Scientific Commission G Meeting of the COSPAR 25th Plenary Meeting.* Oxford: Pergamon Press, 1985.

*Birnbaum, Philip H. "Assessment of Alternative Management Forms in Academic Interdisciplinary Research Projects." *Management Science,* 24 No. 3 (1977), 272–84.

*———. "Academic Contexts of Interdisciplinary Research." *Educational Administration Quarterly,* 14 No. 2 (1978), 80–97.

———. "A Theory of Academic Interdisciplinary Research Performance: A Contingency and Path Analysis Approach." *Management Science,* 25 No. 3 (1979), 231–42.

*———. "Academic Interdisciplinary Research: Problems and Practice." *R&D Management,* 10 No. 1 (1979), 17–22.

*———. "Academic Interdisciplinary Research: Characteristics of Successful Projects." *SRA. Journal of the Society of Research Administrators,* 13 No. 1 (1981), 5–16.

*———. "Integration and Specialization in Academic Research." *Academy of Management Journal,* 24 No. 3 (1981), 487–503.

*———. "Contingencies for Interdisciplinary Research: Matching Research Questions with Research Organizations." *Management Science,* 27 No. 11 (1981), 1279–93.

*————. "The Organization and Management of Interdisciplinary Research: A Progress Report." *SRA. Journal of the Society of Research Administrators,* 13 No. 4 (1982), 11–23.

*————, and David Gillespie. "Status and Performance in Small Professional Organizations: The Case of Scientific Research Projects." *Social Science Quarterly,* 60 No. 1 (1979), 105–12.

*————, W.T. Newell, and B.O. Saxberg. "Managing Academic Interdisciplinary Research Projects." *Decision Sciences,* 10 No. 4 (1979), 645–65.

*Birnbaum, Philip H., Frederick A. Rossini, and Donald Baldwin, eds. *International Research Management: Studies in Interdisciplinary Methods.* New York: Oxford University Press, 1990.

Black, R.G. "The Interdisciplinary Communication Problem: Its Etiology and Therapy." *Trend in Engineering,* 21 No. 1 (1969), 10–18.

Blackwell, Gordon W. "Multidisciplinary Team Research." *Social Forces,* 33 No. 4 (1955), 367–74.

Blaschke, Dieter. "Management Problems of Interdisciplinary Basic Research in the Social Sciences." *Interstudy Bulletin,* 1 No. 2 (Aug. 1980), 6+.

Bonnicksen, T.M., and R.H. Becker. "Environmental Impact Studies: An Interdisciplinary Approach for Assigning Priorities." *Environmental Management,* 7 No. 2 (1983), 109–17.

Bradley, Raymond T. "Ethical Problems in Team Research: A Structural Analysis and an Agenda for Resolution." *American Sociologist,* 12 (May 1982), 87–94.

Branin, F.H., Jr., and Huseyin, K. *Problem Analysis in Science and Engineering.* New York: Academic Press, 1977.

Burdge, R.J., and P. Opryszek. "Interdisciplinary Problems in Doing Impact Assessment." In *Coping with Change: An Interdisciplinary Assessment of the Lake Shelbyville Reservoir.* Urbana: Institute for Environmental Studies, University of Illinois at Urbana, June 1981, pp. 349–59.

Bush, G.P., and L.H. Hattery, eds. *Teamwork in Research.* Washington, D.C.: American Univ. Press, 1953.

Cameron, A. "Lubrication: Interdisciplinary Subject." *Lubrication Engineering,* 35 No. 12 (1979), 670–71.

Capener, Harold R., and Robert J. Young. "Interdisciplinary Research in the University." In *Nitrogen and Phosphorous: Food Production, Waste, and the Environment,* ed. Keith S. Porter. Ann Arbor, Mich.: Ann Arbor Science Publishers, 1975.

*Caudill, W., and B.H. Roberts. "Pitfalls in the Organization of Interdisciplinary Research." *Human Organization,* 10 No. 4 (1951), 12–15.

*Chase, S., J. Wright, and R. Ragade. "Decision Making in an Interdisciplinary Team." *Behavioral Science: Journal of the Society for General Systems Research,* 26 No. 3 (1981), 206–15.

*Chen, Robert S. "Interdisciplinary Research and Integration: The Case of CO_2 and Climate." *Climatic Change,* 3 No. 4 (1981), 429–48.

*Chubin, D.E., F.A. Rossini, A.L. Porter, and I.I. Mitroff. "Experimental Technology Assessment: Explorations in Processes of Interdisciplinary Team Research." *Technological Forecasting and Social Change,* 15 (1979), 87–94.

*Chubin, D.E., A.L. Porter, F.A. Rossini, and T. Connolly, eds. *Interdisciplinary Analysis and Research: Theory and Practice of Problem-Focused Research and Development.* Mt. Airy Md.: Lomond, 1986. Includes an "Annotated Bibliography," pp. 441–70.

Cohen, B.P., R.J. Kruse, and M. Anbar. "The Social Structure of Scientific Research Teams." *Pacific Sociological Review,* 25 (1982), 205–32.

Compton, W.D. "Multidisciplinary Research." *Physics Today,* 24 (1971), 11.

"Computerising a Multi-Disciplinary Team (Building Industry)." *Building* (Great Britain), 23 Nov. 1984, p. 49.

Coyne, Dermot P. "Horticulture and Interdisciplinary Research." *Hortscience,* 14 (Dec. 1979), 686.

*Cravens, D.W., K.W. Heatherington, and R.A. Mundy. "Organizing for Interdisciplinary Research in a University Setting." *SRA, Journal of the Society of Research Administrators,* 8 No. 1 (Summer 1976), 3–10.

Crusberg, T.C., A.H. Hoffman, and L.J. Morse. "The Water Quality Resource Study Group: An Interdisciplinary Community Effort in Worcester, Massachusetts, USA." *Environmental Professional,* 5 No. 2 (1983), 162–67.

Cunningham, D.E. "Federal Support of Interdisciplinary Research in Universities." United States Department of Commerce, National Bureau of Standards, Oct. 1969, N70-21072.

Dailey, R.C. "A Path Analysis of R&D Team Co-ordination and Performance." *Decision Sciences,* 1 No. 2 (1980), 357–69.

———. "The Role of Team and Task Characteristics in R&D Collaborative Problem Solving and Productivity," *Management Science,* 24 No. 15 (1978), 1579–88.

Darbellay, Charly. "Ecological Problems in the Swiss Alps: The Pays d'Enhaut Project." *International Social Science Journal,* 34 No. 3 (1982), 427–39.

Davis, W.E., III. "Interdisciplinary Research in Theory and Practice: A View From the University." M.A. Thesis, Syracuse University, April 1970. NASA Project. National Technical Information Service N70-33934.

Day, Douglas H., Jr. "The Management of Organized Research Units at the University of California, Berkeley: Size, Politics, and Interdisciplinarity." Center for Research in Management Science, University of California, Berkeley. Revised Mar. 1977. Working Paper CP-399.

DiCastri, Francesco. "International, Interdisciplinary Research in Ecology: Some Problems of Organization and Execution. The Case of the Man and the Biosphere (MAB) Programme." *Human Ecology,* 4 No. 3 (1976), 235–46.

Eaton, J.W. "Social Processes of Professional Teamwork." *American Sociological Review,* 16 (Oct. 1951), 707–13.

Ellis, Robert H. *The Planning and Management of Problem-Oriented, Interdisciplinary Research at Academic Institutions.* Hartford: Connecticut Renssalaer Hartford Graduate Center, 1974.

*Epton, S.R., R.L. Payne, and A.W. Pearson. "The Management of Cross-Disciplinary Research." *R&D Management,* 14 No. 2 (1984), 69–79.

*Epton, S.R., A.W. Pearson, and R.L. Payne, eds. *Managing Interdisciplinary Research.* Chichester: John Wiley & Sons, 1984.

Everest, F.H. "How to Demonstrate the Importance of Fishing Resources to Interdisciplinary Planning Teams." *Fisheries,* 4 No. 1 (1979), 15–20.

Fenner, E.H. "A Project Accounting System That Encourages Multidisciplinary Research." *Engineering Education,* 71 (Nov. 1980), 167–69.

Fennell, Mary L., and Gary D. Sandefur. "Structural Clarity of Interdisciplinary Teams: A Research Note." *Journal of Applied Behavioral Science,* 19 No. 2 (1983), 193–202.

Floret, C., and M.S. Hadjej. "An Attempt to Combat Desertification in Tunisia." *Ambio,* 6 No. 6 (1977), 366–68.

Fundamental Research on Estuaries: The Importance of an Interdisciplinary Approach. Washington, D.C.: National Academy Press, 1983.

Giacomini, V. "Man and the Biosphere: An Amplified Ecological Vision." *Landscape Planning,* 5 No. 2–3 (1978), 193–211.

*Gillespie, D.F., and Philip H. Birnbaum. "Status Concordance, Coordination, and Success in Interdisciplinary Research Teams." *Human Relations,* 33 No. 1 (1980), 41–56.

*Gillespie, D.F., and Brian Mar. "Interdisciplinary Team PreProposal Management." *SRA, Journal of the Society of Research Administrators,* 9 (Fall 1977), 33–40.

Golubev, G., and O. Vasiliev. "Interregional Water Transfers as an Interdisciplinary Problem." *Water Supply and Management,* 2 No. 2 (1978), 67–77.

Gulf Universities Research Consortium (James Sharp). "Methods to Support Multidisciplinary University Interdisciplinary Research Program." *Interstudy Bulletin,* 2 No. 4 (1981), 5+.

Gummick, J.L., S.G. Appan, and C.S. Dunn. "Computerized Mind Support to Interdisciplinary Consensus Formation Processes." *Journal of Energy and Environment,* 1 (Sept. 1982), 37–60.

Gunz, H.P., and A.W. Pearson. "Introduction of a Matrix Structure into an R&D Establishment." *R&D Management,* 7 No. 3 (1977), 173–81.

Hagstrom, Warren O. "Traditional and Modern Forms of Scientific Teamwork." *Administrative Science Quarterly,* 9 No. 3 (1964), 241–63.

Hargis, William J., Jr. *A Benchmark Multidisciplinary Study of the Interaction between the Chesapeake Bay and Adjacent Waters of the Virginian Sea. NASA Conf. Publ* (1981), NASA-CP2188. Chesapeake Bay Plume Study, N82-10622, pp. 1–14.

Harriott, B.L. "Interdisciplinary Research: The USDA-ARS Plan." *Agricultural Engineering,* 64 No. 9 (1983), 7.

Harrold, A.H. "Multidisciplinary Engineering in the Process Industries." *Radio and Electronic Engineering,* 51 No. 9 (1981), 416.

Heathington, K.W., et al. "Management of Interdisciplinary Research in Universities: The State of the Art." *Educational Researcher,* 7 No. 1 (1978), 11–14.

Heller, S.R., and S.L. Rawlins. "Agriculture Systems Research – A New Initiative." *Human Systems Management (Netherlands),* 6 No. 4 (1986), 289–96.

Helmer, O. "The Need for Interdisciplinarity." In *Looking Forward: A Guide to Future Research.* New York: Sage, 1983.

Henschel, Richard L. "Effects of Disciplinary Prestige on Predictive Accuracy: Distortions from Feedback Loops." *Futures,* 7 No. 2 (1975), 92–106.

Higgins, J.C. "University Courses Combining Engineering with Management." *IEE Proceedings, Part A: Physical Science, Measurement and Instrumentation, Management and Education, Reviews,* 129 No. 4 (1982), 213–18.

Hoddeson, Lillian. "The Discovery of the Point-Contact Transistor." *Historical Studies in the Physical Sciences,* 12 No. 1 (1981), 41–76.

Holton, Gerald. "Niels Bohr and the Integrity of Science." *American Scientist,* 74 No. 3 (1986), 237–43.

Hopeman, Richard J., and David L. Wilemon. "Reflection on Interdisciplinary Research." Occasional Paper No.2. Syracuse University. Apr. 1969. Available as "Reflecting on Interdisciplinary Research," NASA document N70-18480, 1970.

Ikenberry, Stanley I., and Renee C. Friedman. *Beyond Academic Departments: The Story of Institutes and Centers.* San Francisco: Jossey Bass, 1972.

*Interdisciplinary Research Tools. Santa Barbara, Calif.: ABC – CLIO. MNUG83-B48082.

Jackson, F.H. "Interdisciplinary Environmental Analysis for Timber Sale Planning." *Water Resources Bulletin,* 17 No. 2 (1981), 301–06.

Jeffs, George W. "Space Shuttle: Its Interdisciplinary Design and Construction." *Interdisciplinary Science Reviews,* 4 No. 3 (1979), 208–38.

*Jurkovich, R., and J.H.P. Paelinck, eds. *Problems in Interdisciplinary Studies: Issues in Interdisciplinary Studies, No. 2.* Hampshire, Eng.: Gower, 1984. (Steering Committee in Interdisciplinary Studies, Erasmus University, Rotterdam)

Kade, Gerhard. "Introduction: The Economics of Pollution and the Interdisciplinary Approach to Environmental Planning." *International Social Science Journal,* 22 No. 4 (1970), 563–73.

Kamen, Charles S. "The Effect of a 'Social Problem' Orientation on the Organization of Scientific Research." *Journal of Environmental Systems,* 7 (1977–78), 309–22.

Kappeler, T. "The World Ecotoxicology Watch." *Environmental Science and Technology,* 13 No. 4 (1979), 412–15.

Kash, Don E., and Irvin L. White. "Technology Assessment: Harnessing Genius." *Chemical Engineering News,* 49, 29 Nov. 1971, 36–41.

*Kast, F.E., J.E. Rosenzweig, and J.W. Stockman. "Interdisciplinary Programs in a University Setting." *Academy of Management Journal,* 13 No. 3 (1970), 311–24.

*Kendall, Stephen, and E.E. Mackintosh. *Management Problems of Polydisciplinary Environmental Research Projects in the University Setting.* Guelph, Ont.: University of Guelph, 1978. Centre for Resources Development Publication No. 86 (May 1978). Also listed as Canada/Man and the Biosphere Committee Report No. 13 (31 Nov. 1979).

Khush, G.S., and W.R. Coffman. "Genetic Evaluation and Utilization (GEU) Program. The Rice Program of the International Rice Research Institute." *Theoretical and Applied Genetics,* 51 No. 3 (1977), 97–110.

Klassen, Waldemar. "Interdisciplinary Programs in Insect Mass Rearing and in Insect Population Management." *Entomology Society of America Bulletin,* 24 No. 1 (1978), 63–65.

*Klein, Julie Thompson. "The Evolution of a Body of Knowledge: Interdisciplinary Problem-Focused Research." *Knowledge: Creation, Utilization, and Diffusion,* 7 No. 2 (1985), 117–42.

Kloza, Marian, Czeslaw Sztukowski, and Ryszard Wasniowski, eds. *Management of Research, Development, and Education, IV. International Conference Proceedings.* Wroclaw, Poland: Futures Research Center of Wroclaw Technical University, 1980. No. 13.

Knott, K., and B. Feuerbacher. "Spacelab-1: An Early Space Station for Science and Technology," *Acta Astronautica,* 9 No. 6–7 (1982), 347–52.

*Kruse, R.J., et al. "Interdisciplinary Research Teams as Status Systems." Paper presented at the Annual Meeting of the American Society for Engineering Education, Ft. Collins, Colo., 16–19 June 1975. Technical Report No. 56. Laboratory for Social Research, Stanford University, 1977. ERIC ED 118 450.

Kruse, Ronald J., Michael Anbar, and Bernard Cohen. "Threats to the Promise of Synergy in Interdisciplinary Research." Technical Report No. 57. Laboratory for Social Research. Stanford University, 1977.

Larsson, P., et al. "The Lake Ecosystem of Ovre, Heimdalsvatn, Norway." *Holarctic Ecology,* 1 No. 2–3 (1978), 304–20.

Linstone, H.A., et al. "The Multiple Perspective Concept with Applications to Technology Assessment and Other Decision Areas." *Technological Forecasting and Social Change,* 20 (1981), 275–325.

Loeb, E. "Some Concepts for Interdisciplinary Practice." *Social Work,* 5 (1960), 83.

Lomas, T. "Multidisciplinary Engineering in the Process Industries." *Radio and Electronic Engineer,* 51 No. 9 (1981), 417.

*London, Manuel, and W. Bruce Walsh. "The Development and Application of a Model of Long-Term Group Process for the Study of Interdisciplinary Teams." *Catalog of Selected Documents in Psychology,* 5 (Winter 1975), 1–35.

Long, F.A. "Interdisciplinary Problem Oriented Research in the University." *Science,* 12 March 1971, p. 961.

Loveday, D. "Factors Affecting the Management of Interdisciplinary Research in the Pharmaceutical Industry." *R&D Management,* 14 No. 2 (1984), 93–103.

*Luszki, Margaret Barron. *Interdisciplinary Team Research Methods and Problems.* Washington, D.C.: National Training Laboratories, 1958.

*McCorcle, Mitchell. "Critical Issues in the Functioning of Interdisciplinary Groups." *Small Group Behavior,* 13 (Aug. 1982), 291–310.

McDole, R.E., and S.A. Reinertsen. "Steep: An Interagency, Multidisciplinary Approach to Soil Conservation." *Journal of Soil and Water Conservation,* 38 No. 3 (1983), 244–45.

*MacDonald, William R. *The Management of Interdisciplinary Research Teams: A Literature Review.* Report prepared on behalf of the Department of the Environment and the Department of Agriculture, Government of Alberta. Edmonton, Alberta, Canada, Jan. 1982.

*McEvoy, James III. "Multi- and Interdisciplinary Research: Problems of Initiation, Control, Integration and Reward." *Policy Sciences,* 3 (July 1972), 201–08.

McGrath, Dorn C., Jr. "Multidisciplinary Environmental Analysis: Jamaica Bay and Kennedy Airport." *Journal of the American Institute of Planners,* 37 No. 4 (1971), 343–52.

Mar, Brian. "Problems Encountered in Multidisciplinary Resources and Environmental Simulation Model Development." *Journal of Environmental Management,* 2 (1974), 82–100.

*———, et al. "Applied Interdisciplinary, Interdepartmental Management." *INTERSTUDY Bulletin,* 4 (1983), 3.

*———, W.T. Newell, and B.O. Saxberg. "Interdisciplinary Research in the University Setting." *Environmental Science and Technology,* 10 No. 7 (1976), 650–53

*———, eds. *Managing High Technology: An Interdisciplinary Perspective.* Amsterdam: Elsevier, 1985.

Martin, J.N., et al. "The Structural Engineer in a Multidisciplinary Practice." *Structural Engineer: Part A,* 59 No. 5 (1981), 177–80.

Martino, J.P. "Managing Interdisciplinary Research Teams." *Proceedings of the IEEE 1978 National Aerospace and Electronics Conference NAECON 78, Volume I* (May 1978), 280–85.

Materials Science and Engineering, 37 (Jan. 1979), 56–70. (Case studies.)

Mead, Margaret. "Can Research Institutions Accommodate Interdisciplinary Researchers?" Symposium at 143rd Annual Meeting of the American Association for the Advancement of Science, Denver, Colo., 20–25 Feb. 1977. Taped transcript available from AAAS.

Meadows, A.J. "Scientific Collaboration and Status." *Communication Science* (1974), 172–206.

*Meechan, C. "Interdisciplinary Problem Solving: Some Actual Teaming Experiences." *SRA, Journal of the Society of Research Administrators,* 10 No. 1 (1978), 19–25.

Michaelis, Anthony. "Great Problems and Interdisciplinary Solutions." *Interdisciplinary Science Reviews,* 3 No. 1 (1978), 1–2.

———. "Interdisciplinary Disaster Research." *Interdisciplinary Science Reviews,* 9 No. 3 (1984), 193–94.

*Mitchell, R. "The Maintenance of Personal Integrity in the Interdisciplinary Team Research Effort." *HortScience,* 12 No. 1 (1977), 36–37.

Morphet, C. "Positivist and Political Approaches to Interdisciplinarity." *Science and Science Policy,* Feb. 1981, pp. 18–22.

Morris, J.W. "The United States Army Corps of Engineers: Two Centuries of Interdisciplinary Engineering." *Interdisciplinary Science Reviews,* 5 No. 4 (1980), 269–80.

Murray, Keith A., and Brian J. Rothschild. *Policy Issues in Resource Management, Vol. 4. World Fisheries Policy: Multidisciplinary Views.* Seattle: Univ. of Washington Press, 1972.

Narayan, L.R.A., and B. Sahai. "Integrated Resources Survey and Applications." *Proceedings of the Indian Academy of Sciences. Engineering Sciences,* 6 No. 4 (1983), 287–95.

Neumann, Klaus-Kurt, and Hans-Joachim, Neumann. "Interdisciplinary Chemical Engineering: Present and Future." *Interdisciplinary Science Reviews,* 8 No. 3 (1983), 231–34.

*Newell, William T., et al. "Management of Interdisciplinary Research in Universities Faces Problems." Paper presented at the Annual Meeting of the American Society for Engineering Education, Colorado State University, Ft. Collins. 16–19 June 1975. ERIC ED 118 395.

*———. "Guidelines for Applied Interdisciplinary Research in the University: How to Manage the University Role in Solving Society's Problems." Project Report No. 11. July 1980. Seattle: Graduate School of Business Administration, College of Engineering, University of Washington. NSF Grant NM44380. See also in the *INTERSTUDY Bulletin,* 1 No. 2 (1980).

Nicholas, D.D. "Multidisciplinary Approach to the Development of New Wood Preservatives." *Forest Products Journal,* 31 No. 9 (1981), 28–33.

Nilles, Jack M. "Interdisciplinary Policy Research and the Universities." *IEEE, Transactions on Engineering Management,* EM 23 No. 2 (1976), 74–84.

*————. "Interdisciplinary Research and the American University." *Interdisciplinary Science Reviews,* 1 No. 2 (June 1976), 160–66.

*————. "Interdisciplinary Research Management in the University Environment." *SRA, Journal of the Society of Research Administrators,* 6 No. 9 (1975), 9–16.

Norman, Colin. "NSF Readies New Engineering Program; A Major Effort to Establish Multidisciplinary Centers on University Campuses Is Being Viewed with Some Apprehension." *Science,* 4 Jan. 1985, p. 38.

Norstrom, R.J. "Multidisciplinary vs. Interdisciplinary Research." *Journal of Great Lakes Research,* 12 No. 1 (1986), 1.

*Odhner, Fred. "Group Dynamics of the Interdisciplinary Team." *American Journal of Occupational Therapy,* 24 (Oct. 1970), 484–87.

Oeschger, H. "The Carbon-Dioxide Problem: An Interdisciplinary Survey." *Experientia,* 36 No. 7 (1980), 808–12.

Orme, G.R., and J.R. Hails. "Great Barrier Reef Project: An Exercise in Interuniversity Interdisciplinary Research." *Search,* 17 Nos. 1–2 (1986), 36–40.

*Peston, Maurice. "Some Thoughts on Evaluating Interdisciplinary Research." *Higher Education Review,* 10 (Spring 1978), 55–60.

*Pignataro, Louis J., and William R. McShane. "Interdisciplinary Research: Transcending Departmental Conflicts." *Engineering Education,* 69 No. 4 (1979), 349–51.

Polishuk, Paul. "Problems in Interdisciplinary Policy Research and Management in Government." *IEEE. Transactions on Engineering Management,* EM 23 No. 2 (1976), 92–100.

*Porter, Alan L. "Interdisciplinary Research: Current Experience in Policy and Performance." *Interdisciplinary Science Reviews,* 8 No. 2 (1983), 158–67.

*————, et al. "Between Disciplines." *Science,* 29 Aug. 1980, p. 966.

*————, and F.L. Rossini, "Interdisciplinary Research Redefined: Multi-Skill, Problem-Focused Research in the STRAP Framework." *R&D Management,* 14 No. 2 (1984), 105–11.

*————, and D.E. Chubin, "An Indicator of Cross-Disciplinary Research." *Scientometrics,* 8 Nos. 3–4 (1985), 161–76.

Potchen, E.J., et al. "Management of Large-Scale Interdisciplinary Activities in Medicine." Final Report. NSF Grant NM 44353. 109, PB 262 205.

Povsner, A.D. "Interdisciplinary Research Project as a System." *Systems Research* (Yearbook). Moscow: Nauka, 1976, pp. 91–103. In Russian.

Purschwitz, M.A. "National Dairy Housing Conference Attracts Wide Interdisciplinary Support." *Agricultural Engineering,* 64 No. 5 (1983), 15.

R&D Management, 14 No. 2 (1984). Special issue.

Rajagopal, R. "Interdisciplinary Research and Education for Ecosystems Management." *Urban Systems,* 4 No. 1 (1979), 43–52.

Redding, D.S. "Setting Up the Maintenance Organization in a Multidisciplinary Project." *Terotechnica,* 2 No. 2 (1981), 105–19.

*Regier, Henry A. *A Balanced Science of Renewable Resources with Particular Reference to Fisheries.* Seattle: Univ. of Washington Press, 1978. A Washington Sea Grant Publication.

*Reisenburg S. "Interdisciplinary Research Groups: International Comparison of Their Organization and Management." *R&D Management,* 10 No. 1 (1979), 35–41.

*Riesenhuber, Heinz. "Interdisciplinary Co-operation Between Industry and Government in the FRG." *Interdisciplinary Science Reviews,* 8 No. 2 (1982), 102–104.

Riley, M.W. "Phases Encountered by a Project Team." *IEEE. Transactions on Education,* 23 (Nov. 1980), 212–13.

*Robertson, Ivan T. "Some Factors Associated with Successful Interdisciplinary Research." *SRA, Journal of the Society of Research Administrators,* 13 (Fall 1981), 44–50.

Roether, W. "The Carbon-Dioxide Problem. An Interdisciplinary Survey: The Effect of the Ocean on the Global Carbon Cycle." *Experientia,* 36 No. 9 (1980), 1017–25.

*Rose, Richard. "Disciplined Research and Undisciplined Problems." *International Social Science Journal,* 28 No. 1 (1976), 99–121.

Rossi, P.H. "Researchers, Scholars, and Policy Makers: The Politics of Large-Scale Research." *Daedalus,* 93 (Fall 1964), 1142–61.

*Rossini, F.A., and A.L. Porter. "Frameworks for Integrating Interdisciplinary Research." *Research Policy,* 8 No. 1 (1979), 70–79.

*———, and Alan Porter. "Interdisciplinary Research: Performance and Policy Issues." *SRA, Journal of the Society of Research Administrators,* 13 No. 2 (1981), 8–24.

*———, et al. "Interdisciplinary Integration within Technology Assessments." *Knowledge: Creation, Diffusion, Utilization,* 2 No. 4 (1981), 503–28.

———, et al. "Technology Assessment." In *Research in Philosophy and Technology,* ed. Paul T. Durbin. Vol. 2. Greenwich, Ct.: JAI Press, 1979, pp. 341–56.

*Roy Rustum. "Interdisciplinary Science on Campus: The Elusive Dream." *Chemical & Engineering News,* 29 Aug. 1977, pp. 28–40. See also under the same title in *Interdisciplinarity and Higher Education,* ed. Joseph Kockelmans. University Park: The Pennsylvania State Univ. Press, 1979, pp. 161–96.

Roy, W.R., and R.A. Griffin. "A Proposed Classification System for Coal Fly Ash in Multidisciplinary Research." *Journal of Environmental Quality,* 11 No. 4 (1982), 563–68.

Russell, M.G., and R. J. Sauer. "Creating Administrative Environments for Interdisciplinary Research." *SRA, Journal of the Society of Research Administrators,* 14 No. 4 (Spring 1983), 21–31.

*———, John M. Barnes, and John R. Cornwell, eds. *Enabling Interdisciplinary Research: Perspectives from Agriculture, Forestry, and Home Economics.* St. Paul, Minn.: Agricultural Experiment Station, University of Minnesota, 1982. Miscellaneous Publication No. 19.

*———. *Bridging Disciplinary Strengths.* St. Paul, Minn.: Agricultural Experiment Station, University of Minnesota, 1986. Miscellaneous Publication No. 39.

Savile, D. "Communication Problems in Interdisciplinary Research." *Proceedings of the Indian Academy of Sciences: Plant Sciences,* 93 No. 3 (1984), 223–30.

Saxberg, Borje O. "The Action Research Model Applied to the Management of Interdisciplinary Research in University and Industrial Settings." *R&D Management,* 15 No. 1 (Jan. 1985), 31–39.

*———, William T. Newell, and B.W. Mar. "Interdisciplinary Research: A Dilemma for University Central Administration." *SRA, Journal of the Society of Research Administrators,* 13 No. 2 (1981), 25–43.

Sbragia, R. "Clarity of Manager Roles and Performance of R&D Multidisciplinary Projects in Matrix Structures." *R&D Management,* 14 No. 2 (1984), 113–28.

Scarff, J.E. "International Management of Whales, Dolphins, and Porpoises: An Interdisciplinary Assessment.2." *Ecology Law Quarterly,* 6 No. 3 (1977), 571–638.

Schneider, Stephen H. "Climatology and Glaciology: An Interdisciplinary Opportunity – An Editorial." *Climatic Change,* 4 No. 4 (1982), 327–28.

*———. "Climate Change and the World Predicament: A Case Study for Interdisciplinary Research." *Climatic Change,* 1 (1977), 21–43.

———. "Quality Review Standards for Interdisciplinary Research." Paper presented at Symposium, "Can Research Institutions Accommodate Interdisciplinary Researchers?" 143rd annual meeting of the American Association for the Advancement of Science. Denver, Colo., 20–25 Feb. 1977. Taped transcript available from AAAS.

Schyttt, Valter. "Ymer-80: A Swedish Expedition to the Arctic Ocean." *Geographical Journal* (Great Britain), 149 No. 1 (1983), 22–28.

*Scribner, R.A., and R.A. Chalk, eds. *Adapting Science to Social Needs: Conference Proceedings.* Washington, D.C.: American Association for the Advancement of Science, 1977. Report No. 76-R-8. See especially C.W. Churchman, "Toward a Holistic Approach," pp. 11–24; D.E. Kash, "Observations on Interdisciplinary Studies and Government Roles," pp. 147–67; W.A. Hahn, "Observations on Interdisciplinarity: Its Need, Management, and Utilization," pp. 253–63.

Semple, J. "Smoke Control: An Interdisciplinary Concept." *Ashrae Journal: American Society of Heating, Refrigerating, and Air Conditioning EN,* 25 No. 5 (1983), 60.

Sharp, James M., and James L. Gumnick. "University-Industry Connections: The GURC Example." *SRA, Journal of the Society of Research Administrators,* 12 No. 2 (Fall 1980), 15–21.

————. "A Method for Peer Group Appraisal and Interpretation of Data Developed in Interdisciplinary Research Programs." *SRA, Journal of the Society of Research Administrators,* 13 No. 2 (1981), 51–66.

Simeonova, Kostadinka. "The Inter-disciplinary Movement and the Organization of Scientific Research Problems of the Science of Science, 1972–1973." Ossolineum, 1973. By The Polish Academy of Sciences Press.

*Simonton, Dean Keith. "Interdisciplinary Creativity over Historical Time: A Correlational Analysis of Generational Fluctuations." *Social Behavior and Personality,* 3 No. 2 (1975), 181–88.

Smythe, G.E. "Multidisciplinary Engineering in the Process Industries." *Radio and Electronic Engineer,* 51 No. 9 (1981), 416–17.

SRA, Journal of the Society of Research Administrators (Fall 1981). Special issue on management of interdisciplinary research.

Stankiewicz, R. "The Effects of Leadership on the Relationship between the Size of Research Groups and Their Performance." *R&D Management,* 9 (1979), 207–12.

Steck, R. "How Can Research on Research Contribute to a Better Management of University Research?" *R&D Management,* 6 (Feb. 1976), 81–86.

*————. "R&D Coordination in Industry and University." *Research Policy,* 3 No. 4 (1975), 360–71.

*————, and J. Sundermann. "The Effects of Group Size and Cooperation on the Success of Interdisciplinary Groups in R&D." *R&D Management,* 8 No. 2 (1978), 59–64.

Stoddard, Ellwyn R. "Multidisciplinary Research Funding: A 'Catch 22' Enigma." *American Sociologist,* 17 (Nov. 1982), 210–16.

*Stone, Anthony R. "The Interdisciplinary Research Team." *Journal of Applied Behavioral Science,* 5 No. 3 (1969), 351–65.

Technological Forecasting and Change, 2 (1979). Problem-focused research.

Thurman, E.M. "Multidisciplinary Research: An Experiment." *Environmental Science and Technology,* 17 No. 11 (1983), 511.

Toft, Graham, and R. Tomlinson Sparrow. "University Interdisciplinary Engineering Centers: New Directions — Persistent Organizational Problems." Paper presented at the Third International Conference on Interdisciplinary Research. Seattle, Wash., 1 Aug. 1984.

Tomczak, M., Jr. "Some Conclusions From the Port Hacking Estuary Project." In *Synthesis and Modelling of Intermittent Estuaries: A Case Study From Planning to Evaluation,* ed. W.R. Cuff and M. Tomczak. Berlin: Springer-Verlag, 1983, pp. 293–302.

*Törnebohm, Hakan, et al. "Researcher Roles and the Organization of Interdisciplinary Groups. R&D for Higher Education." Stockholm: Research and Development Unit, National Swedish Board of Universities and Colleges, 1980. ERIC ED 201 235.

United States Library of Congress. Legislative Reference Series. Interdisciplinary Research: An Exploration of Public Policy. NYPG734445477-B.

Valaskakis, K. "Rewards and Tribulations of Interdisciplinary Futures Studies." *Industrialization Forum,* 6 (1975), 41–46.

Vitzthum, E.F., and R.E. Gold. "Environmental Programs within the Institute of Agriculture and Natural Resources, University of Nebraska, Lincoln." *Environmental Professional,* 9 No. 3 (1987), 250–53.

Volker, E.J., and C. Schultz. "Microbial Conversion of D-Sorbitol to L-Sorbose: Interdisciplinary Experiment Illustrating an Industrial Process." *Journal of Chemical Education,* 55 No. 10 (1978), 673–74.

Walker, B.H., et al. "A Procedure for Multidisciplinary Ecosystem Research: With Reference to the South African Savannah Ecosystem Project." *Journal of Applied Ecology,* 15 (1978), 481–502.

Walsh, John. "New R&D Centers Will Test University Ties: Interdisciplinary Research Labs Are Campus Fixtures, But Industry, Government Involvement Gives a New Twist." *Science,* 11 Jan. 1985, p. 150.

Walsh, W.B., G.L. Smith, and M. London. "Developing an Interface between Engineering and the Social Sciences: An Interdisciplinary Approach to Solving Societal Problems." *American Psychologist,* 30 No. 11 (1975), 1067–71.

Walters, C. "Interdisciplinary Approach to Development of Watershed Simulation Models." *Journal of the Fisheries Research Board of Canada,* 32 (1975), 177–95.

Warrick, Richard A., and William E. Riebsami. "Societal Response to CO_2-Induced Climate Change: Opportunities for Research." *Climatic Change,* 3 No. 4 (1981), 387–446.

Weingert, Jerome M. "Transdisciplinary Science: Some Recent Experiences with Solar Energy Conversion Research." Paper presented at 143rd Annual Meeting of the American Association for the Advancement of Science. Denver, Colo., 20–25 Feb. 1977. Taped Transcript available from AAAS.

Wheeler, Lawrence, and Ewing Miller. "Multi-Disciplinary Approach to Planning." Paper presented at Council of Education Facilities Planners 47th Annual Conference. Oklahoma City, Okla., 6 Oct. 1970, pp. 1–3. ERIC ED 044 814.

*White, Irvin L. "An Interdisciplinary Approach to Applied Policy Analysis." *Technological Forecasting and Social Change,* 2 (Sept. 1979), 95–106.

Wilbanks, Tom. "Communications between Hard and Soft Sciences." *Oak Ridge National Laboratory Review,* Spring 1979, pp. 24–29.

*Williams, Anne S., et al. "Guidelines for Conducting Interdisciplinary Applied Research in a University Setting." *Review of Public Data Use,* 6 No. 2 (1978), 3–12.

Wilson, R. R. "My Fight against Team Research." *Daedalus,* Fall 1970, 1076–87.

Winnicki, T., and B. Glowiak. "Management of Large-Scale Interdisciplinary Environmental Programs." *R&D Management,* 8 No. NS 1 (1978), 127–32.

*Wohl, R. Richard. "Some Observations on the Social Organization of Interdisciplinary Social Science Research." *Social Forces,* 33 (1955), 374–83.

*Wolfle, Dael L. "Interdisciplinary Research as a Form of Research." *SRA, Journal of the Society of Research Administrators,* 13 (Fall 1981), 5–7.

Woodrow, Raymond J. "Interdisciplinary Research." *Management for Research in U.S. Universities.* Washington, D.C.: National Association of College and University Business Officers, 1978. Pp. 33–41.

Wymore, A.W. *Systems Engineering Methodology for Interdisciplinary Teams* New York, 1976.

Note: For reports on the findings of the National Science Foundation's Research Management Improvement Program:

- Original copies filed with the National Technical Information Service of the U.S. Department of Commerce.
- A file of these and other reports on IDR management is also available in the Center for Technology and Administration at American University in Washington, D.C.

Interdisciplinary Care and Services

Accardi, R.F., and R.L. Munch. "Pastoral Communication: A Method of Evaluation and Reporting at Interdisciplinary Staffings." *Archives of Physical Medicine and Rehabilitation,* 64 No. 10 (1983), 508.

*Ackerman, L., et al. "Role Clarification: A Procedure for Enhancing Interdisciplinary Collaboration on the Rehabilitation Team." *Archives of Physical Medicine and Rehabilitation,* 64 No. 10 (1983), 514.

*Allen, K.E., V.A. Holm, and R. Schiefelbusch, eds. *Early Intervention: A Team Approach.* Baltimore: University Park Press, 1978. See especially V.A. Holm and R. McCartin, "Interdisciplinary Child Development Team: Team Issues and Training in Interdisciplinariness," pp. 99-122.

Amsterdam, J.T., D.K. Wagner, and L.F. Rose. "Interdisciplinary Training: Hospital DentalGeneral Practice/Emergency Medicine." *Annals of Emergency Medicine,* 9 No. 6 (1980), 310-13.

Andrus, P.L., C.E. Fasser, and L. Yeoman. "Interdisciplinary Learning in Pharmacology: Analysis of MD and PA Student Performance." *Journal of Medical Education,* 56 No. 9 (1981), 757-61.

*Appleyard, J., and J.G. Maden. "Multidisciplinary Teams." *British Medical Journal,* 2 (1979), 1305-07.

Armer, B., and B.J. Thomas. "Attitudes toward Interdisciplinary Collaboration in Pupil Personnel Services Teams." *Journal of School Psychology,* 16 No. 2 (1978), 167-76.

Aronoff, G.M., and W.O. Evans. "The Prediction of Treatment Outcome at a Multidisciplinary Pain Center." *Pain,* 14 No. 1 (1982), 67-73. See also (with R.L. Enders) "A Review of Follow-up Studies of Multidisciplinary Pain Units." *Pain,* 16 No. 1 (1983), 1-11.

*Bailey, D.B., et al. "Measuring Individual Participation on the Interdisciplinary Team." *American Journal of Mental Deficiency,* 88 No. 3 (1983), 247-54.

Baker, S.R., and N.A. Swanson. "Management of Nasal Cutaneous Malignant Neoplasms: An Interdisciplinary Approach." *Archives of Otolaryngology,* 109 No. 7 (1983), 473-79.

Bardon, Jack I. "Viewpoints of Multidisciplinary Teams in Schools." *School Psychology Review,* 12 No. 2 (1983), 186-89.

Barnett, S.E, W.E. Eden, and J. McGill. "The Reciprocal Benefits of Nutrition: Student Participation in an Interdisciplinary Migrant Health Program." *Journal of Nutrition Education,* 12 No. 3 (1980), 153-56.

Baust, J.G. "Interdisciplinary Nature of Cryobiology." *Cryo-Letters,* 4 No. 5 (1983), 269-71.

Bax, D.D., and F. Kalil. "An Interdisciplinary Approach to Group Therapy." *Journal of Visual Impairment and Blindness.* 75 No. 4 (1981), 169–72.

Beale, P.P., and M.I. Gulley. "Discharge Planning Process: An Interdisciplinary Approach." *Military Medicine,* 146 No. 10 (1981), 713–16.

*Beardsley, Robert, et al. "The Interdisciplinary Approach." *American Pharmacy,* 21 No. 11 (1981), 54–55.

Becker, A., E. Bimstein, and A. Shteyer. "Interdisciplinary Treatment of Multiple Unerupted Supernumerary Teeth: Report of a Case." *American Journal of Orthodontics,* 81 No. 5 (1982), 417–22.

Bellanti, J.A. "Bela Schick Memorial Lecture: Allergy and Clinical Immunology – Interdisciplinary Concept." *Annals of Allergy,* 41 No. 3 (1978), 129–35.

Bennett, F.C. "The Pediatrician and the Interdisciplinary Process." *Exceptional Children,* 48 No. 4 (1982), 306–14.

*Benor, D.E. "Interdisciplinary Integration in Medical Education: Theory and Method." *Medical Education,* 16 No. 6 (1982), 355–61.

Berard, C.W., et al. "A Multidisciplinary Approach to Non-Hodgkins Lymphomas." *Annals of Internal Medicine,* 94 No. 2 (1981), 218–35.

Bergmann, Garrett E., et al. "An Adjunct Humanities Faculty in Medical School." *Journal of Medical Education,* 57 No. 5 (1982), 413–15.

*Bernstein, Barton E. See articles on the lawyer and other professionals as an interdisciplinary team in *Family Coordinator,* 26 No. 4 (1977), 415–20, 421–27; *Journal of Marriage and Family Counseling,* 3 No. 3 (1977), 29–40; *Death Education,* 1 No. 3 (1977), 277–91, 3 No. 1 (1979), 11–19, and 4 No. 2 (1980), 179–88; *Journal of Marital and Family Therapy,* 5 No. 4 (1979), 93–100; *Social Casework – Journal of Contemporary Social Work,* 61 No. 7 (1980), 416–22; *Health and Social Work,* 5 No. 3 (1980), 68–72; (with B.G. Haberman) *Child Welfare,* 60 No. 4 (1981), 211–19.

Beynon, G.P.J., and J. Croker. "Multidisciplinary Education in Geriatric Medicine: Continuing Experience at the Middlesex Hospital." *Age and Aging,* 12 No. 1 (1983), 26–29.

"Beyond the Ordinary: The Preparation of Professionals to Educate Severely and Profoundly Handicapped Persons – toward the Development of Standards and Criteria." From the American Association for the Education of the Severely/Profoundly Handicapped, 1977. ERIC ED 182 373.

Bisiachi, P., C. Semenza, and F. Denes. "First European Workshop on Cognitive Neuropsychology: An Interdisciplinary Approach – 23–28 January 1983 – Bressanone, Italy." *Neuropsychologica,* 21 No. 5 (1983), 573–74.

Blanchard, E.B., et al. "Interdisciplinary Agreement in the Diagnosis of Headache Types." *Journal of Behavioral Assessment,* 3 No. 1 (1981), 5–9.

Blattner, W.A. "Etiology and Prevention of Acquired Immunodeficiency Syndrome: The Path of Interdisciplinary Research." *Journal of Chronic Diseases,* 39 No. 12 (1986), 1125–44.

Blight, E.M., and J.R. Davis. "Treatment of Male Sexual Dysfunction: Interdisciplinary Undertaking in a Military Hospital." *Military Medicine,* 143 No. 5 (1978), 322–24.

Bloom, B., and H. Parad. "Interdisciplinary Training and Interdisciplinary Functioning." *American Journal of Orthopsychiatry,* 46 (1976), 669–76.

*Bottom, P.A., et al. "Curriculum Development for Interdisciplinary Health Team Education." *Alabama Journal of Medical Sciences,* 15 No. 1 (1978), 98–100.

———. "Interdisciplinary Health Care: Adjunct to Family Medicine." *Alabama Journal of Medical Sciences,* 15 No. 2 (1978), 134–36.

*Braithwaite, Ronald L., and Euolinda R. Logan. "Hospital Based Interdisciplinary Education for Health Science Majors." In *Non-Traditional and Interdisciplinary Programs,* comp. James W. Fonseca. Fairfax, Va.: Division of Continuing Education, George Mason

University, 1984. Selected papers from the Second Annual National Conference on Non-Traditional and Interdisciplinary Programs. Arlington, Va., 27–29 June 1984.

Brookehughes, C. "Interdisciplinary Approach to Deaf Children and Their Families." *Teacher of the Deaf,* 2 No. 3 (1978), 88–91.

Buckalew, L.W., and Sherman Ross. "Behavioral Teratology: An Interdisciplinary Frontier." *Journal of Alcohol and Drug Education,* 27 No. 3 (1982), 34–40.

Burridge, P., and R. Logan. "A Multidisciplinary Coronary Rehabilitation Program: Three Years Initial Experience." *New Zealand Medical Journal,* 93 No. 686 (1981), 411–13.

Burtenica, N. "A Multidisciplinary Training Team in the Public School." *Journal of School Psychology,* 8 (1970), 220–25.

Campbell, L.S., and D.C. Whitenack. "An Interdisciplinary Approach for Consultation on Multiproblem Patients." *North Carolina Medical Journal,* 44 No. 2 (1983), 81–87.

Campion, E.W., A. Jette, and B. Berkman. "An Interdisciplinary Geriatric Consultation Service: A Controlled Trial." *Journal of the American Geriatrics Society,* 31 No. 12 (1983), 792–96.

*Case, R. Maynard. "'Cell Calcium': A New International, Interdisciplinary Journal." *Cell Calcium,* 1 No. 1 (1980), 1–5.

Casotto, A., and P. Buoncristiani. "Medulloblastoma in Children: Multidisciplinary Treatment." *Child's Brain,* 9 No. 3–4 (1982), 299–308.

Cassidy, Robert C., David G. Swee, and Marian Stuart. "Teaching Biopsychoethical Medicine in a Family Practice Clerkship." *Journal of Medical Education,* 58 No. 10 (1983), 778–83.

*Chamberlain, H.R. "The Interdisciplinary Team: Contributions by Allied Medical and Non-Medical Disciplines." In *Child Development and Developmental Disabilities,* ed. S Gabel and M. Erickson. Boston: Little, Brown, 1980.

Change, C.H., et al. "Comparison of Postoperative Radiotherapy and Combined Postoperative Radiotherapy and Chemotherapy in the Multidisciplinary Management of Malignant Gliomas: A Joint Radiation Therapy Oncology Group and Eastern Cooperative Oncology Group Study." *Cancer,* 52 No. 6 (1983), 997–1007.

Chapuis, P., and M.T. Pheils. "Report of a Multidisciplinary Research Program for Colorectal Cancer." *Anticancer Research,* 1 No. 1 (1981), 11–13.

Cheung, A., et al. "Clinical Pharmacist as an Interdisciplinary Primary Care Provider." *Military Medicine,* 144 No. 5 (1979), 297–301.

Cohen, Cynthia B. "Interdisciplinary Consultation on the Care of the Critically Ill and Dying: The Role of One Hospital Ethics Committee." *Critical Care Medicine,* 10 No. 11 (1982), 776–84.

Cohen, F.G., R.D. Walker and S. Stanley. "The Role of Anthropology in Interdisciplinary Research on Indian Alcoholism and Treatment Outcome." *Journal of Studies on Alcohol,* 42 No. 9 (1981), 836–45.

Coleman, J.V., and D.L. Patrick. "Integrating Mental Health Services into Primary Medical Care." *Medical Care,* 14 (1976), 654–61.

Collins, M., G.R. Hodas, and R. Liebman. "Interdisciplinary Model for the In-Patient Treatment of Adolescents with Anorexia Nervosa." *Journal of Adolescent Health Care,* 4 No. 1 (1983), 3–8.

*Connelly, Thomas R. "Interdisciplinary References III, A Reference Document for Those Contemplating Interdisciplinary Educational Programs in the Health Sciences." Appendix 6 in the Proceedings of the Workshop on Interdisciplinary Education: Kentucky January Prototype. Lexington, Ky., 17 Apr. 1975. Lexington College of Allied Health Professions. ERIC ED 129 134.

Cooley, D.A. "Concepts of Health and Disease in Medicine: Interdisciplinary Perspectives." *Cardiovascular Diseases,* 7 No. 2 (1980), 123–26.

*Cowie, G.B.A. "The Multidisciplinary Team." *New Zealand Medical Journal,* 96 No. 731 (1983), 359–60.

Cox, G.B., R.J. Hanley and B.V. Riefler. "An Integrated Data Base for an Interdisciplinary Geriatric Clinic." *Journal of Psychiatric Treatment and Evaluation,* 4 No. 2 (1982), 149–53.

Critchley, Deane L., and Irving N. Berlin. "Day Treatment of Young Psychotic Children and Their Parents: Interdisciplinary Issues and Problems." *Child Psychiatry and Human Development,* 9 No. 4 (1979), 227–37.

Cromes, G.F. "Implementation of Interdisciplinary Cancer Rehabilitation." *Rehabilitation Counseling Bulletin,* 21 No. 3 (1978), 230–37.

Crooks, V., P. Lee, and T.T. Yoshikawa. "Geriatric Medicine: A Multidisciplinary Training and Education Model in an Acute Care Medical Center." *Journal of the American Geriatrics Society,* 30 No. 12 (1982), 774–80.

Dauber, L.G., et al. "Hospice in Hospital: Interdisciplinary Group for Delivery of Care to Terminally Ill in Acute-Care (Community) Hospital, *New York State Journal of Medicine,* 80 No. 11 (1980), 1721–23.

David, J.R., and E.M. Blight. "Interdisciplinary Treatment of Male Sexual Dysfunction in a Military Health-Care Setting." *Journal of Sex and Marital Therapy,* 4 No. 1 (1978), 29–34.

*Day, Donald W. "Perspectives on Care: The Interdisciplinary Team Approach." *Otolaryngologic Clinics of North America,* 14 No. 4 (1981), 769–75.

DeBlassie, Richard R., and Juan N. Franco. "An Interdisciplinary Graduate Program for Mexican-American Researchers-Evaluators." *American Journal of Orthopsychiatry,* 51 No. 4 (1981), 730–33.

Delany, G.M., and Goldblatt, L.I. "Fused Teeth: A Multidisciplinary Approach to Treatment." *Journal of the American Dental Association,* 103 No. 5 (1981), 732–34.

*DeWachter, Maurice. "Interdisciplinary Bioethics: But Where Do We Start? A Reflection on Epochè as Method." *Journal of Medicine and Philosophy,* 7 No. 3 (1982), 275–87.

*DeWachter, M. "Interdisciplinary Team Work." *Journal of Medical Ethics,* 2 (1976), 52–57.

Dimitrov, N.V., S.M. McMahon, and D.T. Carr. "Multidisciplinary Approach to Management of Patients with Mesothelioma." *Cancer Research,* 43 No. 8 (1983), 3974–76.

*Dobson, J.R.E., et al. "The Multidisciplinary Team," *New Zealand Medical Journal,* 95 No. 707 (1982), 319.

Donovan, W.H., et al. "A Multidisciplinary Approach to Chronic Low Back Pain in Western Australia." *Spine,* 6 No. 6 (1981), 591–97.

*Ducanis, Alex J., and Anne K. Golin. *The Interdisciplinary Health Care Team: A Handbook.* Germantown, Md.: Aspen Systems Corp., 1979.

Duhl, L.J. "Interdisciplinary Teaching in Health." *Interdisciplinary Science Reviews,* 4 No. 2 (1979), 155–57.

[Reports from] Dunedin Multidisciplinary Child Development Study. In *Australian Paediatric Journal,* 18 No. 1 (1982), 35–36, and 18 No. 4 (1982), 247–49; 19 No. 4 (1983), 237–40; *New Zealand Medical Journal,* 93 No. 680 (1981), 180–82; 93 No. 684 (1981), 344–47; 95 No. 709 (1982), 371–73; 95 No. 713 (1982), 533–536; 95 No. 716 (1982), 655–57; 95 No. 717 (1982), 693–96; and 96 No. 729 (1983), 252–55; *Journal of Human Movement Studies,* 8 No. 4 (1982), 187–94; *British Journal of Disorders of Communication,* 17 No. 3 (1982), 133–39; *British Journal of Psychiatry,* 143 (November 1983), 473–79; *Developmental Medicine and Child Neurology,* 25 No. 6 (1983), 783–93; *Journal of Pediatric Psychology,* 8 No. 2 (1983), 181–90.

Eagen, Carol S., et al. "The Transdisciplinary Training, Assessment, and Consultation Model. Preschool Program: A Regional Demonstration Program for Preschool Handicapped Children." Putnam and Northern Westchester Counties Board of Cooperative Education (Dec. 1980). ERIC ED 217 597.

Eckert, G.M., F. Gutmann, and M. Kabos. "Some Physical Methods in an Interdisciplinary Approach to Drug Interactions." *Applied Physics Communications,* 1 No. 1 (1981), 105–20.

Edinberg, M.A., S.E. Dodson, and T.L. Veach. "Preliminary Study of Student Learning in Interdisciplinary Health Teams." *Journal of Medical Education,* 53 No. 8 (1978), 667–71.

Edinberg, M.A., M.K. Tsuda, and E.S. Gallagher. "Training Interdisciplinary Student Health Teams in a Gerontological Setting." *Educational Gerontology,* 3 No. 3 (1978) 203–13.

Ellenor, G.L., S. Zimmerman, and J. Kriz. "Interdisciplinary Approach to Dental Care of Mentally Disabled." *Journal of the American Dental Association,* 97 No. 3 (1978), 491–95.

Elmer, E., et al. "Child Abuse Training: Community Based Interdisciplinary Program." *Community Mental Health Journal,* 14 No. 3 (1978), 179–89.

*Engel, George L. "The Clinical Application of the Biopsychosocial Model." *American Journal of Psychiatry,* 137 No. 5 (1980), 535–44. See also "A Unified Concept of Health and Disease." *Perspectives in Biology and Medicine,* 3 (1960), 459–85.

Escalante, P., et al. "Reliability Assessment of Two Clinical Psychological Methods: Individual versus Interdisciplinary Team." *Archivos de Investigacion Medica* (Mexico), 10 No. 3 (1979), 46–47.

Evers, Cate. "Low Vision Services: An Interdisciplinary Approach to Quality." *Journal of Visual Impairment and Blindness,* 76 No. 6 (1982), 224–28.

Fabrega, Horacio. *Disease and Social Behavior: An Interdisciplinary Perspective.* Cambridge, Mass.: MIT Press, 1974.

Farrell, M.K., et al. "Prepubertal Gonorrhea: A Multidisciplinary Approach." *Pediatrics,* 67 No. 1 (1981), 151–53.

Feiger, S.M., and M.H. Schmitt. "Collegiality in Interdisciplinary Health Teams: Its Measurement and Its Effects." *Social Science and Medicine: Medical Psychology and Sociology,* 13 No. 2A (1979), 217–29.

Fenwick, A.M. "Interdisciplinary Tool for Assessing Patients' Readiness for Discharge in the Rehabilitation Setting." *Journal of Advanced Nursing,* 4 No. 1 (1979), 9–21.

Ferguson, D.G., et al. "Effects of Data Based Interdisciplinary Medication Reviews on the Prevalence and Pattern of Neuroleptic Drug Use with Institutionalized Mentally Retarded Persons." *Education and Training for the Mentally Retarded,* 17 No. 2 (1982), 103–08.

Ferguson, L.R. "Family Life Cycle: Orientation for Interdisciplinary Training." *Professional Psychology,* 6 (1979), 863–67.

Fitzsimons, R.M. "Fostering Productive Interdisciplinary Staff Conferences." *Academic Therapy,* 12 (1977), 281–87.

Fleming, D.C., and E.R. Fleming. "Consultation with Multidisciplinary Teams: A Program of Development and Improvement of Team Functioning." *Journal of School Psychology,* 21 No. 4 (1983), 367–76.

Forbes, Ian J., et al. "Multidisciplinary Approach to Phototherapy of Human Cancers." *Progress in Clinical and Biological Research,* 170 (1984), 693–708.

*Fordyce, W.E. "Interdisciplinary Process: Implications for Rehabilitation Psychology." *Rehabilitation Psychology,* 27 No. 1 (1982), 5–11.

*———. "On Interdisciplinary Peers." *Archives of Physical Medicine and Rehabilitation,* 62 No. 2 (1981), 51–53.

Forness, S.R., et al. "Identifying Children with School Learning and Behavior Problems Served by Interdisciplinary Clinics and Hospitals." *Child Psychiatry and Human Development,* 11 No. 2 (1980), 67–78.

Frei, E. "Multidisciplinary Treatment for Cancer: New Opportunities." *International Journal of Radiation Oncology, Biology, Physics,* 8 No. 5 (1982), 951–52.

Frenkiel, S., et al. "Nasal Polyposis: A Multidisciplinary Study." *Journal of Otolaryngology,* 11 No. 4 (1982), 275–78.

Fry, Lincoln, and Jon P. Miller. "The Impact of Interdisciplinary Teams on Organizational Relationships." *Sociological Quarterly,* 15 No. 3 (1974), 417–31.

Gallagher, James J. "The Interdisciplinary Sharing of Knowledge." *Journal of Special Education,* 13 No. 1 (1979), 41–43.

Gardner, J.M., and A. Veno. "Interdisciplinary Multilevel, University-Based Training Program in Community Psychology." *American Journal of Community Psychology,* 6 (1979), 605–20.

Geis, W.P., et al. "An Integrated University Emergency Medicine-Trauma Program." *Journal of Trauma,* 22 No. 4 (1982), 295–302.

Gerard, A., et al. "Prospective and Controlled Studies on Multidisciplinary Treatment in Gastro-Intestinal Cancer." *Recent Results in Cancer Research,* 79 (1981), 19–27.

Gerosa, M.A., et al. "Multidisciplinary Treatment of Medulloblastoma: A Five-Year Experience with the SIOP Trial." *Child's Brain,* 8 No. 2 (1981), 107–18.

Gilpin, D.C., and J.M. Schachtman. "Interdisciplinary Collaborative Process in Therapy with Families." *Journal of Psychiatric Treatment and Evaluation,* 3 No. 1 (1981), 67–71.

Gold, Lois. "The Psychological Context of the Interdisciplinary Co-Mediation Team Model in Marital Dissolution." *Conciliation Courts Review,* 20 No. 2 (1982), 45–53.

Goldberg, R.J., et al. "Defining Discipline Roles in Consultation Psychiatry: The Multidisciplinary Team Approach to Psychosocial Oncology." *General Hospital Psychiatry,* 6 No. 1 (1984), 17–23.

Graham, Peter. "The Place of the Humanities in Medical Education." *Liberal Education,* 66 No. 4 (1980), 388–93.

Graninger, G. and P.G. Svensson. "Exploration of an Interdisciplinary Research Theme: The Case of Public Health and Health Care in the Society." *Scandinavian Journal of Social Medicine Supplement,* 18 (1980), 3–24.

*Greden, John F., et al. "Interdisciplinary Differences on a General Hospital Psychiatry Unit." *General Hospital Psychiatry,* 1 No. 1 (1979), 91–97.

Grenvik, A., et al. "Critical Care Medicine: Certification as a Multidisciplinary Subspecialty." *Critical Care Medicine,* 9 No. 2 (1981), 117–25.

Grossarth-Maticek, R., et al. "Psychosomatic Factors in the Process of Cancerogenesis: Theoretical Models and Empirical Results." *Psychotherapy and Psychosomatics,* 38 Nos. 1–4 (September 1982), 284–302.

Guindi, G.M. "Acute Orbital Cellulitis: A Multidisciplinary Emergency." *British Journal of Oral Surgery,* 21 No. 3 (1983), 201–07.

Hagerstam, G., et al. "Placebo in Clinical Drug Trials: A Multidisciplinary Review." *Methods and Findings in Experimental and Clinical Pharmacology,* 4 No. 4 (1982), 261–78.

Haizlip, Thomas M., Billie R. Corder, and Ralph Dixon. "Staff Evaluation and Classification, Issues Created by Multi-Level, Interdisciplinary Psychotherapy Programs." *Psychiatric Forum,* 8 No. 1 (1978–79), 42–46.

Hallett, E.C., and I. Pilowsky. "The Response to Treatment in a Multi-Disciplinary Pain Clinic." *Pain,* 12 No. 4 (1982), 365–74.

Hamad, B. "Interdisciplinary Field Training Research and Rural-Development Programme." *Medical Education,* 16 No. 2 (1982), 105–107.

Hart, L.L., et al. "The Clinical Pharmacist on an Interdisciplinary Primary Health-Care Team." *Drug Intelligence and Clinical Pharmacy,* 13 No. 7–8 (1979), 414–19.

Hart, V. "The Use of Many Disciplines with the Severely and Profoundly Handicapped." In *Educational Programming for the Severely and Profoundly Handicapped,* ed. E. Sontag, J. Smith, and N. Certo. Reston, Va.: Division on Mental Retardation of the Council for Exceptional Children, 1977.

Hellmuth, Jerome, ed. *Exceptional Infant.* Vol. 1. Seattle, Wash.: Bernie Straub and Jerome Hellmuth Co., 1967. Special Child Publications of the Seattle Seguin School. See especially Martin A. Mendelson, "An Interdisciplinary Approach to the Study of the Exceptional Infant: A Large-Scale Project."

Hill, Gayle W. "Interdisciplinary Field Training for Social Change: A Case Study for Psychology and Law." *American Journal of Community Psychology,* 7 No. 2 (1979), 223–30.

Hinsenkamp, M.G., and Burny, F. "Electromagnetic Stimulation of Bone-Growth and Repair: An Interdisciplinary Study—Preface." *Acta Orthopaedica Scandinavica,* 53 No. 196 (1982), 7–8.

Hoch, Z., et al. "An Interdisciplinary Approach to the Study of Sexual Dysfunction in Couples. Preliminary Findings." In *Medical Sexology: The Third International Conference,* ed. R. Forleo and W. Pasini. Rome, Italy, 1978. Littleton, Mass.: PSG Pub., 1980, pp. 553–58.

Hoge, A.F., et al. "Multidisciplinary Approach to Breast-Cancer Control." *Southern Medical Journal,* 74 No. 2 (1981), 136–43.

Hogenson, D. "A Multidisciplinary Approach to the Inschool Management of Acutely Anxious and Depressed Students in a Large Urban Senior High School Setting." *Pupil Personnel Services Journal,* 3 (1973), 29–31.

Holmstedt, B., S.H. Wassen, and R.E. Schultes. "Jaborandi: An Interdisciplinary Appraisal." *Journal of Ethnopharmacology,* 1 No. 1 (1979), 3–22.

Horwitz, John J. *Team Practice and the Specialist: An Introduction to Interdisciplinary Teamwork.* Springfield: Ill.: Charles C. Thomas, 1970.

Hunter, Kathryn and Diana Axelsen. "The Morehouse Human Values in Medicine Program, 1978–1980: Reinforcing a Commitment to Primary Care." *Journal of Medical Education,* 57 No. 2 (1982), 121–23.

Hutchinson, D.A. *A Model for Transdisciplinary Staff Development: A Nationally Organized Collaborative Project to Provide Comprehensive Services to Atypical Infants and Their Families.* New York: United Cerebral Palsy Associates, 1974. Technical Report No. 8.

Hutchinson, J.C., D.D. Caldarelli, and H.J. Gould. "Classification and Multidisciplinary Management of Microtia." *Otolaryngologic Clinics of North America,* 14 No. 4 (1981), 885–93.

Iizuka, T. "Preliminary Report on Multidisciplinary Treatment for Esophageal Carcinoma." *Japanese Journal of Clinical Oncology,* 10 No. 2 (1980), 215–20. See also "Multidisciplinary Treatment for Esophageal Carcinoma." *Japanese Journal of Clinical Oncology,* 13 No. 2 (1983), 417–23.

Infante, M., K. Speranza, and P. Gillespie. "An Interdisciplinary Approach to the Education of Health Professional Students." *Journal of Allied Health,* 5 (Fall 1976), 13–22.

Interdisciplinary Glossary on Child Abuse and Neglect: Legal, Medical, Social Work Teams. United States Department of Health and Human Services. Publication (OHDS) 80-30137 (April 1980). ERIC ED 212 105.

Interdisciplinary Topics in Gerontology. A series published by Karger.

Iyengar, G.V., and L.E. Feinendegen. "Human Health and Trace Element Research: A Multidisciplinary Task in Its Perspective." *Transactions of the American Nuclear Society,* 41 (1982), 203–04.

Jacobs, J.A., et al. "A Multidisciplinary Approach to the Evaluation and Management of Male Sexual Dysfunction." *Journal of Urology,* 129 No. 1 (1983), 35–38.

James, H.E., and W.L. Nyhan. "Spinal Dysraphism: Interdisciplinary Diagnostic Approach." *Western Journal of Medicine,* 129 No. 6 (1978), 475–79.

Jensen, T.G., and S.J. Dudrick. "Implementation of a Multidisciplinary Nutritional Assessment Program." *Journal of the American Dietetic Association,* 79 No. 3 (1981), 258–66.

Johnston, R.B., and P.R. Magrab, eds. "Introduction to Developmental Disorders and the

Interdisciplinary Process." In *Developmental Disorders: Assessment, Treatment, and Education,* ed. R.B. Johnston and P.R. Magrab. Baltimore: University Park Press, 1976.

Jolly, P.A., and A.N. Galanos. "Neurotic Excoriators: Advantages of an Interdisciplinary Treatment Approach." *Alabama Journal of Medical Sciences,* 20 No. 2 (1983), 180–81.

Jose, R.T., J. Cummings, and L. MacAdams. "The New Model Low Vision Clinic Service: An Interdisciplinary Vision Rehabilitation Program." *New Outlook for the Blind,* 68 (1974), 97–103.

Kaiser, S.M., and R.W. Woodman. "Multidisciplinary Teams and Group Decision-Making Techniques: Possible Solutions to Decision-Making Problems." *School Psychology Review,* 14 No. 4 (1985), 457–70.

Kalick, S. Michael. "Toward an Interdisciplinary Psychology of Appearances." *Psychiatry,* 41 No. 3 (1978), 243–53.

Kaltreider, Nancy B., et al. "The Integration of Psychosocial Care in a General Hospital: Development of an Interdisciplinary Consultation Program." *International Journal of Psychiatry in Medicine,* 5 No. 2 (1974), 125–34.

Kaplan, R. "Interdisciplinary Course for Optometry Students Specializing in Vision Training." *American Journal of Optometry and Physiological Optics,* 55 No. 7 (1978), 466–68.

Kaplan, R.M. "Interdisciplinary Modified Motor Evaluation." *Academic Therapy,* 14 No. 1 (1978), 67–72.

Kaplow, M., et al. The Dysvascular Amputee: Multidisciplinary Management." *Canadian Journal of Surgery,* 26 No. 4 (1983), 368–69.

Karki, Myron, and Christine Mayer. "Assessing Reuse of Disposables: An Interdisciplinary Challenge for the 1980's." *Medical Instrumentation,* 15 No. 3 (1981), 153–55.

Karlen, J.R., G.B. Williams, and J.L. Summers. "The Multidisciplinary Team Approach to Exenteration of the Pelvis." *Surgery, Gynecology and Obstetrics,* 156 No. 6 (1983), 789–94.

Kay, L. "Electronic Aids for Blind Persons: An Interdisciplinary Subject." *IEEE Proceedings A.,* 131 No. 7 (1984), 559–76.

Kessler, D.M., and R.J. Murphy. "Interdisciplinary Management Group Design." *Hospital and Health Services Administration,* 27 No. 2 (1982), 33–42.

Koepp-Baker, H. "Cleft Palate: Multidisciplinary Management." In *Cleft Palate: Criteria for Physical Management: Conference Report.* Iowa City: Iowa University, 1963.

*———. "The Craniofacial Team." In *Communicative Disorders Related to Cleft Lip and Palate,* ed. Kenneth R. Bzoch. Boston: Little, Brown, 1979.

———. "The Multidisciplinary Approach to the Treatment of the Child with Cleft Palate." *Journal of International College of Surgeons,* 24 No. 3 (1955).

Kramer, S. "Reflections on Multidisciplinary Management of Cancer: Presidential Address, 1981." *Cancer,* 49 No. 6 (1982), 1276–77.

Kroeger, A. "Workshop. Primary Health Care in the Developing World: Aspects of Community Participation, Interdisciplinary Approach, and Integration into the Health Services Pyramid." *Arbeitsmedizin Socialmedizin Praventivmedizin,* 18 No. 9 (1983), 216–17.

Labianca, D.A. "The Chimney Sweepers Cancer: An Interdisciplinary View of Chemical Carcinogenesis." *Journal of Chemical Education,* 59 No. 10 (1982), 843–46.

Langdon, E.J., and R. MacLennan. "Western Biomedical and Sibunody Diagnosis: An Interdisciplinary Comparison." *Social Science and Medicine,* 13B (1979), 211–20.

Larsen, S., and J. Wilson. "Interdisciplinary Conference." *Division for Children with Learning Disabilities Newsletter,* 1 (1976), 22–24.

*Layton, Richard H. and Schubert, Mark M. "Integrated Residency Training in Family Medicine and General Practice Dentistry." *Journal of Practice,* 7 No. 2 (1978), 333–36.

LeClerc, G. "Multidisciplinary Approaches to the Alpha Adrenergic Receptor Using Clonidine-like Compounds." *Periodicum Biologorum,* 85 No. 2 (1983), 83–90.

Lee, S. "Interdisciplinary Teaming in Primary Care: A Process of Evolution and Resolution." *Social Work in Health Care,* 3 (1980), 237–44.

Levi, Lennart. *Society, Stress, and Disease. I. The Psychological Environment and Psychosomatic Diseases: Proceedings of an International Interdisciplinary Symposium Held in Stockholm. April 1970.* New York: Oxford Univ. Press, 1971.

Levine, D.M., and L.W. Green. "Cardiovascular Risk Reduction: An Interdisciplinary Approach to Research Training." *International Journal of Health Education,* 24 No. 1 (1981), 20–25.

Levine, David. "The Dangers of Social Action." In *Behavior Analysis and Systems Analysis: An Integrative Approach to Mental Health Programs,* ed. D. Harshbarger and R.F. Maley. Kalamazoo, Mich.: Behaviordelia, 1974.

Levine, E.M. "The Role of Cultural-Values in the Etiology of Psychopathologies: An Inter-Disciplinary Approach." *International Journal of Sociology of the Family,* 12 No. 2 (1982), 189–200.

Levine, M.D., et al. "The Longitudinal Study of Findings in Childhood: Analysis of an Interdisciplinary Process." *American Journal of Diseases of Children,* 136 No. 4 (1982), 303–09.

*Lincoln, J.A., and M.N. Werblun. "Interdisciplinary Family Practice Rounds." *Journal of Family Practice,* 6 No. 4 (1978), 899–91.

Locke, D.C., C.E. Bazemore, and E.M. Clarke. "Interdisciplinary PPS Training Team." *Counselor Education and Supervision,* 18 No. 1 (1978), 65–69.

*Logan, R.L., and M. McKendry. "The Multidisciplinary Team: A Different Approach to Patient-Management." *New Zealand Medical Journal,* 95 No. 722 (1982), 883–84.

Lubin, Gerald I., James F. Magary, and Marie K. Poulsen. *Proceedings, Fourth Interdisciplinary Seminar: Piagetian Theory and Its Implications for the Helping Professions. February 15, 1974. University of Southern California.* Los Angeles, Calif.: University of Southern California, 1975.

Ludwig, S. "A Multidisciplinary Approach to Child Abuse." *Nursing Clinics of North America,* 16 No. 1 (1981), 161–65.

Lutz, R.W., M. Silbret, and N. Olshan. "Treatment Outcome and Compliance with Therapeutic Regimens: Long-Term Follow-Up of a Multidisciplinary Pain Program." *Pain,* 17 No. 3 (1983), 301–08.

Lynch, E., et al. "Interdisciplinary Services Provided to Handicapped Children by University Affiliated Facilities." *Education and Training of the Mentally Retarded,* 17 No. 1 (1982), 61–64.

Lyon, Steve, and Grace Lyon. "Team Functioning and Staff Development: A Role Release Approach to Providing Integrated Services for Severely Handicapped Students." *Journal of the Association for the Severely Handicapped,* 5 No. 3 (1980), 250–63.

McBroom, E. "Interdisciplinary Learning in Rehabilitation Hospital." *Social Work in Health Care,* 3 No. 4 (1978), 385–94.

McCormick, Linda, and Ronald Goldman. "The Transdisciplinary Model: Implications for Service Delivery and Personnel Preparation for the Severely and Profoundly Handicapped." *AAESPH Review* [See *Journal of the Association for Persons with Severe Handicaps (JASH)*], 4 No. 2 (1979), 152–61.

McDougall, G.M., and D.E. Taylor. "Interdisciplinary Team in General Hospital." *Canada's Mental Health,* 26 No. 2 (1978), 12–15.

*McKendry, M., and R.L. Logan. "The Multidisciplinary Team." *New Zealand Medical Journal,* 96 No. 731 (1983), 359.

Magraw, Richard M. "Interdisciplinary Teamwork for Medical Care and Health Services: Components and Organization." *Annals of Internal Medicine,* 69 No. 4 (1968), 821–35.

Mann, R.W. "Biomedical Engineering: A Cornucopia of Challenging Engineering Tasks—

All of Direct Human Significance." *IEEE Engineering, Medicine, and Biology Magazine,* 4 No. 3 (1985), 43–45.

Manni, J.L., and J.P. Kender. "Lehigh University Diagnostic Interdisciplinary Classroom." *Journal of Learning Disabilities,* 13 No. 7 (1980), 403–06.

Marsh, J.L. "Interdisciplinary Care for Craniofacial Deformities." *Missouri Medicine,* 79 No. 9 (1982), 623–28, 630.

Maull, K.I., and Yarbrough, B. "Experience with a Multidisciplinary Emergency Medicine Clerkship." *Southern Medical Journal,* 76 No. 7 (1983), 876–78.

Mazur, H., J.J. Beeston, and E.J. Yerxa. "Clinical Interdisciplinary Health Team Care: Educational Experiment." *Journal of Medical Education,* 54 No. 9 (1979), 703–13.

Medawar, Peter B. " 'Neuroimmunologic' Diseases: Conference Provides an Interdisciplinary Overview." *Hospital Practice,* 17 No. 1 (1982), 17, 20, 24, 31.

Mello, Nancy K., and Jack H. Mendelson. *Recent Advances in Studies of Alcoholism: An Interdisciplinary Symposium.* Washington, D.C: U.S. Government Printing Office, 1971.

Melville, Robert S. "The Interdisciplinary Approach to Laboratory Medicine." *American Journal of Medical Technology,* 44 No. 3 (1978), 196–200.

*Melvin, J.L. "Interdisciplinary and Multidisciplinary Activities and the ACRM." *Archives of Physical Medicine and Rehabilitation,* 61 No. 8 (1980), 379–80.

Micu, D. "Symposium on the Contribution of Interdisciplinary Research to the Progress of Internal Medicine (Bucharest, October 23 and 24, 1981)." *Revue Romaine de Medecine-Medecine Interne,* 20 No. 2 (1982), 167. See also G. Popa et al., "Interdisciplinary Research in the Interpretation of Some Lymphoproliferative Diseases," pp. 167–68.

Millington, M. "Client-Centered Counseling: An Interdisciplinary Examination." *International Journal for the Advancement of Counselling,* 3 No. 2 (1980), 107–18.

Morse, B.W., and E. Vandenberg. "Interpersonal Relationships in Nursing Practice: Interdisciplinary Approach." *Communication Education,* 27 No. 2 (1978), 158–63.

*Mullen, Peter W. "An Immunopharmacology Journal: Reflections on Its Interdisciplinary and Historical Context." *International Journal of Immunopharmacology,* 1 No. 1 (1979), 1–4.

Muller, H.F., et al. "A Psychogeriatric Assessment Program. IV. Interdisciplinary Aspects." *Journal of the American Geriatrics Society,* 24 No. 2 (1976), 54–57.

Nagi, S.Z. "Teamwork in Health Care in the United States: A Sociological Perspective." *Milbank Memorial Fund Quarterly,* 53 (1975), 75–91.

Nath, R.L., et al. "The Multidisciplinary Approach to Vasculogenic Impotence." *Surgery,* 89 No. 1 (1981), 124–33.

Notter, Robert H., and Jacob N. Finkelstein. "Pulmonary Surfactant: An Interdisciplinary Approach." *Journal of Applied Physiology: Respiratory, Environmental, and Exercise Physiology,* 57 No. 6 (1984), 1613–24.

Oberfield, R.A., R.N. Reuben, and L.J. Burkes. "Interdisciplinary Approach to Conversion Disorders in Adolescent Girls." *Psychosomatics,* 24 No. 11 (1983), 983–89.

*Odhner, Fred. "Group Dynamics of the Interdisciplinary Team." *American Journal of Occupational Therapy,* 24 No. 7 (1970), 484–87.

Ogura, M., et al. "Ethnopharmacologic Studies. 1. Rapid Solution to a Problem: Oral Use of Heliopsis Longipes By Means of a Multidisciplinary Approach." *Journal of Ethnopharmacology,* 5 No. 2 (1982), 215–19.

Pace, D.W., et al. "NHS Reorganization: A Multidisciplinary Reorganization." *British Medical Journal,* 283 No. 6299 (1981), 1134–37.

Page, T.J., et al. "Evaluating and Training Interdisciplinary Teams in Writing IPP Goals and Objectives." *Mental Retardation,* 19 No. 1 (1981), 25–27.

*Pantell, M., et al. "Resolving Role Conflict: An Interdisciplinary Approach." *American Pharmacy,* 21 No. 7 (1981), 41.

Parker, Alberta W. *The Team Approach to Primary Health Care.* Berkeley: University Extension, University of California, 1972. Neighborhood Health Center Seminar Program, Monograph Series No. 3.

*Parker, Marie, and R.C. Hindle. "Multidisciplinary Team." *New Zealand Medical Journal,* 96 No. 728 (1983), 224–25.

*Pearson, Paul H. "The Interdisciplinary Team Process, Or the Professionals' Tower of Babel." *Developmental Medicine and Child Neurology,* 25 No. 3 (1983), 390–95.

Perske, Robert, and Judy Smith, eds. "Beyond the Ordinary: The Preparation of Professionals to Educate Severely and Profoundly Handicapped Persons toward the Development of Standards and Criteria." American Association for the Education of the Severely/Profoundly Handicapped, 1977. ERIC ED 182 873.

Petrella, Russell C., and Norman G. Poythress, Jr. "The Quality of Forensic Evaluations: An Interdisciplinary Study." *Journal of Consulting and Clinical Psychology,* 51 No. 1 (1983), 76–85.

Pfeiffer, Steven I. "The Multidisciplinary Team and Non-Discriminatory Assessment." *Arizona Personnel and Guidance Journal,* 7 (1981), 22–23.

———. "The Problems of Multidisciplinary Teams: As Perceived by Team Members." *Psychology in the Schools,* 18 No. 3 (1981), 330–33.

———. "The School-Based Interprofessional Team: Recurring Problems and Some Possible Solutions." *Journal of School Psychology,* 18 (1980), 388–94.

———, and Bennett I. Tittler. "Utilizing the Multidisciplinary Team to Facilitate a School-Family Systems Orientation." *School Psychology Review,* 12 No. 2 (1983), 168–73.

*Pheby, Derek P.H. "Changing Practice on Confidentiality: A Cause for Concern." *Journal of Medical Ethics,* 8 No. 1 (1982), 12–17.

Piergeorge, A.R., F.L. Cesarano, and D.M. Casanova. "Designing the Critical Care Unit: A Multidisciplinary Approach." *Critical Care Medicine,* 11 No. 7 (1983), 541–45.

Pochyly, D.F., J.S. Albert, and B.B. Blivaiss. "Use of Interdisciplinary Faculty Groups in Curricular Evaluation." *Journal of Medical Education,* 54 No. 7 (1979), 587–89.

Politzer, P., P.H. Reggio, and I.R. Politzer. "Interdisciplinary Cancer Research Workshop." *Cancer Research,* 39 No. 10 (1979), 4291–92; (Politzer, Politzer, and Seybold) "Third Annual Interdisciplinary Cancer Research Workshop." *Cancer Research,* 40 No. 8 (1980), 2943–44; (Politzer, Politzer, and Parkanyi) "Fourth Annual Interdisciplinary Cancer Research Workshop." *Cancer Research,* 41 No. 11 (1981), 4740–41, and "Fifth Annual Interdisciplinary Cancer Research Workshop." *Cancer Research,* 42 No. 11 (1982), 4867–68.

Popkin, M.K., et al. "An Interdisciplinary Comparison of Consultation Outcomes: Psychiatry vs. Cardiology." *Archives of General Psychiatry,* 38 No. 7 (1981), 821–25.

Powell, M.F., et al. "Pharmacist Participation in a Multidisciplinary, Community Health Education Project." *American Journal of Hospital Pharmacy,* 39 No. 5 (1982), 851–52.

*"Proceedings. Workshop on Interdisciplinary Education: Kentucky January Prototype. University of Kentucky, April 15–17, 1975." Lexington, Ky.: College of Allied Health Professions. ERIC ED 129 134.

*Pruzansky, Samuel. "Center for Craniofacial Anomalies: Spinoffs for Medical Education and Delivery of Health Care." *Otolaryngologic Clinics of North America,* 14 No. 4 (1981), 777–82.

*Rae-Grant, Q.A., and Marcuse, D. "The Hazards of Teamwork." *American Journal of Orthopsychiatry,* 38 (1968), 4–8.

Raffoul, P.R., and G.L. Ellenor. "Drug Use among Older People: An Interdisciplinary Paradigm." *Educational Gerontology,* 17 No. 2–3 (1981), 275–83.

Rammage, L.A., H. Nichol, and M.D. Morrison. "The Voice Clinic: An Interdisciplinary Approach." *Journal of Otolaryngology,* 12 No. 5 (1983), 315–18.

Ratzenhofer, Max, Heinz Hoefler, and Gerhard F. Walter, eds. *Frontiers of Hormone Research, V. 12: Interdisciplinary Neuroendocrinology.* Basel, Switzerland: Karger, 1984.

Reeber, B., and D. Custer. "Interdisciplinary Treatment of Closed Head Injured Patients: A Model for Documentation." *Archives of Physical Medicine and Rehabilitation,* 61 No. 10 (1980), 482–83.

Reed, D. Cramer. "Integrated Teaching for Medicine and Allied Health." *Journal of Allied Health,* Fall 1973, pp. 159–62.

Reich, Warren T. "A Laboratory for Humanities and the Health Professions." *MOBIUS: A Journal for Continuing Education of Professionals in the Health Sciences,* 2 No. 3 (July 1982), 61–71.

Renne, Diane J., and Jean J. Moore. "Transdisciplinary Evaluation of Children: Final Report of the Southwest Regional Resource Center's Involvement with the Central Arizona Child Evaluation Center." November 1977. ERIC ED 150 799.

Ringert, R.H., R. Hartung, and W. Havers. "Interdisciplinary Treatment of Wilms Tumor." *British Journal of Urology,* 55 No. 4 (1983), 347–48.

Robinson, K., and P. Rudge. "The Differential Diagnosis of Cerebellopontine Angle Lesions: A Multidisciplinary Approach with Special Emphasis on the Brain Stem Auditory Evoked Potential." *Journal of the Neurological Sciences,* 60 No. 1 (1983), 1–21.

Romankiewicz, J.A., V. Gotz, and H.S. Carlin. "To Improve Patient Adherence to Drug Regimens: Interdisciplinary Approach." *American Journal of Nursing,* 78 No. 7 (1978), 1216–19.

Rose, L.F., I.S. Brown, and M.A. Lynch. "An Interdisciplinary Training Program in a Hospital." *Journal of Dental Education,* 38 (1974), 156–60.

Rosenberg, J.C., R. Franklin, and Z. Steiger. "Squamous Cell Carcinoma of the Thoracic Esophagus: An Interdisciplinary Approach." *Current Problems in Cancer,* 5 No. 11 (1981), 1–52.

Ross, S., H.S. Dorfman, and K.G. Palanis. "Orthodontic Extrusion: A Multidisciplinary Treatment Approach." *Journal of the American Dental Association,* 102 No. 2 (1981), 189–91.

Rosse, Cornelius. "Integrated Versus Discipline-Oriented Instruction in Medical Education." *Journal of Medical Education,* 49 (October 1974), 995–98.

*Rotberg, J., et al. "Status of Interagency Cooperation between Interdisciplinary Clinics or Hospitals and the Public Schools." *Child Psychiatry and Human Development,* 12 No. 3 (1982), 153–59.

Roush, Robert E. "Interdisciplinary Education in the Health Professions: A Caveat from Research." *Journal of Allied Health,* Fall 1973, pp. 150–54.

Rowe, V.K. "Industrial Hygiene: Truly an Interdisciplinary Science." *American Industrial Hygiene Association Journal,* 40 No. 9 (1979), 751–56.

Royal Society of Medicine International Concerns and Symposium Series No. 55. Osteoporosis: A Multidisciplinary Problem. Ed. A. Dixon, R. Russel, and T. Stamp. London: Royal Society of Medicine, 1983.

Rubin, I., and R. Beckhard. "Factors Influencing Effectiveness of Health Teams." In *Organizational Psychology: An Experimental Approach,* 2nd ed., Englewood Cliffs, N.J.: Prentice Hall, 1974, pp. 202–12.

Rutz, W. "Interdisciplinary Cooperation in an Integrated Psychiatric Rehabilitation Program." *International Journal of Rehabilitation Research,* 2 No. 2 (1979), 169–76.

Rycroft, R.J.G. "The College of Medicine of South Africa Interdisciplinary Symposium on Rehabilitation 1981." *Clinical and Experimental Dermatology,* 8 No. 1 (1983), 111–12.

Sabin, James E., and Steven S. Sharfstein. "Integrating Community Psychiatry into Residency Training." *Hospital and Community Psychiatry,* 26 No. 5 (1975), 289–92.

Sakai, S., et al. "Multidisciplinary Treatment of Maxillary Sinus Carcinoma." *Cancer,* 52 No. 8 (1983), 1360–64.

*Salinas, C.F., and R.J. Jorgenson, eds. *Dentistry in the Interdisciplinary Treatment of Genetic Diseases.* New York: Alan R. Liss, 1980. See especially H.L. Morris, "Structure and Function of Interdisciplinary Teams," pp. 105–10; R.S. Sobel, "Hemophilia Interdisciplinary Programs: The Role of the Dentist," pp. 147–50.

Scaggs, C.G., et al. "Insulin Dependent Diabetes Mellitus in a Young Woman: The Interdisciplinary Approach." *Journal of the American Podiatry Association,* 71 No. 9 (1981), 514–19.

Scalley, R.D., E. Kearney, and E. Jakobs. "Interdisciplinary Inpatient Warfarin Education Program." *American Journal of Hospital Pharmacy,* 36 No. 2 (1979), 219–20.

Schauss, Alexander G. "Nutrition and Behavior: Complex Interdisciplinary Research." *Nutritional Health* (Great Britain), 3 No. 1–2 (1984), 9–37.

Schirren, C. "The Interdisciplinary Cooperation between Andrology and Gynecology in Considering the Effectiveness of the Treatment of Sterility." *International Urology and Nephrology,* 12 No. 2 (1980), 181–84.

Schlesinger, Z. "An Interdisciplinary Approach to Cardiac Rehabilitation." *Heart and Lung,* 12 No. 4 (1983), 336–37.

Schmitt, G., et al. "Present Interdisciplinary Treatment Regimen for Advanced Head and Neck Tumors at the West German Tumour Centre." *Journal of Maxillofacial Surgery,* 11 No. 2 (1983), 51–53.

Schoenberg, H.W., C.K. Zarins, and R.T. Segraves. "Analysis of 122 Unselected Impotent Men Subjected to Multidisciplinary Evaluation." *Journal of Urology,* 127 No. 3 (1982), 445–47.

Schwartz, Gary E., and Stephen M. Weiss. "Yale Conference on Behavioral Medicine: A Proposed Definition and Statement of Goals." *Journal of Behavioral Medicine,* 1 No. 1 (1978), 3–12; *Journal of Behavioral Medicine,* 1 No. 3 (1978), 249.

Scofield, Michael E., and Timothy J. Hynick. "A Multidisciplinary Perspective on Rehabilitation Research Needs." *Journal of Rehabilitation,* 49 No. 2 (1983), 15–18, 24.

Scott, David. M., et al. "The Development and Evaluation of an Interdisciplinary Health Training Program: A Pharmacy Perspective." *American Journal of Pharmaceutical Education,* 47 No. 1 (1983), 42–48.

Sears, Carol J. "The Transdisciplinary Approach: A Process of Compliance with Public Law 94-142." *Journal of the Association for the Severely Handicapped,* 6 No. 1 (1981), 22–29.

Seattle Indian Alcoholism Program. "The Role of Anthropology in Interdisciplinary Research on Indian Alcoholism and Treatment Outcome." *Journal of Studies on Alcohol,* 42 No. 9 (1981), 836–45.

Segev, U., and Z. Schlesinger. "Rehabilitation of Patients After Acute Myocardial Infarction: An Interdisciplinary, Family-Oriented Program." *Heart and Lung,* 10 No. 5 (1981), 841–47.

Shiveley, J.A. "Pathology in Interdisciplinary Courses." *Pahlavi Medical Journal,* 9 No. 1 (1978), 104–11.

Sifneos, Peter E. "The Interdisciplinary Team and Educational Experience for Mental Health Professionals." *Psychiatry Quarterly,* 43 (1969), 123–30.

Siggers, Walter W. "The Role of the Psychologist in Advocacy for the Handicapped." *Professional Psychology,* 10 No. 1 (1979), 80–86.

Singer, J., M. Bossard, and M. Watkins. "Effects of Parental Presence on Attendance and Input of Interdisciplinary Teams in an Institutional Setting." *Psychological Reports,* 41 No. 3 (1977), 1031–34.

Sinson, J.C. "Downs Patients: Interdisciplinary Approach Involving Parents." *International Journal of Rehabilitation Research,* 1 No. 1 (1978), 59–69.

Sirvis, Barbara. "Developing IEP's for Physically Handicapped Students: A Transdisciplinary Viewpoint." *Teaching Exceptional Children,* 10 No. 3 (1978), 78–82.

Slaby, Andrew B. "The Team Approach to the Treatment of the Rape Victim." *Connecticut Medicine,* February 1978, pp. 135–36.

———, Richard J. Goldberg, and Stephen R. Wallace. "Interdisciplinary Team Approach to Emergency Psychiatric Care." *Psychosomatics,* 24 No. 7 (1983), 627–37.

Snodgrass, J. "Interprofessional Stereotyping in the Hospital." *Nursing Research,* 15 (1966), 350–54.

Stahl, S.M., et al. "A Model for the Social Sciences and Medicine: The Case for Hypertension." *Social Science and Medicine,* 9 No. 1 (1975), 31–38.

Stanton, K.M., et al. "Wheelchair Transfer Training for Right Cerebral Dysfunctions: An Interdisciplinary Approach." *Archives of Physical Medicine and Rehabilitation,* 64 No. 6 (1983), 276–80.

Steinberg, J.L. "Towards an Interdisciplinary Commitment: A Divorce Lawyer Proposes Attorney-Therapist Marriages or, at the Least, an Affair." *Journal of Marital and Family Therapy,* 6 No. 3 (1980), 259–68.

Stieg, R.L., R.C. Williams, and L.A. Gallagher. "Multidisciplinary Pain Treatment Centers." *Journal of Occupational Medicine,* 23 No. 2 (1981), 94–102.

Stile, Stephen W., and E. Ann Olson. "The Transdiciplinary Model: An Alternative Approach for Meeting the Needs of Children in Early Childhood Education Programs for the Handicapped." Las Cruces: New Mexico State University, 1980. ERIC ED 189 803.

Stone, N.D. "Effecting Interdisciplinary Coordination in Clinical Services to the Mentally Retarded." *American Journal of Orthopsychiatry,* 40 (1970), 835–40.

Sumner, E.D. "Teaching an Interdisciplinary Gerontological Course to Pharmacy Students." *American Journal of Pharmaceutical Education,* 42 No. 2 (1978), 135–37.

Sumner, E.D., E.C. Toporek, and J.D. James. "Elective Course for an Interdisciplinary Approach to Family Health Care." *American Journal of Pharmaceutical Education,* 42 No. 1 (1978), 49–52.

Swazey, Judith P., and Renée C. Fox. "Medical Sociology." *JAMA (Journal of the American Medical Association),* 247 No. 21 (1982), 2959–62.

Szaz, G. "Interprofessional Education in the Health Sciences." *Milbank Memorial Fund Quarterly,* 47 No. 4, Pt. 1 (1969), 449–75.

Tichy, M.K. *Health Care Teams: An Annotated Bibliography.* New York: Prager, 1974.

Tognetti, F., M. Poppi, and V. Poppi. "A Multidisciplinary Approach for the Treatment of Metastatic Brachial Plexus Neuropathy from Breast Cancer: Neurosurgical, Plastic, and Radiotherapeutic." *Neurochirurgia,* 26 No. 3 (1983), 86–88.

Tonkin, R. "Interdisciplinary Approach to Dental Care." *Canadian Journal of Public Health,* 69 No. 2 (1978), 158–62.

Toshifumi, I., et al. "Multidisciplinary Treatment for Esophageal Carcinoma." *Japanese Journal of Clinical Oncology,* 13 No. 2 (1983), 417–24.

Tremblay, E., et al. "A Multidisciplinary Study of Folic Acid Neurotoxicity: Interactions with Kainate Binding Sites and Relevance to the Etiology of Epilepsy." *Neuroscience* (Great Britain), 12 No. 2 (1984), 569–89.

*Udziela, A.D., T.K. Shinn, and B.Y. Whitman. "The Psychologist on the Multidisciplinary Development-Disabilities Team." *Professional Psychology,* 13 No. 6 (1982), 782–88.

*Urschel, Harold C. "Interdisciplinary University without Walls: Current Status of the ACCP." *Chest,* 75 No. 4 (1979), 495–99.

*Valletutti, Peter J., and Florence Christopolos, eds., *Interdisciplinary Approaches to Human Services.* Baltimore: University Park Press, 1977.

Vanbladeren, P.J. "The Dual Role of Glutathione Conjugation in the Biotransformation of

Xenobiotics: A Multidisciplinary Investigation," *Pharmaceutisch Weekblad: Scientific Edition,* 4 No. 5 (1982), 137–38.

Vanbrievingh, R.R.V. "A Multidisciplinary Program for Hospital Safety Education." *Medical Progress through Technology,* 8 No. 4 (1982), 189–91.

Van Cauwenberge, H., C. Lambotte, and A. André. "Interdisciplinary Colloquium on HLA Group and Its Importance in Adult and Child Pathology. Liège, Belgium. December 4, 1981." *Revue Médicale Liège,* 38 No. 4 (1983), 117–43. (In French.)

*Van Krevelen, Nellis, and Eric R. Harvey. "Integrating Clinical Pharmacy Services into the Interdisciplinary Team Structure." *Mental Retardation,* 20 No. 2 (1982), 64–68.

Van Praag, H.M. *Research in Neurosis: Symposium Organized by the Interdisciplinary Society of Biological Psychiatry.* Utrecht, Netherlands: Bohn, Scheltema, and Holkema, 1976.

Vichinsky, E.P., R. Johnson, and B.H. Lubin. "Multidisciplinary Approach to Pain Management in Sickle-Cell Disease." *American Journal of Hematology Oncology,* 4 No. 3 (1982), 328–33.

Vinsonhaler, J.F. *Implications of an Interdisciplinary Theory of Clinical Inquiry for Diagnostic Efficacy.* Amsterdam: North-Holland, 1979, pp. 93–104.

Wallace, Gerald. "Interdisciplinary Efforts in Learning Disabilities: Issues and Recommendations." *Journal of Learning Disabilities,* 9 No. 8 (1976), 59–65.

Wallgren-Pettersson, Carina, et al. "Interdisciplinary Teaching of Community Pediatrics." *Medical Education,* 16 No. 5 (1982), 290–95.

Wehrmacher, W.H., C.N. Peiss, and W.C. Randall. "Weekly Interdisciplinary Colloquy on Cardiology: A Decade of Experiment." *Journal of Medical Education,* 56 No. 10 (1981), 846–50.

Weisenburger, T.H., et al. "Multidisciplinary Limb Salvage Treatment of Soft Tissues and Skeletal Sarcomas." *International Journal of Radiation Oncology, Biology, Physics,* 7 No. 11 (1981), 1495–99.

Werner, Paul T., Ronald W. Richards, and Barbara Fogle. "Ambulatory Family Practice Experience as the Primary and Integrating Clinical Concept in a Four-Year Undergraduate Curriculum." *Journal of Family Practice,* 7 No. 2 (1978), 325–32.

West, M., R. McIlvaine, and C.J. Sells. "Interdisciplinary Health Care Settings: Experience with Groups for Parents of Children Having Specific Disabilities." *Social Work in Health Care,* 4 No. 3 (1979), 287–98.

White, R.B., D.A. Cornely, and A. Gately. "Interdisciplinary Training for Child Welfare and Health." *Child Welfare,* 57 No. 9 (1978), 549–62.

Whitehead, E.D., et al. "Male Sexual Dysfunction and Diabetes Mellitus: Multidisciplinary Approach to Diagnosis and Management." *New York State Journal of Medicine,* 83 No. 11-1 (1983), 1174–79.

*Whitehouse, F.A. "Teamwork: A Democracy of Professions." *Exceptional Children,* 18 (1951).

Williamson, G.G. "The Individualized Education Program: An Interdisciplinary Endeavor." in *Unique Aspects of the Individualized Educational Program for the Physically Handicapped, Homebound and Hospitalized.* Ed. B. Sirvis, J.W. Baken, and G.G. Williamson. Reston, Va: Council for Exceptional Children, 1979.

Wise, H., et al. *Making Health Teams Work.* Cambridge: Balinger, 1974. See also "Making Health Teams Work," *American Journal of Diseases of Children,* 127 (1974), 537–42.

Wolfendale, S. "Interdisciplinary Approaches to Preschool Developmental Surveillance: Recent Trends in the UK." *Early Child Development and Care,* 6 No. 3–4 (1980), 135–46.

*Wong, S.B. "Interdisciplinary Health Care." *Journal of the American Optometric Association,* 49 No. 9 (1978), 1001–06. See also "Interdisciplinary Health Care 1," *Journal of the American Optometric Association,* 49 No. 7 (1978), 803–07; "Interdisciplinary

Health Care 2." *Journal of the American Optometric Association,* 49 No. 8 (1978), 895–900.

Wood, B.G., et al. "Surgical Problems of the Base of the Skull: Interdisciplinary Approach." *Archives of Otolaryngology,* 106 No. 1 (1980), 1–5.

Woodruff, Geneva. "Transdisciplinary Approach for Preschool Children and Parents." *Exceptional Parent,* 10 No. 3 (1980), 13–16.

Young, C.W., et al. "Multidisciplinary Treatment of Advanced Hodgkins Disease by an Alternating Chemotherapeutic Regimen of Mopp ABDV and Low-Dose Radiation Therapy Restricted to Originally Bulky Disease." *Cancer Treatment Reports,* 66 No. 4 (1982), 907–14.

Young, R., E. Freiberg, and P. Stringham. "The Home Visit in the Multidisciplinary Teaching of Primary Care Physicians." *Journal of Medical Education,* 56 No. 4 (1981), 341–46.

Zavattoni, V., V.L. Grillo, and E. Figini. "Advances in Interdisciplinary Diagnostic Therapeutic Research in Psychosomatic Obstetric Gynecologic Diseases." *Galini,* 11 No. 1 (1979), 17–32.

Zipko, S.J. "Interdisciplinary Research Reports on Bioethical Controversies." *American Biology Teacher,* 45 No. 1 (1983), 47–48.

Education

Abbey, David S. *Designing Interdisciplinary Studies Programs.* Albany, N.Y.: State University of New York, 1976.

Adams, Charles. "The Inquiry Program at the University of Massachusetts – Amherst." *Association for Integrative Studies Newsletter,* 6 No. 4 (1984), 1, 6–9.

Adams, R.S. "An Interdisciplinary Taped Closed-Circuit Television Course," *National Association of College Teachers of Agriculture Journal,* 26 No. 3 (1982), 22–26.

Almy, Millie. "Survey of Selected Interdisciplinary Programs." Report to the Carnegie Corporation and the Grant Foundation. New York, 1978. ERIC ED 158 880.

Ansboro, J.J. "Experiment in Interdisciplinary Liberal Education." *Liberal Education,* 54 (1968), 521–27.

*Armstrong, Forrest. "Faculty Development through Interdisciplinarity." *JGE, The Journal of General Education,* 32 No. 1 (1980), 52–63.

*Assimopoulos, Nadia, and Charles H. Berlanger. "Interdisciplinary Policies and Practices." Paper presented at the Eighteenth Annual Association for Institutional Research Forum in Houston, Texas, 21–25 May 1978. ERIC 161 366.

Ault, David, and Rutman, Gilbert. "The Role of Economics in Interdisciplinary and Problem-Oriented Programs." *Journal of Economic Education,* 9 No. 2 (1978), 96–101.

Austenson, Roy A. "History and the Humanities: An Integrative Approach." *Social Studies,* 66 (Sept./Oct. 1974), 210–14.

Babb, Lawrence A. "Interdisciplinary Studies: Proceed with Caution." *Independent School,* 38 (May 1979), 23–27.

Balogh, S. "The Multi-Disciplinary Approach in History and Ethnic Studies," *Community College Social Science Journal,* 3 (1980–81), 62–69.

Bannister, Sharon. "Images of Society: An Experimental Interdisciplinary Course Using Historical Novels." *History Teacher,* 6 No. 3 (1973), 365–74.

Barman, C.R., R.E. Harshman, and J.J. Rusch. "Attitudes of Science and Social-Studies Teachers toward Interdisciplinary Instruction." *American Biology Teacher,* 44 No. 7 (1982), 421–426.

Barsch, Ray H. "The Concept of Multidisciplinariness." *Academic Therapy,* 6 No. 2 (1970–71), 187–91.

Baum, Joan. "Interdisciplinary Studies, The Latest Experimental Rage." *College Composition and Communication,* 26 (Feb. 1975), 30–33.

Baum, Robert J. "Teaching Philosophy of Science in an Interdisciplinary Context." *Teaching Philosophy,* 2 (1977), 126–30.

Bayerl, Elizabeth. *Interdisciplinary Studies in the Humanities: A Directory.* Metuchen, N.J.: Scarecrow Press, 1977.

*Beck, Clive. "Educational Studies and the Cult of Specialization." *Educational Studies,* 5 (Winter 1974–75), 189–96.

Beck, James P. *"Thinking* across the Curriculum." in *California English,* Jan.-Feb. 1982.

———. "Theory and Practice of Interdisciplinary English." *English Journal,* 69 No. 2 (1980), 28–32.

*Becker, Samuel L. "Innovations in Administration Used and Being Used by Other Departments." Paper presented at the 63rd Annual Meeting of the Speech Communication Association. Washington, D.C., 1–4 Dec. 1977. ERIC ED 147 885.

Beckwith, M.M. "Integrating the Humanities and Occupational Programs: An Inventory of Current Approaches, Project Report No. 12." Los Angeles: Center for the Study of Community Colleges, 1980. ERIC ED 196 489.

———. "Science Education in Two-Year Colleges: Interdisciplinary Social Sciences." Los Angeles: ERIC Clearinghouse for Junior Colleges and Center for the Study of Community Colleges, 1980. ERIC ED 181 955.

*Benson, Thomas L. "Five Arguments against Interdisciplinary Studies." *Issues in Integrative Studies,* 1 (1982), 38–48.

*Berquist, William H. "Curricular Practice." In *Developing the College Curriculum: A Handbook for Faculty and Administrators,* ed. Arthur Chickering et al. Washington, D.C.: Council for the Advancement of Small Colleges, 1977, pp. 77–109.

Betts, Francis M. "A Qualitative Model of the Integrative Learning Process." *Issues in Integrative Studies,* 2 (1983), 93–122.

Bie, Karen Nossum. *Creating a New University: The Establishment and Development of the University of Tromso.* Oslo: Institute for Studies in Research and Higher Education, 1981.

Biggs, A.L. "An Interdisciplinary Course in Big Bend National Park, Texas." *American Biology Teacher,* 44 No. 4 (1982), 219–33.

Bingham, Nelson. "Preparing Society's Servants." *Earlhamite Magazine,* Summer 1983, 20–22.

Blum, Mark E. "Introducing the Liberal Arts through Interdisciplinary Inquiry: Proposal for an Integrative General Education Experience." *Issues in Integrative Studies,* 3 (1984/85), 57–89.

Blyth, W.A.L. "Integrated Study and Educational Research: Some Observations on the British Scene." *British Journal of Educational Studies* (Great Britain), 25 No. 2 (1977), 109–23.

Boebler, Bettie Anne. "Skinning Cats and Interdisciplinary Studies: A Caveat," *Change, The Magazine of Higher Learning,* 12 (Nov./Dec. 1980), 10–12.

Boger, Robert P. "Organizational Policy Issues Affecting Interdisciplinary Educational Research and Research Training." Boulder, Colorado University. Feb. 1973. ERIC ED 077 422.

Bonner, Thomas P. "Delta College at SUNY-Brockport." *Association for Integrative Studies Newsletter,* 7 No. 4 (1985), 4–7.

*Boyer, Ernest, ed. *Common Learning: A Carnegie Colloquium on General Education.* Washington, D.C.: Carnegie Foundation for the Advancement of Teaching, 1981.

Bradie, Michael, and Comer Duncan. "A Course on the Philosophy and Physics of Space and Time." *Teaching Philosophy,* 5 (Apr. 1982), 109–16.

Bridges, J.D.F. "An Interdisciplinary Curriculum Linking Geology with Prehistoric Archaeology." *Journal of Geological Education,* 27 (Sept. 1979), 160–61.

Brillhart, L., and M.B. Debs. "An Engineering-Rhetoric Course: Combining Learning-Teaching Styles," *Improving College and University Teaching,* 30 No. 2 (1982), 80–85.

————. "Team Teaching and Faculty Development: A Simultaneous Process." *Educational Research and Methods,* 2 (1979), 18–20.

Brinker, Paul. "Our Illiberal Liberal Arts Colleges: The Dangers of Undergraduate Over-specialization." *Journal of Higher Education,* 31 (1960), 133–38.

Brock, D. Heyward. "Program in the Culture of Biomedicine at the University of Delaware." *Liberal Education,* 65 (Spring 1979), 92–97.

Brock, T.C., et al. *Interdisciplinary Research and Doctoral Training: A Study of the Linköping University (Sweden) Tema Departments.* Stockholm: Swedish National Board of Universities and Colleges, 1986.

Broderick, Francis L. "A New Moment for the Humanities: An Introduction to the Symposium." *Liberal Education,* Spring 1979, pp. 1–9.

*Brooks, Anne, and Un-chol Shin. "Past, Present, and Future of Interdisciplinary Humanities." *Humanities Education,* Sept. 1984, pp. 3–9.

Brown, Elizabeth A.R. "Interdisciplinary Studies and the Undergraduate Reflections from Brooklyn College." *Centerpoint,* 1 No. 4 (1975–76), 45–49.

Brown, Peggy. "Graduate Liberal Studies," *Forum for Liberal Education,* 4 No. 4 (1982).

Brownell, Judith. "Elwood Murray's Interdisciplinary Analogue Laboratory." *Communication Education,* 28 (Jan. 1979), 9–21.

Bundy, Barbara K. "The One and the Many: A Colloquia Program in Humanities at Dominican College of San Rafael." *Liberal Education,* 65 No. 1 (1979), 30–44.

Byrne, Lee. "An Educational Application of Resources of the Unity of Science Movement." *Philosophy of Science,* 7 (Apr. 1940), 241–62.

Calvert, J.B., et al. "The Age of Newton: An Intensive Interdisciplinary Course." *History Teacher,* 14 No. 2 (1981), 167–90.

Cantor, Harold. "Reintegrating the Humanities." *Change,* 10 (1978), 54–55.

Carleton, William. "Rhetorical Rationale for Interdisciplinary Graduate Study in Communication." *Communication Education,* 28 No. 4 (1979), 332–38.

*"The Case For and Against Interdisciplinary Studies." *Issues in Integrative Studes,* 2 (1983), 1–34. A series of articles by William H. Newell, Jerry L. Petr, Raymond C. Miller, and Thomas Benson.

Case Studies in Interdisciplinarity. London: Group for Research and Innovation in Higher Education, Nuffield Foundation, 1975. Vol. 1: *Environmental Sciences and Engineering,* Sept. 1975; Vol. 2: *Science, Technology and Society,* Oct. 1975; Vol. 3: *Integrated Social Sciences,* Sept. 1975; Vol. 4: *National and International Studies,* Sept. 1975; Vol. 5: *Humanities and Cognitive Studies,* Sept. 1975.

Cassidy, Harold G. "A Natural Philosophy Course in Physics and Chemistry." *Journal of Chemical Education,* 46 (Feb. 1969), 64–66.

Caswell, Hollis L. "The Generalist: His Unique Contribution." *Educational Leadership,* 24 (Dec. 1966), 213–15.

Cawelti, John, et al. "National Humanities Faculty Working Papers." National Humanities Faculty. Concord, Mass. ERIC ED 098 128.

Change Magazine. Aug. 1978. Report on Teaching: 6. Issue on Interdisciplinary Studies. ERIC ED 157 461.

*Ciccorico, Edward. "'Integration' in the Curriculum." *Main Currents in Modern Thought,* 27 (Nov.-Dec. 1970), 60–62.

Cliff, Rosemary. "Interdisciplinary and Multidisciplinary Programs: Attitudes and Experiences of USC Faculty." National Science Foundation Report USC-OIS-741. ERIC ED 093 250.

Cook, E.E. "An Engineering Educator's Experience in Interdisciplinary Team Teaching." *Engineering Education,* 65 (Dec. 1974), 230–32.

*Counelis, James Steve. "Education about Education." *Educational Studies,* 9 (Winter 1979), 407–24.

———. "What Is an Interdisciplinary Course in the Social Sciences?" *Community College Social Science Quarterly,* 3 (Winter 1973), 29–31.

*Crandall, Deborah, and Elizabeth Rinnander. "Interdisciplinary Humanities: Sources and Information." *New Directions for Community Colleges,* 12 (Winter 1975), 95–102.

Cravens, Raymond L. "The Battle over Turf." *Association of Governing Boards of Universities and Colleges,* 20 No. 2 (1973), 41–44.

*Crawford, Bryce. "The Support of Interdisciplinary and Transdisciplinary Programs." Washington, D.C. Address to the Ninth Annual Meeting of the Council of Graduate Schools in the United States. 5 Dec. 1969. ERIC ED 035 364.

*"Creating an Integrated Curriculum: The 'Higher' in Higher Education." *Current Issues in Higher Education,* No. 2 (1981). ERIC ED 213 324.

Dale, J.E. "The Case for an Interdisciplinary Approach to Social Science." *Community College Social Science Journal,* 2 No. 3 (1980–81), 34–38.

Dallas, Susan, ed. "What Are Interdisciplinary Studies?" *Center for the Study of Community Colleges Bulletin,* 2 (1982), ERIC document ED 219 116.

Davis, David J. "The Cluster College Revisited: A Dream Falls on Hard Times." *College Teaching,* 33 No. 1 (1985), 15–20.

*"Developments in Interdisciplinarity." *Group for Research and Innovation in Higher Education Newsletter,* 4 (April 1974). Published in London by the Nuffield Foundation.

Diamond, Irene, et al. "Interdisciplinary Writing: A Guide to Writing across the Curriculum." Madison: University of Wisconsin, 1980. ERIC ED 193 655.

Dick, B.G. "An Interdisciplinary Science Humanities Course." *American Journal of Physics,* 51 No. 8 (1983), 702–08.

*Dill, Stephen H. *Integrated Studies: Challenges to the College Curriculum,* ed. Stephen H. Dill. Washington, D.C.: University Press of America, 1982.

Dill, Stephen H. "The Role of History in the Integrated Humanities Program." *Network News Exchange,* 4 (Fall 1979), 16–17.

Douglass, Robert W. "Whose Turf Is This?" Paper presented at the Society of Professional Recreation-Educators Symposium on Leisure Research: Curriculum Planning and Evaluation, 1979. ERIC ED 193 220.

*Doyal, Len. "Interdisciplinary Studies in Higher Education." *Universities Quarterly, Higher Education and Society,* 28 No. 4 (1974), 470–87.

Drake, Miriam. "The Librarian's Role in Interdisciplinary Studies," *Special Libraries,* 66 No. 3 (1975), 116–20.

Duncan, W. Jack. "Professional Education and the Liberating Tradition: An Action Alternative." *Liberal Education,* 43 (Oct. 1977), 453–61.

Dunstone, J. "A Course in Chemistry of Silicates for Beginning Undergraduate Students: An Interdisciplinary Study." *Journal of Chemical Education,* 50 (1973), 362–64.

Eason, D.O. "Charting the Territory: Interdisciplinary Studies." Paper Presented at the Annual Meeting of the Southeastern Conference on English in the Two-Year College, in Biloxi, Miss., 1981. ERIC ED 208 914.

Eckenrod, James S., and James F. Holmes. "Interdisciplinary Teaching Strategies." *Special Education,* 37 No. 7 (1973), 622–34.

Eckhardt, Caroline D. *Interdisciplinary Programs and Administrative Structure: Problems and Prospects for the 80's.* University Park: Center for the Study of Higher Education, Pennsylvania State Univ. Press, 1978.

Edington, W.F., and E.J. Preville. "A Journey toward Unity." *Engineering Education,* 65 (Dec. 1974), 213–15.

Ellington, H.I., and E. Addinall. "The Multi-Disciplinary Multi-Project Pack: A New Concept in Simulation Gaming." *Programmed Learning and Educational Technology,* 14 (1977), 213–22.

Ellington, H.I., E. Addinall, and M.C. Hately. "The Project Scotia Competition." *Physics Education* (Great Britain), 15 No. 4 (1980), 220–22.

Epstein, Richard. "Incorporating Recent Political Theory into the Social Studies Curriculum." *Social Studies,* 66 No. 2 (1975), 51–53.

Erickson, Mildred B., and John N. Winburne. "General Studies: A Trend in Higher Education in the Seventies." Michigan State University, East Lansing, University College (Sept. 1972) ERIC ED 076 134.

Estep, Myrna L. "A Multidisciplinary Approach to Teaching Introductory Philosophy." *Aitia,* 4 (Spring 1976), 13–17.

Estus, Charles, et al., "An Interdisciplinary Approach to Community Studies." *History Teacher,* 13 No. 1 (1979), 37–48.

Eurich, Alvin C. "Ideas: The Key to Interdisciplinary Studies." *Learning Today,* 5 (Fall 1972), 45–53.

Fedo, David A. "Learning for Careers and Life: Liberal Arts in the Professional Institutions," *College Board Review,* 105 (Fall 1977), 28–33.

Fethe, Charles. "Curriculum Theory: A Proposal for Unity." *Educational Theory,* 27 (Spring 1977), 96–102.

*Fethe, Charles B. "A Philosophical Model for Interdisciplinary Programs." *Liberal Education,* 59 No. 4 (1973), 490–97.

Finn, Peter. "Alcohol Education in the School Curriculum: The Single Discipline versus the Interdisciplinary Discipline." *Journal of Alcohol and Drug Education,* 24 No. 2 (1979), 41–57.

Fischer, J. "Survival U Is Alive and Burgeoning in Green Bay, Wisconsin." *Harpers,* 242 (1971), 20–27.

*Flexner, Hans, and Gerald A. Hauser. "Interdisciplinary Programs in the United States: Some Paradigms." In *Interdisciplinarity and Higher Education,* ed. Joseph Kockelmans (University Park: The Pennsylvania State Univ. Press, 1979), pp. 328–50.

*Foa, Lin. "The Integrated Humanities in Higher Education: a Survey." *Journal of Aesthetic Education,* 7 (July 1973), 85–98.

Ford, G.W., and Lawrence Pugno, eds. *The Structure of Knowledge and the Curriculum.* Chicago: Rand McNally, 1964.

The Forum for Liberal Education, 8 No. 4 (1986). Special issue on interdisciplinary education.

*Fox, W.M., and J.A. Stewart. "Practitioners' Views on Interdisciplinary Studies at the College Level." Kansas Center for Faculty Evaluation and Development in Higher Education, Kansas State University, June 1978. ERIC ED 172 598.

Frederick, William C. "Education for Social Responsibility: What the Business Schools Are Doing about It," *Liberal Education,* 63 (May 1977), 190–203.

*Fulcher, James. "Liberal Education: Interdisciplinary Study of Integrative Topics." *Improving College and University Teaching,* 26 (Winter 1978), 44–47.

Gaff, Jerry G. "Avoiding the Potholes: Strategies for Reforming General Education." *Educational Record,* 61 No. 4 (1980), 50–59.

———, et al. *The Cluster College.* San Francisco: Jossey Bass, 1967.

———. *General Education Today: A Critical Analysis of Controversies, Practices, and Reforms.* San Francisco: Jossey Bass, 1983.

———, and Robert C. Wilson. "Faculty Cultures and Interdisciplinary Studies." *Journal of Higher Education,* 42 No. 3 (1971), 186–201.

Gallagher, J.J. "Interdisciplinary Sharing of Knowledge: Response." *Journal of Special Education,* 13 No. 1 (1979), 41–43.

Gallant, T.F. "Interdisciplinary Boom in Higher Education: Reincarnation of John Dewey and the Progressives' Core Program?" *Liberal Education,* 58 No. 3 (1972), 347–58.

*Galverstein, Carolyn. "Interdisciplinarity at the Graduate Level." *Perspectives, Journal of the Association for General and Liberal Studies,* 11 No. 3 (1981), 18–23.

*Garkovich, Lorraine. "A Proposal for Building Interdisciplinary Bridges." *Teaching Sociology,* 9 No. 2 (1982), 151–68.

*Goodwin, William M., and William K. LeBold. "Interdisciplinarity and Team Teaching." *Engineering Education,* 66 (Dec. 1975), 247–54.

Gordon, Joseph T. "The Colorado College Southwestern Studies Program." *Liberal Education,* 65 No. 1 (1979), 20–29.

Gordon, Robert I. "Emerging Black Colleges: an Interdisciplinary Approach." *Negro Education Review,* 21 No. 1 (1970), 30–37.

Gosselin, Edward A., and Lawrence S. Lerner. "History of Science as a Device for Reconciling the Sciences and the Humanities." *Teaching History: A Journal of Methods,* 2 (Fall 1977), 41–49.

Graham, Peter. "The Place of the Humanities in Medical Education." *Liberal Education,* 66 No. 4 (1980), 388–94.

Grant, Gerald, and David Riesman. *The Perpetual Dream: Reform and Experiment in the American College.* Chicago: Univ. of Chicago Press, 1978.

Greeley, Warren, et al. Final Report (1975). Unified Studies Program. *United Studies Report,* I:10. Boston State College. ERIC ED 118 034.

Gregory, Michael W. "NEXA: The Science-Humanities Convergence Program at San Francisco State University." *Liberal Education,* 65 No. 1 (1979), 66–91.

Grogan, J. "Teacher Inservice for Nutrition Education: Interdisciplinary Approach in School System," *Journal of Nutrition Education,* 10 No. 3 (1978), 119–20.

Gross, Ronald. "Columbia's University Seminars: Creating a 'Community of Scholars.'" *Change, The Magazine of Higher Learning,* 14 No. 2 (1982), 43–45.

Guidry, Rosaline. "A Design for Teaching Human Behavior in a Generalist Undergraduate Program." *Journal of Education for Social Work,* 15 (Spring 1979), 45–50.

*Guroff, Katherine S., and Margaret C. Boker, eds. *Quality in Liberal Education: Curricular Innovations in Higher Education.* A Report of Project QUILL. Washington, D.C.: Association of American Colleges, 1981. ERIC ED 212 189.

Hain, W.F., et al. "Design Considerations for Multidisciplinary Continuing Nutrition Education Programs," *Journal of Parenteral and Enteral Nutrition,* 6 No. 6 (1982), 522–25.

*Halliburton, David. "Interdisciplinary Studies." In *The Modern American College,* ed. Arthur Chickering. San Francisco: Jossey Bass, 1981, pp. 453–71.

Haning, B.C. "Interdisciplinary Curricula: Ingredients for Success." *National Association of College Teachers of Agriculture Journal,* 25 No. 3 (1981), 10–14.

Hanisch, Thor Einar, and Wolfgang Vollman, eds. *Interdisciplinarity in Higher Education.* Bucharest, Romania: European Centre for Higher Education, UNESCO-CEPES, 1983. ERIC ED 249 864. Proceedings from symposium on "Interdisciplinarity in Higher Education in Europe," held in Bucharest, 24–26, Nov. 1981.

Hansen, Desna W. "New Directions in General Education." *Journal of General Education,* 33 No. 4 (1982), 249–62.

Hays, Garry D., and C. Robert Haywood. "Liberal Education at Southwestern: An Interdisciplinary Approach." *Liberal Education,* 53 (Dec. 1967), 526–39.

*Hazzard, George W. "Quality in Lifelong Learning. A Report of Project QUILL," *Forum for Liberal Education,* 2 No. 3 (1979). ERIC ED 180 380.

Hill, Brian. "Multi-Disciplinary Courses: Mush or Muscle?" *Australian University,* May 1976, pp. 48–57.

Hinden, Michael, "Bridges: A Modest Proposal to Connect the Disciplines," *Liberal Education,* 70 (Spring 1984), 13–16.

Hirst, Paul H. *Knowledge and the Curriculum: A Collection of Philosophical Papers.* London. Routledge and Kegan Paul, 1974.

Hopkins, T.L. *Integration: Its Meaning and Application.* New York: Appleton Century Crofts, 1937.

Howe, E., et al. "The Development of an Interdisciplinary Social Planning Concentration." *Journal of Education for Social Work,* 16 No. 1 (1980), 13–18.

Huber, Curtis E. "The Dynamics of Change: A Core Humanities Program." *Liberal Education,* 63 (May 1977), 159–70.

Huckaba, C.E., and A. Griffin, "The Infusion of Socio-Humanistic Concepts Into Engineering Courses via Horizontal Integration of Subject Matter." *Chemical Engineering Education,* 17 No. 2 (1983), 74–76.

Hughes, L.J., J.W. Frank, and A.T. Wilson. "Origin of Life: An Interdisciplinary Course in Chemical Evolution for Undergraduates." *Journal of Chemical Education,* 55 No. 8 (1978), 521–24.

"A Humanistic Perspective on the Professions." *Change, The Magazine of Higher Learning,* Aug. 1978, pp. 40–41.

*Humphreys, Les. "Concepts of Unified Education." *Unified Studies Report,* 1:3 (1974). Boston, Mass.: Boston State College. ERIC ED 118 037.

*———. "Interdisciplinarity: A Selected Bibliography for Users." Resource Directory Number 1. Change in Liberal Education Project. January 1976. ERIC ED 115 536.

*———. "Resources for Renewal: Interdisciplinarity." *Change in Liberal Education.* 1977. An Action Research Project for the Renewal of Undergraduate Liberal Education. ERIC ED 167 002.

*Hursh, Barbara, Paul Haas, and Michael Moore. "An Interdisciplinary Model to Implement General Education." *Journal of Higher Education,* 54 (1983), 42–59.

"IDS. (Interdisciplinary Studies in General Education): A Program for the 1980's," Orlando, Fla.: Valencia Community College, 1980. ERIC ED 207 635.

Improving College and University Teaching, 30 No. 1 (1982). Issue on interdisciplinary studies.

Interdisciplinarity. Papers presented at the Society for Research into Higher Education, European Symposium on Interdisciplinary Courses in European Education, held at City University, London, Sept. 1975. Surrey: SRHE at the University of Surrey, 1977. ERIC ED 165 212. See especially Rolf Schulmeister, "Methodological Issues in Evaluating Interdisciplinary Studies."

Interdisciplinarity, Problems of Teaching and Research in Universities. Paris: Organization for Economic Cooperation and Development, 1972.

"Interdisciplinary Approaches to University Physics." *Physics in Technology,* 9 No. 2 (1978), 92.

Jackel, Susan. "Making Connections." *Journal of Canadian Studies* (Canada), 15 No. 3 (Fall, 1980), 34–38.

Jencks, Christopher, and David Riesman. *The Academic Revolution.* New York: Doubleday, 1968.

Jenkins, Evan. "A Guided Tour through the Academic Mind." *Change, The Magazine of Higher Learning,* 6 (Aug. 1978), 11–14. Report on teaching.

*Josephs, Mary Jim. "Curricular Integration: Mortar for the Ivory Tower." *Current Issues in Higher Education,* 2 (1981), 5–8.

Kahne, Stephen. "Introducing Systems Concepts to All University Students." *Engineering Education,* 70 (Feb. 1980), 427–29.

Kantor, Kenneth J. "The English Curriculum and the Structure of the Disciplines." *Theory into Practice,* 22 No. 3 (1983), 174–81.

Kells, H.R., and C.T. Stewart. "An Experiment in Intercollegiate Interdisciplinary Doctoral Study." *Journal of General Education,* 20 (Apr. 1968), 1–12.

Killian, C. Rodney, and Catherine M. Warrick. "Steps to Abstract Reasoning: An Interdisciplinary Program for Cognitive Development." *Alternative Higher Education: The Journal of Non-Traditional Studies,* 4 (Spring 1980), 189–200.

*Klein, Thomas, and Jack Nachbar. "In Search of Technology." *Science, Technology, and Society* [Curriculum Newsletter of the Lehigh University STS Program], 29 (1982), 1–9.

*Kockelmans, Joseph J., ed. *Interdisciplinarity and Higher Education.* University Park: Pennsylvania State Univ. Press, 1979.

Kornfield, Milton. "A New Opportunity for General Education." *Alternative Higher Education: The Journal of Non-Traditional Studies,* 3 (Summer 1979), 254–59.

LaBianca, D.A. "An Interdisciplinary Approach to Science and Literature." *Journal of Chemical Education,* 52 No. 1 (1975), 66–67.

———. "A Non-Traditional Science Laboratory for the Non-Science Major." *Journal of Chemical Education,* 57 No. 3 (Mar. 1980), 198–99.

———. "Science for the Non-Science Major through Interdisciplinary Study: The Interrelationship of Science and Art." *Science Education,* 59 (1975), 187–90.

———, and W.J. Reeves. "Chemistry and Detective Fiction: An Interdisciplinary Program for the Nonscience Major." *Journal of Chemical Education,* 58 No. 9 (1981), 683–86.

Langerak, Edward. "An Interdisciplinary Experiment in Values Education." *Teaching Philosophy,* 1 (Fall 1976), 423–33.

Langford, Thomas A. "A Model for Interdisciplinary Study in the Fine Arts." *Journal of Aesthetic Education,* 16 No. 3 (1982), 115–18.

Larson, R.C. "Challenges for a Geography Instructor in an Interdisciplinary Public Affairs Program." *Journal of Geography,* 2 (1980), 70–72.

Leacock, Robert A., and Harold I. Sharlin. "The Nature of Physics and History: A Cross-Disciplinary Inquiry." *American Journal of Physics,* 45 No. 2 (1977), 146–53.

Lee, Calvin. "Knowledge Structure and Curriculum Development." *Educational Record,* 47 (1966), 347–60.

Lerner, Lawrence S., and Edward A. Gosselin. "Physics and History as a Bridge across the 'Two-Cultures' Gap." *American Journal of Physics,* 43 No. 1 (1975), 13–17.

Lesher, J.H. "An Interdisciplinary Course on Classical Athens." *Teaching Philosophy,* 5 No. 3 (1982), 203–10.

Levensky, Mark. "Trying Hard: Interdisciplinary Programs at the Evergreen State College." *Alternative Higher Education,* 2 (Fall 1977), 41–46.

*Levin, Lennart, and Ingemar Lind, eds. *Inter-Disciplinarity Revisited: Re-Assessing the Concept in the Light of Institutional Experience.* Stockholm: OECD/CERI, Swedish National Board of Universities and Colleges, Linköping University, 1985.

Levine, Donald. "The Physical Sciences among the Liberal." Paper presented at the Symposium on Undergraduate Education in Chemistry and Physics at the University of Chicago, 18 Oct. 1985.

Liberal Education. Spring 1979. Special issue on interdisciplinary education.

Lieberman, Janice E. "The Pathology of Innovation." *Liberal Education,* 62 No. 3 (1976), 380–84.

Lind, Joan Dyste. "Confusion, Conflict: Cooperation?" *Improving College and University Teaching,* 30 No. 1 (1982), 17–22.

Lindemann, S.K. "Philosophy and Mathematics: An Interdisciplinary Experiment." *Teaching Philosophy,* 2 No. 3–4 (1977–78), 321–22.

Lindner, Carl M. "The Industrial Society Program at the University of Wisconsin-Parkside," *Liberal Education,* 60 No. 3 (1974), 340–47.

Lingren, Wesley E., and Robert C. Hughson. "Chemistry in a Large, Multidisciplinary Laboratory." *Journal of Chemical Education,* 59 No. 12 (1982), 1018–20.

Logan, Richard D. "Bridging the Traditional and Non-Traditional: A Model for Higher Education." *Liberal Education,* 69 No. 3 (1983), 233–43.

Lombardo, Joseph. "Possible Basis: Interdisciplinary Approach to Philosophy." *Aitia,* 1 (Dec. 1973), 6–9.

Lowry, George G. "An Integrated Physics-Chemistry Curriculum for Science Majors." *Journal of Chemical Education,* 46 (June 1969), 393–95.

Lumsden, C.J., L.E.H. Trainor, and M. Silverman. "Physical Theory in Biology: Interdisciplinary Course." *American Journal of Physics,* 47 No. 4 (1979), 302–08.

Lutz, John E. "The Potential for Improving Science Education through Transdisciplinary Integration with Art Education." Paper presented at the 49th meeting of the National Association for Research in Science Teaching, San Francisco, Calif., 23–25 Apr. 1976. ERIC ED 127 139.

Lyman, Richard W. "New Trends in Higher Education: The Impact on the University Library." *College and Research Libraries,* 33 No. 4 (1972), 298–304.

Lynch, James. "Recent Integrative Trends in Further Education in England and Wales." *International Review of Education,* 24 (1978), 177–85.

MacAndrew, Donald A. "Measuring Growth in an Interdisciplinary Humanities Course." *English Journal,* 69 No. 2 (1980), 52–56.

McCormack, A.J., and T. Smucker. "Biology and Art: Interdisciplinary Challenges." *American Biology Teacher,* 44 No. 2 (1982), 112–15.

*McGrath, Earl M. "Interdisciplinary Studies: An Integration of Knowledge and Experience," *Change, The Magazine of Higher Learning,* Aug. 1978, pp. 6–9.

Magada, Virginia, and Michael Moore. "The Humanities Cluster College at Bowling Green State University: Its Middle Years." *Liberal Education,* 62 (Mar. 1976), 100–112.

Magery, Susan. "Women's Studies in Australia: Towards Trans-disciplinary Learning." *Journal of Educational Thought,* 17 No. 2 (1983), 162–71.

*Maher, Thomas. "Creating Connections: An Experiment in Interdisciplinary Education." Report of a project sponsored by FIPSE and Wichita State University, 1981–84.

Malcolm, A., et al. "A Comparison of English-Language Skill Improvement between Interdisciplinary and Non-Interdisciplinary English Classes." *American Annals of the Deaf,* 3 (1980), 435–38.

Marx, Leo. "Amherst's Kenan Colloquium: Can We Create Together What We Can't Create Alone?" *Change,* 7 No. 6 (Summer 1975), 30–38.

*Mayville, William. *Interdisciplinarity: The Mutable Paradigm.* Washington, D.C.: American Association for Higher Education, 1978.

*Meeth, L. Richard. "Interdisciplinary Studies: A Matter of Definition." *Change, The Magazine of Higher Learning,* Aug. 1978, p. 10.

*Milicic, Vladimir. *Symposium on Interdisciplinary Aspects of Academic Disciplines.* Bellingham: Western Washington University, 1973.

Miller, A.J. "Interdisciplinary Graduate Program of the Institute of Paper Chemistry." *Abstracts of Papers of the American Chemical Society,* Apr. 1979, p. 103.

*Miller, Marjorie C. "On Making Connections," *Liberal Education,* 69 No. 2 (1983), 101–07.

Mohrig, J.R., and Nancy M. Tooney. "Biochemistry in the Undergraduate Curriculum: An Interdisciplinary Course." *Journal of Chemical Education,* 46 No. 1 (1969), 33–35.

*Mohrman, Kathryn, et al., eds. "Integrating Sciences and Humanities." *Forum for Liberal Education,* May 1979. ERIC ED 172 614.

Moline, Lorraine G., et al. "Standpoints: A Model for Common Learning." Paper presented at the Conference of the Association for General and Liberal Studies. Rochester, N.Y., 5–7 Nov. 1981. ERIC ED 210 072.

Monts, J.K., M.S. Lynn, and C.S. Burrus. "Interdisciplinary Instruction on Dynamic Simulation of Social Systems." *Teaching Sociology,* 4 No. 4 (1977), 315–32.

Moore, L.D. "Improving Graduate Education in Plant Physiology through an Interdisciplinary Approach." *National Association of College Teachers of Agriculture Journal,* 27
No. 1 (1983), 27–29.

Morehouse, Ward. "The Challenge of Intellectual Provincialism in the Colleges," *Educational Record,* 47 (Spring 1966), 263–74.

Morgan, George. "A New Interdisciplinary Curriculum." In *New Teaching, New Learning.*
Ed. G. Smith. San Francisco: Jossey-Bass, 1971, pp. 70–71.

Morrison, James L., and Tamara Swora. "Interdisciplinarity and Higher Education," *Journal of General Education,* 26 (Apr. 1974), 45–52.

Morton, Richard K. "Interdepartmental Relationships." *Improving College and University
Teaching,* 13 (Spring 1965), 116–17.

Murchland, Bernard. "The Liberal Arts and Career Education," *Thought, A Review of Culture and Idea,* 65 No. 225 (1982), 196–204.

Musil, Robert K. "Teaching in a Nuclear Age." *Teachers College Record,* 84 No. 1 (1982),
79–101.

Nae, N., A. Hofstein, and D. Samuel. "Chemical Industry: A New Interdisciplinary Course
for Secondary Schools." *Journal of Chemical Education,* 57 No. 5 (1980), 366–68.

Nash, Philip C., and Grant L. Voth. "GENTRAIN: An Instructional Delivery System at
Monterey Peninsula College." *Liberal Education,* 65 No. 1 (1979), 45–52.

Nauta, Doede. "Toward an Interdisciplinary Reconstruction of Frameworks." In *Graduate
Studies, Texas Tech University,* ed. Kenneth L. Ketner. Lubbock: Texas Tech Press,
pp. 121–26.

Neal, C.E. "Where We Have Been . . . Where Are We Going?" *Journal of Aerospace Education,* 4 No. 2 (1977), 8–9.

Nelson, Rex A. " Polydisciplinary Approach for the General Study Area of Higher Education." Monograph, Mar. 1973. ERIC ED 088 768.

*Newell, L. Jackson, and Karen I. Spear. "New Directions for Academic Careers: Rediscover-
ing Intrinsic Satisfactions." *Liberal Education,* 69:2 (Summer 1983), 109–116.

Newell, William H. "Interdisciplinary Curriculum Development in the 1970's: The Paracol-
lege at St. Olaf and the Western College Program at Miami University." In *Against the
Current: Reform and Experimentation in Higher Education,* ed. Richard M. Jones and
Barbara Leigh Smith. Cambridge: Schenkman, 1984, pp. 127–47.

*———. "The Role of Interdisciplinary Studies in the Liberal Education of the 1980's." *Lib-
eral Education,* 69 No. 3 (1983), 245–55.

*———, ed. and comp. *Interdisciplinary Undergraduate Programs: A Directory.* Oxford,
Ohio: Association for Integrative Studies, 1986.

*———. "Interdisciplinary Studies are Alive and Well." *Association for Integrative Studies
Newsletter,* 10 No. 1 (1988), 1, 6–8.

*———, and William J. Green. "Defining and Teaching Interdisciplinary Studies." *Improv-
ing College and University Teaching,* 30 No. 1 (1982), 23–30.

*Nicholson, Carol. "Post-Modernism and the Present State of Integrative Studies: A Reply
to Benson and His Critics." *Issues in Integrative Studies,* 5 (1987), 19–34. See also response by William Newell, "The Case for Agreement about Interdisciplinarity," 35–39.

*[*Proceedings from the . . . Annual Conference on*] *Non-Traditional and Interdisciplinary
Programs.* Fairfax, Va.: Department of Continuing Education, George Mason University. A series of published papers from annual national conferences under the editor-
ship of James Fonseca and, later, Kathleen McGuinness.

Noonan, John F. "The Impact of Curricular Change on Faculty Behavior." *Liberal Education,* 57 No. 3 (1971), 344–58.

Norton, Frank, and Marjorie White. "January Term." *American Biology Teacher,* 38 No. 5 (1976), 297–98.

*O'Callaghan, Phyllis. "Graduate Liberal Studies: Graduate Liberal Arts." In *Non-Traditional Graduate Education: A Frontier for the 1980's,* ed. James W. Fonseca. Fairfax, Va.: George Mason University, 1985, pp. 28–36.

Ogren, P.J., and D.L. Bunse. "An Interdisciplinary Course in Art and Chemistry." *Journal of Chemical Education,* 48 No. 10 (1971), 681–82.

Ohmer, Milton. *Alternatives to the Traditional.* San Francisco: Jossey-Bass, 1973.

*Palmer, James C. "Interdisciplinary Studies: An Eric Review." *Community College Reivew,* 11 No. 1 (1983), 59–64.

*Parker, Alice, and Elizabeth A. Meese. "A Re-valuation of Values through Interdisciplinary and Team Teaching." University of Alabama Teaching-Learning Center, Monograph Series, Summer 1976.

Parsons, M.H. "A Sense of Perspective: Four Years of Experience with an Integrated Humanities Course for Career Students." Paper presented at the conference "Whatever Happened to the Humanities?" Catonsville, Md., 1978. ERIC ED 156 281.

Pecorino, Philip. "Philosophy and Interdisciplinary Studies." *Aitia,* 4 No. 5 (1976/77), 10–14.

Peel, Malcolm L., and Leo L. Nussbaum. "The Core Course Redivius." *Liberal Education,* 60 No. 4 (1974), 478–88.

Perren, G.E., et al., eds. "Interdisciplinary Approaches to Language." Centre for Information on Language Teaching. Papers read at a conference held in London, England, 4–6 Apr. 1971. ERIC ED 054 696.

Peterson, G. "Integrating a Professional Program in an Interdisciplinary Environmental Studies Program." *Journal of Environmental Education,* 9 No. 2 (1978), 37–47.

Peterson, Roy P., and Stephen K. Hall. "Environmental Education for the Non-Science Major." *Science Education,* 58 (Jan./Mar. 1974), 57–63.

Petr, Jerry C. "Can Progress toward Interdisciplinary Education Be Built on a Disciplinary Base?" *Issues in Integrative Studies,* 1 (1982), 68–78.

Pezaro, P., et al. "Chemistry of Rocks and Minerals: New Interdisciplinary Curriculum for Secondary Schools." *Journal of Chemical Education,* 55 No. 6 (1978), 383–85.

Pfuister, A.O. *The Influence of Departments and Disciplinary Perspectives on Curriculum Formation.* Toledo, Ohio: Center for the Study of Higher Education, University of Toledo, 1969.

*Phenix, Philip. "Use of the Disciplines as Curriculum Content," *Educational Forum,* 26 (1962), 273–80.

Pitzl, Gerald R. "Revitalizing Interdisciplinary Offerings." 15 Nov. 1977. ERIC ED 173 306.

*Porter, Arthur. "The Expansion of Interdisciplinary Studies." *Transactions of the Royal Society of Canada,* 11 (1973), 11–20.

*Potter, George. "The Promise of Interdisciplinarity and Its Problems." *Ramapo Papers,* 1 (1977), 1–23.

Prange, W.W., et al. *Tomorrow's Universities: A Worldwide Look at Educational Change.* Boulder: Westview Press, 1982. ERIC ED 232 488.

Press, Harriet Baylor. "Basic Motivation for Basic Skills: The Interdependent Approach to Interdisciplinary Writing." *College English,* 41 (Nov. 1979), 310–13.

*Pring, Richard. "Curriculum Integration." *Proceedings of the Philosophy of Education Society of Great Britain, Supplemental Issue,* 5 No. 2 (1971), 170–200.

"A Program for Integrative Education: Satisfying the Search for Unity." *Change,* Aug. 1978, pp. 44–45.

Radest, Howard B. "On Interdisciplinary Education." In *The Philosophy of the Curriculum: The Need for General Education,* ed. Sidney Hook, Paul Kurtz, and Miro Todorovich. Buffalo, N.Y.: Prometheus, 1975, pp. 227–33.

Ratcliffe, G. "Crossdisciplinary Courses for Polytechnics." *Physics Education,* 10 (June 1975), 272–73.

"Reflections on Interdisciplinary Studies." *Southern Humanities Review,* 15 (Winter 1981), 26–31.

Rhyner, C.R., et al. "The Chemistry-Physics Program at the University of Wisconsin–Green Bay." *American Journal of Physics,* 42 (Dec. 1974), 1106–11.

Riesman, David. *Constraint and Variety in American Education.* New York: Doubleday, 1958.

Ritcheson, Charles R. "The Southwestern Consortium for History Education: A Model of Interdisciplinary and Interinstitutional Cooperation." *History Teacher,* 6 No. 2 (1973), 219–26.

Robbins, Larry M. "Integrating Communication Instruction in the Wharton MBA Curriculum." *ABCA Bulletin,* 42 (Sept. 1979), 1–2.

Romey, William D. "Transdisciplinary Problem-Centered Studies: Who Is the Integrator?" *School Science and Mathematics,* 75 No. 1 (1975), 30–38.

Rosenthal, L.A. "A Course in Technology for Non-Technology Students," *Engineering Education,* 64 (1974), 270–72.

———. "Technics: A Course in Technology for Art Students," *Engineering Education,* 61 (1971), 281–83.

Salder, W.A., Jr. "Tapping the Potentials of Interdisciplinary Studies in a Freshman Core Program." Unpublished paper, 1978. ERIC ED 167 231.

Saeger, Wain. "Interdisciplinary (That Much Abused Word)." *Teaching-Learning Issues,* 30 (Winter 1976), 1–30.

*Salmon-Cox, Leslie, and Burkhart Holzner. "Managing Multidisciplinarity: Building and Bridging Epistemologies in Educational R&D." Paper presented at the American Education Research Association in New York, 4–8 Apr. 1977. ERIC ED 135 760.

Salmon, Wesley C. "Philosopher in a Physics Course." *Teaching Philosophy,* 2 No. 2 (1977), 139–46.

Sanacore, J. "Interdisciplinary Strategies, Independent Study, and Career Planning." *Phi Delta Kappan,* 59 No. 6 (1978), 403–04.

Sanford, Nevitt. "The Human Problems Institute and General Education." *Daedalus,* Summer 1965, 642–62.

Sbaratta, P.A. "The Interdisciplinary Cornucopia." Paper presented at the Annual Conference on English in the Two Year College, Baltimore, Md., 1981. ERIC ED 211 156.

Scheinman, L. "Science and Society at Cornell: Interdisciplinary Excursion." *Bulletin of the American Physical Society,* 25 No. 1 (1980), 20.

Scott, Peter. "The Rediscovery of the Liberal University: Popular Higher Education in a Post-Industrial World." *Soundings,* 64 (Spring 1981), 5–28.

Secrest, Leigh. "The Rationale for Polydisciplinary Programs." Address to the Ninth Annual Meeting of the Council of Graduate Schools in the United States, Washington, D.C. Dec. 1969. ERIC ED 037 151.

Shapiro, Beth J., and John Whaley, eds. *Selection of Library Materials in Applied and Interdisciplinary Fields.* Chicago: American Library Association, 1987.

Shaplin, Judson T., and Henry F. Olds, Jr. *Team Teaching,* New York: Harper & Row, 1964.

Shaw, Gary C., and William D. Crist. "An Interdisciplinary Team Teaching Experiment." *Improving College and University Teaching,* 21 No. 2 (1973), 159–60.

Sheppard, Nathaniel, Jr. "A Thematic Approach to Concerns of the Future." *Change, The Magazine of Higher Learning,* Aug. 1978, pp. 30–33.

Short, E., and T. Jennings, Jr. "Multidisciplinarity: An Alternative Approach to Curriculum Thought." *Educational Leadership,* 33 No. 8 (1976), 590–94.

Shumway, Keith C. "Collegiality, Community, and the Climate for Learning at Ottawa University. Final Report to the National Endowment for the Humanities." Ottawa University, Kans. ERIC ED 089 613.

Simpson, M.H. "Faculty Requirements for an Interdisciplinary Environmental Sciences Engineering Curriculum." *Journal of Environmental Sciences,* 21:4 (1978), 19–22.

Singleton, Rivers, Jr., "Interdisciplinary Teaching with Humanists: Reflections of a Biological Scientist." *Perspectives in Biology and Medicine,* 26 No. 2 (1983), 304–14.

*――――, and Heyward D. Brock. "Teaching Bioethics from an Interdisciplinary Perspective." *American Biology Teacher,* 44 No. 5 (1982), 280–85, 313.

Sladky, J.F. "Engineering Design Education: A Multidisciplinary Perspective." *Mechanical Engineering,* 104 No. 9 (1982), 54–57.

Slaughter, John B. "Interdisciplinary Science for the Future." *Interdisciplinary Science Reviews,* 8 No. 2 (1983), 105–07.

Soundings, 54 No. 1 (1971), 82–123. Issue on experimental interdisciplinary programs.

Southern Regional Education Board. "Interdisciplinary Explorations in the South." *Regional Spotlight,* 2 (Dec. 1976).

Spratlen, Thaddeus H. "The Educational Relevance of Black Studies: An Interdisciplinary and Inter-Cultural Interpretation." *Western Journal of Black Studies,* 1 (Mar. 1977), 38–45.

Spurlock, Karla J. "Toward the Evolution of a Unitary Discipline: Maximizing the Interdisciplinary Concept in African/Afro-American Studies." *Western Journal of Black Studies,* 1 (Sept. 1977), 224–28.

Stafford, Roger. "Green Bay's Interdisciplinary Faculty." *Change,* 4 (Apr. 1972), 20–22.

Stansfield, Charles A., Jr. "Using Census Data in Geography-Oriented Interdisciplinary Social Studies, *Social Studies,* 63 No. 5 (1972), 202–08.

Stevens, W.F., and J.B. Cohen. "A Synergistic Approach for Freshman Engineers." *Engineering Education,* 64 (1974), 577–79, 583.

Sullivan, Malachy R. "The Implementation of the Integration Program in a Catholic Liberal Arts College." *Proceedings of the Catholic American Philosophical Association,* 24 (1950), 58–61.

Takakura, Sho. "Innovation of Higher Education in Japan." In *Comparative Approaches to Higher Education.* Hiroshima: Research Institute for Higher Education, Hiroshima University, 1983, pp. 101–03.

Taylor, Alastair. "Education and the Search for Order." *Main Currents in Modern Thought,* 27 No. 4 (1971), 125–31.

*――――. "Integrative Principles and the Educational Process." *Main Currents in Modern Thought,* 25 No. 5 (1969), 126–33.

Teachers College Record, 73 No. 2 (1971). Special Issue: "Curriculum: Interdisciplinary Insights."

Thomas, D.E. "An Interdisciplinary Course in Real-Time Computing." *IEEE Transactions on Education,* 24 No. 1 (1981), 69–74.

Thompson, Lee. "International Environmental Problems." *International Educational and Cultural Exchange,* 7 (Summer 1971), 61–66.

Thoroughman, Thomas V. "Values and Issues: The Humanities Program at Wofford College." *Liberal Education,* 65 No. 1 (1979), 98–110.

Toombs, William. "Interdisciplinarity in General Education: Problems in Curriculum Design." Paper Presented in Caracas, Venezuela, May 1980. ERIC ED 188 572.

"Tracking Civilization on Gentrain: Snapshots of Global History." *Change, The Magazine of Higher Learning,* Aug. 1978, 38–39.

Travis, Thomas, Peter A. Facione, and James L. Litwin. "Beyond the Core Curriculum: An Outcomes Approach to General Education." *Liberal Education,* 64 No.4 (1978), 435–46.

Troutman, Benjamin I., Jr. "An Interdisciplinary Approach to Curriculum and Instruction: From Purpose to Method." *Clearing House,* 50 (Jan. 1977), 200–201.

*Trow, Martin. "Interdisciplinary Studies as a Counterculture: Problems of Birth, Growth, and Survival," *Issues in Integrative Studies,* 4 (1984–85), 1–15.

Trumbore, C.N. "A Chemistry Course for Non-Science Majors Based upon Student Concerns." *Journal of Chemical Education,* 52 No. 7 (1975), 450–51.

Vander Wilt, R.B. "Student-Faculty Cooperation in an Interdisciplinary Experiment." *National Association of Student Personnel Administration Journal,* 8 (1970), 115–18.

Vatanno, Frank J., and Robert W. Titley. "An Interdisciplinary Seminar for Preparing College Teachers." *Improving College and University Teaching,* Apr. 1977, pp. 197–203.

Von Blum, Paul. "Marginality, Survival or Prosperity: Interdisciplinary Education in Large Research Universities—Berkeley and U.C.L.A." In *Against the Current: Reform and Experimentation in Higher Education,* ed. Richard M. Jones and Barbara Leigh Smith. Cambridge, Massachusetts: Schenkman, 1984. Pp. 227–48.

Walsh, W.B., G.L. Smith, and M. London. "Developing an Interface between Engineering and the Social Sciences: An Interdisciplinary Team Approach to Solving Societal Problems." *American Psychologist,* 30 (1975), 1067–71.

Walton, John. "A Confusion of Contexts: The Interdisciplinary Study of Education." *Educational Theory,* 24 (Summer 1974), 219–29.

Warriner, Helen P. "Foreign Language Interdisciplinary Programs and Activities." In *Britannica Review of Foreign Language Education,* ed. Dale L. Lange. Chicago: Encyclopedia Britannica, 1971, vol. 3.

Weaver, Frederick S. "Academic Disciplines and Undergraduate Liberal Arts Education." *Liberal Education,* 67 No. 2 (1981), 151–65.

*———. "Inquiry, Interdisciplinary Study, and Minor Programs of Study." *Issues in Integrative Studies,* 4 (1986), 37–55.

Weidner, E. "Interdisciplinarity and Higher Education." *International Journal of Environmental Studies,* 5 (1973), 205–14.

Wenner, Gene C. "Interdisciplinary Approaches to Teaching and Learning: Where Do the Arts Fit?" *Arts Education,* 29 (Nov. 1976), 4–8.

———. "Interdisciplinary Courses: Mythology and Methodology." *Arts Education,* 26 No. 6 (1973), 19–21.

*White, Alvin, ed. *Interdisciplinary Teaching.* San Francisco: Jossey Bass, 1981. No. 8 in the New Directions for Teaching and Learning Series.

White, William A. "[Interdisciplinary Studies:] A Case Study of Three Approaches." *Improving College and University Teaching,* 30 No. 1 (1982), 31–33.

Wiebe, Paul. "Knowledge, The Disciplines, and the University." *Soundings,* 65 (Fall 1982), 292–315.

Wiley B. "The Intercurriculuar Studies Division: An Interdisciplinary Success." 1981. ERIC ED 207 643.

Wilson, John. "Orthodox, General, or Integrated?" *University Quarterly,* 21 (1967), 445–52.

Wilson, R.S. "Bridging the Gap between Technology and the Humanities." *Engineering Education,* 63 (1973), 349–51.

Winquist, Robert B. "What are Transdisciplinary Principles?" *Issues in Integrative Studies,* 1 (1982), 49–67.

Winthrop, Henry. *Education and Culture in the Complex Society: Perspectives on Interdisciplinary and General Education.* Tampa: Univ. of South Florida Press, 1979.

*———. "Methodological and Hermeneutic Functions in Interdisciplinary Education." *Educational Theory,* 14 (Apr. 1964), 118–27.

———. "New World-A-Coming: Can Academia Adapt?" *Systematics,* 7 No. 3 (1969), 189–208.

————. "Specialization and Intellectual Integration in Liberal Education." *Educational Theory,* 17 (Jan. 1967), 25–31.

Wise, Gene. "Integrative Education for the Disintegrated World." *Teachers College Record,* 67 (1966), 391–401.

Wolman, M. Gordon. "Interdisciplinary Education: A Continuing Experiment." *Science,* 25 Nov. 1977, pp. 800–804.

Wooton, Lutian R., et al. "A Response to Student Needs for Knowledge and Innovations in Education." *Contemporary Education,* 50 (Spring 1979), 166–68.

"Workshop on Interdisciplinary Education: Kentucky January Prototype. Proceedings." University of Kentucky, 15–17 Apr. 1975. Lexington, Ky., 17 Apr. 1975, College of Allied Health Professions, ERIC ED 129 134.

Zander, Arlen R. "Science and Fiction: An Interdisciplinary Approach." *American Journal of Physics,* 43 No. 1 (1975), 9–12.

Zipko, S.J. "An Interdisciplinary Approach to Forestry Education." *American Biology Teacher,* 45 No. 7 (1983), 387–92.

Zoller, U. "Smoking and Cigarette-Smoke: Innovative, Interdisciplinary, Chemically-Oriented Curriculum." *Journal of Chemical Education,* 56 No. 8 (1979), 518–19.

The Humanities

Including American Studies, Language and Literature, Linguistics, Philosophy, Religion

Aiken, H.D. "A Pluralistic Analysis of Aesthetic Value." *Philosophical Review,* 59 (1950), 493–513.

Alexander, R.J. "Towards a Multidisciplinary View of Language: Some Biolinguistic Reflections," *Linguistiche Berichte,* 25 (1973), 1–21.

Babossov, Evgueni. "Man as a Subject of Interdisciplinary Studies." Trans. Nina Godneff and Barbara Thompson. *Diogenes,* 104 (Winter 1978), 23–35.

*Bailis, Stanley. "The Social Sciences in American Studies: An Integrative Conception." *American Quarterly,* 26 No. 3 (1974), 202–24.

Barricelli, Jean-Pierre, and Gibaldi, Joseph. *Interrelations of Literature.* New York: The Modern Language Association of America, 1982.

Barricelli, Jean-Pierre, et al., "The Place of Comparative Literature in Interdisciplinary Studies: A Symposium." *Yearbook of Comparative and General Literature,* 24 (1975), 36–55.

*Barzun, Jacques. "Cultural History as a Synthesis." In *The Varieties of History: From Voltaire to the Present.* London: Macmillan, 1956, 1970, pp. 387–402.

Baxter, Annette. "Women's Studies and American Studies: The Uses of the Interdisciplinary." *American Quarterly,* 26 No. 4 (1974), 433–39.

Bayerl, Elizabeth. *Interdisciplinary Studies in the Humanities: A Directory.* Metuchen, N.J.: Scarecrow Press, 1977.

Beck, James P. "Theory and Practice of Interdisciplinary English." *English Journal,* 69 No. 2 (1980), 28–32.

———. *"Thinking* across the Curriculum." *California English,* Jan.-Feb. 1982.

Bird, Donald Allport. "A Theory for Folklore in Mass Media: Traditional Patterns in the Mass Media." *Southern Folklore Quarterly,* 40 No. 3-4 (1976), 285–305.

Blancke, Nelson Manfred, and John A. Hague. "How to Learn History from Sinclair Lewis and Other Uncommon Sources." In *American Character and Culture in a Changing World: Some Twentieth Century Perspectives,* ed. John A. Hague. Westport, Conn.: Greenwood Press, 1979, pp. 111–23.

Blumenhagen, Kathleen O'Connor, and Walter D. Johnson, eds. *Women's Studies: An Interdisciplinary Collection.* Westport, Conn.: Greenwood Press, 1978. Contributions in Women's Studies, No. 2.

Bonaparth, Ellen. "Evaluating Women's Studies: Academic Theory and Practice." In *Women's Studies. An Interdisciplinary Collection,* ed. Kathleen O'Connor Blumhagen and Walter Johnson. Westport, Conn.: Greenwood Press, 1978.

*Booth, Wayne C. *Critical Understanding: The Power and Limits of Pluralism.* Chicago: Univ. of Chicago Press, 1979.

Bostock, William. "The Boundary between Languages and the Social Sciences." *Journal of the Australian Federation of Modern Language Teachers' Association,* 11 (April 1975), 14–18.

Boxer, Marilyn J. "For and About Women: The Theory and Practice of Women's Studies in the United States." *Signs,* 7 No. 3 (1982), 661–95.

Briere, Eugene J. "Communicative Competence, Variable Rules, and Interdisciplinary Research," In *Research in Second Language Acquisition,* ed. Robin C. Scarcella and Stephen F. Krashen. Rowley, Mass.: Newbury, 1981.

*Brooks, Anne, and Un-chol Shin. "Past, Present, and Future of Interdisciplinary Humanities." *Humanities Education,* September 1984, pp. 3–9.

Brown, Linda Keller. "American Studies at Douglass College: One Vision of Interdisciplinarity." *American Quarterly,* August 1975, pp. 342–53.

Burgarski, Ranko. "The Interdisciplinary Relevance of Folk Linguistics." In *Progress in Linguistic Historiography,* ed. Konrad Koerner. Amsterdam: Benjamin, 1980, pp. 381–93.

Burke, Kenneth. *Language as Symbolic Action: Essays on Life, Literature, and Method.* Berkeley: Univ. of California Press, 1966.

*Casey, Beth A. "The Quiet Revolution: The Transformation and Reintegration of the Humanities." *Issues in Integrative Studies,* 4 (1986), 71–92.

Caughey, John L. "The Ethnography of Everyday Life: Theories and Methods for American Studies." *American Quarterly,* 34 (Bibliography Issue) (1982), 222–43.

*Cluck, Nancy A. "Reflections on the Interdisciplinary Approaches to the Humanities." *Liberal Education,* 66 No. 1 (1980), 67–77.

Cowan, Michael. "The National Humanities Institute: The First Year." *American Quarterly,* 28 No. 3 (1976), 378–86.

Crane, R.S. *The Idea of the Humanities.* Chicago: Univ. of Chicago Press, 1967.

Dagron, Gilbert. "Inaugural Lecture at the Collège de France." *Social Science Information,* 16 No. 3/4 (1977), 261–78.

*Davis, Walter A. *The Act of Interpretation: A Critique of Literary Reason.* Chicago: Univ. of Chicago Press, 1978. See especially chapter 3, "Critical Theory and Philosophical Method."

Davis, W.E., and P.E. Richter. "Integrating Science and Humanities: A Modular Approach." *Journal of College Science Teaching,* 10 No. 3 (January 1981), 176–77.

Deely, John. *Introducing Semiotics: Its History and Doctrine.* Bloomington: Indiana Univ. Press, 1980.

Deguise, Pierre. *Symposium on Romanticism: An Interdisciplinary Meeting.* New London: Connecticut College, 1977.

Den Ouden, Bernard D. *Language and Creativity: An Interdisciplinary Essay in Chomskyan Humanism.* Lisse, Netherlands: Ridder, 1975.

*Dihle, Albrecht. "Interdisciplinary Scholarship in the Humanities: The *Reallexikon,*" *Interdisciplinary Science Reviews,* 11 No. 2 (1986), 107–109.

Donnell, Carol A. and William Duignan. "Synaesthesia and Aesthetic Education." *Journal of Aesthetic Education,* 11 (July 1977), 69–85.

Dorenkamp, Angela G. "Resisting Closure: Integrating the Humanities and Social Sciences." Paper presented at the thirteenth annual meeting of the College English Association in Houston, Texas, 15–17 April 1982. ERIC ED 217 492.

Eco, Umberto. "Semiotics: A Discipline or an Interdisciplinary Method?" In *Sight, Sound, and Sense,* ed. Thomas A. Sebeok. Bloomington: Indiana Univ. Press, 1980.

*Eighteenth Century Life, 5 No. 3 (1979). Special issue. See especially Richard B. Schwartz, "Contextual Criticism and the Question of Pedagogy"; Arthur H. Scouten, "The Limitations of the Interdisciplinary Approach"; and David Sheehan, "Pope and Palladio, Hogarth and Fielding: Kinds of Discipline in Interdisciplinary Studies."

Eliade, Mircea. "Religion." *International Social Science Journal,* 29 No. 4 (1977), 615–27.

*English Journal, 65 (October 1976). See articles on the humanities and interdisciplinary studies.

Feaver, J. Clayton, and W. Horosz, eds. *Religion in Philosophical and Cultural Perspective: A New Approach to the Philosophy of Religion through Cross-Disciplinary Studies.* Princeton, N.J.: Van Nostrand, 1967.

"A Feminist Perspective in the Acadamy: The Difference It Makes," ed. Elizabeth Langland and Walter Gove. Special Issue of *Soundings,* 64 No. 4 (1981). Appears also as a book under the same title and editors. Chicago: University of Chicago Press, 1983.

Ferguson, Priscilla Parkhurst, Philippe Desan, and Wendy Griswold. "Editors' Introduction: Mirrors, Frames, and Demons: Reflections on the Sociology of Literature." *Critical Inquiry,* 14 (Spring 1988), 421–30.

**Finestone, Harry, and Michael F. Shugrue, eds. *Prospects for the 70's: English Departments and Multidisciplinary Study.* New York: Modern Language Association, 1973.

Fishman, J.A. *The Sociology of Language: An Interdisciplinary Social Science Approach to Language in Society.* Rowley, Mass.: Newbury House, 1972.

Fishwick, Marshall, ed. *American Studies in Transition.* Philadelphia: Univ. of Pennsylvania Press, 1964.

Fukumoto, Hajime. "The Interdisciplinary Relation between Linguistics and Neurophysiology." In *Annual Reports of Studies,* 22 (1971), 287–313. Doshisha Women's College of Liberal Arts.

Galinsky, G.K. "The First Interdisciplinary Field." *ADFL Bulletin,* 13 No. 1 (1981), 29–30.

Garcia, E. "Interdisciplinary Humanistic Research and the Arts and Humanities Citation Index." *Proceedings of the American Society for Information Science,* 18 (1981), 319.

Garfield, Eugene. "Is Information Retrieval in the Arts and Humanities Inherently Different from That in Science? The Effect that ISI's Citation Index for the Arts and Humanities Is Expected to Have on Future Scholarship." *Library Quarterly,* 50 No. 1 (1980), 40–57.

Georgetown University Round Table on Language and Literature. Washington, D.C.: Georgetown Univ. Press, 1974. Special section on linguistics and other disciplines.

*German Quarterly, 62 No. 2 (1989). *Germanistik* as German Studies. Interdisciplinary Theories and Methods.

Gerstenberger, Donna, and Carolyn Allen. "Women's Studies/American Studies, 1970–1975." *American Quarterly,* 29, Bibliography Issue (1977), 262–79.

Glueck, Grace. "Clashing Views Reshape Art History," *New York Times,* 20 Dec. 1987, Section 2:1, pp. 22–23.

Goian, Ion. "Ethnoreligion: An Interdisciplinary Approach." *Philosophie et Logique,* 26 (January–March 1982), 51–56.

Good, Stephen H. and Olaf P. Tollefsen. *Interdisciplinary Essays.* Emmitsburg, Md.: Mt. St. Mary's College, 1973.

Greenberg, J.M. "Interdisciplinary Perspective in African Linguistic Research." *African Studies Bulletin,* 9 No. 1 (1966), 8–23.

Greene, Maxine. "Real Toads and Imaginary Gardens." In *Humanities and the Social Studies.* Bulletin No. 44. Ed. Thomas F. Powell. Washington, D.C.: National Council for the Social Studies, 1969, pp. 15–29.

*Grele, Ronald. "A Surmisable Variety: Interdisciplinarity and Oral Testimony." *American Quarterly,* 27 (Aug. 1975), 275-95.

Griffith, William B. "The Relevance of Professional Philosophy." *Metaphilosophy,* 13 (July/ Oct. 1982), 181-200.

Gunderson, Doris V. *Language and Reading: An Interdisciplinary Approach.* Washington D.C.: Center for Applied Linguistics, 1970.

Hall, Stuart. "Cultural Studies and the Centre: Some Problematics and Problems." In *Culture, Media, Language,* ed. Stuart Hall, et al. London: Hutchinson, 1984, pp. 16-47.

Heelan, Patrick A. "The Need for Pluralism in Academic Philosophy Today." *Main Currents in Modern Thought,* 28 (Sept.-Oct. 1971), 26-27.

Heim, Michael, R. "Some Philosophical Proposals for the Role of the Humanities: Toward a Postmodern Logic." *Kinesis,* 9 (Spring 1979), 39-46.

*Hermand, Jost, and Evelyn Torton Beck. *Interpretive Synthesis: The Task of Literary Scholarship.* New York: Ungar, 1975.

Hoagland, Sarah. "On the Reeducation of Sophie." *Social Science Journal,* 14 No. 2 (1977), 15-22.

*Hufford, David J. "Psychology, Pschoanalysis, and Folklore." *Southern Folklore Quarterly,* 38 No. 3 (1974), 187-97.

Hymes, D. "Why Linguistics Needs the Sociologist." *Social Research,* 34 No. 4 (1967), 632-37.

Ihde, Don, and Richard M. Zaner. *Interdisciplinary Phenomenology.* The Hague: Nijhoff, 1977.

James, A.R. "Compromisers in English: A Cross-Disciplinary Approach to Their Interpersonal Significance." *Journal of Pragmatics,* 7 No. 2 (1983), 191-206.

Jones, W.T. *The Sciences and the Humanities: Conflict and Reconciliation.* Berkeley: Univ. of California Press, 1965.

Kelly, L.G. "Modus Significandi: An Interdisciplinary Concept." *Historiographia Linguistica,* 6 (1979), 159-80.

Kelly, R. Gordon. "Literature and the Historian." *American Quarterly,* 26 (1974), 141-59.

Koenigsberger, Dorothy. *Renaissance Man and Creative Thinking: A History of Concepts of Harmony, 1400-1700.* Atlantic Highlands, N.J.: Humanities Press, 1979.

Kolodny, Annette. "Dancing through the Minefield: Some Observations on the Theory, Practice, and Politics of a Feminist Literary Criticism." *Feminist Studies,* 6 (Spring 1980), 1-25.

Krakowiak, J. "An Interdisciplinary Conference on Creativity." *Dialectics and Humanism,* 4 (Spring 1977), 99-103.

Krieger, Murray, ed. *The Aims of Representation: Subject/Text/History.* New York: Columbia Univ. Press, 1987.

Landry, David M. "American Studies: Its Development and Status as a Discipline." *Southern Quarterly,* 13 No. 2 (1975), 151-57.

Lauer, Janice. "Studies of Written Discourse: Dappled Discipline." Address to the Rhetoric Society of America. Presented at the 34th Meeting of the Conference on College Composition and Communication in Detroit, Mich., on 17 March 1983.

Leavenworth, May. "A Suggestion for an Interdisciplinary Approach to Ethics." *Zygon,* 8 (June 1973), 135-46.

*Lenz, Guenther H. "American Studies—Beyond the Crisis?: Recent Redefinitions and the Meaning of Theory, History, and Practical Criticism." *Prospects, Annual of American Cultural Studies,* 7 (1982), 53-113.

Lewis, Anthony J. "Interdisciplinary Approaches to Shakespeare Studies." *Shakespearean Research and Opportunities: The Report of the MLA Conference,* 7-8 (1972-74), 53-60.

McAndrew, D. "Measuring Growth in an Interdisciplinary Humanities Course." *English Journal,* 69 No. 2 (1980), 52–56.

*McKeon, Richard. "The Uses of Rhetoric in a Technological Age: Architectonic Productive Arts." In *The Prospect of Rhetoric,* ed. Lloyd F. Bitzer and Edwin Black. Englewood Cliffs, N.J.: Prentice Hall, 1971, pp. 44–63.

Malone, David H. "Comparative Literature and Interdisciplinary Research." *Synthesis: Bulletin du Comité National de Litterature Comparée de la République Socialiste de Roumanie,* 1 (1974), 17–26.

Marcell, David W. "Characteristically American: Another Perspective on American Studies." *Centennial Review,* 21 No. 4 (1977), 388–400.

———. "Recent Trends in American Studies in the United States." *American Studies: An International Newsletter,* 8 No. 1 (1970), 5–12.

Marder, Daniel. "The Interdisciplinary Discipline." *ADE Bulletin,* 45 (May 1975), 29–31.

Martensen, Daniel F. "Concerning the Ecological Matrix of Theology." *Zygon: Journal of Religion and Science,* 5 No. 4 (1970), 353–369.

Martindale, Colin. "Sit with Statisticians and Commit a Social Science: Interdisciplinary Aspects of Poetics." *Poetics: International Review for the Theory of Literature,* 7 (1978), 273–82.

Maruyama, Magorah. "Philosophy as an Open Meta-Science of Interdisciplinary Cross-Induction." *Dialectica,* 16 No. 4 (1962), 361–84.

Marx, Leo. "American Studies: A Defense of an Unscientific Method." *New Literary History,* 1 No. 1 (1969), 76–90.

Matthews, Fred. "Polemical Palefaces and Genteel Redskins: The Debate over American Culture and the Origins of the American Studies Movement." *American Quarterly,* 35 No. 5 (1983), 76–90.

Mechling, Jay. "If They Can Build a Square Tomato: Notes toward a Holistic Approach to Regional Studies." *Prospects,* 4 (1979), 59–78.

Mechling, Jay, Robert Meredith, and David Wilson. "American Culture Studies: The Discipline and the Curriculum." *American Quarterly,* 25 No. 4 (1973), 363–89.

Meeker, Joseph W. "The Imminent Alliance: New Connections among Art, Science, and Technology." *Technology and Culture,* 19 (Apr. 1978), 187–98.

Melczer, William. "The War of the Carrots and the Onions; or, Concentration versus Dispersion: The Methodology of Interdisciplinary Studies Applied to the European Courts." In *The Expansion and Transformation of Courtly Literature,* ed. Nathaniel B. Smith and Joseph T. Snow. Athens: Univ. of Georgia Press, 1980.

*Messmer, Michael W. "The Vogue of the Interdisciplinary." *Centennial Review,* 12 No. 4 (1978), 467–78.

Michelfeld, Ted. "An Interdisciplinary Approach to Science Fiction." *Ramapo Papers,* 2 No. 1 (1978), 1–33.

Miller, Joan. *French Structuralism: A Multidisciplinary Bibliography.* New York: Garland, 1981.

Mink, Louis O. "History and Fiction as Modes of Comprehension." *New Literary History,* 1 (Spring 1970), 541–64.

Minshull, Roger. "The Functions of Geography in American Studies." *Journal of American Studies* (Great Britain), 7 No. 3 (1973), 267–78.

Mitchell, W.J.T. "Critical Inquiry and the Ideology of Pluralism." *Critical Inquiry,* 8 No. 4 (1982), 609–18.

Mitroff, I., and R.D. Mason. "Dialectical Pragmatism: A Progress Report on an Interdisciplinary Program of Research on Dialectical Inquiring Systems." *Synthese,* 47 No. 1 (1981), 29–42.

Munsey, Brenda. "Multidisciplinary Interest in Moral Development." In *Moral Develop-*

ment, Moral Education, and Kohlberg. Ed. Brenda Munsey, Birmingham, Ala.: Religious Education Press, 1980, pp. 1–11.

Murray, Elwood. "An Operational Meta-Language for Interdisciplinary Cross-Cultural Communications." *Eco-logos* (Incorporates *Biophilist and International Language Reporter*), 17 No. 1x (1971), 1, 3, 5–9.

Nash-Webber, Bonnie, and Roger Schank. *Theoretical Issues in Natural Language Processing.* Cambridge, Mass.: Mathematical Society Sciences Board, Yale University, 1975.

Nauta, Doede. "Toward an Interdisciplinary Reconstruction of Frameworks." In *Graduate Studies Texas Tech. University.* Ed. Kenneth L. Ketner. Lubbock: Texas Tech. Press, 1981, pp. 121–26.

New Literary History, 12 No. 1 (1980). Special Section on Psychology and Literature: Some Contemporary Directions.

O'Kell, Robert. "The Victorian Counter Culture: An Interdisciplinary Conference." *Victorian Studies,* 17 No. 4 (1974), 431–35.

Orchard, Cecil C. "Recent Trends in Cultural Studies: The New American Approach." *Cultures, Aspects of Culture in Modern Society* (France), 2 No. 2 (1975), 143–55.

Ornstein, Jacob. "Toward an Inventory of Interdisciplinary Tasks in Research on U.S. Southwest Bilingualism/Biculturalism." In *Bilingualism in the Southwest,* ed. Paul R. Turner. Tucson: Univ. of Arizona Press, 1973, pp. 321–39.

*Parsons, Talcott. "Theory in the Humanities and Sociology." *Daedalus,* Spring 1970, 495–523.

Paulson, William R. *The Noise of Culture: Literary Texts in a World of Information.* Ithaca: Cornell University Press, 1988.

Peckham, Morse. "Victorian Counterculture." *Victorian Studies.* 18 No. 3 (1975), 257–76.

Petrus, Leon C. "The Word as Metaphor: An Interdisciplinary Theory." *Soundings,* 55 (1972), 269–91.

Praz, Mario. *Mnemosyne: The Parallel Between Literature and the Visual Arts.* Princeton: Princeton Univ. Press, 1970.

Prior, M.E. *Science and the Humanities.* Evanston, Ill.: Northwestern Univ. Press, 1963.

Puka, Bill. "An Interdisciplinary Treatment of Kohlberg." *Ethics,* 92 (Apr. 1982), 468–90.

Pulgram, E. "Sciences, Humanities, and the Place of Linguistics." *Linguistics,* 53 (1969), 70–92.

Rajnath, Metah, ed. *Twentieth Century American Criticism: Interdisciplinary Approaches.* New Delhi, India: Gulab Vazirani for Arnold Heinemann, 1977. See especially Jonathan Culler, "American Interdisciplinary Criticism, 1940-1974," pp. 17–30.

Raval, Sesh. *Metacriticism.* Athens: Univ. of Georgia Press, 1981.

*"Reading the Bible: An Interdisciplinary Experience." A special section of *Issues in Integrative Studies,* 5 (1987). Christopher Becker, "An Introductory Comment: Integration, Cultural and Academic," 69–75; Mary Savage, "Controversy and Canon in the Undergraduate Humanities Curriculum: The Example of Biblical Studies," 77–90; Stephen Gottlieb, "Reading the Bible, Writing the Self: George Herbert's *The Temple,*" 91–103; Christopher Becker, "Origen: Reading as Discipline and as Sacrament," 105–28.

Ricoeur, Paul, et al. *The Rule of Metaphor: Multi-Disciplinary Studies of the Creation of Meaning in Language.* Toronto: Univ. of Toronto Press, 1978. University of Toronto Romance Series, No. 37.

Ritsch, Frederick F. "A New Emphasis for the Humanities." *Humanities in the South,* 40 (1974), 2–3, 7–8.

Royce, Joseph R. *The Encapsulated Man: An Interdisciplinary Essay on the Search for Meaning.* Princeton, N.J.: Van Nostrand, 1964.

Said, Edward. *The World, the Text, and the Critic.* Cambridge: Harvard Univ. Press, 1983.

*———. *Orientalism.* New York: Pantheon Books, 1978. See also "Orientalism Reconsidered." *Cultural Critique,* 1 (Fall 1985), 89–107.

*Saint Clair, Robert. "On the Nature of Interdisciplinary Linguistics." Lektos: Interdisciplinary Working Papers in Language Series, vol. 1, no. 2. Louisville, Ky.: Interdisciplinary Program in Linguistics (Oct. 1975), ERIC ED 123 887.

Salomone, Ronald E. "The Humanities: Interconnections," *Teaching English Language Arts,* 11 No. 2 (1985), ERIC ED 254 850.

Schoeck, Richard J. "The Ironic and the Prophetic: Towards Reading More's Utopia as a Multidisciplinary Work." *Albion,* 10 Suppl. (1978), 124–34.

Schwadron, Abraham A. "Comparative Music Aesthetics: Toward a Universality of Musicality." *Music Man,* 1 (December 1973), 17–31.

Sederberg, Peter, and Nancy B. Sederberg. "Transmitting the Nontransmissable: The Function of Literature in the Pursuit of Social Knowledge." *Philosophy and Phenomenological Research,* 35 No. 2 (1975), 173–96.

Sheridan, H.W., and B.A. Hill, *Widening the Circle: The Humanities in American Education. A Report of the Wingspread Conference on the Humanities in Higher Education.* Washington, D.C.: Association of American Colleges, 1981. ERIC ED 216 648.

Singer, Peter. "Ethics and Sociobiology." *Philosophy and Public Affairs,* 11 (Winter 1982), 40–64.

Sklar, Robert. "The Problem of an American Studies 'Philosophy': A Bibliography of New Directions." *American Quarterly,* 27 No. 3 (1973), 245–46.

Soundings, 58 No. 2 (1975). Special Issue on Structuralism: An Interdisciplinary Study. See especially Susan Wittig, "Structuralism: An Interdisciplinary Study."

Spiller, Robert E. "Unity and Diversity in the Study of American Culture: The American Studies Association in Perspective." *American Quarterly,* 25 No. 5 (1973), 611–18.

Steinberg, Danny D., and Leon A. Jakobovits. *Semantics: An Interdisciplinary Reader in Philosophy, Linguistics, and Psychology.* Cambridge: Cambridge University Press, 1971.

Stevenson, Leslie. "Applied Philosophy." *Metaphilosophy,* 1 No. 3 (1970), 258–67.

Stock, Brian. "Literary Discourse and the Social Historian." *New Literary History,* 8 No. 2 (1977), 183–94.

Stone, James H. "Integration in the Humanities: Perspectives and Prospects." *Main Currents in Modern Thought,* 26 No. 1 (1969), 14–19.

Teeter, K.V. "Linguistics and Anthropology." *Daedalus,* 102 No. 3 (1973), 87–97.

*Thorpe, James, ed. *Relations of Literary Study: Essays on Interdisciplinary Contributions.* New York: Modern Language Association, 1967.

Turner, Frederick. *Natural Classicism: Essays on Literature and Science.* New York: Paragon House, 1985.

Vandamme, F. "On Negation, An Interdisciplinary Study." *Logique et Analyse,* 15 (Mar./ June 1972), 39–98.

Vercruysee, Jeroom. "Why the Enlightenment: An Introduction." *Arizona Quarterly,* 31 No. 2 (1975), 104–105.

Walker, W.B. "Art Libraries: International and Interdisciplinary." *Special Libraries,* 69 No. 12 (1978), 475–81.

Wallace, Dawn. "Finding the Common Ground." *English Journal,* 69 No. 2 (1980), 24–61. Special issue on interdisciplinary English.

Walzer, Judith B. "New Knowledge or a New Discipline? Women's Studies at the University." *Change, The Magazine of Higher Learning,* Apr. 1982, pp. 21–23.

Warriner, Helen P. "Foreign Language Interdisciplinary Programs and Activities." In *Britannica Review of Foreign Language Education,* ed. Dale L. Lange. Chicago: Encyclopedia Britannica, 1971, vol. 3.

Weigl, E., and M. Bierwisch. "Neuropsychology and Linguistics: Topics of Common Research." *Foundations of Language,* 6 No. 1 (1970), 1–18.

White, Hayden. "The Absurdist Movement in Contemporary Literary History." *Contemporary Literature,* 17 No. 3 (1976), 378-403.

*——. *Metahistory: The Historical Imagination in Nineteenth-Century Europe.* Baltimore: Johns Hopkins Univ. Press, 1973.

*White, James Boyd. *The Legal Imagination: Studes in the Nature of Legal Thought and Expression.* Boston: Little, Brown, 1973.

Winthrop, H. "The Interdisciplinary Nature of the Sociology of Religion." *Sociologia Religiosa,* 15-16 (1967), 59-68.

*Wise, Gene. "Some Elementary Axioms for an American Culture Studies." *Prospects, The Annual of American Cultural Studies,* 4 (Winter 1978), 517-47.

*Wolff, Michael. "Victorian Study: An Interdisciplinary Essay." *Victorian Studies,* 8 No. 1 (1964), 59-70.

Zagrando, Joanne Schneider. "Women's Studies in the United States: Approaching Reality." *American Studies International,* 14 No. 1 (1975), 15-36.

History

*Abrams, Philip. "History, Sociology, Historical Sociology." *Past and Present,* 87 (May 1980), 3-16.

Alagoa, E.J. "The Inter-disciplinary Approach to African History in Nigeria." *Présence Africaine,* 94 (1975), 171-83.

Alagoa, E.J. "The Relationship between History and Other Disciplines." *Tarikh* (Nigeria), 6 No. 1 (1978), 12-20.

Albrecht-Carrie, René. "The Social Sciences and History." *Social Education,* 16 (1952), 315-18.

Appleby, Andrew. "Disease, Diet, and History." *Journal of Interdisciplinary History,* 8 No. 4 (1978), 725-35.

Arzt, Donna. "Psychohistory and Its Discontents." *Biography,* 1 No. 3 (1978), 1-36.

Berkhofer, R.F., Jr. *A Behavioral Approach to Historical Analysis.* New York: Free Press, 1969.

Bourne, L.S. "The Centre for Urban and Community Studies." *Urban History Review* (Canada), 78 no. 2 (1978), 100-104.

*Braudel, Fernand. *On History.* Trans. Sarah Matthews. Chicago: University of Chicago Press, 1980.

Brown, Richard Harvey, and Stanford M. Lyman, eds. *Structure, Consciousness, and History.* Cambridge: Cambridge University Press, 1978.

Bryson, R.A., and C. Padoch. "On the Climates of History." *Journal of Interdisciplinary History,* 10 (1980), 583.

Challener, R.D., and M. Lee, Jr. "History and the Social Sciences: The Problem of Communications." *American Historical Review,* 60 (1956), 331-38.

Clough, Shepard B. "A Half Century in Economic History: Autobiographical Reflections." *Journal of Economic History,* 30 No. 1 (1970), 4-17.

Cohen, Charles. "Essays on Metapsychology." *History and Theory,* 17 No. 1 (1978), 113-20.

Cohn, Bernard S. "History and Anthropology: The State of Play." *Comparative Studies in Sociology and History* (Great Britain), 22 No. 2 (1980), 198-221.

Cook, Charles O., and James Friguglietti. "History, Literature, and the Franco-American War: An Interdisciplinary Methodology." *Proceedings of the Annual Meeting of the Western Society for French History,* 8 (1980), 11-19.

Darnton, Robert. *The Great Cat Massacre and Other Episodes in French Cultural History.* New York: Vintage Books, Random House, 1985.

Ebner, Michael H. "Urban History: Retrospect and Prospect." *Journal of American History,* 68 No. 1 (1981), 69–84.

Embree, Ainslie T. "Studies in Indian History." *Journal of Interdisciplinary History,* 2 No. 4 (1972), 477–82.

Emteen, George. "History and the Social Sciences: Emerging Patterns." *History of European Ideas* (Great Britain), 1 No. 4 (1981), 345–66.

Fichtner, Paula Sutter. "Dynastic Marriage in the Sixteenth Century Habsburg Diplomacy and Statecraft: An Interdisciplinary Approach." *American Historical Review,* 81 No. 2 (1976), 243–65.

Fox-Genovese, Elizabeth, and Eugene D. Genovese. "The Political Crisis of Social History." *Journal of Social History,* 10 No. 2 (1976), 205–20.

Frederickson, George M. "Two Southern Historians." *American Historical Review,* 75 No. 5 (1970), 1387–92.

Goranov, Krastio. "History and The Sociology of Art." *International Social Science Journal* (France), 33 No. 4 (1981), 611–23.

Gordon, Martin. "American Military History." *American Studies International,* 15 No. 1 (1976), 3–16.

Graff, Harvey J. *Literacy in History: An Interdisciplinary Research Bibliography.* New York: Garland, 1981.

Graham, Otis L. "The Seventeenth Annual Meeting of the Organization of American Historians." *Journal of American History,* 64 No. 4 (1978), 1031–44.

*Hareven, Tamara. "The History of the Family as an Interdisciplinary Field." *Journal of Interdisciplinary History,* 2 No. 2 (1971), 399–414.

Harrigan, Patrick J. "Historians and Compilers Joined: The Historiography of the 1970's and the French Enquétes of the Nineteenth Century." *Historical Reflections* (Canada), 7 No. 2–3 (1980), 3–21.

Harth, Philip. "Clio and the Critics." *Studies in Eighteenth Century Culture,* 10 (1981), 3–15.

Hartman, Geoffrey H. "History Writing as Answerable Style." *New Literary History,* 2 No. 1 (1970), 73–84.

Hays, Samuel P. "History and Genealogy: Patterns of Change and Prospects for Cooperation." *Prologue,* 7 No. 1 (1975), 39–43.

Henretta, James. *The Evolution of American Society, 1700–1815: An Interdisciplinary Analysis.* Lexington, Mass.: Heath, 1973.

Hershberg, Theodore. "The New Urban History: Toward an Interdisciplinary History of the City." *Journal of Urban History,* 5 No. 1 (1978), 3–40.

*———, ed. *Philadephia: Work, Space, Family, and Group Experience in the Nineteenth Century. Essays toward an Interdisciplinary History of the City.* New York: Oxford University Press, 1981.

———. "Toward the Historical Study of Ethnicity." *Journal of Ethnic Studies,* 1 No. 1 (1973), 1–5.

"History of Planning Group: A Summary of Its Aims and Activities." *Urban History Review (Canada),* 76 No. 2 (1976), 89–94.

Hobsbawm, E.J. "From Social History to the History of Society." *Daedalus,* 100 No. 1 (1971), 20–45.

Holt, W. Stull. "History and the Social Sciences." *Kyklos,* 4 (1955), 389–96.

*Horn, T.C.R., and Harry Ritter. "Interdisciplinary History: A Historiographical Review," *History Teacher,* 19 No. 3 (1986), 427–48.

Hughes, H. Stuart. "The Historian and the Social Scientist." *American Historical Review,* 66 (1960), 20–46.

Hundert, E.J. "History, Psychology, and the Study of Deviant Behavior." *Journal of Interdisciplinary History,* 2 No. 4 (1972), 453–72.

Iggers, Georg G., and Harold T. Parker, eds. *International Handbook of Historical Studies: Contemporary Research and Theory.* Westport, Conn.: Greenwood Press, 1979.

Imhof, Arthur E., and Olivind Larsen. "Social and Medical History: Methodological Problems in Interdisciplinary Quantitative Research." *Journal of Interdisciplinary History,* 7 No. 3 (1977), 493–98.

Interdisciplinary Urban History Series. See individual titles in the series, published by Kennikat (Port Washington, N.Y.). Selected titles: *America and the New Ethnicity* (1979); *Cities and Schools in the Gilded Age: the Evolution of an Urban Institution* (1974); *The City in Southern History: The Growth of Urban Civilization in the South* (1977); *Franklin D. Roosevelt and the City Bosses* (1977); *From Main Street to State Street: Town, City, and Community in America* (1977); *The Paradox of Progressive Education: The Gary Plan and Urban Schooling* (1979): *Socialism and the Cities* (1975).

*Journal of Interdisciplinary History.

Kerridge, Eric. "British Field Systems." *Agricultural History Review.* (Great Britain) 24 No. 1 (1976), 48–50.

Kewenig, Wilhelm. "The Contribution of International Law to Peace Research." *Journal of Peace Research* (Norway), 10 No. 3 (1973), 227–34.

Kilunov, A.F. "The Use of Concrete Sociological Research in Historical Scholarship." *Soviet Studies in History,* 11 No. 4 (1973), 291–318.

Kinser, Samuel. "*Annaliste* Paradigm? The Geohistorical Structure of Fernand Braudel." *American Historical Review,* 86 (1981), 63–105.

Ladurie, Emmanual B. "Recent Historical 'Discoveries.'" *Daedalus,* 106 No. 4 (1977), 141–55.

*Lankford, John. "The Writing of American History in the 1960's: A Critical Bibliography of Materials of Interest to Sociologists." *Sociological Quarterly,* 14 No. 1 (1973), 99–126.

Laslett, Peter. "History and the Social Sciences." In *International Encyclopedia of the Social Sciences,* ed. David L. Sills. New York: Macmillan, The Free Press, 1968. Vol. 6, pp. 434–40.

Lauren, Paul Gordon, ed. *Diplomacy: New Approaches in History, Theory, and Policy.* New York: Free Press, 1979.

Lemarchand, René. "African Armies in Historical and Contemporary Perspectives: The Search for Connections." *Journal of Political and Military Sociology,* 4 No. 2 (1976), 261–75.

*Leontief, Wassily. "Note on the Pluralistic Interpretation of History and the Problem of Interdisciplinary Cooperation." *Journal of Philosophy,* 45 No. 23 (1948), 617–23.

*Lepenies, Wolf. "History and Anthropology: A Historical Appraisal of the Current Contact between the Disciplines." *Social Science Information,* 15 No. 213 (1976), 287–306.

*Lotchin, Roger W., and David J. Webber. "The New Chicano History: An Urban History Perspective." *History Teacher,* 16 No. 2 (1983), 219–47.

Lynch, Katherine A. "Local and Regional Studies in Historical Demography." *Historical Methods,* 15 No. 1 (1982), 23–29.

Macfarlane, Alan. "History, Anthropology, and the Study of Communities." *Social History* (Great Britain), 5 (1977), 631–52.

McGrew, R.E. "History and the Social Sciences." *Antioch Review,* 18 (1958), 276–89.

MacPherson, Mary. "Historiography: Its Implications for Building Library Collections." *Canadian Library Journal,* 33 No. 1 (1976), 39–45.

Mannion, John J. "Multidisciplinary Dimensions in Material History." *Material History Bulletin* (Canada), 8 (1979), 21–25.

Manuel, Frank E. "The Use and Abuse of Psychology in History." *Daedalus,* 100 No. 1 (1971), 187–213.

Mitchell, David J. "'Living Documents': Oral History and Biography." *Biography, An Interdisciplinary Quarterly,* 3 No. 4 (1980), 283–96.

Mitroff, I.I., and R.O. Mason. "Dialectical Pragmatism: A Progress Report on an Interdisciplinary Program of Research on Dialectical Inquiring Systems." *Synthese,* 47 (1981), 29–42.

Monkkonen, Eric H. "Blood and Space: More Studies of Nineteenth Century Crime and Justice." *Journal of Urban History,* 7 No. 2 (1981), 239–45.

Munro, William B. "Clio and Her Cousins." *Pacific Historical Review,* 10 (1941), 403–10.

Nemec, Thomas F., and Neil V. Rosenberg. "A Multi-Disciplinary Approach to the Reconstruction of the History and Culture of Rural Population: A Newfoundland Example." In *Folklore and Oral History,* ed. Neil V. Rosenberg. St. John's Memorial University of Newfoundland, 1978.

Newell, Dianne. "Published Government Documents as a Source of Interdisciplinary History: A Canadian Case Study." *Government Publications Review, Part A: Research Articles,* 8A No. 5 (1981), 381–93.

Patterson, James T. "The Uses of Techno-Psychohistory." *Journal of Interdisciplinary History,* 2 No. 4 (1972), 473–76.

Perry, P.J. "Agricultural History: A Geographer's Critique." *African History,* 46 No. 2 (1972), 259–67.

Rabb, Theodore K. "The Historian and the Climatologist." *Journal of Interdisciplinary History,* 10 No. 4 (1980), 831–37.

*————, and Robert I. Rotberg, eds. *Climate and History: Studies in Interdisciplinary History.* Princeton, N.J.: Princeton Univ. Press, 1981.

*————. *The Family in History, Interdisciplinary Essays.* New York: Harper and Row, 1971.

Reid, John G. "'The Beginnings of the Maritimes': A Reappraisal." *American Review of Canadian Studies,* 9 No. 1 (1979), 38–51.

Rurup, Reinhard. "Historians and Modern Technology: Reflections on the Development and Current Problems of the History of Technology." *Technology and Culture,* 15 No. 2 (1974), 161–93.

Rutman, Darrett B. "Notes on the Underground: Historiography," *Journal of Interdisciplinary History,* 3 No. 2 (1972), 373–83.

Schaeper, Thomas J. "Interuniversity Centre for European Studies. Centre Interuniversitaire d'études Européennes." *French Historical Studies,* 12 No. 1 (1981), 139–43.

Schumann, Hans-Gerd. "The Problem of Conservatism: Some Notes on Methodology." *Journal of Contemporary History* (Great Britain), 13 No. 4 (1978), 803–17.

Shapiro, Martin, and Barbara Shapiro. "Interdisciplinary Aspects of American Legal History." *Journal of Interdisciplinary History,* 4 No. 4 (1974), 611–26.

Sharlin, Allan N. "Historical Demography as History and Demography," *American Behavioral Scientist,* 21 No. 2 (1977), 245–62.

Small, Melvin, ed. *Public Opinion and Historians: Interdisciplinary Perspectives.* Detroit: Wayne State Univ. Press, 1970.

Smith, John David. *Black Slavery in the Americas: An Interdisciplinary Bibliography, 1865–1980.* 2 vols. Westport, Conn.: Greenwood Press, 1982.

Snell, B. "On the Unity of History." *Special Research,* 39 No. 4 (1972), 679–95.

The Social Sciences in Historical Study. Bulletin 64. Social Science Research Council, 1954, pp. 4–16.

Social Science Quarterly, 50 No. 1 (1969), 6–58. Special section on some convergences in history and sociology.

Stone, Albert E. "Visions and Versions of Childhood." In *American Character and Culture in a Changing World: Some Twentieth Century Perspectives,* ed. John A. Hague. Westport, Conn.: Greenwood Press, 1979, pp. 275–92.

Swierenga, Robert P. "Computers and Comparative History." *Journal of Interdisciplinary History,* 5 No. 2 (1974), 267–86.

Theilman, John M. "Crossing the Sacred Boundary between the Disciplines: Medieval History and Symbolic Anthropology." *Midwest Quarterly,* 24 No. 1 (1982), 28–38.

Tittler, Robert. "Recent Research in English Urban History, c. 1450–1650." *Urban History Review* (Canada), 11 No. 2 (1982), 31–39.

Waddell, Louis M. "The Thirteenth Annual Research Conference at Harrisburg." *Pennsylvania History,* 45 No. 4 (1978), 333–50.

Weaver, John. "Urban Canada: Recent Historical Writing." *Queen's Quarterly* (Canada), 86 No. 1 (1979), 75–97.

Weber, David J. "Mexico's Far Northern Frontier, 1821–1854: Historiography Askew." *Western Historical Quarterly,* 7 No. 3 (1976), 276–93.

Weber, Eugen. "About Marc Bloch." *American Scholar,* 51 No. 1 (1981–82), 73–82.

Weinstein, Allen. "The Sixty-Fifth Annual Meeting of the Organization of American Historians." *Journal of American Historians,* 60 No. 2 (1973), 373–408.

Wells, Robert V. "Birth Control: Different Conceptions." *Journal of Interdisciplinary History,* 10 No. 3 (1979), 511–16.

White, Hayden. "The Historical Text as Literary Artifact." *Clio,* 3 No. 3 (1974), 277–303.

———. "The Politics of Contemporary Philosophy of History." *Clio,* 3 No. 1 (1973), 35–54. See also W.H. Dray, "The Politics of Contemporary Philosophy of History," pp. 55–76.

Wiener, Philip P. "Centenary of A.O. Lovejoy's Birthday (October 10, 1873)." *Journal of the History of Ideas,* 34 (Oct.-Dec. 1973), 591–98.

The Social Sciences

Including Economics, Geography, Law, Political Science, General Systems

Ackoff, Russell L. "Systems, Organizations, and Interdisciplinary Research." *General Systems* (Yearbook), 5 (1960), 1-8.

Adams, John. "The Analysis of Rural Indian Economy: Economics and Anthropology." *Man in India,* 52 No. 1 (1972), 1-20.

Adler, L.L. "Plea for Interdisciplinary Cross-Cultural Research: Some Introductory Remarks." *Annals* [of the New York Academy of Sciences], 285 (Mar. 1977), 1-2.

Alexander, Jeffrey C. *The Modern Reconstruction of Classical Thought: Talcott Parsons.* Berkeley: Univ. of California Press, 1983.

Alker, H.R., K.W. Deutsch, and A.H. Stoetzel, eds. *Mathematical Approaches to Politics.* Amsterdam: Elsevier, 1973.

Allen, Richard, Terry Copp, and John H. Thompson, eds. *The Social Gospel in Canada: Papers of the Inter-Disciplinary Conference on the Social Gospel in Canada. March 21-24, 1973 at the University of Regina.* Ottawa: National Museum of Man, 1975. Mercury Series, No. 9.

Ambraseys, N.M. "A Test Case of Historical Seismicity: Isfahan and Cahar Mahal, Iran." *Geographical Journal* (Great Britain), 145 No. 1 (1979), 56-71.

American Behavioral Scientist, Sept./Oct. 1976. Political Decision Making: Interdisciplinary Development from a Microanalytic Perspective.

Andersson, L. "Interdisciplinary Study of Loneliness: With Evaluation of Social Contacts as a Means towards Improving Competence in Old Age." *Acta Sociologica,* 25 No. 1 (1982), 75-80.

Apostel, Leo. "The Difficulty and the Necessity of a Synthetic Theory of Action." *Communication and Cognition,* 9 No. 3-4 (1976), 377-417.

Apostle, C.N. "Is Sociology a Deviant of Economics?" *Journal of Human Relations.* 15 No. 2 (1967), 210-22.

Archibald, K.A. "Three Views of the Expert's Role in Policymaking: Systems Analysis, Incrementalism, and the Clinical Approach." *Policy Sciences,* 1 (1970), 73-86.

Ashby, W. Ross. "General System Theory as a New Discipline." *General Systems* (Yearbook), 3 (1958), 2-6.

Bahm, Archie J. "Holons: Three Conceptions." *Systems Research,* 1 No. 2 (1984), 145-50.

Bailey, K.D. "Equilibrium, Entropy and Homeostasis: A Multidisciplinary Legacy." *Systems Research* (GB), 1 No. 1 (1984), 25–43.

Bailliet, Gary Charles. "Economic Growth in Nineteenth-Century America: A Bibliography for an Inter-Disciplinary Studies Unit." *History Teacher,* 6 No. 4 (1973), 575–86.

Banton, Michael. "The Future of Race Relations Research in Britain: The Establishment of a Multidisciplinary Research Unit." *Race,* 15 No. 2 (1973), 221–29.

Battista, John R. "The Holistic Paradigm and General System Theory." *General Systems,* 22 (1977), 65–71.

*Baumann, Bedrich. *Imaginative Participation: The Career of an Organizing Concept in a Multidisciplinary Context.* The Hague: Martinus Nijhoff, 1975.

Becker, E. *The Structure of Evil: An Essay on the Unification of the Sciences of Man.* New York: Braziller, 1978.

*Bellah, Robert, et al. *Habits of the Heart: Individualism and Commitment in American Life.* Berkeley: Univ. of California Press, 1985.

Benedon, W. "Management in Information: Interdisciplinary Research." *Journal of Micrographics,* 12 No. 5 (1979), 293–99.

*Benson, Oliver, and Charles M. Bonjean. "The *Social Science Quarterly,* 1920–1970: A Case History in Organizational Growth." *Social Science Quarterly,* 50 No. 4 (1970), 806–25.

Berk, Richard A. "On the Compatibility of Applied and Basic Sociological Research: An Effort in Marriage Counseling." *American Sociologist,* 16 No. 4 (1981), 204–11.

Bernard, Harold W., and Wesley C. Huckins. *Exploring Human Development: Interdisciplinary Readings.* Boston, Mass.: Allyn and Bacon, 1972.

Bhola, H.S. "Theoretical Perspectives for Transdisciplinary Social Science Research." *Indian Educational Review,* 2 No. 2 (1967), 1–12.

*Binder, Arnold. "Criminology and Interdisciplinarity." *Issues in Integrative Studies,* 5 (1987), 41–67.

———. "A New Context for Psychology: Social Ecology." *American Psychologist,* 27 No. 9 (1972), 903–908.

*———, et al. "Social Ecology: An Emerging Multidiscipline." *Journal of Environmental Education,* 7 (1975), 32–43.

Blackburn, Richard S., and Michelle Mitchell. "Citation Analysis in the Organizational Sciences." *Journal of Applied Psychology,* 66 No. 3 (1981), 337–42.

Blanchard, Paul D. "Small Group Analysis and the Study of School Board Conflict: An Interdisciplinary Approach." *Small Group Behavior,* 6 No. 2 (1975), 229–37.

Blunt, P. "Methodological Developments in the Social Sciences: Some Implications for Interdisciplinary Study." *New Zealand Psychologist,* 10 No. 2 (1981), 55–70.

Borrie, W.D. "The Place of Demography in the Development of the Social Sciences," In *International Population Conference.* Liège: International Union for the Scientific Study of Population, 1973. Vol. 1.

Bostock, William. "The Boundary Between Languages and the Social Sciences." *Babel: Journal of the Australian Federation of Modern Language Teachers' Associations,* 11 (Apr. 1974), 14–18.

Boulding, Kenneth. "Economics and the Behavioral Sciences: A Desert Frontier." *Diogenes,* 15 (Fall 1956), 1–14.

———. "Peace Research." *International Social Science Journal* (France), 29 No. 4 (1977) 601–14.

*Brody, Alexander. Appendix: "Toward Integration of the Social Sciences." In Ralph Borsodi, *The Definition of Definition: A New Linguistic Approach to the Integration of Knowledge.* Boston: Porter Sargent, 1967, pp. 112–17.

Bronfenbrenner, Martin. "Radical Economics in America: A 1970 Survey." *Journal of Economic Literature,* 8 No. 3 (1970), 747–66.

Bronfenbrenner, Urie, and Edward C. Devereux. "Interdisciplinary Planning in Team Research on Constructive Community Behavior." *Human Relations,* 5 No. 2 (1952), 187–203.

Bulick, Stephen Lynn. *Structure and Subject Interaction: Toward a Sociology of Knowledge in the Social Sciences.* New York: Marcel Dekker, 1982.

*Bunge, Mario. "General Systems and Holism." *General Systems,* 22 (1977), 87–90.

———. "The Role of Forecast in Planning." *Theory and Decision,* 3 (1973), 207–21.

Cain, Stanley. "Can Ecology Provide the Basis for Synthesis among the Social Sciences?" In *Social Sciences and the Environment.* Ed. Morris E. Gurnsey and James R. Hibbs. Boulder: Univ. of Colorado Press, 1967, pp. 27–52.

Carlson, Eric T., and Simpson, Meribeth M. "Interdisciplinary Approach to the History of American Psychiatry." in *Psychiatry and Its History: Methodological Problems in Research,* ed. G. Mora and J.L. Brand. Springfield, Ill.: C.C. Thomas, 1970, pp. 119–48.

Carroll, Lucy. "Caste, Social Change, and the Social Scientist: A Note on the Ahistorical Approach to Indian Social History." *Journal of Asian Studies,* 35 No. 1 (1975), 63–84.

Cazden, Courtney B. "Subcultural Differences in Child Language: An Interdisciplinary Review." *Merrill-Palmer Quarterly,* 12 No. 3 (1966), 185–219.

"The Centre for Urban and Community Studies." *Urban History Review,* 2 No. 78 (1978), 100–104.

Cernea, M. "Sociology, Economic Psychology, and Economic Consciousness." *Rumanian Journal of Sociology,* 4–5 (1966), 207–15.

Charlesworth, James C., ed. *Integration of the Social Sciences through Policy Analysis.* Philadelphia: American Academy of Political and Social Science, 1972.

Claude, Richard Pierre. "Comparative Civil Liberties: The State of the Art." *Policy Studies Journal,* 4 No. 2 (1975), 175–80.

Cobb, Loren, and Ragade Rammohan. *Contributions to Applications of Catastrophe Theory in the Behavioral Sciences.* Louisville, Ky.: Society for General Systems Research, University of Louisville, 1978. See especially pp. i–ii, 291–419.

Cohen, Bernice. *The Cultural Science of Man: A New Synthesis.* London: Codek Publications, forthcoming. Vol. I: *The Seamless Web: Discovering Cultural Man;* Vol. II: *The Origin of Civilisation: An Explanation of Dynamic Cultural Change*; Vol. III: *Global Perspectives: The Total Culture System in the Modern World.*

Cope, Robert G. "Strategic Planning, Management, and Decision Making." AAHE-ERIC/Higher Education Research Report No. 9, 1981. Washington, D.C., American Association for Higher Education. ERIC ED 217 825.

*Crow, John E. "Interdisciplinary Research and Arid Lands Studies." *Social Science Journal,* 15 No. 3 (1978), 49–54.

Curlin, James A. "Fostering Understanding between Science and Law." *American Bar Association Journal,* 59 No. 2 (1973), 157–61.

Cutler, Neal E. "Demographic Social-Psychological and Political Factors in the Politics of Aging: A Foundation for Research in Political Gerontology." *American Political Science Review,* 71 No. 3 (1977), 1011–25.

Dahl, Robert A. "The Behavioral Approach in Political Science." *American Political Science Review,* 55 (1961), 771.

Daniel, Philip T.K. "Theory Building in Black Studies." *Black Scholar,* 12 No. 3 (1981), 29–36.

Dewey, Clive. "Annals of Rural Punjab." *Modern Asian Studies,* 10 No. 1 (1976), 131–38.

*Dinges, Norman. "Interdisciplinary Collaboration in Cross-Cultural Social Science Research." In *Research in Culture Learning: Language and Conceptual Studies,* ed. Michael P. Hamnett and Richard W. Brislin. Hawaii: East-West Center, Univ. of Hawaii Press, 1980, pp. 166–73. See also in *Topics in Culture Learning,* 5 (August 1977), 136–43.

*DiRenzo, Gordon J. "Toward Explanation in the Behavioral Sciences." In *Concepts, Theory and Explanation in the Behavioral Sciences,* ed. Gordon J. DiRenzo. New York: Random House, 1966, pp. 229–91.

Doornkamp, J.C., and K. Warren. "Geography in the United Kingdom, 1976–1980: Report to the 24th International Geographical Congress in Tokyo, Japan, In August 1980." *Geographical Journal* (Great Britain), 146 No. 1 (1980), 94–110.

Duncan, W. Jack, W.T. Edwards, and J. Wayne Flynt. "An Experiment in Large Group Interdisciplinary Investigations into Contemporary Social Issues." *Social Science,* 46 No. 4 (1971), 216–22.

Eadington, William R. *Gambling and Society: Interdisciplinary Studies on the Subject of Gambling.* Springfield, Ill.: Charles C. Thomas, 1976.

Eckhardt, William. "Changing Concerns in Peace Research and Education." *Bulletin of Peace Proposals* (Norway), 5 No. 3 (1974), 280–84.

Efron, Arthur. "The Mind-Body Problem in Lawrence, Pepper, and Reich." *Journal of Mind and Behavior,* 1 No. 2 (1980), 247–70.

Ehmke, I. "Results and Problems of Information Provision for the Management and Planning of Interdisciplinary Research Projects in Social Sciences." *International Forum on Information and Documentation,* 9 No. 4 (1984), 8–10.

Eulau, Heinz. *Behavioralism in Political Science.* New York: Atherton Press, 1969.

Fei, John C.H., et al. "An Experience of Interdisciplinary Approach to Research in Chinese Economic History." In *Modern Chinese Economic History: Proceedings of the Conference on Modern Chinese Economic History.* Taipei: Institute of Economic Academia Sinica, 1979, pp. 669–74.

Feldman, Laurence P., and Jacob Hornik. "The Use of Time: An Integrated Conceptual Model." *Journal of Consumer Research,* 7 No. 4 (1981), 407–19.

Ferber, Robert. "Uses of Applied Mathematics in Political Science." *Policy Studies Journal,* 2 No. 1 (1973), 48–51.

*Firestone, F.N. "Academic Structures and the Integration of the Social Sciences." In *Man in Systems,* ed. M. Rubin. New York: Gordon and Breach, 1971.

Fraser, J.T., ed. *The Voices of Time: A Cooperative Survey of Man's Views of Time as Expressed by the Sciences and by the Humanities.* New York: Braziller, 1966.

Friedrich, C.J., and M. Horwitz. "Some Thoughts on the Relations of Political Theory to Anthropology." *American Political Science Review,* 62 No. 2 (1968), 536–45.

Friend, Theodore. "Southeast Asia: Integration, Development, and the Terror of Time." *Journal of Interdisciplinary History,* 3 No. 3 (1973), 585–90.

Furbey, R.A. "An Examination of Some Influential Views on the Relationship between Sociology and History and the Use of Historical Material in Sociological Research." *Sociological Analysis* (Great Britain), 2 No. 3 (1972), 59–63.

Furtado, Celso. "Development." *International Social Science Journal,* 29 No. 4 (1977), 628–50.

Garcia, Gillian. "Credit Cards: An Interdisciplinary Inquiry." *Journal of Consumer Research,* 6 No. 4 (1980), 327–37.

*Geertz, Clifford. "Blurred Genres: The Refiguration of Social Thought." *American Scholar,* 49 No. 2 (1980), 165–79.

Ghaem-Maghami, F. "Toward an Interdisciplinary Model of Political Behavior: a New Approach." *Sociological Focus,* 6 No. 3 (1973), 1–22.

Gordon, Martin K. "American Military Studies." *American Studies International,* 15 No. 1 (1976), 3–16.

Graves, N.J. "Geography, Social Science, and Inter-Disciplinary Inquiry." *Geographical Journal,* 134 No. 3 (1968), 390–94.

Grinker, Roy, ed. *Toward a Unified Theory of Human Behavior: An Introduction to General Systems Theory.* New York: Basic Books, rpt. 1967.

Groh, Dieter, and Rolf-Peter Sieferle. "Experience of Nature in Bourgeois Society and Economic Theory: Outlines of an Interdisciplinary Research Project." Trans. Peter Vintilla. *Social Research,* 47 No. 3 (1980), 557–81.

Gudykunst, William B., et al. "An Analysis of an Integrated Approach to *Cross-Cultural Training." International Journal of Inter-Cultural Relations,* 1 (Summer 1977), 99–110.

*Hall, Robert B. *Area Studies: With Special Reference to Their Implications for Research in the Social Sciences.* Social Science Research Council Pamphlet No. 3 (1947).

Harris, Marvin. *Cultural Materialism: The Struggle for a Science of Culture.* New York: Vintage-Random House, 1980.

*Harvey, John H., ed. *Cognition, Social Behavior, and the Environment.* Hillsdale, N.J.: Lawrence Erlbaum, 1981. See especially Baruch Fischoff, "No Man is a Discipline," pp. 579–83.

Hediger, H. "Biological Glimpses of Some Aspects of Human Sociology." *Social Research,* 36 No. 4 (1969), 530–41.

Heims, Steve. "Encounter of the Behavioral Sciences with New Machine-Organism Analogies in the 1940's." *Journal of the History of the Behavioral Sciences,* 11 No. 4 (1975), 368–73.

———. "Gregory Bateson and the Mathematicians: From Interdisciplinary Interaction to Societal Functions." *Journal of the History of the Behavioral Sciences,* 13 No. 2 (1977), 141–59.

Herring, Fred H., Donald J. Mason, and John H. Doolittle. "The Virginia Opposum in Psychological Research." *Psychological Reports,* 19 No. 3 (1966), 755–57.

Hibbard, D.O., and R.J. Meadows. "Interdisciplinary Approach to Police Communication: Perspectives for Curriculum Development." *Police Chief,* 1 (1980), 62–66.

Hill, G.W. "Interdisciplinary Field Training for Social Change: Case Study for Psychology and Law." *American Journal of Community Psychology,* 7 No. 2 (1979), 223–30.

Holsti, O.R. "Historians, Social Scientists, and Crisis Management: An Alternative View." *Journal of Conflict Resolution,* 24 No. 4 (1980), 665–82.

Horn, Marilyn J., and Sharon Y. Nichols. "Interdisciplinary Research: Have We Lost Our Focus?" *Home Economics Research Journal,* 11 No. 1 (1982), 9–14.

"How 'Interdisciplinary' Are We at Chicago?" Document A in A Report on the Behavioral Sciences at the University of Chicago. Chicago: University of Chicago, 1954, pp. 64–83.

*Humphreys, S.C. "History, Economics, and Anthropology: The World of Karl Polanyi." *History and Theory,* 8 No. 2 (1969), 165–212.

*Hunter, Albert. "Why Chicago? The Rise of the Chicago School of Urban Social Science." *American Behavioral Scientist,* 24 No. 2 (1980), 215–27.

Huntington, Samuel P. "The Change to Change: Modernization, Development, and Politics." *Comparative Politics,* 3 No. 3 (1971), 283–322.

*Ichimura, Shinichi. "Interdisciplinary Research and Area Studies." *Journal of Southeast Asian Studies* (Singapore), 6 (Sept. 1975), 112–20.

International Social Science Journal, 16:4 (1964). Special issue on problems of surveying the social sciences and humanities.

**International Social Science Journal,* 20 (1968), 192–210. Special issue on multidisciplinary problem-focused research.

**International Social Science Journal,* 29 No. 4 (1977). Special issue on facets of interdisciplinarity.

Istock, C., and W. Rees. In *Towards the Urban Ecosystem: A Holistic Approach,* ed. F. Stearns and T. Montag. Stroudsburg, Pennsylvania, 1974.

Jackson, Maurice. "Toward a Sociology of Black Studies." *Black Scholar,* 1 (Dec. 1970).

Jacoby, Jacob, George J. Szybillo, and Carol K. Berning. "Time and Consumer Behavior: An Interdisciplinary Overview." *Journal of Consumer Research,* 2 No. 4 (1976), 320–39.

James, B.J. "Niche Defense among Learned Gentlemen." *Human Organization,* 30 (Fall 1971), 223–28.

*Jeffery, C.R. "Criminology as an Interdisciplinary Behavioral Science." *Criminology: An Interdisciplinary Journal,* 16 No. 2 (1978), 146–69.

Jeffery, I.A. "Advocates' Defense of an Interdisciplinary Perspective." *American Sociologist,* 14 No. 2 (1979), 118–19.

Jeffery, K.G. "Multidisciplinary Spatial Data Presentation." *Journal of the Geological Society,* 138 (July 1981), 495.

Juznic, S. "Some Questions of Method in Studying Developing Countries." *International Problems* (Yugoslavia) (1973), 89–100.

Kade, Gerhard. "Introduction: The Economics of Pollution and the Interdisciplinary Approach to Environmental Planning." *International Social Science Journal,* 22 No. 4 (1970), 561–725.

Kapp, K. William. *Toward a Science of Man in Society: A Positive Approach to Integration of Social Knowledge.* The Hague: Martinus Nijhoff, 1961.

Kates, Robert. "Geography: The Case for the Specialized Generalist." In *Social Sciences and the Environment.* Ed. Morris E. Gurnsey and James R. Hibbs. Boulder: Univ. of Colorado Press, 1967, pp. 53–76.

Kellner, Hanfried. "On the Sociolinguistic Perspective of the Communicative Situation." *Social Research.* 37 No. 1 (1970), 71–87.

Kilson, Martin. "Reflections on Structure and Content in Black Studies." *Journal of Black Studies,* 3 No. 3 (1973), 297–314.

Kimmel, Douglas C. *Adulthood and Aging: An Interdisciplinary Developmental View.* New York: John Wiley, 1974.

*Koopmans, Tjalling C. "Economics among the Sciences: Interaction Between Natural and Social Scientists." *American Economics Review,* 69 No. 1 (1979), 1–13.

Krishna, Daya. "Culture." *International Social Science Journal,* 29 No. 4 (1977), 651–70.

Kuhn, Alfred. "Dualism Reconstructed." *General Systems* (Yearbook), 22 (1977), 91–97.

*Kuhn, Alfred. *The Logic of Social Systems: A Unified Deductive, System-Based Approach to Social Science.* San Francisco: Jossey Bass, 1974.

*———. "A Manifesto for System-Based Unified Knowledge," and "A Unified System View: A Short Summary." *Association for Integrative Studies Newsletter,* 1 (September 1979), 1–2, 10–12.

———. *The Study of Society: A Unified Approach.* Homewood, Ill.: Irwin-Dorsey, 1963.

*———. *Unified Social Science: A System-Based Introduction.* Homewood, Ill.: Dorsey Press, 1975.

Kuklick, Henrietta. "The Organization of Social Science in the United States." *American Quarterly,* 28 No. 1 (1976), 124–41.

*Landau, Martin, Harold Proshansky, and William H. Ittelson. "The Interdisciplinary Approach and the Concept of Behavioral Science." In *Decisions, Values, and Groups,* ed. Norman F. Washburne. New York: Macmillan, 1962, II, pp. 7–25.

Langdon, E. Jean, and Robert MacLennan. "Western Biomedical and Sibunody Diagnosis: An Interdisciplinary Comparison." *Social Science and Medicine,* 13B (1979), 211–20.

*Lankford, John. "The Writing of American History in the 1960s: A Critical Bibliography of Materials of Interest to Sociologists." *Sociological Quarterly,* 14 No. 1 (1973), 99–126.

Lazarsfeld, Paul. "A Note on Empirical Social Research and Interdisciplinary Relationships." *International Social Science Journal,* 16 (1964), 529–33.

Laszlo, Ervin. "Systems Philosophy." *Ultimate Reality and Meaning,* 11 No. 3 (1978), 223–30.

Lemon, J.T. "Study of the Urban Past: Approaches by Geographers." *Canadian Historical Association Historical Papers,* 1973, 179–90.

*Lepenies, Wolf. "History and Anthropology: A Historical Appraisal of the Current Contact between the Disciplines." *Social Science Information,* 15 No. 213 (1976), 287–306.

Lerner, Richard M. "Adolescent Development: Scientific Study in the 1960's," *Youth and Society,* 12 No. 3 (1981), 251–75.

Liben, L.S. "Representing, Using, and Designing Space: Review of an Interdisciplinary Life Span Conference." *Human Development,* 3 (1980), 210–16.

*Lipton, Michael. "Interdisciplinary Studies in Less Developed Countries." *Journal of Development Studies,* 7 No. 1 (1970), 5–18. See reply by M.P. Moore, "The Logic of Interdisciplinary Studies." *Journal of Development Studies,* 11 No. 1 (1974), 98–106.

Longest, James W. "The Role of Community Development in Rural Development." Paper presented at the Association of Southern Agricultural Workers Meeting in Atlanta, Georgia, 4–7 February 1973. ERIC ED 072 906.

Lopez, Manuel D. "A Guide to the Interdisciplinary Literature of the History of Childhood." *History of Childhood Quarterly,* 1 No. 3 (1974), 463–94.

*Luszki, Margaret Barron. *Interdisciplinary Team Research: Methods and Problems.* Washington, D.C.: National Training Laboratories. Printed by New York Univ. Press, 1958. Research Training Series, No. 3.

———. "Team Research in Social Science: Major Consequences of a Growing Trend." *Human Organization,* 16 No. 1 (1957), 21–24.

McAlister, Leigh, and Edgar Pessemier. "Variety Seeking Behavior: An Interdisciplinary Review." *Journal of Consumer Research,* 9 No. 3 (1982), 311–22.

*McCool, J.P. "Cybernetics and General Systems: A Unitary Science?" (Cybernetics as a base for integrated science teaching). *Kybernetes* (GB), 9 No. 1 (1980), 67–73.

McNall, Scott G. "A Comment on Research in the Field of Military Sociology." *Pacific Sociological Review,* 16 No. 2 (1973), 139–42.

*Mahan, Jack Lee, Jr. "Toward Transdisciplinary Inquiry in the Humane Sciences." Diss. United States International University, San Diego, 1970.

Marsden, W.E. "Historical Geography and the History of Education." *History of Education* (Great Britain), 6 No. 1 (1977), 21–42.

Masur, Jack D. *Efferent Organization and the Integration of Behavior.* New York: Academic Press, 1973.

Mead, Margaret. "Columbia University Research in Contemporary Cultures." In *Groups, Leadership and Men.* Ed. Harold Guetzkow. N.Y.: Russell and Russell, rpt. 1963, pp. 106–18.

*———. "Crossing Boundaries in Social Science Communications." *Social Science Information,* 8 No. 1 (1969), 7–16.

Meehan, Eugene J. *Explanation in Social Science: A System Paradigm.* Homewood, Ill.: Dorsey Press, 1968.

Metcalfe, William, et al. *Understanding Canada: A Multidisciplinary Introduction to Canadian Studies.* New York: New York Univ. Press, 1982.

Michaels, J.W. "On the Relations between Human Ecology and Behavioral Social Psychology." *Social Forces,* 52 No. 3 (1974), 313–21.

*Mikesell, Marvin W., ed. *Geographers Abroad: Essays on the Problems and Prospects of Research in Foreign Areas.* Chicago: Department of Geography, University of Chicago, 1973. Research Paper No. 153.

Miller, James Grier, and Jesse Louise Miller. "Systems Science: An Emerging Interdisciplinary Field." *Center Magazine,* September/October 1981, pp. 44–55.

*Miller, Raymond C. "Varieties of Interdisciplinary Approaches in the Social Sciences." *Issues in Integrative Studies,* 1 (1982), 1–37.

Mitchell, Jack. *Social Exchange, Dramaturgy, and Ethnomethodology: Toward a Paradigmatic Synthesis.* New York: Elsevier, 1978.

Mitroff, Ian I., and L.V. Blankenship. "On the Methodology of the Holistic Experiment: An Approach to the Conceptualization of Large-Scale Social Experiments." *Technological Forecasting and Social Change,* 4 (1973), 339–53.

Mitroff, Ian I., and Richard O. Mason. "Dialectical Pragmatism: A Progress Report on an Interdisciplinary Program of Research on Dialectical Inquiring Systems." *Synthese,* 47 (Apr. 1981), 29–42.

Montgomery, Edward B., ed. *The Foundations of Access to Knowledge: A Symposium.* Syracuse: Syracuse Univ. Press, 1968, pp. 101–21.

Mooney, G.H., and A.H. Williams. "Economists in Multidisciplinary Teams: Some Unresolved Problems in the Conduct of Health Services Research." *Social Science and Medicine,* 14 (1980), 217–21.

Morgan, Douglas N. "An Interdisciplinary Program for Neopositivistic Social Science." *Ethics,* 68 (July 1958), 292–95.

Moss, Nancy E., and Stephen I. Abramowitz. "Beyond Deficit-Filling and Developmental Stakes: Cross-Disciplinary Perspectives on Parental Heritage." *Journal of Marriage and the Family,* 44 No. 2 (1982), 357–66.

Mott, Frank L., and Sylvia F. Moore. "The Causes of Marital Disruption among Young American Women: An Interdisciplinary Perspective." *Journal of Marriage and the Family,* 41 No. 2 (1979), 355–65.

Multidisciplinary Studies in the Law Series. See individual titles: *The Insular Cases: The Role of the Judiciary in American Expansionism* (1982); *Law and Order in American History* (1979).

Murphy, Lawrence R. "Social Science Research in the Middle East: The American University in Cairo, Egypt." *Journal of the History of the Behavioral Sciences,* 15 No. 2 (1979), 115–27.

Myrdal, Gunnar. *The Political Element in the Development of Economic Theory.* Cambridge: Harvard Univ. Press, 1954.

Nanus, Burt. "Interdisciplinary Policy Analysis in Economic Forecasting." *Technological Forecasting and Social Change,* 13 No. 4 (1979), 285–95.

Naylor, Larry L., et al. "Socioeconomic Evaluation of Reindeer Herding in Northwestern Alaska." *Arctic* (Canada), 33 No. 2 (1980), 246–76.

Neeley, James D., Jr. "The Management and Social Science Literatures: An Interdisciplinary Cross-Citation Analysis." *Journal of the American Society for Information Science,* 32 No. 3 (1981), 217–23.

Nef, John V. "The Rise of the Coal Industry and Its Place in Integral History." (Review article.) *Journal of the History of Geography,* 8 No. 1 (1982), 68–73.

Nettl, J.P. "Centre and Periphery in Social Science: The Problem of Political Culture." *American Behavioral Scientist,* 9 No. 10 (1966), 39–46.

*Neurath, Otto. "Unified Science as Encyclopedic Integration." In *International Encyclopedia of Unified Science. Foundations of the Unity of Science,* Vol. 1, No. 1 Chicago: Univ. of Chicago Press, 1938.

Nicosia, F.M. "Consumer Behavior: Can Economics and Behavioral Science Converge?" *California Management Review,* 16 No. 2 (1973), 71–78.

Norris, Darrell A. "Some Comments Concerning a Meeting of Ontario Historical Geographers." *Urban History Review* (Canada), 76 no. 1 (1976), 14–20.

Nuckton, C.F., R.I. Rochin, and D. Gwynn. "Farm Size and Rural Community Welfare: An Interdisciplinary Approach." *Rural Sociology,* 47 No. 1 (1982), 32–46.

Ocran, Tawia. "Law or Culture?" *African Social Research* (Zambia), 13 (1972), 221–27.

Omvedt, G. "The Social Sciences and Linguistic Revolution." *Berkeley Journal of Sociology,* 12 (Summer 1967), 220–28.

Paillat, Paul. "Gerontological Research: Present Situation and Prospects." *International Social Science Journal,* 20 No. 2 (1968), 263–72.

*Palmer, M., L. Stern, and C. Gaile. *The Interdisciplinary Study of Politics.* New York: Harper & Row, 1974.

Parker, Ian. "Harold Innis, Karl Marx, and Canadian Political Economy." *Queen's Quarterly* (Canada), 84 No. 4 (1977), 545–63.

*Parsons, Talcott, and Edward A. Shils, eds. *Toward a General Theory of Action: Theoretical Foundations for the Social Sciences.* Cambridge: Harvard Univ. Press. 1951.

Paterson, A.C., and R. Gilger. "Expanding Horizons: An Interdisciplinary Approach." *Social Science,* 55 No. 4 (1980), 219–20.

Perry, J.A., and R.K. Dixon. "An Interdisciplinary Approach to Community Resource Management: Preliminary Field Test in Thailand." *Journal of Developing Areas,* 21 No. 1 (1986), 31–47.

Perry, P.J. "Agricultural History: A Geographer's Critique." *Agricultural History,* 46 No. 2 (1972), 259–67.

*Phillips, D.C. *Holistic Thought in Social Science.* Stanford: Stanford Univ. Press, 1976.

*Piaget, Jean. *Main Trends in Interdisciplinary Research.* New York: Harper and Row, 1973.

———. *The Place of the Sciences of Man in the System of Sciences.* New York: Harper and Row, 1970.

Pirtle, Wayne G., and John J. Grant. *The Social Sciences: An Integrated Approach,* New York: Random House, 1972.

Policy Studies Journal, 2 No. 1 (1973). Special issue on interdisciplinary approaches to policy sciences.

*Popper, Karl R. "Unity of Method in the Natural and Social Sciences." *Philosophical Problems of the Social Sciences,* ed. David Braybrooke. New York: Macmillan, 1965.

Porter, Arthur. "Reflections on the Nature and Design of Systems." *Philosophy of the Social Sciences,* 1 (Sept. 1971), 233–43.

Potter, William C., and Patrick W. Murphy. *Nuclear Power and Nonproliferation: An Interdisciplinary Perspective.* Cambridge, Mass.: Oelgeschlager, Gunn, and Hain, 1982.

Professional Socialization in Political Science Departments. Final Report. Graduate Socialization Project of the Department of Political Science, University of Oregon, April 1971. ERIC ED 050 700.

*Pye, Lucian W., ed. *Political Science and Area Studies, Rivals or Partners?* Bloomington: Indiana Univ. Press, 1975.

Ranson, Baldwin. "Choosing Institutions for Development: Five Interdisciplinary Models." *Rocky Mountain Social Science Journal,* 10 No. 2 (1973), 135–41.

Rapoport, Anatol. "General Systems Theory: A Bridge between Two Cultures. Third Annual Ludwig von Bertalanffy Memorial Lecture." *General Systems* (Yearbook), 23 (1978), 149–56.

*Rich, Daniel, and Robert Warren. "The Intellectual Future of Urban Affairs. Theoretical, Normative, and Organizational Options." *Social Science Journal,* 17 No. 2 (1980), 53–66.

Richman, Barry. "Chinese and Indian Development: An Interdisciplinary Environmental Analysis." *American Economic Review,* 65 No. 2 (1975), 345–55.

Rickson, Roy E., and Sarah T. Rickson. "Problems and Prospects of Cross-Disciplinary Research." *Rural Sociologist,* 2 (Mar. 1982), 95–103.

Rieselbach, L.N., and G.I. Balch. *Psychology and Politics.* New York: Holt, Rinehart & Winston, 1969.

*Rigney, Donald, and Donna Barnes. "Patterns of Interdisciplinary Citation in the Social Sciences." *Social Science Quarterly,* 61 No. 1 (1980), 114–27.

Rodgers, H.B., et al. "Recreation and Resources." *Geographical Journal* (Great Britain), 139 No. 3 (1973), 467–97.

*Roeling, N.C. "Towards the Interdisciplinary Integration of Economic Theory and Rural Sociology." *Sociologia Ruralis,* 6 No. 2 (1966), 97–117.

*Rogers, E.S., and H.B. Messinger. "Human Ecology: Toward a Holistic Method." *Milbank Memorial Fund Quarterly,* 45 No. 1 (1967), 25–42.

Rosenberg, S. "Mathematical Models of Social Behavior." In *Handbook of Social Psychology. I. Systematic Positions,* ed. G. Lindzey and E. Aronson. Reading, Mass.: Addison-Wesley, 2nd rev. ed., 1968, pp. 179–244.

Rouse, William B. "On Models and Modelers: N Cultures." *IEEE Transactions: Man, Systems, and Cybernetics,* SMC-12 (Sept./Oct. 1982), 605–10.

Rowney, Don Karl. "Bureaucratic Development and Social Science History." *Social Science History,* 2 No. 4 (1978), 379–84.

Royce, J.R. "A Personal Portrayal of Ludwig Von Bertalanffy: System Theorist and Interdisciplinary Scholar at the University of Alberta." *Journal of the History of the Behavioral Sciences,* 17 No. 3 (1981), 340–42.

Rubinstein, E.A. & Coelho, G.V. "Mental Health and Behavioral Sciences: One Federal Agency's Role in the Behavioral Sciences." *American Psychologist,* 25 No. 6 (1970), 517–23.

Sargent, S. Stansfeld, and Marian W. Smith. *Culture and Personality: Proceedings of an Interdisciplinary Conference Held under Auspices of the Viking Fund. November 7 and 8, 1947.* New York: Cooper Square, 1974.

Scheiber, Harry N. "Regulation, Property Rights, and Definition of 'The Market': 'Law' and the American Economy." *Journal of Economic History,* 41 No. 1 (1981), 103–11.

Scherer, K.R., R.P. Abeles, and C.S. Fischer. *Human Aggression and Conflict: Interdisciplinary Perspectives.* Englewood Cliffs, N.J.: Prentice-Hall, 1975.

Schneider, H.K. *Economic Man: The Anthropology of Economics.* New York Free Press, 1974.

*Schwartz, Benjamin I. "Presidential Address: Area Studies as a Critical Discipline." *Journal of Asian Studies,* 40 No. 1 (1980), 15–25.

Schwartzstein, L.A. "Legal Education, Information Technology, and Systems Analysis." *Rutgers Computers & Technology Law Journal,* 13 No. 1 (1987), 59–71.

Sederberg, Peter C., and Nancy B. Sederberg. "Transmitting the Nontransmissible: The Function of Literature in the Pursuit of Social Knowledge." *Philosophy and Phenomenological Research,* 36 No. 2 (1975), 173–96.

Semmes, Clovis E. "Foundations of an Anthrocentric Social Science: Implications for Curriculum Building, Theory, and Research in Black Studies." *Journal of Black Studies,* 12 No. 1 (1981), 3–17.

*Shapiro, Martin, and Barbara Shapiro. "Interdisciplinary Aspects of American Legal History." *Journal of Interdisciplinary History,* 4 No. 4 (1974), 611–26.

*Sherif, Muzafer, and Carolyn Sherif, eds. *Interdisciplinary Relationships in the Social Sciences.* Chicago: Aldine, 1969.

Shoham, S.G. "The Interdisciplinary Study of Sexual Violence." *Deviant Behavior,* 3 No. 3 (1982), 245–74.

Shorthill, Rachel R. "Unexpected Online Sources for Business Information." *Online (USA),* 9 No. 1 (1985), 68–78.

Simas, Philip W. "A New Supra Discipline, Policy Sciences, Aims to 'Integrate Intelligence and Action.'" *Chronicle of Higher Education,* 5 No. 16 (1971), 1, 5.

Simons, H. "Problems of Interdisciplinary Research in the Field of Sports Examined from the Point of View of the Social Sciences." *International Journal of Sports Medicine,* 3 No. 3 (1982), 182.

Singh, Yogendra. "Constraints, Contradictions, and Interdisciplinary Orientations: The Indian Context." *International Social Science Journal,* 31 (1979), 114–22.

*Skinner, Quentin, ed. *The Return of Grand Theory in the Human Sciences.* Cambridge: Cambridge Univ. Press, 1985.

Slap, Joseph W. "Interdisciplinary Perspectives on Psychoanalytic Theories of Aggression." *Journal of the American Psychoanalytic Association,* 27 No. 3 (1979), 655–64.

Smith, Donald E.P. "Interdisciplinary Approach to the Genesis of Anxiety." *Educational Theory,* 6 (Oct. 1956), 222–31.

Social Science Information. See periodic sections on interdisciplinary research and bibliographies on interdisciplinary relations.

Social Science Quarterly, 50 No. 1 (January 1969), 6–58. Special section on some convergences in history and sociology.

Smolicz, J.J. "Paradigms and Models: A Comparison of Intellectual Frameworks in Natural Sciences and Sociology." *Australian and New Zealand Journal of Sociology,* 6 No. 2 (1970), 100–119.

*"Some Concluding Observations, Especially with Respect to Interdisciplinary Activity." In *The Behavioral Sciences at Harvard.* Cambridge: Harvard University Press, 1954, pp. 259–302.

Spengler, J.J. "Generalists versus Specialists in Social Science: An Economist's View." *American Political Science Review,* 44 (June 1950), 358–79, discussion, 380–93.

Steinitz, C. "Computer Modeling Approach to Managing Urban Expansion." *Geo-Processing,* 1 No. 4 (1981), 341–75.

*Stoddard, Ellwyn R. "Multidisciplinary Research Funding: A 'Catch 22' Enigma." *American Sociologist,* 17 (Nov. 1982), 210–16.

*———, ed. "The Status of U.S.-Mexico Borderlands Studies: Multidisciplinary Symposium." *Social Science Journal,* 12/13 (Oct. 1975/Jan. 1976), 1–112.

Street, Richard Steven. "The Economist as Humanist: The Career of Paul S. Taylor." *California History,* 58 No. 4 (1979–80), 350–61.

*Studdert-Kennedy, Gerald. *Evidence and Explanation in Social Science: An Interdisciplinary Approach.* London: Routledge and Kegan Paul, 1975.

Taylor, Alastair M. "A Systems Approach to the Political Organization of Space." *Social Science Information,* 14 No. 5 (1975), 7–40.

Thorpe, L.P., and A.M. Schmuller. *Personality: An Interdisciplinary Approach.* London: Van Nostrand, 1958.

Thurber, James A. "The Battelle Memorial Institute's Human Affairs Research Centers." *PS,* 14 No. 3 (1981), 584–89.

Toch, H. "Toward an Interdisciplinary Approach to Criminal Violence." *Journal of Criminal Law and Criminology,* 71 No. 4 (1980), 646–53.

*Trent, John E. "Internationalization? Interdisciplinarity? Development? The Social Sciences from 1952-1977. A Report on the 25th Anniversary Round Table." *Social Science Information,* 17 No. 2 (1978), 337–42.

Trigg, Roger. *Understanding Social Science: A Philosophical Introduction to the Social Sciences.* London: Basil Blackwell, 1985.

*Twining, William. "Law and Anthropology: A Case Study in Inter-Disciplinary Collaboration." *Law and Society Review,* 7 No. 4 (1973), 561–84.

Valone, James J. "Parsons' Contributions to Sociological Theory: Reflections on the Schutz-Parsons Correspondence." *Human Studies,* 3 (Oct. 1980), 375–86.

Wakil, Parvez A. "On the Question of Developing a Sociology of the Canadian Family: A

Methodological Statement." *Canadian Review of Sociology and Anthropology,* 7 No. 2 (1970), 154–57.

Waldman, Marilyn Robinson. "Islamic Studies: A New Orientalism?" *Journal of Interdisciplinary History,* 8 No. 3 (1978), 545–62.

Waldo, Dwight. "Developments in Public Administration." *Annals of the American Academy of Political and Social Science,* 404 (Nov. 1972), 217–45.

Walker, Loretta, and David Gerhan. *Multinational Enterprise and Its Implications for Library Research.* Union College, Schenectady, N.Y. Schaffer Library. December 1975. ERIC ED 085 603.

Wandersman, Abraham. "A Framework of Participation in Community Organizations." *Journal of Applied Behavioral Science,* 17 No. 1 (1981), 27–58.

*Weaver, James, and Kenneth Jameson. *Economic Development: Competing Paradigms.* Lanham, Md.: University Press of America, 1981.

Weingrod, A. "Political Sociology, Social Anthropology, and the Study of New Nations." *British Journal of Sociology,* 18 No. 2 (1967), 121–134.

*Wilson, E.O. *Sociobiology: The New Synthesis.* Cambridge, Mass.: Belknap Press of Harvard University Press, 1975.

Winthrop, Henry. "Policy and Planning Programs as Goals of Scientific Work." *American Journal of Economics and Sociology,* 34 No. 3 (1978), 225–45.

Wolfgang, Marvin E., and Franco Ferracuti. *The Subculture of Violence: Towards an Integrated Theory in Criminology.* London: Tavistock, 1967.

World Population Society. *Multidisciplinary Approaches to Population Problems: Global Dialogue of the Disciplines on Population.* Washington, D.C.: World Population Society, 1974.

*Yanitsky, Oleg. "Towards an Eco-City: Problems of Integrating Knowledge with Practice." *International Social Science Journal,* 34 No. 3 (1982), 469–79.

Zurcher, Louis A., and Charles M. Bonjean. *Planned Social Intervention: An Interdisciplinary Anthology.* Scranton, Pa.: Chandler, 1970.

Anthropology, Archaeology, Ethnography

Adams, John. "The Analysis of Rural Indian Economy: Economics and Anthropology." *Man in India,* 52 No. 1 (1972), 1–20.

*Agar, Michael. "Getting Better Quality Stuff: Methodological Competition in an Interdisciplinary Niche." *Urban Life,* 9 No. 1 (1980), 34–50.

———. "Toward an Ethnographic Language." *American Anthropology,* 84 No. 4 (1982), 779–95.

Aikens, C.M., D.D. Fowler, and A. Smith. "Interdisciplinary Models and Great Basin Prehistory: A Comment on Current Orientations." In *Models and Great Basin Prehistory: A Symposium.* Ed. Don D. Fowler and Alma Smith. Reno: Desert Research Institute, 1977, pp. 211–13. Desert Research Institute Publications in Social Sciences No. 12.

Brameld, Theodore. "Cultural Determinism in Puerto Rico: An Inter-Disciplinary Study in Philosophy, Anthropology, and Education." *Proceedings of the Philosophy of Education Society,* 14 (Mar.-Apr. 1958), 69–73.

*Butzer, Karl W. "The Ecological Approach to Archaeology: Are We Really Trying?" *American Antiquity,* 40 No. 1 (1975), 106–11.

*Clifford, James. *The Predicament of Culture: Twentieth-Century Ethnography, Literature, and Art.* Cambridge: Harvard University Press, 1988.

*Clifford, James, and George E. Marcus, eds. *Writing Culture: The Poetics and Politics of Ethnography.* Berkeley: University of California Press, 1986.

Cohn, Bernard S. "History and Anthropology: The State of Play." *Comparative Studies in Sociology and History* (Great Britain), 22 No. 2 (1980), 198–221.

Cohen, R. "Anthropology and Political Science: Courtship or Marriage?" *American Behavioral Scientist,* 11 No. 2 (1967), 1–17.

Cook, Scott. "Production, Ecology, and Economic Anthropology: Notes Toward an Integrated Frame of Reference." *Social Science Information,* 12 No. 1 (1977), 25–52.

*Davy, Douglas M. "Borrowed Concepts: A Comment on Rhoades." *American Antiquity,* 45 No. 2 (1980), 346–49. See also Robert E. Rhoades and David A. Phillips, Jr. "Reply to Davy," 349–50.

Finley, M.I. "Archaeology and History." *Daedalus,* 100 No. 1 (1971), 168–86.

*"Fryxell Award for Interdisciplinary Research." *American Antiquity,* 45 No. 4 (1980), 660–61; 45 No. 2 (1980), 229–30; 48 No. 3 (1983), 453.

Gumerman, George J., and David A. Phillips, Jr. "Archaeology beyond Anthropology." *American Antiquity,* 43 No. 2 (1978), 184–91.

Hoffmann, H. "Mathematical Anthropology." In *Biennial Review of Anthropology, 1969.* Ed. B.J. Siegel. Stanford: Stanford Univ. Press, 1970, pp. 41–79.

Jennings, Francis. "A Growing Partnership: Historians, Anthropologists, and American Indian History." *History Teacher,* 14 No. 1 (1980), 87–104.

King, Thomas F. "A Conflict of Values in American Archaeology." *American Antiquity,* 36 No. 3 (1971), 255–62.

Kroeber, A.L. *Anthropology Today, An Encyclopedic Inventory.* Chicago: Univ. of Chicago Press, 1953.

*Lepenies, Wolf. "History and Anthropology: A Historical Appraisal of Current Contact between the Disciplines." *Social Science Information,* 15 No. 213 (1976), 287–306.

Longacre, William A., and J. Jefferson Reid. "The University of Arizona Archaeological Field School at Grasshopper: Eleven Years of Multidisciplinary Research and Teaching." *Kiva,* 40 No. 1–2 (1974), 3–38.

*Macfarlane, Alan. "History, Anthropology, and the Study of Communities." *Social History* (Great Britain), 5 (1977), 631–52.

MacNeish, Richard S. "An Interdisciplinary Approach to an Archaeological Problem." In *The Prehistory of the Tehuacan Valley, V.I. Environment and Subsistence,* ed. D. Byers. Austin: Univ. of Texas Press, 1967, pp. 14–24.

*Mandelbaum, D.B., G. Lasker, and E.M. Albert. *The Teaching of Anthropology.* Berkeley: Univ. of California Press, 1963. See especially the sections "Interdisciplinary Relations in Teaching Anthropology" and "The Relations of Anthropology with the Social Sciences."

Marcus, G.E., and M.M.J. Fischer. *Anthropology as Cultural Critique: An Experimental Moment in the Human Sciences.* Chicago: Univ. of Chicago Press, 1986.

Mering, O. Von, and L. Kasdan, eds. *Anthropology and the Behavioral and Health Sciences.* Pittsburgh: Univ. of Pittsburgh Press, 1970.

Minderhout, D. "Sociolinguistics and Anthropology." *Anthropological Linguistics,* 16 No. 4 (1974), 168–76.

Moore, S.F. "Law and Anthropology." In *Biennial Review of Anthropology, 1969.* Stanford: Stanford Univ. Press, 1970, pp. 252–300.

Morgan, John Henry. "Religious Myth and Symbol: Convergence of Philosophy and Anthropology." *Philosophy Today,* 18 (Spring 1974), 68–84.

Morwood, M.J. "Analogy and the Acceptance of Theory in Archaeology." *American Antiquity,* 40 No. 1 (1975), 111–16.

Peck, R. "Anthropology and Mass Communication Research." *Sociologus,* 11 No. 2 (1967), 97–115.

Pepper, George B. "Anthropology, Science or Humanity?" *Anthropological Quarterly,* 34 No. 3 (1961), 150–57.

*Pomerance, Leon. "The Need for Guidelines in Interdisciplinary Meetings." *American Journal of Archaeology,* 75 No. 4 (1971), 428–31.

*Rhoades, Robert E. "Archaeological Use and Abuse of Ecological Concepts and Studies: The Ecotone Example." *American Antiquity,* 43 No. 4 (1978), 608–14.

*Schiffer, Michael B. "Some Issues in the Philosophy of Archaeology." *American Antiquity,* 46 No. 4 (1981), 899–908.

Shaw, Thurstan. "In Praise of Interdisciplinary Archaeology." *Interdisciplinary Science Reviews,* 2 No. 2 (1977), 92–93.

*Shawcross, F.W., and Maureen Kaye. "Australian Archaeology, Implications of Current Interdisciplinary Research." *Interdisciplinary Science Reviews,* 5 No. 2 (1980), 112–28.

Southwold, M. "The Boundaries of Social Anthropology." *Man,* 3 No. 4 (1969), 656–57.

*Sturtevant, William C. "Anthropology, History, and Ethnohistory." *Ethnohistory,* 13 No. 1-2 (1966), 1–51.

*Twining, William. "Law and Anthropology: A Case Study in Inter-Disciplinary Collaboration." *Law and Society Review,* 7 No. 4 (1973), 561–84.

Von Mering, O., and L. Kasdan, eds. *Anthropology and the Behavioral and Health Sciences.* Pittsburgh: Univ. of Pittsburgh Press, 1970.

Weakland, J.H. "Anthropology, Psychiatry, and Communication." *American Anthropology,* 71 No. 5 (1969), 880–88.

*Wilderson, Paul W. "Archaeology and the American Historian: An Interdisciplinary Challenge." *American Quarterly,* 27 (May 1972), 115–32.

Williams, L.E., D.C. Parris, and S.S. Albright. "Interdisciplinary Approaches to WPA Archaeological Collections in the Northeast." *Annals of the New York Academy of Sciences,* 376 (Dec. 1981), 141–59.

Wylie, Kenneth C. "The Uses and Misuses of Ethnohistory." *Journal of Interdisciplinary History,* 3 (Spring 1973), 707–20.

Psychology, Sociology, Social Psychology

Apostle, C.N. "Is Sociology a Deviant of Economics?" *Journal of Human Relations,* 15 No. 2 (1967), 210–20.

Back, K.W. "New Frontiers in Demography and Social Psychology." *Demography,* 4 No. 1 (1967), 90–97.

*Blank, Thomas O. "Two Social Psychologies: Is Segregation Inevitable or Acceptable?" *Personality and Social Psychology Bulletin,* 4 No. 4 (1978), 553–56.

Boutilier, R.G., J.C. Roed, and A.G. Svendsen. "Crises in the Two Social Psychologies: A Critical Comparison." *Social Psychology Quarterly,* 43 No. 1 (1980), 5–17.

Brown, Julia S., and Brian G. Gilmartin. "Sociology Today: Lacunae, Emphases, and Surfeits." *American Sociology,* 4 (Nov. 1969), 283–91.

*Brown, Richard Harvey. *A Poetic for Sociology: Toward a Logic of Discovery for the Human Sciences.* Cambridge: Cambridge Univ. Press, 1977.

———. *Society as Text: Essays on Rhetoric, Reason, and Reality.* Chicago: Univ. of Chicago Press, 1987.

———. *Social Science as Civic Discourse: On the Invention, Legitimation, and Uses of Social Theory.* Chicago: Univ. of Chicago Press, forthcoming.

Bruhn, J. "Ecological Responsibility in Sociology." *Sociological Quarterly,* 12 (1971), 77–82.

*Bulmer, M. "Sociology and History: Some Recent Trends." *Sociology,* 8 No. 1 (1974), 138–50.

Carlson, Rae. "What's Social about Social Psychology? Where's the Person in Personality Research?" *Journal of Personality and Social Psychology,* 47 No. 6 (1984), 1304–09.

Chertok. L. "Hypnosis, The Psychobiological Crossroads, A 200-Year Query." *Journal of Nervous and Mental Disease,* 166 No. 4 (1978), 231-33.

Chirot, Daniel. "Introduction: Thematic Controversies and New Developments in the Uses of Historical Materials by Sociologists." *Social Forces,* 55 (Dec. 1976).

Cohen, Charles. "Essays on Metapsychology." *History and Theory,* 17 No. 1 (1978), 113-30.

Furbey, R.A. "An Examination of Some Influential Views on the Relationship between Sociology and History and the Use of Historical Material in Sociological Research." *Sociological Analysis* (Great Britain), 2 No. 3 (1972), 59-63.

Gergen, K.J. "Social Psychology and History." *Journal of Personality and Social Psychology,* 26 (1973), 309-20.

Gnepp, E.H. "Communication among Psychologists: A Study." *Psychology: A Quarterly Journal of Human Behavior,* 18 No. 4 (1981), 30-34.

Greenberg, Neil, and Paul D. MacLean. *Behavior and Neurology of Lizards: An Interdisciplinary Colloquium.* Rockville, Md.: H.E.W. Press, 1978.

Hall, C.S., and Lindzey, G. "The Relevance of Freudian Psychology and Related Viewpoints for the Social Sciences." In *Handbook of Social Psychology. I. Systematic Positions,* ed. G.H. Lindzey and E. Aronson. 2nd rev. ed. Reading, Mass.: Addison-Wesley, 1968, pp. 245-319.

Heath, A. "Economic Theory and Sociology: A Critique of P.M. Blau's *Exchange and Power in Social Life," Sociology,* 2 No. 3 (1968), 273-92.

Horowitz, I.L., and Liebowitz, M. "Social Deviance and Political Marginality: Toward a Redefinition of the Relation between Sociology and Politics." *Social Problems,* 15 No. 3 (1968), 280-96.

House, J.S. "The Three Faces of Social Psychology." *Sociometry,* 40 (1977), 161-77.

*Hufford, David J. "Psychology, Psychoanalysis, and Folklore." *Southern Folklore Quarterly,* 38 No. 3 (1974), 187-97.

Ingarden, Roman. "Psychologism and Psychology in Literary Scholarship." *New Literary History,* 5 No. 2 (1974), 213-23.

Kalick, S.M. "Toward an Interdisciplinary Psychology of Appearances." *Psychiatry,* 41 No. 3 (1978), 243-53.

Kitchener, Richard D., "Holism and the Organismic Model in Developmental Psychology." *Human Development,* 25 (1982), 233-49.

Kluckhorn, Clyde. "An Anthropologist Looks at Psychology." *American Psychologist,* 3 No. 10 (1948), 439-42.

Kunz, G., and S. Halling. "The Development of a Phenomenologically Based Therapeutic Graduate Program: A Contribution to Pluralism in Psychology." Paper presented at the 61st annual meeting of the Western Psychological Association in Los Angeles, California, 10 April 1981. ERIC ED 214 077.

*Lankford, John. "The Writing of American History in the 1960s: A Critical Bibliography of Materials of Interest to Sociologists." *Sociological Quarterly,* 14 (Winter 1973), 99-126.

Levenson, Daniel J. "Toward a New Social Psychology: The Convergence of Sociology and Psychology." *Merrill-Palmer Quarterly of Behavior and Development,* 10 (1964), 77-88.

Levine, Donald N. "Psychoanalysis and Sociology." *Ethos,* 6 No. 3 (1978), 175-84.

McMahon, Frank B. *Psychology: The Hybrid Science.* Englewood Cliffs, N.J.: Prentice-Hall, 1974.

Manuel, Frank E. "The Use and Abuse of Psychology in History." *Daedalus,* 100 No. 1 (1971), 187-213.

Marlowe, Leigh, ed. *Basic Topics in Social Psychology: An Interdisciplinary and Inter-Cultural Reader.* Boston: Holbrook Press, 1972.

Mijuskovic, Ben. "Loneliness: An Interdisciplinary Approach." *Psychiatry,* 40 No. 2 (1977), 113-32.

Mitscherlich, A. et al. "On Psychoanalysis and Sociology." *International Journal of Psychoanalysis,* 51 No. 1 (1970), 33–48.

Moraitis, George. "Introduction: Psychoanalysis and the Promise of Interdisciplinary Research." *Emotions and Behavior Monographs,* 1 No. 2 (1984), 117–26.

Muresan, Paul. "Gheorghe Zapan (1897–1976): Romanian Scholar of Interdisciplinary Formation: Contributions to the Development of Psychology, Pedagogy, and Cybernetics of the Human Activities." *Revue Roumaine des Sciences Sociales—Série de Psychologie,* 26 No. 1 (1982), 75–82.

*Nisbet, Robert. *Sociology as an Art Form.* London: Heinemann, 1976.

O'Toole, Patricia. "The New Psycho-Disciplines." *Change, The Magazine of Higher Learning,* 11 No. 3 (1979), 36–40.

*Parsons, Talcott. "Theory in the Humanities and Sociology." *Daedalus* (Spring 1970), 495–523.

Rabow, Jerome. "Psychoanalysis and Sociology: a Selective Review." *Sociology and Social Research, An International Journal,* 65 No. 2 (1981), 117–28.

Ratliff, F. "Some Interrelations among Physics, Physiology, and Psychology." In *Psychology: A Study of a Science, V. 4,* ed. Sigmund Koch. New York: McGraw-Hill, 1962.

*Rickson, Roy E., and Sarah T. Rickson. "Problems and Prospects of Crossdisciplinary Research." *Rural Sociologist,* 2 (Mar. 1982), 95–103.

Roeling, N.C. "Towards the Inter-Disciplinary Integration of Economic Theory and Rural Sociology." *Sociologia Ruralis,* 6 No. 2 (1966), 97–117.

Rolf, J.E., and P.B. Read. "Programs Advancing Developmental Psychopathology." *Child Development,* 55 No. 1 (1984), 8–16.

Royce, Joseph R., ed. *Psychology and the Symbol: An Interdisciplinary Symposium.* New York: Random House, 1965.

————, et al. "Psychological Epsitemology: A Critical Review of the Empirical Literature and the Theoretical Issues." *Genetic Psychology Monographs,* 97 No. 2 (1978), 265–353.

Sarup, Gian. "Levels of Analysis in Social Psychology and Related Social Sciences." *Human Relations,* 28 No. 8 (1975), 755–69.

Secord, Paul F. "Transhistorical and Transcultural Theory." *Personality and Social Psychology Bulletin,* 2 No. 4 (1976), 418–20.

Shapiro, D. "Psychophysiological Contributions to Social Psychology." *Annual Review of Psychology,* 21 (1970), 87–112.

Simon, H.A., and Stedry, A.C. "Psychology and Economics." In *Handbook of Social Psychology. V. Applied Social Psychology.* 2nd rev. ed. Reading, Mass.: Addison Wesley, 1969, pp. 269–314.

Sinha, Durganand. "Social Psychologists' Stance in a Developing Country." *Indian Journal of Psychology,* 50 No. 2 (1975), 91–107.

Slap, J.W. "Interdisciplinary Perspectives on Psychoanalytic Theories of Aggression." *Journal of the American Psychoanalytic Association,* 27 No. 3 (1979), 655–64.

Smelser, Neil J. "Sociology and the Other Social Sciences." In *The Uses of Sociology,* ed. P.A. Lazarsfeld, W.H. Sewell, and H.L. Wilensky. New York: Basic Books, 1967.

Smith, Donald E.P. "Interdisciplinary Approach to the Genesis of Anxiety." *Educational Theory,* 6 (Oct. 1956), 222–31.

Smolicz, J.J. "Paradigms and Models: A Comparison of Intellectual Frameworks in Natural Sciences and Sociology." *Australian and New Zealand Journal of Sociology,* 6 No. 2 (1970), 100–19.

Sorokin, Pitrim A. *Fad and Foibles in Modern Sociology and Related Sciences.* Chicago: Henry Regnery, 1956. See especially chapter 11.

*Stoddard, Ellwyn R., and C. Lawrence McConville. "The Effectiveness of Sociology in Training and Rewarding Scholars in a Multidisciplinary/Multicultural Field." *Western Sociology Review,* 9 (Fall 1978), 67–75.

Stryker, S. "Developments in 'Two Social Psychologies': Toward an Appreciation of Mutual Relevance." *Sociometry,* 40 (1977), 145–60.

Tien, H.C. "Pattern Recognition and Psychosynthesis." *American Journal of Psychotherapy,* 23 No. 1 (1969), 53–66.

Van Praag, Bernard M. "Linking Economics with Psychology: An Economist's View." *Journal of Economic Psychology,* 6 No. 3 (1985), 289–311.

Von Haller, Gilmer B. "Science-Based, Applications-Oriented Psychology." *Academic Psychology Bulletin,* 2 No. 1 (1980), 95–101.

Waite, Robert G.L. "Interdisciplinary Approaches to the Study of Modern Germany: Psychoanalysis and the Study of Hitler." *Europa (Canada),* 4 No. 1 (1981), 133–38.

Weingrod, A. "Political Sociology, Social Anthropology, and the Study of New Nations." *British Journal of Sociology,* 18 No. 2 (1967), 121–34.

*Wilson, David W., and Robert B. Schafer. "Is Social Psychology Interdisciplinary?" *Personality and Social Psychology Bulletin,* 4 No. 4 (1978), 548–52.

The Sciences

Including the Sciences and Technology

Anderson, Peter Bogh, and Arne Kjaer. "Artifical Intelligence and Self-Management." *Journal of Pragmatics,* 6 (Aug. 1982), 321–55.

Baker, F.W.G. "A Century of International Interdisciplinary Cooperation." (International Polar Year). *Interdisciplinary Science Reviews,* 7 No. 4 (1982), 270–82.

*Baker, Paul T. "Human Population Biology: A Viable Transdisciplinary Science." *Human Biology,* 54 No. 2 (1982), 203–20.

Barigozzi, C. "An Interdisciplinary Symposium on the Brine Shrimp *Artemia* in the USA." *Experientia,* 36 No. 5 (1980), 627.

Barker, E. "Science and Theology: Diverse Resolutions of an Interdisciplinary Gap by the New Priesthood of Science." *Interdisciplinary Science Reviews,* 5 No. 4 (1980), 281–91.

Bastedo, J.D., and J.B. Theberge. "An Appraisal of Inter-disciplinary Resource Surveys (Ecological Land Classification)." *Landscape Planning,* 10 No. 4 (1983), 317–34.

*Bechtel, W. ed. *Integrating Scientific Disciplines.* Dordrecht: Martinus Nijhoof, 1986.

Blanc, R., et al. "A Multidisciplinary Approach to the Characterization of Heavy Oil Deposits from the Tri-State Area (U.S.A.)." In *Future Heavy Crude Tar Sands, International Conference, 2nd.* Ed. R. F. Meyer, J.C. Wynn, and J.C. Olson. New York: McGraw Hill, 1984, pp. 433–57.

Bloch, J.R. "Quality and Quantity in the Analysis of Integrated Science Curricula." *Studies in Education Evaluation,* 2 (1976).

Boulding, Kenneth E. "Science: Our Common Heritage." *Science,* 22 Feb. 1980, pp. 831–36.

Boyden, S. "Integrated Ecological Studies of Human Settlements." *Impact of Science on Society* (UNESCO), 27 No. 2 (1977), 159–69.

Breguet, C.A.J. "The Breguet Dynasty: Two Centuries of Interdisciplinary Scientists and Engineers." *Interdisciplinary Science Reviews,* 5 No. 2 (1980), 149–64.

Bronowski, Jacob. *Science and Human Values.* New York: Messner, 1956.

Brownell, J. "Murray Ellwood Interdisciplinary Analog Laboratory." *Communication Education,* 28 No. 1 (1979), 9–21.

Bunge, Mario. "The Role of Forecast in Planning." *Theory and Decision,* 3 (Mar. 1983), 207–21.

Cadzow, James H. *Discrete-Time Systems: An Introduction with Interdisciplinary Applications.* Englewood Cliffs, N.J.: Prentice-Hall, 1973.

*Caldwell, Lynton K. "Environmental Studies: Discipline or Metadiscipline?" *Environmental Professional,* 5 (1983), 247–59.

Cellular Automata: Proceedings of an Interdisciplinary Workshop. Los Alamos, New Mexico, March 7-11, 1983. Amsterdam: North-Holland Physics Publishers, 1984.

*Chen, Robert S. "Interdisciplinary Research and Integration: The Case of CO_2 and Climate." *Climatic Change,* 3 No. 4 (1981), 429-48.

Cloud, P. "Beyond Plate Techtonics." *American Scientist,* 68 No. 4 (1980), 381-87.

Coyne, D.P. "Horticulture and Interdisciplinary Research." *Hortscience,* 14 No. 6 (Dec. 1979), 686.

Dabat, R. "A New Discipline: Architectural Bioclimatology—Towards an Interdisciplinary Research Program." *Energy and Buildings,* 5 No. 1 (1982), 39-41.

*Darden, Lindley, and Nancy Maull. "Interfield Theories." *Philosophy of Science,* 44 (Mar. 1977), 43-64.

David, Edward E., Jr. "Science Futures: The Industrial Connection." *Science,* 2 Mar. 1979, pp. 837-40.

Dees, B.C. "The Franklin Institute: Commemorating a Great Interdisciplinary Scientist." *Interdisciplinary Science Reviews,* 5 No. 2 (1980), 90-101.

Dirkx, J., et al. "Confirmation of Somatostatin: An Interdisciplinary Approach." *Hormone Research,* 9 No. 2 (1978), 63-64.

Dragoun, O. "Interdisciplinary Applications of Gamma-Ray Internal Conversion." *Europhysics News,* 15 No. 4 (1984), 11-13.

Dreyfus, T. "Introducing Shock Waves: An Interdisciplinary Approach." *Helvetica Physica Acta,* 52 No. 5-6 (1979), 680.

Durbin, Paul T. "Is There a Philosophical Paradigm for Technological Studies?" *Nature and System,* 3 (Mar. 1981), 29-36.

———. "Toward a Social Philosophy of Technology." In *Research in Philosophy and Technology,* Vol. 1, ed. Paul T. Durbin. Greenwich: JAI Press, pp. 67-98.

———, and Carl Mitcham. *Research in Philosophy and Technology.* Greenwich: JAI Press, 1979. See especially Hans Lenk and G. Ropohl, "Toward an Interdisciplinary Pragmatic Philosophy of Technology," pp. 15-52.

Epple, G., et al. "Communication by Scent in Some Callitrichidae Primates: An Interdisciplinary Approach." *Chemical Senses and Flavor,* 6 No. 4 (1981), 377-90.

Fincham, R. "Interdisciplinary Expedition to the Okavango Swamps." *South African Journal of Science,* 76 No. 3 (1980), 101-02.

Finocchiaro, Maurice A. "Galileo's Philosophy of Science. II. A Case Study of Interdisciplinary Synthesis." *Scientia* (Italy), 112 No. 1-4 (1977), 371-99.

Floret, Christian, and Mohamed S. Hadjej. "An Attempt to Combat Desertification in Tunisia." *Ambio,* 6 No. 6 (1977), 366-68.

Fried, Jacob, and Paul Molnar. "A General Model for Culture and Technology." *Technological Forecasting and Social Change,* 8 (1975), 175-88.

Garfield, E. "ISI Compumath: Multidisciplinary Coverage of Applied and Pure Mathematics, Statistics, and Computer Science, In Print and/or Online—Take Your Pick." *Current Contents,* 10 (1982), 5-10.

Gleick, James, *Chaos: Making a New Science.* New York: Viking, 1987.

Goldstein, M., and I. Goldstein. *Experience of Science: An Interdisciplinary Approach.* New York: Plenum, 1984.

Griffith, Belver C., and Nicholas C. Mullins. "Coherent Social Groups in Scientific Change." *Science,* 15 Sept. 1972, pp. 959-64.

Grossberg, S. "Interdisciplinary Aspects of Perceptual Dynamics." *Behavioral and Brain Sciences.* 6 No. 4 (1983), 676-87.

Haaland, K.Y., et al. "Symposium: Motor Control—A Multidisciplinary Look." *International Journal of Neuroscience,* 12 No. 3-4 (1981), 162-63.

*Hadač, Emil, et al. "Complex Interdisciplinary Investigation of Landscape." *Landscape Planning,* 4 No. 4 (1977), 333–48.

Haken, H. "Some Aspects of Synergetics." *Synergetics,* Berlin: Springer, 1977.

Hanson, W.T. "Interdisciplinary Approach: New Photographic Film." *Interdisciplinary Science Reviews,* 4 No. 4 (1979), 290–97.

Hardeland, R., and A. Sollberger. "Ninth International Interdisciplinary Cycle Research Symposium. Tier, West Germany. July 6–11, 1980. *Journal of Interdisciplinary Cycle Research,* 12 No. 2 (1981), 97–192; 12 No. 4 (1981), 257–323.

*Haskell, Edward. "Unified Science." In *Coping with Increasing Complexity,* ed. Donald E. Washburn. New York: Gordon and Breach, pp. 375–77.

Herrick, J.B. "Interdisciplinary Approach." *Journal of the American Veterinary Medicine Association,* 172 No. 11 (1978), 1286.

Hoddeson, Lillian. "The Discovery of the Point-Contact Transistor." *Historical Studies in the Physical Sciences,* 12 No. 1 (1981), 41–76.

Holton, Gerald. "On the Role of Themata in Scientific Thought." *Science,* 188 No. 4186, 25 Apr. 1975, pp. 328–34.

Hull, A.P., and E.S. Martin. "An Interdisciplinary Experimental Station." *Scientific Horticulture,* 31 (1980), 111–17.

"Interdisciplinary Communication. R.F. Rushmer." *Science,* 157 No. 3786, 21 July 1967, p. 252.

"Interdisciplinary Communications: Population; Report of Meeting. Lord Ritchie-Calder." *Science,* 163 No. 3865, 24 Jan. 1969, p. 408.

Interdisciplinary Science Reviews.

Jacobs, S.S. "Interdisciplinary Investigations in Antarctic Oceanography." *Antarctic Journal of the United States,* 15 No. 5 (1981), 87–89.

*Jantsch, Erich, ed. *The Evolutionary Vision: Toward a Unifying Paradigm of Physical, Biological, and Sociocultural Evolution.* Boulder, Colo.: Westview Press, 1981.

Jantsch, Erich. "Integrating Forecasting and Planning Through a Function-Oriented Approach." In *Technological Forecasting for Industry and Government,* ed. J. Bright. Englewood Cliffs, N.J.: Prentice-Hall, 1968. See also "New Organizational Forms for Forecasting," *Technological Forecasting,* 1 (Fall 1969).

––––––. "Integrative Planning of Technology." In *Perspectives of Planning.* Paris: Organization for Economic Cooperation and Development, 1969.

Johnson, C.C. "Interdisciplinary and International Contributions to Research on Biological Effects of Electromagnetic Waves: Past Performances and Future Challenges." *Radio Science,* 14 No. 1 (1979), 1–4.

Jones, W.T. *The Sciences and the Humanities: Conflict and Reconciliation.* Berkeley: Univ. of California Press, 1965.

Journal of Interdisciplinary Cycle Research.

*Kallen, H.M. "The Meanings of Unity among the Sciences." In *Structure, Method, and Meaning: Essays in Honor of Henry M. Sheffer.* Ed. Paul Henle, Horace Kallen, and Susanne Langer. New York: Liberal Arts Press, 1951, pp. 225–241.

Kapitza, Sergei P. "Science and Politics: Interdisciplinary Co-Operation Essential." *Interdisciplinary Science Reviews,* 7 No. 4 (1982), 257–60.

Kargon, Robert H. "Temple to Science: Cooperative Research and the Birth of the California Institute of Technology." *Historical Studies in the Physical Sciences,* 8 (1977), 3–31.

Kelly, Rebecca. "Interface '83 – Humanities and Technology: Southern Technical Institute, Marietta, Georgia, October 20–21, 1983." *Technology and Culture,* 25 No. 4 (1984), 839–45.

Kharaka, R.K., et al. "Hydrogeochemistry of Big Soda Lake, Nevada: An Alkaline Meromictic Desert Lake." *Geochimica and Cosmochimia Acta* (Great Britain), 48 No. 4 (1984), 823–35.

Khush, G.S., and Coffman, W.R. "Genetic Evaluation and Utilization Program, The River Improvement Program of the International Rice Research Institute." *Theoretical and Applied Genetics,* 51 No. 3 (1977), 97–110.

Klopatek, J.M., et al. "A Theoretical Approach to Regional Environmental Conflicts." *Journal of Environmental Management,* 16 No. 1 (1983), 1–16.

Knott, K., B. Feuerbracher, and C.R. Chappell. "Spacelab 1: An Early Space Station for Science and Technology." *Acta Astronautica,* 9 No. 6–7 (1982), 347–52.

Kohn, A. "Humor: The Interdisciplinary Denominator in Science." *Interdisciplinary Science Reviews,* 7 No. 4 (1982), 309–24.

Lacefield, G., et al. "Interdisciplinary Beef Forage Management Demonstrations." *Journal of Animal Science,* 55 Suppl. 1 (1982), 206–207.

Laszlo, Ervin, and H. Margenau. "Discussion: The Emergence of Integrative Concepts in Contemporary Science." *Philosophy of Science,* 39 No. 2 (1972), 252–59.

Leclerc, Gerard. "Multidisciplinary Approaches to the Alpha-Adrenergic Receptor Using Clonidine-Like Compounds." *Periodicum Biologorum,* 85 Suppl. 2 (1983), 83–90.

*Lenk, Hans, and Gunther Ropohl. "Toward an Interdisciplinary, Pragmatic Philosophy of Technology: Technology as a Focus for Interdisciplinary Reflection and Systems Research." *Research in Philosophy and Technology,* 2 (1979), 15–52.

LePair, C. "Switching between Academic Disciplines in Universities in the Netherlands." *Scientometrics,* 2 (May 1980), 177–91.

*Lepenies, Wolf. "Toward an Interdisciplinary History of Science." *International Journal of Sociology,* 8 No. 1–2 (1978), 45–69.

Lodding, Alexander, and Hans Odelius. "Applications of SIMS in the Interdisciplinary Material Characterization." *Mikrochimica Acta, Supplementum,* 10: Progress in Materials Analysis 1 (1983), 21–49.

Lumsden, Charles J., and L.E.H. Trainor. "Nonequilibrium Ensembles of Self-Organizing Systems: A Simulation Study." *Canadian Journal of Physics,* 57 No. 1 (1979), 23–38.

McDole, R.E., and S.A. Reinertsen. "STEEP: An Interagency Multidisciplinary Approach to Soil Conservation." *Journal of Soil and Water Conservation,* 38 No. 3 (1983), 244–45.

Malecki, Ignacy. "Twenty-Five Years of the Institute of Fundamental Technical Research, Polish Academy of Sciences." *Review of the Polish Academy of Sciences,* 23 No. 2 (1978), 83–90.

Markee, K.M., and Janick, J. "Bibliography for Horticultural Therapy (1970–1978): Comparison of Literature Search Techniques in an Interdisciplinary Field." *Hortscience,* 14 No. 6 (1979), 692–97.

Martin, B. "Interdisciplinary Approach to Dairy-Herd Health and Productivity." *Veterinary Record,* 105 No. 9 (1979), 186.

*Meadows, A.J. "Diffusion of Information across the Sciences." *Interdisciplinary Science Reviews,* 1 No. 3 (1976), 259–67.

Meeker, Joseph W. "Science Serves Humanity: Humanity Returns the Serve." *North American Review,* 260 No. 1 (1975), 6–9.

Mehra, Jagdish. "Quantum Mechanics and the Explanation of Life." *American Scientist,* 61 No. 6 (1973), 722–28.

Mehrotra, R.C. "Training and Research in Analytical Chemistry: An Interdisciplinary Science." *Journal of Indian Chemical Society,* 59 No. 11 (1982), 1209–12.

Meinwald, Jerrold, et al. "Chemical Ecology: Studies from East Africa." *Science,* 199 (17 Mar. 1978), pp. 1167–73.

Michaelis, A.R. "Great Problems and Interdisciplinary Solutions." *Interdisciplinary Science Reviews,* 3 No. 1 (1978), 1–2.

———. "Interdisciplinary Biotechnology for Nutrition." *Interdisciplinary Science Reviews,* 5 No. 1 (1980), 1.

———. "Interdisciplinary Freedom." *Interdisciplinary Science Reviews,* 4 No. 2 (1979), 87.

———. "Interdisciplinary Science Policy." *Interdisciplinary Science Reviews,* 4 No. 1 (1979), 1.

———. "1980: Interdisciplinary Debate." *Interdisciplinary Science Reviews,* 4 No. 4 (1979), 263–64.

Monnier, M., et al. "Biology of Sleep: Interdisciplinary Survey." *Experientia,* 36 No. 1 (1980), 1–3.

Morecki, A. "On the Study of the Standardization of Terminology in Interdisciplinary Sciences." *Mechanism and Machine Theory,* 18 No. 3 (1983), 225–27.

Moser, A. "Integrating Strategy, A Basis for Bio-Technological Methodology." *Biotechnology Letters,* 4 No. 2 (1982), 73–78.

Moulton, R. "Computer Abuse: A Multidisciplinary Investigative Approach." *Police Chief,* 50 No. 9 (1983), 48–51.

Narodny, L. "Smell: A Challenge to Interdisciplinary Science." *Interdisciplinary Science Reviews,* 5 No. 1 (1980), 37–48.

*Neurath, Otto. "Unified Science as Encyclopedic Integration." *International Encyclopedia of Unified Science. Foundations of the Unity of Science. V.I.* Chicago: Univ. of Chicago Press, 1938.

Newell, Reginald E. "Introduction." *Journal of Volcanology and Geothermal Research,* 11 No. 1 (1981), 1–2.

Nilsson, S. "Aerobiology: Its International and Interdisciplinary Significance." *Scandinavian Journal of Respiratory Diseases,* 1978 No. s. 102 (1978), 115–18.

Nubbell, J.N., Jr. "The Germ-Plasm Accession Information System at the Asian Vegetable Research and Development Center, Taiwan." *HortScience,* 15 No. 1 (1980), 17–21.

Oppenheimer, Robert. "Analogy in Science." *American Psychologist,* 11 (1956), 127–35.

Pangborn, R.M. "New Interdisciplinary Society Is Organized." *Journal of Nutrition Education,* 11 No. 4 (1979), 168.

Pantin, C.F.A. *The Relations between the Sciences.* New York: Cambridge Univ. Press, 1968.

Porter, Arthur. "Reflections on our Technological Future." *Transactions of the Royal Society of Canada,* 4th Ser., 10 (1973), 179–92.

Prave, P., G.M.V. Rymonlipinski, and W. Sambeth. "Nutrition: An Interdisciplinary Survey." *Interdisciplinary Science Reviews,* 5 No. 1 (1980), 6–23.

Proceedings of the Symposium on Climate and Rice, September 24-27, 1974. International Rice Research Institute. 1976.

Purschwitz, Mark A. "National Dairy Housing Conference Attracts Wide Interdisciplinary Support." *Agricultural Engineering,* 64 No. 5 (1983), 15.

Purushothamen, J. "Multidisciplinary Approach of Exploration in the Manadur Polymetallic Sulfide Deposit, Tamilnadu, India: A Case History." *Geoviews* (India) 11 No. 4 (1983), 145–62.

Radnitzky, Gerard, ed. *Centripetal Forces in the Sciences.* New York: Paragon House (Icus Books), 1987. Vol. I.

Regazzi, J.J., B. Bennion, S. Roberts."On-Line Systems of Disciplines and Specialty Areas in Science and Technology." *Journal of the American Society of Information Sciences (USA),* 31 No. 3 (1980), 161–70.

*Reiger, Henry A. *A Balanced Science of Renewable Resources, With Particular Reference to Fisheries.* Seattle: Washington Sea Grant (distributed by Univ. of Washington Press), 1978.

Reno, R.P., and C.B. Thomiszer. "Can the Marriage Last? Conceptual Problems in Science and Humanities." *Improving College and University Teaching,* 31 No. 1 (1983), 5–8.

Richardson, J.G. "Science and Technology as Integral Parts of Our Culture: Interdisciplinary Responsibilities of the Scientific Communicator." *Journal of Technical Writing and Communication,* 2 (1980), 141–47.

Ritchie-Calder, Lord. "Interdisciplinary Communications: Population." *Science,* 24 Jan. 1969, pp. 408–409.

Rose, David J. "New Laboratories for Old." *Daedalus,* 103 No. 3 (1974), 143–55.

Rouse, William B. "On Models and Modelers: N Cultures." *IEEE Transactions on Systems, Man and Cybernetics,* smc-12 No. 5 (1982), 605–10.

*Roy, Rustum. "Interdisciplinary Science on Campus: An Elusive Dream." *Chemical and Engineering News,* 29 Aug. 1977, pp. 28–40. Also in *Interdisciplinarity and Higher Education,* ed. Joseph Kockelmans. University Park: The Pennsylvania State Univ. Press, 1979, pp. 161–96.

Ruehle, John L., and Donald H. Marx. "Fiber, Food, Fuel, and Fungal Symbionts." *Science,* 26 Oct. 1979, pp. 419–22.

Rurup, Reinhard. "Historians and Modern Technology: Reflections on the Development and Current Problems of the History of Technology." *Technology and Culture,* 15 No. 2 (1974), 161–93.

Rushmer, Robert F. "Interdisciplinary Communication." *Science,* 21 July 1967, p. 252.

*Schneider, Stephen N. "Climate Change and the World Predicament: A Case for Interdisciplinary Research." *Climatic Change,* 1 (1977), 21–43.

**Science and Synthesis.* New York: Springer-Verlag, 1967.

Seymour, P.A.H. "An Historical Framework for an Interdisciplinary Approach to Astronomy." *Quarterly Journal of the Royal Astronomical Society,* 21 No. 1 (1980), 39.

Shaw, D., and C. Davis. "Entropy and Information: A Multidisciplinary Overview." *Journal of the American Society for Information Science,* 34 No. 1 (1983), 67–74.

"Siggraph/Sigart Interdisciplinary Workshop on Motion: Representation and Perception." *Computer Graphics* (USA), 18 No. 1 (1984).

Sigma Xi. *Removing the Boundaries: Perspectives on Cross-Disciplinary Research.* Report of Sigma Xi, the Scientific Research Society. New Haven, Conn., May 1988.

Simonton, Dean K. "Interdisciplinary and Military Determinants of Scientific Productivity: A Cross-Lagged Correlation Analysis." *Journal of Vocational Behavior,* 9 No. 1 (1976) 53–62.

Sladek, C.D., et al. "Maturation of the Supraoptic Nucleus: A Multidisciplinary Analysis." *Peptides,* 1 No. 1 (1980), 51–67.

*Snyder, Solomon H. "Neurosciences: An Integrative Discipline." *Science,* 21 Sept. 1984, pp. 1255–57.

Spalding, I.J. "Laser Applications." *Physics Bulletin* (G.B.), 35 No. 10 (1984), 425–27.

Steiner, J.E., J. Reuveni, and Y. Beja. "Simultaneous Multidisciplinary Measures of Taste Hedonics." In *Determination of Behaviour by Chemical Stimuli: Proceedings of the Fifth European Chemoreception Research Organization Symposium. Jerusalem, Israel, November 8–12, 1981,* ed. J.E. Steiner and J.R. Ganchrow. London: IRL Press, 1982, pp. 149–60.

*Sturmer, Wilhelm. "Interdisciplinary Paleontology." *Interdisciplinary Science Reviews,* 9 No. 2 (1984), 123–36.

Szekely, D.L. "Proto-Model of the Interdisciplinary Unified Science and Its Languages, Unicode." *Cybernetica,* 21 No. 1 (1978), 5–44.

Technological Forecasting and Change, 2 (1979). Special issue.

Thompson, J.M.T., and R. Ghaffari. "Chaotic Dynamics of an Impact Oscillator." *Physics Review A* (USA), 27 No. 3 (1983), 1741–43.

Tromp, S.W., and J.J. Bouma. "Proceedings. Seventh International Interdisciplinary Cycle

Research Symposium Held at Bad-Homburg (Federal Republic of Germany), 23 June–3 July 1976." *Journal of Interdisciplinary Cycle Research,* 8 No. 3–4 (1977), 175–76.

Tungsheng, L., and J. Hungleih. "A Review of the Multidisciplinary Scientific Research on the Qinghai-Xizang Plateau by Chinese Scientists in Recent Years." *Geographical Journal,* 147 (Mar. 1981), 23–26.

Turner, Frederick. *Natural Classicism: Essays on Literature and Science.* New York, Paragon House, 1985.

Van Cleve, K., and C.T. Dryness. "Introduction and Overview of a Multidisciplinary Research Project: The Structure and Function of a Black Spruce (Picea Mariana) Forest in Relation to Other Fire-Affected Taiga Ecosystems." *Canadian Journal of Forest Research,* 13 No. 5 (1983), 695–702.

Vyskocyl, P. "Proceedings of the IUGG Interdisciplinary Symposium No. 9, Recent Crustal Movements, Canberra, ACT, Melbourne, Australia, December 13–14. 1979 – Preface." *Techtonophysics,* 71 No. 1–4 (1981), 7.

Walsh, John. "Social Studies of Science: Society Crosses Disciplinary Lines." *Science,* 18 Nov. 1977, pp. 706–07.

Wartofsky, Marx W., ed. *Boston Studies in the Philosophy of Science: Proceedings of the Boston Colloquium for the Philosophy of Science, 1961/1962.* Dordrecht: Reidel, 1963.

Weisz, Paul B. "The Interdisciplinary Tetrakaide Kahedra." *Chemtech,* May 1980, pp. 270–71.

Wilkinson, J.W., and K.D. Kumar. "Role of Data Management and Data-Analysis in an Interdisciplinary Program." *Biometrics,* 34 No. 1 (1978), 168.

William, R.D., and Crabtree, G. "Sods and Living Mulches in Vegetables and Fruits: A Multidisciplinary Extension Approach." *Hortscience,* 18 No. 4 (1983), 621.

*Wilson, E.O. *Sociobiology: The New Synthesis.* Cambridge, Mass.: Belknap Press of Harvard University Press, 1975.

Winthrop, Henry. "Policy and Planning Programs as Goals of Scientific Work." *American Journal of Economics and Sociology,* 34 No. 3 (1978), 225–45.

Wolf, Charles P., and Frederick Rossini. "Conceptual Difficulties in Problem-Oriented Research: Formulating the 'Holistic' Question." In *Adapting Science to Social Needs: Conference Proceedings,* ed. R.A. Scribner and R.A. Chalk. Washington, D.C.: American Association for the Advancement of Science, 1977.

Wolfle, Dale. "The Supernatural Department." *Science,* 173, 9 July 1971.

Woo, Sly. "Biorheology of Soft Tissues: The Need for Interdisciplinary Studies." *Biorheology,* 15 No. 5–6 (1978), 448; 17 No. 1–2 (1980), 39–43.

Zipko, S.J. "An Interdisciplinary Approach to Dinosaur Fossils, Morphology, Ethology, and Energetics." *American Biology Teacher,* 43 No. 8 (1981), 430–39.

———. "Interdisciplinary Study of Nesting Birds." *American Biology Teacher,* 40 No. 9 (1978), 546.

Biology, Chemistry, Physics

*Baker, D. James. "Resource Letter PB-1 on Physics and Biology." *American Journal of Physics,* 34 No. 2 (1966), 83–93.

Beljanski, Mirko. *The Regulation of DNA Replication and Transcription: The Role of Trigger Molecules in Normal and Malignant Gene Expression.* Experimental Biology and Medicine Monographs on Interdisciplinary Topics, Vol. 8. Basel: Karger, 1983.

Beroza, M. "Some Techniques and Interdisciplinary Aspects of Pesticide Chemistry." *Abstracts of Papers of the American Chemical Society,* 174 (Sept. 1977), PEST 046.

Billmeyer, F.W. "Interdisciplinary Program in Color Science and Technology." *Abstracts of Papers of the American Chemical Society,* 177, pt. 2 (Apr. 1979), 100.

Cizek, Jiri, and Edward R. Vrscay. "Large-Order Perturbation Theory in the Context of Atomic and Molecular Physics: Interdisciplinary Aspects." *International Journal of Quantum Chemistry,* 21 No. 1 (1982), 27–68.

"Criteria for Evidence of Chemical Carcinogenicity: Interdisciplinary Panel on Carcinogenicity." *Science,* 17 Aug. 1984, pp. 682–87.

*Donamura, L.G. "Some Problems Encountered in Interdisciplinary Searches of Polymer Literature." *Journal of Chemical Information and Computer Sciences,* 19 No. 2 (1979), 68–70.

Dragoun, O. "Interdisciplinary Applications of Gamma-Ray Internal Conversion." *Europhysics News* (Switzerland), 15 No. 4 (1984), 11–13.

*Dreyfus, T. "Introducing Shock Waves: An Interdisciplinary Approach." *Helvetica Physica Acta,* 52 No. 5–6 (1979), 680.

Dufy, Bernard. "Multidisciplinary Analysis of Pituitary Cells in Culture." *Current Methods in Cell Neurobiology,* 4 (1983), 49–79.

Edmonds, R.L. *International Biological Program Synthesis Series No. 10, Aerobiology. The Ecological Systems Approach.* US-IBP (International Biol. Program). Synth. Ser. 1979, p. 386.

Epple, G., et al. "Communication by Scent in Some Callitrichidae (Primates): An Interdisciplinary Approach." *Chemical Senses,* 6 No. 4 (1981), 377–90.

Ericson, J.E. "Conservation Chemistry as an Interdisciplinary Course." *Abstracts of Papers of the American Chemical Society,* 175 (Mar. 1978), 3.

Farmer, D., T. Toffoli, and S. Wolfram. *Cellular Automata. Proceedings of an Interdisciplinary Workshop. 1983: Los Alamos, New Mexico, USA.* Amsterdam: North-Holland Physics Publishing, 1984. See in *Physica D* 10 (1984), 1–2.

Friar, D.E., and D.F. Cronin. "Criticality Safety Experience Adapted to Interdisciplinary Safety Administration." *Transactions of the American Nuclear Society,* 45 (1983), 336.

*Hackerman, Norman. "Interdisciplinary Chemistry." *Interdisciplinary Science Reviews,* 3 No. 4 (1978), 332–34.

Hayashi, I. "Heterostructure Lasers History of Development." *IEEE Transactions on Electron Devices (USA).* ED-31 No. 11 (1984), 1630–42.

*Holmes, Frederic L. "The History of Biochemistry: A Review of the Literature of the Field." In *Biochemistry Collections. A Cross-Disciplinary Survey of the Literature.* New York: Haworth, 1982.

Izydore, R.E., et al. "Scientific Instrumentation in Chemistry, Biology, and Physics: An Interdisciplinary Approach." *Journal of Chemical Education,* 60 No. 12 (1983), 1065–67.

Jahne, B. "Image Sequence Analysis of Complex Physical Objects: Nonlinear Small Scale Water Surface Waves." *Proceedings of the First International Conference on Computer Vision.* Washington, D.C.: IEEE Computer Society Press, 1987, pp. 191–200.

Jasinki, Donald R., et al. "Interdisciplinary Studies on Phencyclidine." *PCP (Phencyclidine) Historical and Current Perspectives* (workshop), ed. Edward F. Domino. Ann Arbor, Mich.: NPP Books, (1981), pp. 331–400.

Keller, H. "Trends and Aspects in Clinical Chemistry." *Journal of Clinical Chemistry,* 16 No. 13 (1978), 687–92.

Kiss, D.L., and L.M. Zskajcsos. "Positron Annihilation: A Toll in the Interdisciplinary Investigations." *Acta Physica Hungarica,* 55 No. 1–4 (1984), 51–62.

Kleiner, Scott A. "Essay Review: The Philosophy of Biology." *Southern Journal of Philosophy,* 13 (Winter 1975), 523–42.

Kloos, A. "Multidisiciplinary Systematic Research in Moreae (Moraceae): Leaf Anatomy of the Maclura Group." *Acta Botanica Neerlandica,* 31 No. 1–2 (1982), 145.

Leclerc, Gerard. "Multidisciplinary Approaches to the Alpha-Andrenergic Receptor Using Clonidine Like Compounds." *Periodicum Biologorum,* 85 Suppl. 2 (1983), 83–90.

Levins, Richard, and Richard Lewontin. *The Dialectical Biologist.* Cambridge, Mass.: Harvard Univ. Press, 1985.

Longworth, J.F., and J. Kalmakoff. "Insect Viruses for Biological Control: An Ecological Approach." *Intervirology,* 8 No. 2 (1977), 68–72.

Macchia, B., et al. "An Interdisciplinary Approach to the Design of New Structures Active at the Beta-Adrenergic Receptor. Aliphatic Oxime Ether Derivatives." *Journal of Medical Chemistry,* 28 No. 2 (1985), 153–60.

Mehra, Jagdish. "Quantum Mechanics and the Explanation of Life." *American Scientist,* 61 No. 1 (1973), 722–28.

Mienwald, Jerrold, et al. "Chemical Ecology Studies from East Africa." *Science,* 199 No. 4334 (March 1978), 1167–73.

*Milazzo, Giulio. "Bioelectrochemistry and Bioenergetics: An Interdisciplinary Survey." *Ettote Majorana International Science Series: Life Sciences,* 11: Bioelectrochem. 1: Biol. Redox React. (1983), 5–14. See also in *Bioelectrochemistry and Bioenergetics,* 8 No. 5 (1981), 507–13; and *Experientia,* 36 No. 11 (1980), 1243–47.

Monnier, M., and J.M. Galliard. "Biology of Sleep: An Interdisciplinary Survey." *Experientia* (Basel), 36 No. 1 (1980), 3–6, 11–26.

Nicolini, C.A. "Chromatin: A Multidisciplinary Approach to Its Native Structure." *Basic and Applied Histochemistry,* 25 No. 4 (1981), 319–22.

Oeschger, H. "The Interdisciplinary Impact of C-14." *Abstracts of Papers of the American Chemical Society,* 182 (Aug. 1981), 21; *Vacuum,* 31 (1981), 10–12.

Pfeifer, Harry. "Adsorption and Catalysis: Use and Trouble of Interdisciplinary Research." *Spectrum (Berlin),* 17 No. 12 (1986), 1–4.

*Physics Survey Committee. *Physics in Perspective,* Vol. 1. Washington, D.C.: National Academy of Sciences, 1975.

*Pilet, Paul-Emile. "The Multidisciplinary Aspects of Biology: Basic and Applied Research." *Scientia,* 116 (1981), 629–36.

Rohrmann, B. "Design and Preliminary Results of an Interdisciplinary Field Study on Urban Noise." *Journal of Sound and Vibration,* 59 No. 1 (1978), 111–13.

*Roller, M.B. "Thermostat and Coatings Technology: The Challenge of Interdisciplinary Chemistry." *Abstracts of Papers of the American Chemical Society,* 175 (Mar. 1978), 45. See also in *Polymer Engineering and Science,* 19 No. 10 (1979), 692–98.

Schreiber, H.D. "Properties of Redox Ions in Glasses: An Interdisciplinary Perspective — Introduction." *Journal of Non-Crystalline Solids,* 42 No. 1-3 (1980), 175–83.

Sievert, M.E.C., and A.F. Verbeck. "Online Databases in Physics: An Overview of What Is Available in the United States, Both Core Databases and Those Containing a Specialized Area of Orientation." *Database USA,* 7 No. 4 (1984), 54–63.

Spalding, I.J. "Laser Applications." *Physics Bulletin* (Great Britain), 35 No. 10 (1984), 425–27.

Tett, P., and A. Edwards. "Mixing and Plankton: An Interdisciplinary Theme in Oceanography." *Oceanographic Marine Biology,* 22 (1984), 99–123.

Thompson, J.M.T., and R. Ghaffari. "Chaotic Dynamics of an Impact Oscillator." *Physics Review A,* 27 No. 3 (1983), 1741–43.

Thorne, G.N. "Confessions of a Narrow-Minded Applied Biologist, Or Why Do Interdisciplinary Research." *Annals of Applied Biology,* 108 No. 2 (1986), 205–17.

Trimble, Michael R., ed. *Benzodiazepines Divided: A Multidisciplinary Review.* Chichester, U.K.: John Wiley and Sons, 1983.

Venables, J.D. "Adhesions and Durability of Metal Polymer Bonds." *Journal of Materials Science,* 19 No. 8 (1984), 2431–53.

*Vlachy, J. "Interdisciplinary Approaches in Physics: The Concepts." *Czechoslovak Journal of Physics, Section B,* B32 No. 11 (1982), 1311–18.

———. "World Publication Output in Cross-Disciplinary Physics: Materials Science, Physical Chemistry, Energy Research, Biophysics." *Czechoslovak Journal of Physics,* B33 No. 2 (1983), 247–50.

Volker, E.J., and C. Schultz. "Microbial Conversion of D-Sorbitol to L-Sorbose: Interdisciplinary Experiment Illustrating an Industrial Process." *Journal of Chemical Education,* 55 No. 10 (1978), 673–74.

Weisz, P.B. "The Interdisciplinary Tetrakaidekahedra." *Chemical Technology,* 10 No. 5 (1980), 270–71.

Williams, R.H., D.A. King, and J.E. Inglesfield, eds. "Proceedings of the Fifth Interdisciplinary Surface Science Conference, ISSC-5 6–9 April 1981, University of Liverpool — Preface." *Vacuum,* 31 (1981), 10–12.

Mathematics

Adkins, W., A. Andreotti, and J.V. Leahy. *Weakly Normal Complex Spaces.* Rome: Accademia Nazionale dei Lincei, 1981.

Batchelor, Bruce G. *Pattern Recognition.* New York: Plenum Press, 1978.

Booss, Bernhelm, and Mogens Niss. *Mathematics and the Real World.* Basel: Birkhauser, 1979.

Garrido, L., P. Seglar, and P.J. Shepherd. *Stochastic Processes in Nonequilibrium Systems.* Berlin: Springer, 1978.

Gewirtz, Allan, and Louis V. Quintas. *Second International Conference on Combinatorial Mathematics.* New York: New York Academy of Sciences, 1979.

*Haken, H. "Synergetics and Bifurcation Theory." In *Bifurcation Theory and Applications in Scientific Disciplines.* New York: New York Academy of Sciences, 1979, pp. 357–75.

*Hermann, Robert. See individual publications in a series on interdisciplinary mathematics: *Algebraic Topics of Importance in Systems Theory* (1975); *Algebraic Topics in Systems Theory* (1973); *Cartanian Geometry, Nonlinear Waves and Control Theory. Part A* (1979); *Differential Geometry and the Calculus of Variations* (1977); *Energy Momentum Tensors* (1973); "Fiber Spaces, Connections and Yang-Mills Fields," in *Geometric Techniques in Gauge Theories* (1981); *General Algebraic Ideas* (1973); *Geometric Structures* (1974, 1976); *The Geometry of Nonlinear Differential Equation Backlund Transformations, and Solitons. Part B* (1977); *Linear and Tensor Algebra* (1973); *Linear Systems Theory and Introductory Algebraic Geometry* (1974); *Quantum and Fermion Differential Geometry. Part A* (1977); *Spinors, Clifford and Cayley Algebras* (1977); *Toda Lattices, Cosymplectic Manifolds, Backlund Transformations and Kinks. Part B* (1977); *Topics in General Relativity* (1973); *Topics in the Geometric Theory of Integrable Mechanical Systems* (1984); *Topics in the Geometric Theory of Linear Systems* (1984); *Topics in the Mathematics of Quantum Mechanics* (1973); *Yang-Mills, Kaluza-Klein, and the Einstein Program* (1978) (with Norman Hurt); *Quantum Statistical Mechanics and Lie Group Harmonic Analysis, Part A* (with Norman Hurt) (1980).

Irons, B.M. "Hyper-beams, Generalized Splines, and Practical Curve Fitting." In *Energy Methods in Finite Element Analysis.* Chichester: John Wiley and Sons, 1979, pp. 297–307.

Journal of Combinatorics, Information, and Systems Sciences. Delhi: Forum for Interdisciplinary Mathematics.

Kacprzyk, Janusz. *Multistage Decision-Making under Fuzziness. Theory and Applications.* Cologne: Verlag TUB Rheinland GmbH, 1983.

Kalorkoti, K.A. "Decision Problems in Group Theory." *Proceedings of the London Mathematical Society,* 3rd Series, 44 No. 2 (1982), 312–22.

Kamoi, K., and S. Kamefuchi. "Tachyons as Viewed from Quantum Field Theory." In *Tachyons, Monopoles, and Related Topics* (Proc. First Session, Interdisciplinary Seminar, Erice, 1976). Amsterdam: North-Holland, 1978, pp. 159–67.

Kruskal, W.H. "Mathematical Sciences and Social Sciences: Excerpts from the Report of a Panel of the Behavioral and Social Sciences Survey." *Items,* 24 No. 3 (1970), 25–30.

Kulli, V.R., and N.S. Annigeri. "Reconstruction of a Pair of Connected Graphs from their Line-Concatenations." In *Combinatorics and Graph Theory.* Berlin: Springer, 1981, pp. 301–37.

Lofgren, Lars. "Some Foundational Views on General Systems and the Hempel Paradox." *Journal of General Systems,* 4 No. 4 (1977), 243–53.

Marschak, Jacob. "Personal Probabilities of Probabilities." *Theory and Decision,* 6 (1975), 121–53.

Morava, Jack. "Hypercohomology of Topological Categories." In *Geometric Applications of Homotopy Theory. Proceedings of Conference, Evanston, Illinois. 1977. II.* Berlin: Springer, 1978, pp. 383–403.

National Academy of Sciences. *Interdisciplinary Research in Mathematics, Science and Technology Education.* Washington, D.C.: National Academy Press, 1987.

Negoita, C.V., and D.A. Ralescu. *Applications of Fuzzy Sets to Systems Analysis.* Basel: Birkhauser, 1975.

Prasad, Tribhuan. "Nonlinear Stochastic Modeling in Physiological Systems Using Martingales." *Applications and Research in Information Systems and Sciences (Proceedings First International Conference, Univ. Patras Patras, 1976).* Vol. 3. Washington, D.C.: Hemisphere, 1977, pp. 869–74.

Quantum Dynamics: Models and Mathematics (Proceedings of Symposium, Centre for Interdisciplinary Research. Bielefeld University, Bielefeld, 1975). Vienna: Springer, 1976.

Renfrew, Colin, and Kenneth L. Cooke. *Transformations.* New York: Academic Press-Harcourt, 1979.

Ruegg, H. "Octonionic Quark Confinement." *Acta Physica Polonica B.,* 9 No. 12 (1978), 1037–50.

Shurig, R. "Morphology: A Knowledge Tool." *Systems Research,* 3 No. 1 (1986), 9–19.

Tachyons, Monopoles, and Related Topics (Proceedings First Session, Interdisciplinary Seminar Erice, 1976). Amsterdam: North Holland, 1978.

Wu, Xue Mou. "Pansystems Methodology: A Transfield Investigation of Generalized System Transformation Symmetry." In *Fuzzy Information and Decision Processes.* Eds. Madan A. Gupta and Elie Sanchez. Amsterdam: North Holland, 1982, pp. 423–33.

Index

Agar, Michael, 111, 117

Alabama, University of: New College, 165; women's studies program, 172

Alaska Pacific University: core curriculum of, 167

Alpert, Daniel, 58, 63

American studies: compared to urban affairs and environmental studies, 111–16; educational programs in, 173; evolution of, 31; identified with one of its parts, 109; as an interdiscipline, 43; and variations in integrative levels, 64

Anatomy, 42–43

Annales school of history, 30, 117

Anthropology, 43; relations with history, 43, 106

Apostel, Leo, 36, 80

Archaeology, 14; borrowing in, 86, 89–93; exchanges between geology and, 88–89; relations with history, 57

Area studies, 58, 98–102

Aristotle, 19–20

Arizona State University: Master of Arts in the Humanities, 170

Association for Integrative Studies, 37, 49

Bailis, Stanley, 53, 179

Behavioral medicine, 44

Bell Telephone Laboratories, 29, 58, 126

Bennett College: Interdisciplinary Studies Program, 176

Berger, Guy, 36, 44, 55

Bielefeld, University of: Center for Interdisciplinary Research, 48, 49, 64–65

Biochemistry, 12, 13–14, 32, 43

Biology: biochemistry, 12, 13–14, 32, 43; biophysics, 32, 43; molecular biology, 43; relations with physics and chemistry, 12

Biophysics, 32, 43

Borrowing, 41–42, 85–94; common problems of, 88

Boulding, Kenneth, 106–07, 186

Bowling Green State University: major in American Studies, 173

Brandeis University: department of American Studies, 173; humanities center, 48

Braudel, Fernand, 30, 186, 187–88

Brown, Richard Harvey, 31

Burke, Kenneth, 32, 55–56, 182, 186

California, University of (Davis): program in American Studies, 173

California, University of (Irvine): humanities center, 48; Program in Social Ecology, 174–75, 178

California, University of (Santa Cruz): program in the history of consciousness, 169

California Lutheran College: "loop" sequence, 169

California State University (Fullerton): Department of American Studies, 173

California State University (Hayward):

Department of Human Development, 174, 176–78

Campbell, Donald, 82–83, 116

Canadian studies, 96

Chemistry: relations with physics and biology, 12, 45, 81. *See also* Biology.

Chicago, University of: Committee on Social Thought, 48; curricula as model for interdisciplinary programs, 23, 28–29, 167, 168; graduate research workshops, 169, 171; as an interdisciplinary institution, 47–48; medical center, 47; social sciences, 48

Child abuse: interdisciplinary training workshop, 154

Child development, 14, 66–67

Clark University: Science, Technology, and Society Program, 173

Coldwater Regional Center for Development Disabilities, (MI), 149

Columbia University: curricula as model for interdisciplinary programs, 23–24, 28–29; general and interdisciplinary education, 156, 169, 171

Communication: importance of iteration in, 190; importance of role clarification in, 144, 190; models and patterns of, 129–30; techniques for improving, in teamwork, 135–36, 144, 146–47, 153–54, 189–91. *See also* Teamwork

Community-based interdisciplinary care models, 150, 151–52

Community-University Health Care Center (MINN), 152

Computer data bases: and computer modeling, 42, 106; use of, 14, 59–60, 190–91

Darnton, Robert, 186, 187

Dentistry, 152–53

Developing countries, 45–46; in context of modernization, 99–102

Developmentally disabled, 141, 148–49

Dialectic: as interdisciplinary process, 93–94, 194–95

Disciplinarity: concept of discipline and specialization, 20–22, 104–07; disciplinary paradox defined, 106–07; "discipline" as confused with "department," 107; fission and fusion of disciplines, 43; language of, 77–79; relations with interdisciplinarity, 38–39, 75–117; role of specialization in promoting interdisciplinarity, 43

Dominican College (CA): Colloquium Program, 168

Earlham College: Human Development and Social Relations Program, 174, 175–76, 178

Earth sciences: interdisciplinarity in, 33

East Anglia, University of, 158

Ecology: borrowing from, in archaeology, 90–92; Swedish ecosystem project, 61–63. *See also* Environment

Economics, 12, 43, 85, 86; economic history, 30, 44, 85

Education, general, 22–24, 28–29

Education, interdisciplinary, 156–81; concentrations, 172–79; core curricula and clustered courses, 167–69; early history of, 12, 22–24, 28–29, 35–36; and graduate and professional programs, 56, 169–72; and health care, 151–54; and liberal studies, 163–72; and types of curricula, 156–57, 163–64; and universities, 157–63

Eighteenth-century studies: "contextual" vs. "interdisciplinary" and "soft" vs. "hard" approaches, 64

Encylopedists, French, 20

Engineering, 12, 14, 43, 122; multidisciplinary engineering centers, 34, 138. *See also* Materials science

Environmental studies: compared to urban affairs and American studies, 111–16. *See also* Ecology

Ethnic studies, 44, 95–98

Ethnography, 110–11

Evaluation of interdisciplinary work, 73, 136, 138

Florida State University: program in humanities, 169

Folklore: borrowing from psychology, 87

Foundation (Center) for Integrative Education, 26–27

Fryxell Award for interdisciplinary research in archaeology, 89

Futures research: used to illustrate levels of integration, 68–71

Geertz, Clifford, 11, 31, 53
General systems theory, 24; as a discipline, 106–07; as an example of "transdisciplinarity," 65; as foundation for holistic health care model, 140–41; language of, in interdisciplinary discourse, 80–81; as used in Swedish ecosystem project, 61–63; emergence of, 29; and systems engineering, 43; and value of systems specialists, 190–91
Geography, 30; and patterns of borrowing, 86–87, 88, 92
Geology: earth sciences, 33; exchanges between archaeology and, 88–89
Georgetown University: Master of Arts in Liberal Studies, 169, 170–71
Griffith, University of, 157, 158–59
Group for Research into Higher Education (Nuffield Foundation), 27–28
Gusdorf, Georges, 19, 63

Handicapped, education of, 66–68
Harvard University: Center for Entrepreneurial Studies, 30; Department of Social Relations, 48; general education at, 28–29; humanities center, 48
Health care: 140–55; education and training in, 151–54; integration of services in teamwork, 146–50; teamwork, 141–50. See also Child development; Handicapped, education of; immunopharmacology
Heckhausen, Heinz, 56, 64–65
Hegel, 19, 21, 24
Helsinki, University of: Children's Hospital, 152
Hershberg, Theodore, 59, 60, 117
History, 30; African, 14, 58–59; agricultural, 46; Annales school of, 30, 117; and demography, 42, 44; economic, 30, 44, 85; material, 46; oral, 44, 109; Philadelphia Social History Project, 59–61; regional, 46; relations with anthropology and archaeology, 43, 57, 106; rela-

tions with sociology, 86; urban, 45, 59–61, 117
History of the family as an interdisciplinary field, 108–09, 117
Hobart and William Smith Colleges, 47
Hoebel, E.A.: collaboration with W.K. Llewellyn, 185–86
Holton, Gerald, 33, 38, 138
Humanities, 30–32; centers and institutes of, 48; literary studies in, 31–32. See also American studies; Eighteenth-century studies; Folklore; History; History of the family as an interdisciplinary field; Oral testimony; Structuralism; Theology; Women's studies; Written discourse, the study of
Hutchins, Robert Maynard, 23, 29

IDR (problem-focused research), 121–39; early history of, 32–35; leadership of, 131–33; life cycle of, 133–38; structure of, 123–26; teamwork in, 126–30; variables of, 122–23
Illinois, University of (Chicago): Center for Craniofacial Anomalies, 142–43
Immunopharmacology, 44; as an interdisciplinary field, 108
Information theory, 29
Integration: and achieving synthesis, 84, 116–17, 166, 191–95; idea of, 19, 24–28; levels of, 57; process of, 188–95. See also Interdisciplinarity
Interdisciplinarity: conceptually based definitions of, in education and social sciences, 22–28; definitions by nation and type, 12, 40–42; dialectic nature of, 93–94, 192–95; forums for interdisciplinary discourse, 48–52; historical foundation of concept, 19–22; interdisciplinary individuals, 182–88; interdisciplinary institutions, 47–48; interdisciplinary skills, 182–83; interdisciplines, 24, 43; language and metaphoric structure of, 77–84, 93–94; levels of integration, 57 (see also Nomenclature); literature on, 13–14, 38, 122, 140; OECD definition of, 37, 38, 63; organizations, 37, 47–52, 123–25; patterns of

disciplinary regrouping in, 44; process, 188-95; publications, 26, 30, 36-37, 49-51; scope of, 11-12, 13-14, 40-52, 196; significance of, 52-54, 196; "synoptic" versus "instrumental" types of, 41-42, 53; variety of interdisciplinary fields, 44, 46; ways of defining, 55

INTERSTUDY, 37, 49

Iowa, University of: program in American studies, 173

Iowa State University: history and physics course, 174

Iteration, 135, 190

Jantsch, Erich, 36, 66-67; use of his graphic model, 68-71

Johns Hopkins University: program in liberal studies, 170

Kean College: program in liberal studies, 170

Knowledge, general, 19-20

Kockelmans, Joseph, 13, 57

Kroker, Arthur, 96

Kuhn, Thomas, 33, 110

Linköping, University of: TEMA program, 175, 178-79

Llewellyn, W.K.: collaboration with E.A. Hoebel, 185-86

Los Medanos College: general education program, 168

Loyola College (Baltimore): program in liberal studies, 170

Luszki, Margaret Barron, 127

Lynton, Ernest, 73

Maine, University of (Orono): program in liberal studies, 170

Manhattan Project, 34

Marianjoy Rehabilitation Hospital, 146

Marxism, 29, 30, 32, 65

Maryland, University of, 149, 166

Massachusetts, University of (Amherst): Inquiry Program, 166

Materials science, 44, 58, 117

Mathematics, 42, 81-105

Matrix structure, 126

Meikeljohn, Alexander, 23, 80

Merton, Robert, 97; and *theories of the middle range,* 117

Metalanguage, 117

Metropolitan College (Boston): program in liberal studies, 170

Miami University: Western College (School of Interdisciplinary Studies), 165, 167

Michigan, University of, 125; program in American studies, 169, 173

Michigan State University: Upper Peninsula Medical Education Program, 152

Middle-range theory, 117

Miller, Raymond, 52, 65-66

Minnesota, University of: program in American studies, 169

Missouri, University of (Kansas City): Integrated Studies in the Humanities, 169

Modeling: computer modeling, 42; in Swedish ecosystem project, 61-63

Modernization and development, 86, 99-102

Molecular biology, 43

Mount Ida Senior College, 165-66

Murray, Thomas, 145, 184

Muskegon Regional Center for Developmentally Disabled, 148-49

NASA (National Aeronautics and Space Administration), 123, 126; Apollo Project, 122

NATO (North Atlantic Treaty Organization), 34

NEA (National Education Association), 26

NEH (National Endowment for the Humanities), 36, 174

NSF (National Science Foundation), 34-35, 36, 37; multidisciplinary engineering centers of, 34, 138

New Mexico State University: medical training, 151-52

New School for Social Research: program in liberal studies, 170

New York, State University (Stony Brook): Federated Learning Communities, 168-69; humanities center, 48

Newell, William H., 179-80, 195

Nomenclature: 15, 25-28, 55-73; "consulting" versus "contractual" modes, 58; "contextual" versus "interdisciplinary" and "soft" versus "hard" ap-

Nomenclature (*continued*)
proaches, 64; "correlation," 26; "crossdisciplinary," 55; "endogenous" versus "exogenous," 37–38; "holistic," "humanistic," "integrative," and "interdisciplinary" used interchangeably in health care, 140–41; "instrumental," 24, 41–42; "integrative," "integrated," and "integration" versus "interdisciplinary," 25–27; "multidisciplinary" versus "interdisciplinary" discussed, 56–63; "multidisciplinary" versus "interdisciplinary" versus "transdisciplinary" illustrated, 66–71; OECD typology of terms, 36–37, 63; "restructuring" versus "bridge-building," 27–28; "synoptic" versus "instrumental," 41–42, 53; "synthetic" versus "holistic," 113–14; "transdisciplinary" versus "interdisciplinary" discussed, 63–71; "vacant" versus "critical" interdisciplinarity, 96

Northwestern University: Integrated Science Program, 173; Honors Mathematical Models in the Social Sciences Program, 174, 177

Nuffield Foundation. *See* Group for Research into Higher Education

Ohio Dominican College: freshman core in liberal studies, 168

Ohio University (Athens): Tier II Synthesis, 166

Oklahoma, University of, 173

Operations research, 32, 44, 117

Oral history, 44; oral testimony as an interdisciplinary field, 109

Organicism, 21

Organization for Economic Cooperation and Development (OECD), 28, 36–38, 40–41, 44, 58, 63

Parsons, Talcott, 46

Pennsylvania State University: Interdisciplinary Graduate Program in the Humanities, 37, 169, 171–72; Science, Technology, and Society Program, 173–74; variety of interdisciplinary research institutes, 47

Pharmacy, 14, 148–50

Philadelphia Social History Project, 59–61

Physical chemistry, 43, 44

Physics, 12, 44–45, 81. *See also* Materials science

Piaget, Jean, 29, 36, 63

Pittsburgh Child Guidance Center, 154

Plato, 19–20, 186

Political science, 43; and area studies, 99–103; borrowing from economics and sociology, 86

Portland State University: Science and Humanities sequence, 174

Project life cycles, 71–73, 133–38, 188–89

Psychology, 105; environmental psychology, 45; folklore borrowing from, 87

Public health, 12, 44, 56

Riesman, David, 95; and Gerald Grant, 36, 157; and Christopher Jencks, 183

Roskilde, University Centre, 157–59, 160–61

Roy, Rustum, 33, 35

Said, Edward, 186, 187, 188

Saint Johns (MD): "great books" curriculum, 168

Saint Josephs (Indiana): core curriculum of, 167

St. Olaf College: Paracollege, 164–65, 166–67

San Francisco State University: interdisciplinary programs, 47; NEXA Science-Humanities convergence, 174

Science, Technology, and Society programs, 173–74

Sciences, 33; borrowing, 42, 85; cytology and biology, 104–05; modern developments in, 42–43, 45; relationship of physics, chemistry, and biology, 12, 44–45, 81; subdivisions of, 104–05. *See also* Anatomy; Biology; Chemistry; Earth sciences; Ecology; Engineering; Futures research; Geology; Immunopharmacology; Materials science; Physical chemistry; Physics; Sociobiology; Technology assessment

Sherif, Muzafer and Carolyn, 86, 105

Shimer College, 167, 168

Sjölander, Sverre, 71–72, 193–94

Social psychology, 12, 14, 24, 43, 109
Social Science Research Council, 24, 30, 98–99
Social sciences: applied social science, 24; borrowed methodologies, 42; and borrowing by political scientists, 86; historical background of interdisciplinarity in, 24–26; integrative concepts in, 26; relationships between anthropology and history, 43; relationships between history and sociology, 86; Social Science Research Council, 24, 30, 98–99; sociolinguistics and psycholinguistics, 43. *See also* American studies; Anthropology; Archaeology; Area studies; Behavioral medicine; Developing countries; Economics; Ethnography; Futures research; Geography; Modernization; Oral testimony; Psychology; Social psychology; Sociobiology; Urban affairs
Sociobiology, 43, 44, 65
Sonoma State University: Hutchins School of Liberal Studies, 164–65, 166
Southern California, University of: interdisciplinary programs, 47; program in liberal studies, 170
Squires, Geoffrey, 12
Stanford University: Center for Interdisciplinary Studies, 47; humanities center, 48; Stanford Research Institutes, 131; Values, Technology, and Society Program, 174
Statistics, 42
Status issues in teamwork, 126–28, 143–45. *See also* Teamwork
Structuralism, 29, 31, 32, 65
Sussex, University of, 157–58
Synthesis. *See* Integration

Teamwork: communication in, 149, 150, 189–90; in health care, 141–50; in IDR, 126–30; leaders, 131–33; team size, 129. *See also* Communication
Technology assessment, 34
Texas, University of (Dallas): Master of Arts program, 170
Texas Tech University: program in the arts, 169–70

Theology, 30
Theory of internal relations, 21, 24
Toronto, University of: course on physics and biology, 174
Toulmin, Stephen, 38, 49, 104, 110
Tromso, University of, 157, 159, 161–63, 175
Trow, Martin, 180–81
Tsukuba, University of, 157, 160, 161

United States Department of Agriculture, 34, 58; agricultural field stations, 48
Unity: idea of, 11, 19, 20–21, 22; of knowledge, 11, 12; of science, 19; of science movement in the 1930s, 25
Urban affairs, compared to American and environmental studies, 111–16
Utah, University of: Vernal Family Health Center, 150

Vitalism, 21
VonHumboldt, Wilhelm: concept of universal education, 22
Vosskamp, Wilhelm, 21, 22

Washington, University of: interdisciplinary medical programs, 147–48, 152–53
Wayne State University: University Studies/Weekend College Program, 166
Wesleyan University: humanities center, 48; program in graduate liberal studies, 169
West Virginia University: women's studies program, 173
White, Hayden, 31, 186, 187, 188
White, James Boyd, 31, 186
"Whole" person: concept of, in education, 23
Willamette University: College of Liberal Arts, 166
Williams, Raymond, 187
Winthrop, Henry, 186–87, 195
Wisconsin, University of (Green Bay), 157–58, 159–60
Wissenschaft, 21, 22, 116
Women's studies: discussed with ethnic studies, 95–98; educational programs in, 172–73
Worcester Polytechnic Institute, 173
Written discourse: the study of, 109–10

Julie Thompson Klein is Professor of Humanities in the interdisciplinary University Studies/Weekend College program within the College of Lifelong Learning at Wayne State University. She is also a senior editor of *Issues in Integrative Studies* and associate editor of *The Interstudy Bulletin,* as well as a former president of the Association for Integrative Studies. Dr. Klein has been a Visiting Foreign Professor at Shimane University in Japan and Senior Fulbright Lecturer in American Studies and English as a Second Language at Tribhuvan University in Nepal. Dr. Klein received the D.A. and Ph.D. degrees from the University of Oregon. She compiled *John Gay: An Annotated Checklist of Criticism* and has contributed chapters to several books on interdisciplinarity. Her articles on literary criticism, pedagogy, and interdisciplinary history, theory, and method have appeared in such journals as *Southern Review, Teaching History Today, Perspectives, Issues in Integrative Studies,* and *Knowledge.*

The manuscript was edited for publication by Robert S. Demorest. The book was designed by Joanne Elkin Kinney. The typeface for the text is Times Roman and the display is Letraset compacta. The book is printed on 60-lb Glatfelter Spring Forge and is bound in Holliston Roxite B Grade Linen cloth.

Manufactured in the United States of America.